THE ROLE OF GOVERNANCE
IN ASIA

The **Japan Institute of International Affairs (JIIA)** is a private, non-profit, and independent research organization founded in 1959 through the initiative of former Prime Minister Shigeru Yoshida, the first president of the JIIA.

The JIIA's mission is to contribute to the formulation of Japan's foreign policy through organizing study groups on regional and global issues, international conferences, symposiums and seminars, and joint research projects with other domestic and overseas research organizations and universities. The JIIA also invites foreign researchers to Japan and assists them with their research activities, and it issues a wide range of publications as a result of these activities.

The **ASEAN Foundation** was established by ASEAN leaders in 1997 to boost ASEAN's effort to promote regional co-operation in various fields of social and human development such as science and technology, youth, women, health and nutrition, education, labour affairs, disaster management, HIV/AIDS prevention and control, children, population, and rural development and poverty eradication, culture and information, environment, drug matters, and civil service. The Foundation was established to promote greater awareness of ASEAN, greater interaction among the peoples of ASEAN as well as their wider participation in ASEAN activities.

The ASEAN Foundation deems that the most beneficial and effective means to attain its objectives is focusing on human resources development projects such as education, training, seminars, workshops, exchanges, network-building, fellowships and information dissemination.

The **Institute of Southeast Asian Studies (ISEAS)** was established as an autonomous organization in 1968. It is a regional centre dedicated to the study of socio-political, security and economic trends and developments in Southeast Asia and its wider geostrategic and economic environment.

The Institute's research programmes are the Regional Economic Studies (RES, including ASEAN and APEC), Regional Strategic and Political Studies (RSPS), and Regional Social and Cultural Studies (RSCS).

ISEAS Publications, an established academic press, has issued more than 1,000 books and journals. It is the largest scholarly publisher of research about Southeast Asia from within the region. ISEAS Publications works with many other academic and trade publishers and distributors to disseminate important research and analyses from and about Southeast Asia to the rest of the world.

Asian Development Experience Vol. 2

THE ROLE OF GOVERNANCE
IN ASIA

Edited by

Yasutami Shimomura

JAPAN INSTITUTE OF INTERNATIONAL AFFAIRS

ASEAN FOUNDATION

INSTITUTE OF SOUTHEAST ASIAN STUDIES, Singapore

First published in Singapore in 2003 by
Institute of Southeast Asian Studies
30 Heng Mui Keng Terrace
Pasir Panjang
Singapore 119614
http://bookshop.iseas.edu.sg

*The responsibility for facts and opinions expressed in this publication rests
exclusively with the authors whose interpretations do not necessarily reflect the
views or the policy of ISEAS.*

ISEAS Library Cataloguing-in-Publication Data

Asian Development Experience. Volume 2, The Role of Governance in
    Asia / edited by Yasutami Shimomura.
    1. Decentralization in government—Asia, Southeastern.
    2. Decentralization in government—Asia.
    3. Asia, Southeastern—Economic policy.
    I. Shimomura, Yasutami.
    II. Title: The Role of Governance in Asia
HC412 A865 v. 2   2003

ISBN 981-230-197-6 (soft cover)
ISBN 981-230-200-X (hard cover)

Printed in Singapore by Utopia Press Pte Ltd
Typeset by International Typesetters Pte Ltd

Contents

List of Tables

List of Figures

Contributors

Alex ARIFIANTO is a Researcher at the SMERU Research Institute, Indonesia

Juichi INADA is Professor at the School of Economics, Senshu University, Japan

Ikuo IWASAKI is Professor at the Department of Asia-Pacific Studies, Takusyoku University, Japan

Kyoko KUWAJIMA is the Director of the Japan International Co-operation Agency, Japan

Tommy A. LEGOWO is Head of the Department of Politics and Social Change at the Centre for Strategic and International Studies, Indonesia

Mahani ZAINAL ABIDIN is Professor at the Department of Applied Economics, University of Malaya, Malaysia

Yuri SATO is a Senior Research Fellow at the Institute of Developing Economies, Japan

Yasutami SHIMOMURA is Professor at the Faculty of Humanity and Environment, Hosei University, Japan

Hideaki SHIMOMURA is Associate Professor at the Faculty of Law, Tokyo University, Japan

Sudarno SUMARTO is the Director of the SMERU Research Institute, Indonesia

Asep SURYAHADI is Senior Researcher and Deputy Director for Research at the SMERU Research Institute, Indonesia

Jorge V. TIGNO is Assistant Professor at the Department of Political Science, University of the Philippines

Acknowledgements

The three volumes bring together essays from a two-year research project, "Asian Development Experience" that commenced in November 2001. The principal objective of the project was to investigate the dynamic factors contributing to the remarkable success of ASEAN economies. We particularly focused on the role of external factors, domestic policy reforms and governance as well as regional co-operation, which have received lesser attention in the past literature of the field.

We would like to thank Saori Honma and Katsuya Ohara of the Japan Institute of International Affairs for their dedication to this research project and the contributors to the volumes for making the editors' job so easy. We would also like to acknowledge the tireless support of Triena Ong and Dayaneetha De Silva of the Institute of Southeast Asian Studies for realizing the publication.

The research project was undertaken with the financial support of the Japan-ASEAN Solidarity Fund, contributed by the Japanese Government and managed by the ASEAN Foundation.

Introduction

Yasutami Shimomura

1. Objectives

This book attempts to cast light on the complicated realities of the relations between governance and development, through conducting case studies of ASEAN countries. Its main objective is to explore a theoretical framework to overcome the limitation of mainstream approach to the issue.

Since the beginning of the 1990s, aid donors have increasingly stressed that "good governance", together with democracy and protection of basic human rights, is indispensable for sustainable economic development.

In 1991, the Development Assistance Committee (DAC) of Organization for Economic Co-operation and Development (OECD) emphasized that the concept of "governance" has assumed a more central focus as an area of key attention by both bilateral and multilateral donors, and participatory development cannot be achieved without the development of good governance, which is composed of competence and honesty, public accountability, broader participation in discussion and decision making on central issues (OECD 1991, pp. 33, 44). Lewis Preston, former President of the World Bank stated "good governance is an essential complement to sound economic policies" (World Bank 1992, p. v). G8 leaders in their summit statements repeatedly stressed that good governance is indispensable for development.

While the international aid community has proposed a number of definitions of good governance, it should be admitted the definition of governance or good governance is complex, broad, and vague to a certain extent. The following issues are frequently referred to as basic components of good governance:

a)   Accountability, transparency, openness etc., in exercising power of government
b)   Rule of law, competent and credible judiciary, and predictable public conduct
c)   Sufficient institutional capacity of the public sector to ensure effective administrative behaviour
d)   Corruption control
e)   Control of excessive military expenditures

In addition to the above issues, democracy has been repeatedly raised as an important element of good governance. However, the World Bank and, to a lesser extent, the IMF have carefully avoided commitment to political regime agenda, due to the essence of the Bretton Woods System. The position of OECD to regard democracy as a part of good governance could be labelled as "broad" definition, and the World Bank's position as "narrow".

Reflecting these trends, a wide variety of research has been done on the relationship between good governance and development. While various important findings have been made, these studies have basically failed to show the specific process of how the deference in governance influences development performance in the real world in which we actually live. Our knowledge is still very limited in this regard. In our opinion, this is not irrelevant to the structure of mainstream approach. This issue will be treated in the following section.

2. Understanding the impact of governance on development: why case studies on ASEAN countries?

When we review the huge stock of empirical studies on the relationship between governance and development, we find that most of them are regression analyses; governance indicators on the one hand and development achievement on the other. Let us see some examples. Robert Barro showed positive relationships between the growth rate and democracy indicators (Barro 1997, p. 60). Kaufmann, Kraay, and Zoido-Lobaton illustrated positive relations between (i) voice and accountability and infant mortality; and (ii) rule of law index and per capita income (Kaufmann, Kraay, and Zoido-Lobaton 2000, p. 12). In its *Human Development Report 2002*, the United Nations Development Program (UNDP) showed there is no automatic link between (i) democracy scores and equity; and (ii) democracy scores and human development indicators

(UNDP 2002, p. 60). According to Beatrice Weder, the proposition that property rights and the rule of law are important for development were strongly supported, while there is only weak support of the proposition that high levels of corruption reduce growth, and neither democracies nor autocracies are superior at generating higher growth (Weder 1999, pp. 61–62). In short, the results are mixed.

These mainstream approaches have three basic shortcomings in our opinion.

First, there is a notable mismatch between the problem structure and analytical tools. A set of elegant and highly sophisticated analytical tools, which are effective in treating "well-structured" problems are applied to highly complicated and "ill-structured" problems of governance and development with a lot of unknowns. Admittedly, under such conditions, the prospects of uncovering the essential aspects is quite limited.

Second, they do not pay due attention to the stages of development. In most cases, advanced economies (such as United States, Sweden, and Singapore), and Least Developed Countries (LLDC such as Afghanistan, Sierra Leone, and Congo) are dealt with in the same way, although the structure of the problem in the two groups is completely different. This is a serious handicap in the pursuit of the critical variables which differentiate the development performance among developing countries.

Third, the standard approach to comparing the countries with good governance/performance with ones with bad governance/performance is excessively simplistic. Under this approach, a group of high performing developing countries including ASEAN countries is simply regarded as statistically exceptional, as their governance indicators are generally low from the viewpoint of the international community. As a result, the relationship between governance and development in these most dynamic economies is not studied in detail. This inevitably causes significant opportunity cost, as their experiences could lead to valuable policy implications, if studied in-depth.

This is the reason why this book focuses on the ASEAN countries.

The purpose of this book is to propose a supplement to the mainstream approach. We believe that the accumulation of case studies is crucial in the attempt to overcome the weaknesses of the mainstream approach. An in-depth case study of a specific problem in a specific country and period would provide a vivid and realistic picture of the role of governance in the improvement or deterioration of development, and the accumulation of case studies would provide various hints of general theory on the issue. Such data is valuable for functional policy recommendation to address the question of governance and development.

3. The composition of this book

A group of twelve scholars[1], five from ASEAN countries and seven from Japan, launched the research project "Governance in Asia Revisited", which is a part of "The Asian Development Experience Research Project" of Japan Institute of International Affairs (JIIA), with financial support from the Japan-ASEAN Solidarity Fund, in 2001. This book is based on the outcomes of the studies, which were presented at a workshop in May 2003 in Tokyo.

A basic idea behind this research project is that the concept of (good/bad) governance is to be broadly defined, as it consists of various dimensions (political, economic, social, cultural and so on) and is the result of interrelated actions of various actors or stakeholders. It should be noted however that our purpose is not to address the agenda of definition; we adopt the broad definition of governance, which is basically shared in the international community, as the working definition. Rather, our focus is on the multi-dimensional complication of governance.

The centre of the traditional view of governance is public governance, in particular the exercise of authority, control, management, power of the central government. To grasp a total picture of the interaction between governance and development, however, it is not enough to deal with a single dimension, i.e., public governance or the administrative behaviour of the public sector. To fully understand the meaning of different development performance among developing countries, the behaviour of other actors or stakeholders such as private companies, local communities, community-based organizations, non-profit and non-governmental organizations (NPOs and NGOs) are also relevant. In particular, the dynamic and complicated interrelations with public governance in the form of joint governance have an important role. From this viewpoint, this book highlights a group of crucial governance aspects in five "old" ASEAN members, and analyzes how these are relevant to good/bad development performances.

It is notable that five chapters (Kuwajima, Legowo, Shiroyama, Sumarto, and Tigno) deal with decentralization. This reflects the fact that decentralization is a crucial as well as highly controversial issue in the context of reform endeavours in ASEAN countries, particularly in the post East Asian crisis era. Three chapters (Abidin, Inada, Iwasaki) treat the orthodox agenda of macroeconomic management. In particular, Abidin and Inada focus their attention on crisis management in the late 1990s, which had overwhelming importance in this region. Sato examines the essential features of corporate governance in Indonesia, through testing various hypotheses to explain corporate behaviour. Sato's subject is also closely related to the experiences of the East Asian crisis and current structural reform attempts. Shimomura and Kuwajima focus on foreign aid management, which has been one of the central policy agendas in this region.

In this way, the chapters examine the relationship between governance and development from diverse angles, paying due attention to fundamental policy agenda such as economic transformation, the East Asian crisis, and structural reform.

Readers will recognize that these chapters imply that fundamental characteristics of individual society have significant meaning.

While this book represents a small step forward, persistent accumulation of findings through a variety of case studies will reveal essential features of the relationship between governance and development.

Note

[1] Juichi Inada (Japan), Ikuo Iwasaki (Japan), Kyoko Kuwajima (Japan), Tommy Legowo (Indonesia), Mahini Zainal Abidin (Malaysia), Pitch Pongsawat (Thailand), Yuri Sato (Japan), Yasutami Shimomura (Japan), Hideaki Shiroyama (Japan), Sudarno Sumarto (Indonesia), Jorge Tigno (Philippines), and Matsuo Watanabe (Japan).

References

Barro, R. 1977. *Determinants of Economic Growth: A Cross-Country Empirical Study*. Cambridge, Massachusetts: The MIT Press.

Kaufman, D., A. Kraay, and P. Zoido-Lobatan. 2000. "Governance Matters: From Measurement to Action". *Finance and Development*, Vol. 37, No. 2.

OECD. 1991. *Development Co-operation*. Paris: Organisation for Economic Co-operation and Development.

UNDP. 2002. *Human Development Report: Deepening democracy in a fragmented world*. Oxford: Oxford University Press.

Weder, B. 1999. *Model, Myth, or Miracle? Reassesing the Role of Governments in the East Asian Experience*. Tokyo: United Nations University Press.

World Bank. 1992. *Governance and Development*. Washington D.C.: The World Bank.

1

Regional Governance in Asia: Comparative Analysis of Experiments of Decentralization and Deconcentration in Indonesia, Thailand and Korea

Hideaki Shiroyama

1. Introduction

The international development community has an interest in issues of governance as factors that have an impact on the effectiveness of development efforts. The World Bank defines governance as the manner in which power is exercised in the management of a country's economic and social resources for development. Concretely, it focuses on public sector management, accountability (mainly financial accountability) and legal framework for development (which provides a predictable and transparent framework for the conduct of business) (World Bank 1992). The UNDP (United Nations Development Program) defines governance as the exercise of economic, political and administrative authority to manage a country's affairs at all levels, which incorporates aspects of economic governance (decision-making processes that affect a country's economic activities), political governance (the process of decision making to formulate policy) and administrative governance (the system of policy implementation). It considers participation, rule of law, transparency, responsiveness (to stakeholders), equity, effectiveness and efficiency as major components of governance (UNDP 1997). JICA (Japan International Cooperation Agency) defines governance as attitude of state plus government function. Attitude of state is measured based on basic orientation to democracy. JICA's definition is flexible concerning forms of democracy and the timing of achieving democracy. Government function concerns effectiveness and efficiency. Concretely, legitimacy, accountability, human rights, decentralization and control of excessive military expenditure are used as benchmarks of attitude of state; and law and institution, administrative management, decentralization and effort in ensuring market environment are used as benchmarks of government function.

As the above definitions of governance by organizations imply, regional (provincial and local) governance including decentralization is one of the important aspects of governance in general. So the regional dimension of governance is an essential part for analyzing the overall picture of the recent governance reform in Asia.

Decentralization of Asian governments occurred simultaneously in the 1990s. In Korea, the Local Autonomy Law was revised in 1988; and regional (provincial and local) elections of council members and governors/mayors were resumed in 1991 and 1995. The Law for Promotion and Transfer of the Central Authority to Localities was adopted in 1999 and the Comprehensive Decentralization Law is to be adopted in 2003. In Thailand, the Prime Minister emphasized decentralization as a major issue after the democratization movement in 1992. The Constitution was amended in 1997, prescribing decentralization as a basic policy of the government, and the Act of Decentralization and Procedure was adopted in 1999. In Indonesia, after the downfall of President Soeharto in 1998, decentralization was pursued as a major component of democratization reform; and the Law No. 22/1999 on Regional Governance and the Law No. 25/1999 on Fiscal Balance between the Centre and Regions were adopted in 1999. In addition, even in Japan, a resolution for promoting decentralization was adopted by the Diet in 1993, and the Decentralization Promotion Law was adopted in 1995. Based on the Law, the Decentralization Promotion Committee was established, which produced a series of recommendations, and the Comprehensive Law for Decentralization was adopted in 1999 accordingly.

Various side effects of decentralization have also been identified and observed during decentralization processes. Corruption and the lack of sufficient capable human resources in regional governments are examples of side effects. And the need for national coordination for overall economic development was recognized especially in the light of countries' efforts at responding to the Asian financial crisis.

So far, I have used the concept of decentralization in a vague way. But the phenomenon of regional governance, including so-called decentralization, has several dimensions in an analytical sense. The first dimension is decentralization. Decentralization means the transfer of authority from central government to regional (provincial and local) governments. The second dimension is deconcentration. Deconcentration means the delegation of authority by the central government to regional units. In addition, there are two types of deconcentration. One is deconcentration to field offices of the central government; the other is deconcentration to regional governments. This is the system of agency delegation. Agency delegation is the assignment of authorities by the central government to regional (provincial and local) governments, and provincial governments to local governments to perform certain duties.

Along with the deconcentration would be support in the form of finance, facilities and infrastructures sometimes with human resources.

In this article, I focus on the structure of the interrelationship between decentralization and deconcentration (of the two types) at the regional level, and define the structure as regional governance. Asian cases of so-called decentralization are very rich material for institutional experiments of various combinations of decentralization and deconcentration.

In the following pages, experiments involving Indonesia, Thailand and Korea are analyzed with focus on the background, the contents of decentralization/ deconcentration programmes, the process and the difficulties encountered. These countries are similar in that they had centralized regimes before decentralization. But their experiments are different concerning the forms of combinations of deconcentration and decentralization, the timing and speed of the so-called decentralization, the relationship between councils/ assemblies and chief executives such as governors/ mayors, the personnel system between central and regional governments and the financial system between central and regional governments. The case of Indonesia is the most radical experiment of decentralization, the case of Thailand is the most incremental experiment of decentralization, and the case of Korea is somewhere in between. Therefore, these countries seem to be good targets for comparison. After analyzing the cases of these three countries, comparative analysis is undertaken in the concluding part.

2. Indonesia

2.1 Background

Under President Soeharto's regime, the Law No. 5/1974 stipulated the principles of regional governments. There were two levels of government, that is, provincial governments and local governments. Chief executives of those governments, governors and mayors, were appointed by the upper level of government from several candidates selected by regional councils. The governor of a provincial government was appointed by the President based on the recommendation of the Minister of Interior from several candidates selected by each provincial council, and the chief executive of a local government was appointed by the Minister of Interior based on the recommendation of the governor from several candidates selected by each local council. These provincial and local governments were autonomous bodies. However, they also worked as agents of central governments, performing agency delegation functions (Morita 1998, p. 178).

The Asian financial crisis happened in 1997 and the authoritarian regime of former President Soeharto collapsed in May 1998. Various democratization initiatives were taken after that and the overhaul of the regions and redefinition of the relationship between central, provincial and local governments came up as major issues under new President Habibie. The extraordinary session of Indonesia's highest decision-making body, the People's Consultative Assembly (MPR), was held in November 1998, opening the door for the revision of the Law No.5/1974 on the Principles of Regional Governments, by adopting the MPR Decree No. 15/ MPR/1998 (Okamoto 2001, p. 5).

Following the decision, the Ministry of Home Affairs set up a team of senior civil servants, academics and advisers to formulate the draft of the Law No. 22/1999 on Regional Governance. The Ministry of Finance set up a team of senior civil servants, academics and advisers to formulate the draft of the Law No. 25/1999 on Fiscal Balance Between the Centre and Regions. Both laws were approved by the national parliament in May 1999. In addition to the introduction of new laws, the constitutional amendment concerning regional governments and autonomy was undertaken at the MPR's annual session in August 2000. Article 18 of the Constitution was revised and broad-based autonomy for regional governments was laid down in the Constitution (Okamoto 2001, p. 5).

2.2 Contents

The Law No. 22/1999 on Regional Governance and the Law No. 25/1999 on Fiscal Balance Between the Centre and Regions define the basic structure of decentralization in Indonesia. The Law No. 22/1999 on Regional Governance stipulates following things.

First, the law stipulates the local level as the level of government which has "broad and wide-raging autonomy". Para 7.1 stipulates that the local level has responsibility for governmental matters except in the five areas of foreign affairs — defence and security, justice, monetary and fiscal affairs, religion and other matters. These "other matters" are listed in Para 7.2 as "macro-level planning, fiscal equalization, public administration and economic institutions, human resource development, natural resource utilization, strategic technologies, conservation, and national standardization". Para 11 provides a positive list of local responsibilities that includes public works, health, education and culture, agriculture, transport, industry and trade, investment, environment, land matters, cooperatives and manpower (GTZ 2003). One of the interesting characteristics of the new regime is that there no longer exists a clearly defined hierarchical relationship between provincial and local governments. There are often conflicts between provincial and local governments, and local governments, especially relatively big ones, do not have the inclination to follow the guidance of provincial governments.

Second, many of deconcentrated offices of central government agencies at the regional level were merged with the respective agencies of regional governments. Staff and assets were also transferred to the regional governments. Some of the deconcentrated functions were transferred to regional governments as autonomous units, and others were handled by provincial governments as agency delegation functions. In parallel with this institutional development, the transfer of a large number of central civil servants, roughly 3.2 million central civil servants (roughly 1.9 million, including 1.1 million teachers and 0.2 million working for the Ministry of Health), had to be planned and undertaken (Okamoto 2001, p. 8). Considering that the original number of regional civil servants was 0.7 million, it might be easy to understand how huge the scale of transfer was. Although many of the deconcentrated offices of central government agencies at the regional level were merged with the respective agencies of regional governments, field agencies of ministries managed by central government in the fields of international affairs, defence and security, justice, monetary and fiscal aspects, as well as religious affairs remained in place.

Third, in the previous regime, the chief executives of provincial and local governments were accountable to the President of Indonesia through the Minister of Home Affairs. But now, under the new law, chief executives of provincial and local governments are accountable to their respective councils. If the accountability report provided by the chief executive at the end of the fiscal year is rejected twice by the regional council, the chief executive is forced to resign.

The Law No. 25/1999 on Fiscal Balance between the Centre and Regions aims at generating a financial system for the regions which is "just, proportional, rational, transparent, participatory, accountable and provides certainty". The law stipulates the following matters.

First, the system of revenue sharing is defined. A regional share of the property tax and natural resource revenue are transferred to regional governments. For example, in the case of oil, 85% of the revenue is allocated to the central government, 3% to the provincial government, 6% to the producing local government, and the remaining 6% to the surrounding local governments.

Second, the system of transfer from central to regional governments is re-established. From the central government funds (APBN), 25% of domestic revenue is earmarked for the general transfer grant (DAU: Dana Allocasi Umum). From this 25%, 22.5% is transferred to the local level, and the remaining 2.5% to the provincial level. Allocation to each regional government is determined by calculating the criteria based on need and balancing factors (which is used for each government so that they do not receive a lesser amount compared to the previous regime). There used to be various kinds of specific purpose grants (Inpres, etc.) given by sectoral ministries, but there is now a trend towards integrated/general subsidy, that is, DAU. The ratio of DAK (Dana Allosi Kusus), specific purpose subsidy, is very limited.

Third, the law defines that own revenue of regional governments is local taxes, local charges and fees, and revenue from local enterprises. Based on the law, it is reported that various problematic taxation occurred that became obstacles for internal business practices.

2.3 Process

The downfall of President Soeharto in 1998 and various democratization initiatives following that event were the source of dynamism behind the progress toward decentralization in Indonesia. New President Habibie intended to use this reform as a means to build up political credibility. He used to be Vice-President under the Soeharto regime and it was necessary to compensate for the legitimacy deficit (Shiroyama 2001, p. 43). Another factor is the regional movement for independence. There were growing calls for independence in East Timor and the Special District of Aceh. Decentralization is essential for averting declarations of independence by these provinces (Okamoto 2001, p. 43).

In the hasty drafting of Law No. 22/1999, a group called the Team of Seven played an important role. The Team of Seven was composed of senior officials of the Ministry of Home Affairs, including Mr. Ryaas Rasyid (who later became State Minister for Regional Autonomy), university professors and two experts of GTZ, a German technical cooperation agency. The Law No. 22/1999 and the Law No. 25/1999 originally envisaged a transitional phase of two years (May 1999 to May 2001) to finalize the regulatory framework for decentralization and to prepare the internal arrangement of regions. However, the transitional period was shortened and the new system began to function from January 2001 onwards. An inter-departmental team was established to coordinate the process between the ministries involved and the Ministry of Home Affairs (Shiroyama 2001, p. 42).

One important mechanism for coordinating decentralization is the Advisory Board for Regional Autonomy (DPOD: Dewan Pertimbangan Otonomi Daerah). It conducts studies, formulates policies on regional governments and monitors/evaluates the implementation of policies. The DPOD is made up of 15 members, including Chairman (Minister of Home Affairs and Regional Autonomy), Vice-Chairman (Minister of Finance), central government representatives (Minister of Defence, Minister for Reform of the State Apparatus, National Secretary, the head of the National Development Planning Agency (BAPENAS)), and representatives of regional governments (the head of the association of provincial autonomous bodies, the head of the association of regency autonomous bodies, the head of the municipal autonomous bodies, and two representatives each from the provinces, regencies, and municipalities). As the ratio of representation implies (9 of 15 members are representatives of regional interests), the DPOD can work as a forum putting regional pressure on the central government.

In the process of decentralization, the roles and attitudes of the Ministry of Home Affairs and Regional Autonomy are very important. The Ministry has the DG for Regional Autonomy (incorporating the function of the State Minister for Regional Autonomy) in charge of institutional affairs and the DG of Regional Development in charge of development planning. It is true that the Ministry of Home Affairs and Regional Autonomy has concerns about excessive decentralization. However, it also has clear incentives to push decentralization and deconcentration toward regional governments against sectoral ministries of central government that exercise fragmented and sectoral controls on regional units.

2.4 Difficulties

Several difficulties were noticed through the decentralization efforts in Indonesia.

First, as the collapse of the Soeharto regime and various democratization initiatives following that were the source of political dynamism behind the decentralization, it is very hard to control the process of decentralization from an administrative point of view. It may be true that President Habibie used this decentralization reform issue as a tactical means to build up political credibility. However, now the momentum for decentralization has been released, new political "vested interests" have been quickly embedded around regional councils, and it is very hard to control it despite the intentions of donors and central ministries (Shiroyama 2001, p. 44).

Second, there is an issue of redefining the roles of provincial governments. In the process of decentralization in Indonesia, emphasis has been placed on the autonomy of local governments rather than on the autonomy of provincial governments, partly because of fears that provinces might go for independence if they are allowed wide autonomy (Shiroyama 2001, p. 44). In addition to that, no vertical relationship between provincial and local governments is defined in the laws, and conflicts between provincial governments and local governments have emerged. But thinking of equitable national development, there is still a clear need for strengthening the powers and capabilities of provincial governments for coordination and facilitating capacity building of local governments. It is also true that provincial governments perform the dual function, through agency delegation arrangements, the deconcentrated functions of central government in addition to the inherent functions even though that fact is not highlighted.

Third, there is an issue of the capabilities of regional governments (especially local governments). As many of the deconcentrated offices of central government agencies at the regional level were merged with the respective agencies of regional governments, and staff were also transferred to the regional governments, regional governments have to perform new functions with their newly-won responsibilities. For example, health policy is one such area. The Ministry of Health in the central government used to have its own field offices but those are now merged into regional governments so that local governments have to manage health policy including personnel management by themselves. However, it is reported that officials without any expertise in the health area are appointed to the post of director of health policy in local governments because of inadequateness and politicization of personnel management.

Next, there is an issue of local taxation. As already discussed, it was reported that various problematic taxation was undertaken, that became obstacles in internal business practices. Examples are the tax on car licence plates, tax on non-smoking signs of factories, and tax on river freight crossing borders of regional governments (Shiroyama 2001, p. 41).

In addition to those, there is the problem of financial management of regional councils (especially local councils). The regional budget over which a local council has the auditing power has been increased after the regional allocations increased in absolute terms and the ratio of block grants to total subsidies from the central government has grown. And various political parties now have representation in the council, and the local council has the right to decide the salaries of their members. Under those conditions, many local councils have increased their own salaries (Okamoto 2001, p. 27) but many stories of "money politics" were reported (Okamoto 2001, p. 8).

3. Thailand

3.1 Background

The centralized regional administration system remained for nearly a century since the Chakri reformation at the end of the 19th century in Thailand. There is a parallel system of regional administration and regional autonomous government in the regional governance of Thailand.

According to Article 51 of the National Administration Organization Act of 1991, the regional administration consists of provinces and districts. Provinces and districts consist of offices of the various ministries, agencies, and departments of the central government. The governors at the provincial level and district officers at the district level are the heads of these regional administrative units. Provinces and districts are not local governments but field agencies of the central government. Governors of provinces and district officers were the Interior Ministry's bureaucrats appointed by the central government. There are 75 provinces and 769 districts (Hashimoto 1998, p. 200).

As the lowest unit below districts, *tambons* and villages have been established. Heads of these units (*kamnan* and village head) are elected by residents, but they are paid by the central Ministry of Interior and also supervised by a district officer (Hashimoto 1999a, p. 7). The basic structure of administrative units of province, district, *tambon* and village is based on the Local Administration Act of 1914 (Nagai 2001, p. 55; Hashimoto 1999a, p. 7).

There has also been gradual development of a regional autonomous government system to a limited extent. In urban areas, sanitary districts were experimented with in Bangkok in 1897 and institutionalized by law in 1908. The number was 35 in 1908 (Hashimoto 1998, p. 202). The main function of a sanitary district was waste disposal. In 1933, *thesaban* (municipalities) were established by law. A *thesaban* had its own council, and mayors of *thesaban* were elected from the council members who were elected by the residents. The number of *thesaban* was 33 in 1935, 115 in 1945 and 149 in 1998 (Nagai 2001, p. 44). Provincial Administration Organizations (PAOs) were originally established in 1955 to establish an autonomous organization in rural areas that did not belong to either *thesaban* or sanitary districts, since there were no local governments equivalent to *thesaban* or sanitary districts in rural areas. Governors who were dispatched from the Ministry of Interior were the chief executives of PAOs but provincial councils elected by residents were established at PAOs (Nagai 2001, p. 44).

In Bangkok, a special system was established based on the Bangkok Metropolitan Administration Law in 1985. The governor of the Bangkok Metropolitan Administration is directly elected and does not belong to the Ministry of Interior, but still has to be supervised by the Minister of Interior as well (Nagai 2001, p. 53; Hashimoto 1999a, p. 14).

Thailand experienced rapid economic development in the late 1980s and 1990s. Since after the political turmoil in 1992 for democratization, various democratization initiatives have been undertaken. The decentralization movement is closely linked with democratization in the 1990s. Prime Minister Chuan said in October 1992, "Decentralization should be achieved through the implementation of public elections for the heads of local governments and executive bodies at all levels" (Nagai 2001, p. 42; Hashimoto 1999a, p. 19).

Under the trends above, the Constitution was amended in 1997 to pay more attention to decentralization. Article 78 of the Constitution prescribes the promotion of decentralization as a basic policy of the government. Articles 282–290 are articles related to local autonomy. Article 284 requires the definition of plans and procedures for decentralization as a separate Act. After the adoption of the Constitution in 1997, Prime Minister Chuan established the Committee of Revision of Local Government Acts and Decentralization Promotion. Based on the deliberation in the committee, the Act of Decentralization Plan and Procedures was adopted in November 1999.

Gradual progress toward decentralization can be noticed through the developments above. But now under new Prime Minister Thaksin, there are some uncertainties about the future direction of decentralization in Thailand.

3.2 Contents

The Constitution in 1997 had many articles relating to local autonomy but there was no such comprehensive law as a Local Government Act or Local Autonomy Act in Thailand. Amendments of relevant acts were required of the Constitution in 1997 by October 1999. There are several aspects of the regional structure of decentralization and deconcentration that have been reconstructed from around 1997.

First, TAOs (*Tambon* Administration Organizations) were established in 1994 based on the *Tambon* Administration Organization Act of 1994. *Tambons* are administrative units of central government below district level. Although TAOs share similar territorial extensions with *tambons*, they have independent judicial person status and are local autonomous bodies. This creation of TAOs tremendously increased the number of autonomous bodies. There were 6,746 TAOs in 2000 (Nagai 2001, p. 54). Financial grants to TAOs are also established by the central government. In 2001, general grants of 10 billion Baht were provided by the DOLA (Department of Local Administration) of the Ministry of Interior. In addition, specific grants of 23 billion Baht were provided by the Office of Accelerated Rural Development of the Public Works Department of the Ministry of Interior, and other ministries (Nagai 2001, p. 61).

Second, *thesaban* were restructured. The number of *thesaban* was limited and there were only 149 *thesaban* even in 1998. But in May 1999, sanitary districts were upgraded to *thesaban*, and as a result there were 1,129 *thesaban* (Nagai 2001, p. 44). *Thesaban* had their own councils, and chief executives of *thesaban* were elected from the council members who were elected by the residents. But now direct election of the head of *thesaban* has been introduced. The new Municipality Act was passed in May 2000. In the law, it is stipulated that mayors of *thesaban* (metropolitan municipalities) and cities will be directly elected after their current term, and that mayors of *thesaban* (suburban municipalities) will be directly elected in 2007 (Cuachon 2002, p. 146). *Thesaban* also get general grants and specific grants from the central government (Nagai 2001, p. 62).

Third, Provincial Administration Organizations (PAOs) made a fresh start as provincial autonomous organizations. As already discussed, PAOs were originally established in 1955 to establish a regional autonomous organization in a rural area that did not belong to either *thesaban* or sanitary districts, but the governors of provinces who were dispatched from the Ministry of Interior were also appointed to the chief executives of PAOs. After the establishment of TAOs in 1994 mentioned above, a problem emerged — much of the financial source of PAOs was taken by TAOs. Under those conditions, PAOs restructured themselves. Because of Article 285 of the Constitution in 1997, the chief executives of PAOs have to be elected from among the council members. In addition, according to the Act of PAOs in 1997, a new tax source was granted which enables PAOs to restructure themselves (Nagai 2001, p. 44). There are also grants to PAOs from the central government, but these are only specific grants (Nagai 2001, p. 62).

Fourth, the Act of Decentralization Plan and Procedures adopted in November 1999 prescribed that local governments should be allotted at least 20% of the government budget in 2001, and 35% by 2006. The baseline was 6.3% in 1985 and 8.74% even in 1995 (Hashimoto 1999b, p. 91). Considering those baselines, the magnitude of the increase is large. For example, it was reported that there was a 63.02% increase of local share in 2001 compared to the previous year (Suwanmala 2002, p. 12). The ratio of tax revenue between central and regional governments is decided annually by the NDC (National Decentralization Committee) established by law in 1999.

3.3 Process

After 1992, various democratization initiatives have been taken, and the decentralization movement was closely linked with democratization in 1990s. Political parties promoted public elections for governors when it was a major issue from 1992 to 1994 (Nagai 2001, p. 45).

But when the Democratic Party and the New Aspiration Party became governing parties, they withdrew support for direct elections. One of the reasons for the loss of interest of political parties in direct elections of governors and mayors might be resistance of traditional political elites in local areas. When TAOs (*Tambon* Administration Organization) were introduced in 1994, *kamnan* and village headmen who formed the traditional backbone of the local administration campaigned against the introduction of TAOs. The Ministry of Interior incorporated the *kamnan* and the village headmen into TAOs under the agreement that allowed them to become an "appointed council member" for limited period (Nagai 2001, p. 45).

Article 284 of the Constitution in 1997 requires the definition of plans and procedures for decentralization as a separate Act, the establishment of a committee of three parties (representatives of affiliated government agencies, regional governments, and intellectuals) as part of the process, and the committee would prescribe the allocation of administrative authority as well as taxation and surcharges between the central government and local governments. Based on the Article, after the adoption of the Constitution in 1997, Prime Minister Chuan established the Committee of Revision of Local Government Acts and Decentralization Promotion. Based on the discussion at the Committee, the Act of Decentralization Plan and Procedures was adopted in November 1999, which defined six areas of responsibilities (planning, investment, commerce and tourism; infrastructure construction and maintenance; life quality promotion; security and orderliness; protection of environment; art, culture and local wisdom) to be transferred to regional autonomous organizations depending on the categories of regional governments. The Act also established the National Decentralization Committee (NDC) composed of representatives of relevant ministries, representatives of local autonomous bodies, and representatives of intellectuals (Hashimoto 1999b, p. 89). The plan by the NDC was proposed in August 2000 and was approved by the cabinet.

In an environment of political parties' weakening interests in decentralization, the Ministry of Interior seems to play an important role for decentralization and deconcentration. The Ministry of Interior seems to be promoting decentralization and at the same time carrying out a devolution of authority (deconcentration) to the field agencies of the national government. It is inevitable that the role of the Ministry of Interior will diminish in the long term. But the Ministry of Interior has the large discretional authority to supervise local autonomous bodies even under decentralization.

The Ministry of Interior has made an effort to strengthen the function at the provincial level through deconcentration to the provincial level, and tries to coordinate deconcentrated functions operated by various ministries (Nagai 2001, p. 47; Hashimoto 1999b, p. 81). In addition, governors and district officers dispatched from the Ministry of Interior still enjoy broad authority such as for approval of annual development plans including detailed items in the budget for PAOs, *thesaban*, and TAOs, dissolution of the councils of local autonomous bodies, and dismissal of council members from the local council (Nagai 2001, p. 47). For the administration of deconcentrated functions, the DOLA (Department of Local Administration) of the Ministry of Interior still has a staff of more than 20,000 and strong power (Hashimoto 1999b, p. 83).

In the field of education and public health, there seems to be a trend not towards decentralization, but towards deconcentration of authority. The setting up by the central government of 295 "education areas" or "Area Health Boards" in each province was discussed in the national policy arena (Nagai 2001, p. 64).

Of course, some of the functions were decentralized to regional governments, and institutional reforms were undertaken to respond to the changed functions. For example, transfer of personnel and administration to local governments was undertaken. However, it was reported that there was resistance by civil servants, especially front line bureaucrats (Nagai 2001, p. 48) and strong influence by the Ministry of Interior concerning personnel affairs of regional governments continues through the *Thesaban* Civil Service Committee chaired by the Minister of Interior (Hashimoto 1999b, p. 105) and other channels.

There is also more opportunity for local autonomous bodies to receive grants, not just from the central government but also from local government agencies. The grants for local autonomous bodies were provided until 2001 only through the Department of Local Administration (DOLA) of the Ministry of Interior. However, since 2001, local autonomous bodies can receive grants also from other ministries and agencies as well according to the regulations in the 1999 Act on Decentralization Plan and Procedures (Nagai 2001, p. 47).

3.4 Difficulties

Several difficulties are noticed through the decentralization efforts in Thailand.

First, there is an issue of the relationship between regional administrative units of central government and regional autonomous government bodies that share similar territory, that is, the relationship between provinces and PAOs or the relationship between districts/*tambons* and *thesaban*/TAOs.

Now under the trend of decentralization, financial resources of TAOs are increasing. For example, this is true of the AIDS project in the health sector. However, the TAOs do not have enough technical expertise for performing those responsibilities. So what sometimes happens is that TAOs arrange contracts with provinces and districts for performing those functions in exchange for financial transfer to regional administrative units.

Heads of PAOs were governors of provinces but since 1997, heads of PAOs are elected from council members, and they are different from governors (Hashimoto 1999a, p. 10). The function of the governor who held the dual function of the head of the district and the PAO is now separated into the function of the governor as the head of the regional administrative unit and the function as the head of PAO representing regional autonomous governments. If the heads of provinces are directly elected by the public, as was proposed in the early phase of decentralization efforts, the separated functions will merge again in a different manner (Nelson 2001, p. 8). However, this scenario seems not to be realized.

Second, there is an issue of direct election versus indirect election of chief executives of regional governments. All mayors of *thesabans* will be elected by direct elections in 2007. On the other hand, after 1997, heads of PAOs are elected from council members. Direct election of governors was discussed in 1992 but the issue disappeared afterwards (Hashimoto 1999a, p.19).

Third, there is an issue of corruption. Under the condition of increasing budgets (mainly subsidies) for regional governments, there are increasing opportunities for corruption. It is reported that corruption was discovered in 363 TAOs of a total of 6,397 TAOs between January 1996 and June 1998 (Hashimoto 1999b, p. 120). The Miyazawa Fund, set up for the mitigation of the impacts of the Asian financial crisis, provided additional sources for TAOs. Of the total of 53.6 billion Baht, 20 billion was allocated to the Ministry of Interior, of which 13.3 billion was channelled to TAOs through the DOLA. It is said that there are cases of corruption concerning the use of the Miyazawa Fund (Hashimoto 1999b, p. 128).

4. Korea

4.1 Background

The Local Autonomy Law was enacted in 1949 in Korea. It set up provincial governments ("do") and local governments (cities, etc.) as autonomous bodies. Under the Japanese colonial regime, there used to be "do" as a local administration unit and "do" as a local autonomous unit (separation of administrative units of central government and regional autonomous units). Contrary to that regime, the new law established "do" only as a regional autonomous body, but governors of provinces and the mayor of Seoul special city were national civil servants appointed by the President, although other mayors of cities, etc. were local civil servants elected by a local council (Kan 1999, p. 31). Under the Local Autonomy Law, local council elections were undertaken in 1952, 1956, and 1960 (Okada 2002, p. 7).

The military revolution happened in 1961 and the local autonomy system was suspended through the adoption of a Temporary Law on Local Autonomy. The amended Local Autonomy Law required that all the governors of provinces and mayors of cities be appointed by the central government and related law stipulated that organizational rules of regional governments were set by cabinet order of the central government (Kan 1999, p. 33). Local autonomy had been suspended during the long period of authoritarian regimes from 1961 to 1987.

Under the trends of democratization, the Local Autonomy Law was revised and a separate Law on Election of Local Council was enacted 1988. Through these legislations, local and provincial assemblies were re-established. In June 1991, local assembly elections were held after three decades of suspension. In June 1995, governors and mayors were publicly elected. Governors and mayors became local civil servants (Kan 1999, p. 34–35; Okada 2002, p. 13; Kyoung-Ryung 1998, p. 10).

4.2 Contents

As discussed above, the revised Law on Local Autonomy and related laws re-established the local assemblies at various levels, and enabled the direct election of governors and mayors. Heads of the regional (provincial and local) governments are elected by direct vote of residents. The term is four years, and a maximum of three terms is permitted for the same candidate. Regional (provincial and local) councils are comprised of council members who are also elected by their residents.

On the other hand, there remain various limitations to decentralization. For example, the Local Autonomy Act revised in 1994 stipulates in Articles 15 and 16 that local governments and councils are allowed to make local ordinances only "within the scope of the national laws and presidential (administrative) orders" (Kyoung-Ryung 1998, p. 10). The central government set the basic rules for local organizational and personnel management. For instance, the total number of organizational divisions, requirement for specific divisions (e.g., Division for Planning), the total number of public employees, and the rules for promotion and pay raises are all regulated by the central government. Although these regulations have been weakened to some extent since 1997, the basic institutional structure remains largely intact (Kyoung-Ryung 1998, p. 11).

Article 93 of the amended Law on Local Autonomy established the agency delegation system, and governors and mayors have to perform a dual function (Kan 1999, p. 34–35). As personnel support to the agency delegation system, Articles 103–4 of the Local Autonomy Law and related law stipulates that national civil servants can be allocated to posts of provincial and local governments at a higher level. The total number of national civil servants located at provincial and local governments was 9,730 in January 1995. The number is gradually decreasing (Kan 1999, p. 36). The total number of provincial and local government employees was about 242,000 people. In addition to the loaning of national civil servants, the Ministry in charge (the Ministry of Government Administration and Home Affairs: MOGAHA) of central government manages the recruitment and training of local civil servants above a specific grade, and the Local Senior Civil Service Examination was introduced. MOGAHA also formulates a mid-term finance plan of local government every year.

Concerning the scope of decentralization, some parts of the health sector seem to have been transferred to regional autonomous governments but a major part of the education sector still remains under the purview of the central government.

Financial bases of provincial and local governments have been strengthened gradually. The share of local tax among total tax revenue was 8.3% in 1970, 10.2% in 1975, 11.7% in 1980, 12.2% in 1985, 19.0% in 1990, 21.8% in 1995 and 21.0% in 1998 (Osung 2002, p. 7). In addition, there are various mechanisms of transfer to provincial and local governments. The central government allocates 15% of national tax revenue to local governments. For example, 100% of liquor tax, 14.2% of transportation tax and 15.3% of special agricultural tax are transferred. There are also various subsidy programmes by MOGAHA and other relevant ministries.

4.3 Process

Decentralization in Korea has also progressed under the movements of democratization, the Local Autonomy Law was revised in 1988 by a new democratized administration.

One of the characteristics of the Korean process of decentralization is that the process is gradual. The Local Autonomy Law was amended in 1988, the first local council election was held in June 1991, and governors of provincial governments and mayors of local governments were publicly elected in June 1995. All together it took seven years from legislation to full implementation. In the process, the Ministry of Home Affairs and the re-organized MOGAHA have been key players. Another interesting aspect of Korean decentralization is that large-scale mergers of local governments were undertaken just before the local and provincial elections in 1995 (Okada 2002, p. 13).

Korea is now in the second phase of the decentralization programme. It was facilitated by President Kim and international pressure for adjusting to the Asian financial crisis since 1998 (Okada 2002, p. 17). The Law for the Promotion and Transfer of the Central Authority to Localities was adopted in July 1999. The law established a decentralization promotion committee directly under the President and the committee works on issues for promoting decentralization. It is planned that the Comprehensive Decentralization Law will be adopted in 2003 (Cuachon 2002, p. 39; Ishikawa 2002, p. 2).

4.4 Difficulties

Several difficulties are noticed through the decentralization efforts in Korea.

First, there is an issue of the relationship between chief executives and councils at various levels of regional governments. The relationship in Korea is sometimes characterized as "executive-dominated local government" or "mayor-led local politics". It means that despite the constitution of local councils or assemblies, substantial decision-making powers remain with the elected local leaders, particularly in small to medium-size cities and metropolitan areas (Cuachon 2002, p. 38; Kyoung-Ryung 1998, p. 16). The asymmetry was strengthened by permission of power to chief executives to dissolve councils in the amendment of the Local Autonomy Act in 1999 (Okada 2002, p. 15).

Second, there is an issue of high ratio of agency delegation function in regional government activities and to support the working of the agency delegation system, the system of transfer of national civil servants to regional governments has been preserved.

Third, it is sometimes pointed out that even after the progress of official programmes of decentralization, there is still a tendency in the sentiments of citizens to rely on central government and to blame others rather than to resort to self-help based on the principle of local autonomy (Okada 2002, p. 34).

5. Conclusion – Comparative Analysis

The decentralization and deconcentration experiments of Indonesia, Thailand and Korea have been analyzed in the above sections. These countries are similar in that they had centralized regimes before decentralization, and that decentralization has progressed in parallel with the development of democratization for the last decade. But their experiments are different concerning the timing and speed of decentralization, the combinations of decentralization and deconcentration, the relationship between councils/assemblies and chief executives, the personnel system between central and regional governments, the financial system between central and regional governments, the issue of corruption and needs for capacity building at the local level, and the role of the Ministry of Interior or Home Affairs in the process of managing decentralization and deconcentration. In this concluding section, I would like to compare the cases of Indonesia, Thailand, and Korea in those aspects.

First, concerning the timing and the speed of decentralization, the processes in Korea and Thailand are gradual compared to the very rapid process in Indonesia. Because of the revolutionary nature of regime change to democracy and the inherent heterogeneous nature of Indonesian society, the political momentum pushing forward to decentralization especially at the local level has been very strong, and it is very hard for the ministries of central governments or international donors to control the process.

Second, concerning the combinations of decentralization and deconcentration, it is at least possible to say that there is no simple decentralization in those three countries and that some delicate combinations of decentralization and deconcentration are experimented with in each societal context. It means that textbook application of simple decentralization models does not work in the concrete setting of Asian countries.

Beyond that, the three countries can be characterized in the following way. Korea is a country where decentralization progressed (including the direct election of governors and mayors), and decentralized regional governments also perform the deconcentrated functions of the central government through the arrangement of agency delegation. Thailand is a country where decentralization and deconcentration progressed in a parallel way. That is, decentralization progressed in Thailand through the establishment of TAOs, increasing number of *thesaban*, replacement of heads of PAOs from double appointment of governors of provinces to election by the council members elected by residents. On the other hand, deconcentration progressed through the strengthening of the provincial organizations of the central government by the Ministry of Interior and other sectoral ministries. Indonesia is a country where relatively simple decentralization, especially of local governments, occurred. But still, even in Indonesia, provincial governments perform deconcentrated functions of central government through the arrangement of agency delegation, and the central government has deconcentrated offices in the limited functional area.

Third, concerning the relationship between councils/assemblies and governors/mayors, Korea is a country where chief executives (governors and mayors) are strong, partly because they are directly elected by the public. On the other hand, Indonesia is a country where councils or assemblies are stronger, partly because they have the power to force chief executives to resign if they twice disapprove of the chief executives' accountability reports at the end of each year. In Thailand, it is not clear whether councils/assemblies or chief executives are stronger in regional administrative units such as PAOs and TAOs. But there are strong third actors, that is, the agents of central government (governor or district officer) who still have very strong supervising power over regional autonomous organizations.

Fourth, concerning the personnel system between central governments to regional units, each of the three countries had a system of sending national civil servants to regional units, either to regional offices of the central government or to regional autonomous governments through the personnel support arrangement of agency delegation. Thailand has huge human resources (20,000 staff) in the DOLA of the Ministry of Interior, who are sent to provinces and districts as governors or district officers or junior officers. The health and education sectors are also under the central government's purview via deconcentrated administrative units. Korea has a huge pool of national civil servant teachers, who are mainly stationed in regional units. In addition, Korea has the system of transfer of national civil servants to regional governments even after the decentralization reform. The number of central civil service seconded to regional governments (9,730 staff in 1995) is decreasing, but the system is still preserved. Indonesia had so many central civil servants working in the deconcentrated offices of central ministries or regional government at the higher level, but after the decentralization, a large-scale transfer of central civil servants to regional civil servants had to be planned and implemented. Roughly 1.9 million central civil servants, including 1.1 million teachers and 0.2 million staff working for the Ministry of Health, out of roughly 3.2 million total central civil servants were transferred. The original number of regional civil servants was 0.7 million and that means that the number of regional civil servants increased nearly four times.

Fifth, concerning the financial system between central and regional governments, each government is increasing regional shares of government expenditure. Indonesia allows incremental strengthening of regional tax base, and guarantees at least 25% of central revenue to regional governments (1999 Law No. 25). In Thailand, the Act of Decentralization Plan and Procedure stipulated that local governments should be allotted at least 20% of the government budget in 2001 and 35% by 2006. But it seems that the tax bases of regional autonomous governments are still weak. Contrary to those countries, Korea has a relatively strong regional tax base. The share of regional tax among total tax revenue was 8.3% in 1970, and increased to 10.2% in 1975, 11.7% in 1980, 12.2% in 1985, 19.0% in 1990, 21.8% in 1995 and 21.0% in 1998. In addition, the central government allocates 15% of national tax revenue to regional governments.

Sixth, concerning the issue of corruption and need for capacity building at the regional level, similar issues can be identified in each country. But the issue seems to be most severe in Indonesia and Thailand, especially Indonesia. Because of decentralization, regional governments, especially local governments, have more resources. But they sometimes use the resources to increase their salaries and for corrupt purposes.

Seventh, in each country, the Ministry of Interior or Home Affairs has similar incentives in the process of managing decentralization and deconcentration. The Ministry has incentives to restrain the levels of decentralization and deconcentration against the interests of regional autonomous governments. On the other hand, the Ministry has incentives to promote the levels of decentralization and deconcentration against the interests of line/sectoral ministries.

The combinations of decentralization and deconcentration in Indonesia, Thailand and Korea are interesting in that they show us the institutional range for designing decentralization reform. In addition, those differences concerning various dimensions of regional governance may reflect the difference in the social, political and constitutional conditions of Indonesia, Thailand and Korea. So these cases can be a basis for analyzing further the match and mismatch between institutional arrangements for decentralization and social, political and constitutional conditions.

References

General
JICA. 1995. *Sankagata Kaihatsu to Yoki Touchi* (Participatory Development and Good Governance).
JICA. 2001. *Government Decentralization Reforms in Development Countries*. Institute of International Cooperation (JICA).
Morita, Akira (ed.). *Asia no Chihou Seido* (Local Governments in Asia). Tokyo: Tokyo University Press.
Okada, Yuki. *Hatten Tojoukoku niokeru Bunkenka no Hikaku — Kankoku to Indonesia wo Chushin ni* (The Process of Regional Decentralization in Developing Countries — Focusing on Indonesia and Korea). MA Thesis. Graduate School of Law and Politics, The University of Tokyo.
UNDP. 1997. *Governance for Sustainable Human Development: Policy Document*.
World Bank. 1992. *Governance and Development*, Washington, D.C: The World Bank.

Indonesia
Morita, Akira. 1998. "Indonesia". In *Asia no Chihou Seido*, edited by Akira Morita. Tokyo: Tokyo University Press.
Okamoto, Masaki. 2001. "Decentralization in Indonesia: a Project for National Integration", in JICA.
Shiroyama, Hideaki. 2001. "Gabanansu Kaikaku no Jissenn to Kadai — Indonesia no Chihou Bunken wo Sozai toshite (Practice and Issues of Governance Reforms — the Case of Decentralization in Indonesia)", in *Ajia no Gabanansu (Governance of Asia)*, JIIA.

GTZ. 2003. "Decentralization in Indonesia since 1999 — An Overview", <http://www. gtzsfdm.or.id/dec in ind.htm>, accessed April 2003.

Thailand
Cuachon, Nora. 2002. "Thailand: The Continuing Quest for Local Autonomy", *Sourcebook on Decentralization in Asia*, Asian Resource Center for Decentralization.
Hashimoto. 1998. "Tai (Thailand)", in Morita, ed.
Hashimoto, Takashi. 1999a. "Tai niokeru Chihouseido Kaikaku no Doukou to Kadai (Local Government Reform in Thailand: Trends and Problems) (1)", *Doshisha Hogaku* (Doshisha Law Review), vol. 50–54.
Hashimoto, Takashi. 1999b. "Tai niokeru Chihouseido Kaikaku no Doukou to Kadai (Local Government Reform in Thailand: Trends and Problems) (1)", *Doshisha Hogaku* (Doshisha Law Review), vol. 50–55.
Jichitai Kokusaika Kyoukai. 2000. "Tai no Chihoubunken no ugoki to Jinzai Ikusei (Trends of Decentralization in Thailand and Human Resource Development)".
Nagai, Fumio. 2001. "Decentralization in Thailand", in JICA.
Nelson, Michael H. 2001. "Thailand: Problems with Decentralization?" Paper at the International Conference on Building Institutional Capacity in Asia, Jakarta, 12 March 2001.
Suwanmala, Charas. 2002. "Fiscal Decentralization in Thailand". Paper at Bali Intergovernmental Fiscal Reform Workshop.

Korea
Cuachon, Nora. 2002. "South Korea: Enabling local governments and civil society," *Sourcebook on Decentralization in Asia*, Asian Resource Center for Decentralization.
Ishikawa, Yoshinori. 2002. "Kankoku no Chihou Jichi wo Megutte (Local Autonomy in Korea)", *Chihou Jichi* (Local Autonomy) 657.
Kan Zeho. 1999. "Kankoku no Chihou Jichi to Kyouiku Jichi (Local Autonomy and Education Autonomy in Korea)," *Kikan Gyousei Kanri Kenkyu* (Administrative Management Research Quarterly) no. 87.
Kyoujng-Ryung Seong. 1998. "Delayed Decentralization and Incomplete Consolidation of Democracy: The Case of Korean Local Autonomy." Paper for Hoover Conference on Institutional Reform and Democratic Consolidation in Korea.
Osung Kwon. 2002. "The Effects of Fiscal Decentralization on Public Spending: The Korean Case". Paper for 13th Annual Meeting on Public Budgeting and Financial Management, Washington D.C.

2

Governance and Poverty Reduction: Evidence from Newly Decentralized Indonesia

Sudarno Sumarto, Asep Suryahadi, Alex Arifianto

1. Introduction

This study is the first attempt to systematically examine the impact of bad governance practices in Indonesia on poverty reduction. Indonesia is a country that has endured bad governance for a long period, but which has also sustained significant poverty reduction. Prior to the onset of the economic crisis in mid-1997, the problem of bad governance in Indonesia was apparent but mostly ignored because it was compensated by high economic growth. The advent of the economic crisis, however, has highlighted the seriousness of the problem. This study focuses on the impact of bad governance on the people who are most vulnerable — the poor. By assembling scattered anecdotal evidence on how past and current practices of bad governance in Indonesia have hurt the poor, this study shows that the adverse impact of bad governance on the poor is real, systematically affects many people, and undermines the efforts to reduce poverty in the country. More systematic evidence on how bad governance affects poverty reduction indicates that indeed regions that practise better governance experience faster poverty reduction and *vice versa*.

The ongoing economic crisis in Indonesia, which started in mid-1997, has brought attention back to the issue of poverty reduction. High economic growth during the previous three decades has been successful in reducing absolute poverty in the country. Between the early 1970s and the onset of the crisis, the official poverty rate was reduced by more than 50%. Due to the crisis, however, the poverty rate doubled, wiping out many years of progress and putting the issue of poverty back into prominence.[1]

At the same time, in searching for the causes of the crisis, the issue of governance was brought into the limelight. The hypothesis put forward was that bad governance — popularly known as KKN (corruption, collusion, and nepotism) in Indonesia — has weakened the Indonesian economy, making it prone to suffer from periodic crisis. Corruption was a notorious trademark of the New Order regime, which was famous for tolerating petty corruption by low level officials as a means to supplement their meagre salaries as well as promoting mega corruption by twisting government regulations to support the interests of the first-family and their cronies. Often this was accompanied by collusion with businesses — domestic as well as foreign entities — at the expense of the general public. Nearing its final years, the New Order corruption reached its nadir through the practice of nepotism. Family members and close friends of the first-family were appointed in executive as well as legislative positions.[2]

Bad governance during the regimes of the New Order and its successor governments has placed Indonesia at the top the list of the most corrupt countries in the world for a long time. However, prior to the onset of the economic crisis in mid-1997, the problem was mostly ignored. This was primarily because the economy was expanding, which was a result of the high economic growth experienced by the country. For most people, this was enough to compensate for the losses and inefficiencies due to the bad governance. The advent of the economic crisis, however, has highlighted the seriousness of the problem. The People Consultative Assembly (MPR), the highest representative body in Indonesia, even issued a decree on the need to create clean and good governance in the country. Efforts to achieve this, however, have so far proved difficult and elusive.[3]

Recent thinking on poverty reduction and governance argues that both are interrelated. Bad governance has made poverty reduction efforts ineffective,[4] while poverty reduction projects provide a fertile ground for corruption.[5] The consensus that emerges from this line of thinking is that good governance is necessary for poverty reduction efforts to be effective.

The remainder of this chapter consists of the following. First, it reviews theories and definitions of governance and its links with poverty reduction and corruption. Next, it discusses the existing literature on governance, poverty, and corruption, both internationally and in the Indonesian context. Then, it proceeds with our research on governance and poverty in Indonesia, compiling scattered anecdotal evidence on how bad governance has hurt the poor as well as conducting more systematic analysis on how governance affects poverty reduction. Finally, this chapter provides a conclusion and policy recommendation based on the findings.

2. Theories and definitions of governance, poverty reduction, and corruption

2.1 Governance

Governance is an old concept that originates from early democratic political theory that discusses what the relationship between the rulers and the people they ruled should be like. For instance, in the 19th century Woodrow Wilson defines a government that practises good governance as "a government that can properly and succesfully ... with the utmost possible efficiency and at the least possible cost of either money or of energy" (cited in Laporte 2002, p. 3).

However, only in the past decade or so did governance gain significant attention in the international policy-making arena. This was motivated by a concern that bilateral and multilateral assistance from the developed to developing world had failed to achieve its goals (i.e., reduce poverty and promote sustainable economic growth). This was because of poor administrative capacity of the developing countries' governments to administer these projects and widespread corruption. From this, donors concluded that good governance is essential for the success of their assistance in the developing world. Since then, they have begun linking development assistance to the adoption of good government practices by the developing countries.

There are several definitions of governance that are put forward by different bilateral and multilateral lending agencies. Some of them are described here. The World Bank (1992) defines good governance as:

> A public service that is efficient, a judicial system that is reliable, and an administration that is accountable to its public .... Good governance, for the World Bank, is synonymous with sound development management .... [It] is central to creating and sustaining an environment which fosters strong and equitable development, and it is an essential complement to sound economic policies.

Furthermore, the World Bank (1992) defines three different dimensions of governance. First, the form of a political regime (parliamentary or presidential, military or civilian, and authoritarian or democratic); second, the processes by which authority is exercised in the management of a country's economic and social resources; and third, the capacity of the government to design, formulate, and implement policies, and, in general, to discharge governmental functions.

In 1995, in a speech that outlined his country's new policy on foreign assistance to developing countries, the United States Vice President Albert Gore, Jr. as cited in LaPorte (2002, p. 4) stated the five principles of good governance: (1) The administration of the state must be honest and transparent; (2) The administration of the state should be streamlined and as efficient as possible; (3) The government must decentralize as many functions as possible and deliver services as close to the people as possible; (4) Democratic states must make provisions for the security of their people; and (5) Democratic states must rely on an open and modern judiciary.

Meanwhile, the United Nations Development Program defines governance as:

> The exercise of economic, political, and administrative authority to manage a country's affairs at all levels. It comprises of the mechanisms, processes, and institutions through which citizens and groups articulate their interests, exercise their legal rights, meet their obligations, and mediate their differences (UNDP 1997).

Finally, the World Bank economists Daniel Kaufmann, Aart Kraay, and Pablo Zoido-Lobation (1999) define governance as:

> ... the traditions and institutions by which authority in a country is exercised, including (1) the processes by which governments are selected, monitored, and replaced, (2) the capacity of the government to effectively formulate and implement sound policies, and (3) the respect of citizens and the state for the institutions that govern economic and social interaction among them.

In sum, governance is a multidimensional concept which consists of political, economic and sociocultural variables that determine whether public policy designed by the government could achieve its intended goals and improve the welfare of society. From the various definitions of good governance above, Kinutha-Njenga (date unknown) concluded that the criteria for good governance are as follows:

> (1) The government of the country is democratically elected and promotes/ protects human rights and the rule of law; (2) There is a strong and healthy civil society movement in the country; (3) The government of the country is able to create and implement effective public policy; and (4) The government of the country organizes the country's economy along the premise of free, competitive, and efficient markets.

2.2 Governance and Poverty Reduction

Along with the new thinking on governance, donors also incorporate a new thinking on poverty and the relationship between these two variables. They recognize that poverty is a multidimensional concept and is not limited to economic terms alone. Besides a lack of income, the poor also suffer from a lack, or a complete absence of, services (public utilities, public transportation, healthcare, education, credit, etc.) and a lack of participation in social, economic, and political decisions at the local, regional, and national level. Because of this, the poor often feel that they are excluded, and helpless when their rights are violated and exploited by the wealthy and the powerful (Eid 2000).

Drawing from the experience of more than 50 years of developmental assistance to developing countries, developed countries and multilateral lending institutions now conclude that good governance is a necessary prerequisite for poverty reduction, because of the following: (1) Without good governance, the scarce resources available are not generally put to their best use in combating poverty. This is often due to a lack of transparency, rampant corruption, and an uncertain legal system which hinders the economic growth that could help pull the poor out of poverty; (2) Good governance is necessary if all aspects of poverty are to be reduced, not just through an increase in income, but also through empowerment and increasing the economic, political and social opportunities for the poor (Blaxall 2000; Eid 2000).

To accomplish these goals, institutions that support governance need to be reformed and strengthened. In the past decade, donors have created governance support programmes that assist developing countries in reforming their civil service and strengthening their institutions, with the hope that improved governance will create an economic and political climate that will increase economic growth in these countries and eventually draw the poor populace out of poverty. For instance, the World Bank started its governance programme in 1992 and the Asian Development Bank (ADB) started a similar programme in 1997. On a bilateral level, USAID formally launched its governance programme in 1995, while DFID (United Kingdom), CIDA (Canada) and GTZ (Germany) started their governance programmes in the early 1990s.

The focus of these programmes are: civil service reform both at the central, regional and local government levels; legal and judicial system reform; legislative institutions reform; capacity building of NGOs and other civil society organizations; and government efficiency and effectiveness reform (LaPorte 2002; Eid 2000). On improving the welfare of the poor, the World Bank's governance reform programme has four aims: (1) Empowering the poor; (2) Improving the capacity of the poor by improving basic services; (3) Providing economic opportunities by increasing access to markets; and (4) Providing security from economic shocks and from corruption, crime, and violence (Blaxall 2000).

It is hoped that through these programmes, the goal of lasting poverty reduction and improved governance in the developing world can be finally achieved.

2.3 Corruption

Corruption, as the antithesis of good governance, is defined by the World Bank as the abuse of public office for private gain. Corruption scholar Robert Klitgaard hypothesizes that corruption is more likely to occur in an environment where officials have monopolistic control over state resources and a high level of discretion over who can gain access to those resources, while at the same time the mechanisms for holding these officials accountable for their actions are weak or non-existent.[6] It is widely recognized today as a symptom of poor governance and a major obstacle to poverty reduction efforts. While in the past, some have argued that corruption could increase economic efficiency in countries with burdensome regulations and a dominant government role in the economy,[7] today most scholars studying corruption believe that it curbs economic growth, degrades social and political institutions, and hinders efforts toward poverty reduction. Especially for the poor, corruption could create adverse consequences for them, both directly and indirectly.

There are some avenues through which corruption makes poverty reduction efforts ineffective:

(1) Corruption diverts funds for poverty reduction to the pockets of corrupt officials;

(2) Corruption twists the budget allocation away from poverty reduction to other projects more closely associated with the interests of corrupt officials;

(3) Corruption creates a high-cost economy, obstructs the creation of a healthy and conducive economic environment, which is essential for the poor to work and do business;

(4) Corruption jeopardizes the property rights of the poor, since corrupt officials often force the poor out of their homes and off their land, so that they can be used for development projects sponsored by the developers who bribed them; and

(5) Corruption prevents the poor from getting justice in the court, since corrupt court officials sell their decisions to the highest bidder, which makes court decisions biased toward wealthier parties.

Corruption also hurts the poor indirectly by:

(1) Increasing the prices of goods and services that need to be paid for by the poor;

(2) Reducing incomes of the poor by way of semi-legal and illegal taxes and levies;

(3) Diverting support measures for the poor from the hands of the poor to ineligible parties;

(4) Creating asset-ownership inequality, since the wealthy can influence the government to pursue policies that will increase their wealth (such as favourable tax treatments and exchange rates) that are not available to the poor; and

(5) Discouraging the poor from making new investments or opening new businesses, because they know that the well-connected business people will always win government projects and contracts due to corruption. As a result, they cannot increase their living standards, but remain poor.

In sum, there is a strong consensus that good governance is necessary for poverty reduction efforts to be effective and for reducing corruption.

3. Literature review

3.1 Cross-Countries Macroeconomic Studies on Governance and Corruption

There has been an explosion of literature that studies the impact of corruption and governance on economic growth and various economic and social indicators in the past decade or so. These studies use cross-country data on corruption and data on perceptions of governance collected by both commercial firms that measure political risk for their clients (such as Political Risk Services, Inc) and by international governmental and non-governmental organizations (e.g., The World Bank, Transparency International).

A landmark World Bank study done by Kaufmann, Kraay, and Zoido-Lobaton (1999), which for the first time combined the various governance and political risk indices that measure variables such as political rights, civil liberties, government effectiveness, regulatory burden, rule of law, and graft/corruption into a single index found that good governance does matter for economic outcomes. For example, they found that one standard deviation increase in any one of the governance indicators caused between a two and a half, and four-fold increase in per capita income, between a two and a half and four-fold decrease in infant mortality, and a 15% to 25% increase in literacy. The study showed with clear evidence that good governance is very crucial for economic growth and improved social indicators.

Another study by Rajkumar and Swaroop (2002) found that efficiency in public spending reduced child/infant mortality and increased educational attainment and is positively related to governance. It is more effective if governance is good and less effective if governance is poor. They concluded that well-functioning public institutions are critical for translating public spending into effective services.

Several studies that have linked corruption and good governance with economic and social indicators find that there is an inverse relationship between them. Good governance increases these indicators while corruption decreases them. For instance, Gupta, Davoodi and Alonso-Terne (1998) found that an increase of corruption by one standard deviation is associated with an increase in Gini coefficient of about 4.4% and a reduction in income growth for the bottom 20% of population by 7.8% per year. Meanwhile, Gupta, Davoodi and Tiongson (2000) found that better health and education outcomes — measured by child mortality and drop-out rates — are correlated with lower corruption, while countries with high corruption have worse health outcomes compared with countries with low corruption.

Finally, Huther and Shah (1998) found that decentralized countries have better governance than the more centralized countries. They showed that citizen participation and public sector accountability go hand-in-hand with decentralization of public sector decision making. Decentralized countries are more responsive to a citizen's preferences in service delivery and strive harder to serve people than centralized countries. Furthermore, fiscal decentralization goes hand-in-hand with an increase in the human development index and a decrease in income inequality.

However, to conclude that decentralization per se will increase public participation and accountability and result in better public services is a fallacy. A study done by Crook and Sverrison (2001) found that only in countries with well-established public participation schemes, a local government that practises good governance and is capable of delivering good quality services to the public, and functioning checks and balances mechanisms from both the central government and the general public, that decentralization could be considered successful. In contrast, decentralization without a local government that practises good governance and is accountable to the public would not be successful in achieving its intended goals.

3.2 Empirical Evidence from Governance and Corruption Research in Indonesia

Since the fall of the New Order, there has been a lot of interest in finding out about the numerous aspects of corruption in Indonesia, the exact level of corruption in Indonesia and its implications for Indonesians, especially for the poor. There is also a strong interest in whether anti-corruption and good governance reform proposals created by the

Indonesian government since "reformasi" began in 1998 have made any impact on actually reducing the level of corruption. Regional autonomy, that has been implemented in Indonesia since 2001, has also helped to focus attention on corruption and governance at the local level, since many parties have feared that along with fiscal decentralization, corruption will also be decentralized from the central to the local level. The donor agencies, research institutions, and civil society groups have conducted several studies on the above topics. Some of their findings are summarized below.

Research on the impact of anti-corruption reforms in Indonesia has shown that, so far, they have been ineffective in actually reducing corruption in Indonesia. In fact, one could argue that since 1998 corruption has actually gotten worse. For example, corruption has now spread into the parliament, the institution that is supposed to be a watchdog on the executive branch. While the Indonesian Government has made changes that has promoted democracy and free press in the country, instituting legal reforms,[8] and creating greater fiscal and financial transparency, Hamilton-Hart (2001) found that these reforms have been ineffective in actually reducing corruption in Indonesia. Furthermore, they have failed to result in successful prosecution of any major defendants that were accused of corruption. She believes that these reform measures are ineffective because corruption has become so entrenched in Indonesia that no one within the Indonesian Government is really interested in seriously fighting corruption since such an act would only hurt their own rent-seeking interests.

Sherlock (2002) confirmed this conclusion by pointing out that the two new bodies dedicated to monitoring and fighting corruption — the Indonesian Ombundsman's Commission (KON) and the State Official's Assets Auditing Commission (KPKPN) — were given neither adequate funding nor effective power to conduct thorough investigations and prosecute corrupt officials by the government decrees that mandated their creations. He hypothesizes that this is done deliberately so that these commissions would only become "toothless tigers" that would not seriously combat corruption in Indonesia and, therefore, the practice of corruption by government officials in all levels would continue uninterrupted. Thus, he concluded that merely creating new anti-corruption bodies would not have any actual impact in reducing corruption if there is no political will to make sure that these bodies would function effectively as stated in the statutes that created them.

The Partnership for Governance Reform in Indonesia (PGRI) has conducted a national opinion survey on how public officials, businesses, and the public at large, perceived the level of public sector corruption in Indonesia.[9] The study found that 75% of the public regarded public sector corruption to be very common and that 65% of respondents reported that they have experienced corruption involving public officials. The institutions perceived as corrupt by the people sampled are the traffic police, custom officials, and the judiciary. The study estimated that about 48% of all public officials have received unofficial payments, with bureaucrats from the Departments of Housing and Infrastructure. Industry and Trade, and Home Affairs being more likely to receive such payments. It is also found that corruption imposes high costs on the society: up to 5% of household income was used to pay bribes to public officials and 35% of business enterprises reported that they have not made new investments due to the high cost created by corruption.

The Institute for Economic and Social Research (LPEM) at the University of Indonesia recently conducted research on the business climate in 60 district/city governments (LPEM 2001). It conducted interviews with the owners and managers of 1,736 medium and large companies. The study found that regional autonomy has increased business uncertainty and the cost of doing business at the local level (measured through the increase in the unofficial payments made by businesses). It also found that extra payments made to government officials do not necessarily reduce economic efficiency but rather increases it, since often businesses have to spend more time and paperwork when they are dealing with government officials, even with the unofficial payments. However, the report also discovered that the frequency that unofficial payments must be made is lower in the districts that have better regulations and better governance, so there is evidence that good governance does decrease corruption. However, the ability of the districts to generate their own revenue does not correlate with better governance, because often these are the districts that are more prone to higher levels of unofficial payments and corruption.

Another regional-level business climate survey was conducted by the Regional Autonomy Implementation Monitoring Committee (KPPOD) in 2002. It selected 90 regions (68 districts and 22 cities) and measured the business climate of these regions by measuring their security, economic potential, human resources, local government's culture, infrastructure quality, local government's regulations (Perda), and regional finances. The study used both primary (interviews with business executives, journalists, and economic experts) and secondary sources (news accounts and information from the public). It found that regions that attract more businesses are more likely to have better security, better local government's culture and regulations, and better human resources, which confirms the assertion that good governance is a necessary condition for businesses to invest in a region.

Finally, a study on how public participation affects the level of corruption in local government projects, using the World Bank's *Kecamatan* Development Programme (KDP) as a case study, showed that corruption occurred in KDP projects because of the existence of incentives and opportunities to commit corruption. These included a monopoly over the decision-making process, lack of transparency, and low probability of getting caught and punished. Villagers who were well informed about KDP, its goals, and were participating in its planning, were more likely to challenge corrupt practices by local government officials (Woodhouse 2001). Thus, this study confirmed that if the public are actively involved in the planning of government projects that are intended to benefit their communities, they are more likely to speak up when they detect corrupt practices. This hopefully will deter corrupt practices occurring in the future.

3.3 Some Possible Flaws in Governance and Corruption Studies

There are several caveats that one needs to consider when reviewing these studies. First, the data that is required to construct a good governance study is often hard to find (and for the prevalence of corruption, objective data is impossible to find). Even if found, often it would not satisfactorily explain all the dimensions of good governance, since as noted above, it is a multidimensional concept with multiple interpretations. Since there is no single variable that could measure governance, subjective or proxy indicators are used instead, which means that the variables the studies used are not really the ones that the studies intended to measure. As a result, an inexperienced researcher could be "fooled" by the data, that is, they may think they are measuring one thing when in fact they are measuring another, or they could think that they are measuring a direct, first order effect between two variables when in effect they are second or third order variables (Dethier 1999, pp. 37–38; Kaufmann, Kraay, and Zoido-Lobaton 1999, p. 2).

On the other hand, if a study only focuses on a single country, these problems could be minimized because it is possible to focus the study on a small number of policy variables that are easier to observe. However, at this time single country governance studies are not as plentiful as cross country studies, even though the number of these types of studies is growing (Dethier 1999, pp. 46–47).

In regard to the studies about governance in Indonesia mentioned above, the fact that the LPEM and KPPOD studies are based on the opinions of a selected panel of experts (such as business owners, journalists, and NGO leaders) that might not be representative of the general public as a whole could cause concern. This is because some of them might possess opinions that are not shared by the public at large or they may have information regarding the regions that are being studied that is either out of date or inaccurate. This may occur because they lack a comprehensive understanding of these regions. The PGRI study has more validity because its sample is derived from the general public instead of a group of experts, however it is only a public opinion study regarding the pervasiveness of corruption in Indonesia and does not ask more specific questions about certain aspects of governance and corruption (such as the quality of local regulations) that are being asked in the other studies.

4. Governance and poverty in Indonesia: empirical evidence

This chapter is the first attempt to review the relationship between good governance and poverty in Indonesia, where the paradox has been very profound. During the three decades of the authoritarian New Order Government in Indonesia starting in the late 1960s, the country endured various forms of blatant bad governance. Petty corruption as well as mega corruption were incredibly entrenched and pervasive in the bureaucracy. Yet, at the same time, the country enjoyed a very significant reduction in absolute poverty. This reduction in poverty was driven mainly by high economic growth experienced by the country during this period.

The paradox between bad governance and poverty reduction experienced simultaneously by the country makes the effort to sort out the impact of bad governance on poverty a difficult undertaking. Therefore, the strategy adopted in this study is to utilize variations across districts in their governance practices and the poverty reduction that occurred. The adoption of a wide-ranging decentralization and regional autonomy policy starting in 2001 is beneficial to this strategy as such a policy tends to enhance differences across regions. The first part of this section provides a prologue on the decentralization and regional autonomy policy. It is followed by anecdotal evidence of how the practices of bad governance hurt the poor. The final section investigates the impact of governance on poverty reduction using district level data.

4.1 Prologue: Indonesia's Decentralization

Indonesia's decentralization and regional autonomy policy — which is stipulated in Law No. 22/1999 on Local Government and Law No. 25/1999 on Central-Regional Fiscal Balance, both were enacted in January 2001 — involves not only administrative but also political and fiscal decentralization. Figure 2.1 describes the basic structure of authorities and functions of the central, provincial, and district governments stipulated in both laws. These laws have reversed the New Order's centralized approach. Now the responsibilities and functions of the district governments are by and large expanded, while those of the central and provincial governments are reduced.

Figure 2.1 Basic Structure of Government Authorities According to Law No. 22/1999

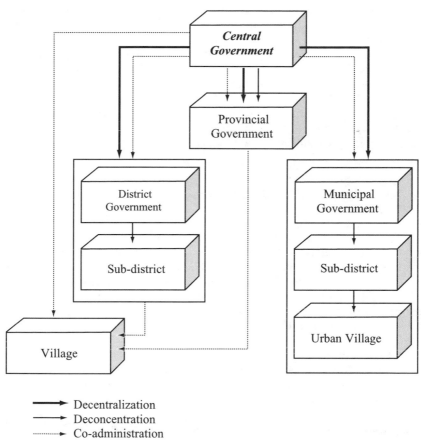

According to Law No. 22/1999, all government authorities are now the authority of autonomous regions, except for five authorities which remain with the central government. These are: foreign affairs, defence and security, justice, fiscal and monetary affairs, religious affairs, and other authorities.[10] Authorities of provincial governments include all authorities with inter-districts coverage, authorities delegated by the central government, and all authorities beyond the capability of district governments.[11]

Since the emphasis of decentralization and regional autonomy policy lies with the district governments, authorities given to the districts are very wide-ranging. In this respect, Law No. 22/1999 grants authorities to district governments which include all other authorities which have not been covered by the central and provincial governments. These include: public works, health, education and culture, agriculture, transportation, industry and trade, investment, environment, land, cooperative, and labour matters.

In line with the expanded local government authorities and functions prescribed by Law No. 22/1999, Law No. 25/1999 sets a new inter-governmental fiscal framework, by drastically changing the disbursement arrangement. A much larger transfer in the form of *Dana Perimbangan* (the equalization fund) replaced the Subsidy for Autonomous Regions (SDO) and the Grants to Local Governments (*Inpres Kabupaten/Kota* and *Inpres Desa*) programmes. The equalization fund consists of three parts:

1.   **Revenue sharing.** The intended purpose of this component is to overcome/reduce vertical imbalance/inequality. This component is introduced in response to the demands of the resource-rich regions for a fair share of revenues extracted from their regions.
2.   **General allocation fund (DAU).** This is a block grant intended to equalize fiscal capacities of regional governments to finance their expenditure needs. The law specifies that DAU should make up at least 25% of the central government revenue and must be distributed among local governments by a formula which takes into account regional needs and potential capacity. In the fiscal year 2001, DAU accounted for around 74% of the equalization fund.
3.   **Special allocation fund (DAK).** This is an earmark grant that is developed to finance special needs that either cannot be determined by formula used for DAU allocations or categorized as national priorities and commitments.

4.2 Bad Governance in Action: Anecdotal Evidence

4.2.1 Pre-Crisis Era

This section presents anecdotal evidence of how bad governance hurts the poor during the pre-crisis era. One source of the anecdotal evidence discussed was Montgomery et al. 2002, which focuses on the agricultural sector, i.e., the sector where most of the poor in Indonesia find their livelihoods. In February 1999, the agricultural sector had the highest sectoral poverty rate as well as the largest number of poor people in the country. The agriculture sector's 1999 head-count poverty rate was 39.7%, and more than 58.4% of the total of poor people gave their primary field of occupation as agriculture.[12] During the economic crisis, agriculture was the only sector to absorb large numbers of the newly unemployed. While other sectors shrank, employment in agriculture rose by 13% or 4.6 million people in just one year, from 34.8 million in 1997 to 39.4 million in 1998.

During the 1980s and much of the 1990s, there was growing concern about the welfare of farmers, based on perceptions that farmers received an increasingly smaller percentage of the final prices for their goods. Incentives to supply the market seemed to be falling over time. Indonesia's economy was not an internal free trade area. The problems fell into two categories: price distortions and non-price distortions. Provincial and district taxes (*pajak*) and levies (*retribusi*) on agricultural trade led to distorted prices. Some of the taxes and levies were legal, but many were not. Among non-price distortions, regulatory controls on national, provincial and district agricultural production and agricultural trade created local monopolies and monopsonies. Other controls such as central government livestock inter-island shipping maximum levels and quota rights presented barriers to entry and restricted competition. Once the regulations were abolished or could be ignored, monopolies and monopsonies disappeared.

Provincial and district governments do not have the authority to tax income or assets. All of them have therefore turned to taxing trade. Regulations authorizing provincial or district governments to apply taxes or levies are officially issued by local parliaments (DPRD). But in the past, most such regulations were drafted by local administrations, then approved by DPRDs without serious review. Seldom were elements of civil society presented with a chance at hearings or feedback on draft revenue legislation before enactment. Trade levies and charges for government-provided services became an important revenue base available to local governments. They became dependent on this restricted fiscal base. Local levies called *retribusi* had a more serious impact than local taxes. Such levies were originally intended by law to be a form of cost-recovery to the Government, a user-charge for facilities or services provided. Over time, *retribusi* levies were extended to include compensation to the Government for extraction of non-renewable natural resource products (since all natural resources belong to the people of Indonesia). The definition of natural resources (*hasil bumi*) then was extended to include agriculture, which is renewable and not owned by government. In fact *retribusi* levies became a trade tax on goods shipped outside of a district. Levies mushroomed. Trucks were stopped at *retribusi* posts every few kilometres along the road. The levies were against physical quantities traded, with no link to profitability, net income or value-added. Ability-to-pay (the level of income of the original producing farmer) was also not taken into account. Methods of collection (stopping trucks along isolated rural roads) led to abuse; much of the money collected did not make its way into official coffers. Agricultural product prices became badly distorted by *retribusi* levies. The impact of levies was highest for forestry, livestock and fishery products.

The first significant reform of local taxes and levies came with the passing of a central government revenue Law No. 18/1997 that restricted the types of local taxes and *retribusi* levies permitted. It reduced regional taxes from the existing 42 to 9. It also reduced *retribusi* levies from the existing 192 items to only 30.

The Government at all levels created, inspired and supported local monopolies, monopsonies and inter-regional trade quotas for the favoured few. These distortions drove wedges between farm-gate prices (driving them lower) and destination market prices (driving them higher). The price difference ("rent") was to the advantage of the holder of the monopoly, monopsony, or quota right. Benefits of these price wedges were shared with the people who gave such rights. Many were specifically created to benefit the children or cronies of the then first-family. The following describes several specific examples of bad governance practices.

Oranges from West Kalimantan.   Until the early 1990s, citrus production was increasing rapidly in West Kalimantan, from just 76,000 tons in 1988 to 199,800 tons in 1991/92. Almost all West Kalimantan's citrus production was shipped to Java. In 1991, the West Kalimantan Governor issued a decree stating that PT Bima Citra Mandiri (a member of the Bimantara group controlled by a son of the then first-family) was appointed to be the official "coordinator" of all citrus trade. All citrus trade had to pass through KUDs (*Koperasi Unit Desa*, Village Unit Cooperatives). Farmers could sell only to KUD-appointed collection-traders, who were then required to sell to Bima Citra Mandiri for inter-island trade. Farm-gate prices dropped precipitately. Exports from the province fell by 63%. Angry orange producers brought truckloads of oranges into Pontianak and dumped them in front of government offices in protest. Many orange producers abandoned their trees, not tending them since. The 1991 monopsony right granted to PT Bimantara Citra Mandiri was abolished by a Governor's decree that "encouraged" (but no longer required) marketing through KUDs. But the orange trade has never recovered.

Required local processing of cocoa and cashew nuts in South Sulawesi. Cocoa and cashew nuts are important export crops for Sulawesi. They are particularly important in isolated upland poverty stricken districts that do not have much flat or gently rolling land suitable for rice or other grain cultivation. For instance in Polmas district, in the hilly northwestern part of South Sulawesi, there were 27,764 hectares of cocoa, grown by 43,361 families in 1998, about 30% of all Polmas farm families. Polmas had a smaller area of cashew (2,914 ha) but it was the main source of income for another 6,700 poor upland farm families. In another poor area surveyed, Bone district, cocoa was important for 25,192 farm families (27% of all farm families), who operated 10,490 hectares of cocoa trees. In Bone, cashew was the main source of income for another 11,706 families (13%) who tended 9,050 hectares of cashew trees.

South Sulawesi's smallholder plantation crop producers were faced with a regulation that required cocoa beans and cashew nuts to be processed within the province. The largest cashew nut processing factory in Ujung Pandang benefiting from the regulation was PT Citra Sekarwangi Agro Persada, part of the Citra group and owned by a daughter of the then first-family. Cashew nut buyers wanted unprocessed cashew nuts (for export in the raw state to lower-cost processors in India) and were willing to pay higher prices than South Sulawesi's cashew processing factories were willing to pay. Also the main cocoa bean importing country, the United States, wants only unfermented cocoa beans. Required local processing in this case was not value-adding but instead was value-subtracting.

After experiencing the impact of *de facto* deregulation, the cocoa bean and cashew nut processing industries tried again in 1999 to ask the Government to force high-cost local processing. It requested the government to impose a 20% to 30% export tax on unprocessed cocoa beans and cashew nuts to help guarantee supplies of raw materials to existing (favoured) processing factories. By this time, elements of civil society were more vocal about the impact of government-created marketing restrictions. Many saw this move as one-sided, helping local processing firms but harming farmers, forcing down the farm-gate price received. The Cocoa Association of Indonesia (*Askindo*) objected strongly to the proposal, as did both the Indonesian Farmers Union (HKTI) and the Association of Indonesian Food and Beverage Producers. Only the Cashew Nut Industry Association of Indonesia supported the move to impose an export tax. The secretary-general of this association stated that the farm-gate price of cashew nuts was rocketing upward, benefiting the farmers, to the detriment of processors. As of July 2001, it appears that the lobbying by the Association has not been successful and there are no new export taxes on cashew nuts. There are also no new export taxes on cocoa beans.

Clove Marketing. Cloves were an important source of income for upland farming areas in Sulawesi. For instance in impoverished Polmas in South Sulawesi, cloves were the main source of income for 2,000 farming families (growing 882 ha). In another district studied in South Sulawesi (Bone), cloves were also important, grown by 5,776 families operating about 4,000 hectares. Cloves were even more important in North Sulawesi. A total of 43,000 hectares was dedicated to planting cloves, but by the period just before deregulation only 20,000 ha were productive, producing just 7,000 tons. The remaining 23,000 hectares of clove plantations had been largely abandoned because of the disincentive effect of low farm-gate prices.

Before deregulation, clove producers were required to sell their clove output to a much-criticized Clove Marketing Board (*Badan Penyangga Pemasaran Cengkeh* or BPPC), controlled by another son of the then first-family. Clove prices at the producer level plummeted, but clove prices to the *kretek* cigarette manufacturers in Java did not fall commensurately. There was suspicion of super-normal profits made by the BPPC monopsony right holder, whose accounts were never made transparent.

The measures taken to break the power of the Clove Marketing Board appear to have been both complete and effective. Presidential Decree No. 21/1998 established the right of all farmers to sell cloves to anyone, and for traders to buy cloves from all agents at a freely determined market price. An instruction letter from the Minister of Industry and Trade supported this Presidential Decree. The Clove Marketing Board wound up its affairs by the end of June 1998, after which time supervision of the clove trade became the responsibility of the Director General of Domestic Trade. A site investigation in North Sulawesi showed no residual trace of the Clove Marketing Board monopsony. Farmers and traders said the trade is now free from interference by the Government.

Smallholder Tea Processing in West Java.   Tea is an important export crop for Indonesia. Exports in 1998 earned $108 million. West Java is the most important producing province. In the 1980s, PT Tehnusamba Indah, a company controlled by a crony of the then first-family, built four tea-processing factories in West Java, a region known already to have excess processing capacity (tea area had declined over the years). Farmers said Tehnusamba's factories offered lower prices than competitors for fresh tea leaves and so they declined to sell to them. In 1990, the Governor of West Java issued a letter instructing District Heads to implement *rayonisasi*, or market "rationalisation", which prescribed area allocations for the collective buying of fresh tea leaves. The District Heads in turn issued letters telling farmers near Tehnusamba factories to sell only to Tehnusamba, thus creating a local monopsony position.

The letter from the Governor of West Java requiring this geographic market allocation for fresh tea leaves has never been formally withdrawn. Also district government market-area-allocation letters in favour of Tehnusamba have not been cancelled. But farmers now disregard these instructions and sell to whomever they want. This is one example where legislation was created to benefit private parties with political clout.

Heavily taxed plantation sector in North Sumatra.[14]   While the North Sumatra provincial government has not profited directly from the plantation sector, the commodities produced in this industry have been the target of various levies, at both the local (*kabupaten*) and the central level of government. Levies are imposed on the plantation industry starting at the production level, through to distribution and marketing of their products. According to the latest inventory released by the management of the Association of Indonesian Rubber Producers (Gapkindo) in North Sumatra, there are at least nine kinds of official levies imposed on rubber commodities (see Table 2.2).

Non-Tariff Trade Restriction in North Sulawesi.[15] The implementation of decentralization and regional autonomy has resulted in several major changes in the way that local governments exercise their autonomous rights. One of these changes has been that local governments are creating a larger number of new local laws. In the case of North Sulawesi, so far only the provincial governments have begun to create regulations that result in non-tariff barriers. However, there are also indications that district governments are also proposing to create non-tariff regulations at this level. The following is an example of non-tariff barrier found in the Province of North Sulawesi concerning regulation on pharmacies, outlined in the Governor's Decree No.4dz/03/891, 13 September 2001 (Temporary Postponement of the Establishment of Large Pharmacies in North Sulawesi). The Province of North Sulawesi has placed restrictions on the ownership of pharmacies by those who do not reside in North Sulawesi, with the aim of protecting local entrepreneurs. The following is a summary of the contents of the Governor's Decree:

1) Licences for Large Pharmacies in the Province of North Sulawesi are only to be issued to those large businesses with a central office, which own or control assets, and whose owners reside in North Sulawesi. However, these licences are not to be issued to those who reside outside of the Province of North Sulawesi, even though they may own and control assets within the province. Instead they are to be accorded the status of Large Pharmacy Branches or Representatives.

2) Large pharmacies must own a building or business location in accordance with the stipulations on ownership status.

3) Large local pharmacies are to be given priority as partners with the government in acquiring pharmacies with a value of up to Rp4 billion.

4) The establishment of Large Pharmacy Branches has to be based on the recommendation of the North Sulawesi Association of Large Indonesian Pharmacies.

Inter-Island Livestock Trade.   Inter-island livestock trade is important for farmers in the dry provinces of West and East Nusa Tenggara (NTT). These relatively poor islands export livestock, mostly to Java. In 1998, NTT had a large livestock population of 803,000 (almost all cattle). Producing slaughter cattle for market was important to more than 200,000 NTT farmers (although this is merely a rough estimate). In NTB the large livestock population numbered 470,000 and was a major source of income for more than an estimated 150,000 farmers. Most of NTB's cattle were on Lombok Island (280,000).

Livestock trade was subject to both local trade taxes and inter-island shipping quotas. By mid 1997, just before the crisis, East Nusa Tenggara cattle farmers and traders had to pay a total of US$40 per cattle through 16 different kinds of taxes and levies, amounting to about 13% of the farm-gate value of a slaughter animal. On Lombok Island in West Nusa Tenggara farmers and traders paid 24 different taxes and *retribusi* on livestock trade: 3 to the central government, 9 to the province and 12 to the district. The total cost was about $31 per cattle in taxes and levies, or 5% of the $570 farm-gate value of a typical slaughter animal. In Bima (Sumbawa Island), traders and farmers had to pay the same 3 central and 9 provincial taxes and levies, plus 18 district charges. In South Sulawesi, traders bringing cattle from Bone to Ujung Pandang (five hours away) had to pay 31 different taxes and levies along the road. Of these, 6 were legal and 25 illegal. Twenty of the posts charging illegal levies were police and military checkpoints. The sum paid represented about 4% of the farm-gate value of the typical animal. A tandem-trailer truck carrying 18 cattle from Bone to Ujung Pandang had to be prepared to pay $228 in taxes and levies.

Until deregulation in 1998, the Ministry of Agriculture's Director General of Livestock set inter-island livestock trade quotas. These severely limited the number that could be marketed to at most about 5% to 6% of the local livestock populations. In fact, a well-managed herd in NTT should be able to reach between 10% and 13% off-take from a stable livestock population (ACIAR January 1998) under extensive grazing, not intensive stall-feeding management systems. Each year the DG issued a letter giving provinces annual maximum quotas for shipments. He even determined destinations (not permitting NTT to ship to East Kalimantan despite high prices and a shortage of beef for instance). Trade was restricted. The cattle quota for NTT kept decreasing each year, from 67,000 in 1994 to only 41,000 in 1997. The livestock populations were increasing, but the opportunity to market was decreasing. Livestock (and meat) prices in Jakarta rose and farm-gate prices in the outer islands fell as a result of this quota system. A large price wedge was formed, that benefited only the inter-island shipping quota rights-holders.

4.2.2 Decentralization Era

Efforts to reform various market distortions that proliferated in the 1980s and 1990s gained momentum between 1998 and 2000, in particular after the fall of the New Order Government. This is understandable as many of the distortions were created by or related to the then first-family or their cronies. These reforms have had some successes, resulting in improving prices received by farmers. However, the implementation of a wide-ranging decentralization and regional autonomy policy — which granted much power to district governments — starting in 2001 seems to have reversed the trend. Various forms of market distortions, which have been dismantled previously, have now revived. The only difference is that now most of the distortions are created by the district governments rather than the central government as had been the case in the past. This section discusses some examples of the new forms of bad governance but with same adverse consequences for the poor.

The costs of transporting goods from North Sumatra to Jakarta.[13] The abundant agricultural commodities from the Karo district in North Sumatra are mostly perishable goods. Therefore, it is crucial to secure smooth and rapid distribution of these goods to maintain both the quality and the selling price at the consumer level. Consequently, farmers and traders will make every effort to expedite the delivery of these goods to the buyers, even if they have to pay various taxes and levies *en route*. These additional charges will add to the distribution cost, and will eventually lead to a higher price at the consumer level. The amount of the levies extracted is determined by measuring the tonnage of the truck at various weighing stations along the routes. Table 2.1 illustrates the number of weighing bridges and the amount of taxes and levies paid by a truck driver at each location travelling from Kabajahe, Karo district to Jakarta. A truck driver who regularly carries oranges from Kabupaten Karo to Jakarta reports that there are at least 16 truck weighing stations and several other levy checkpoints that have to be passed along the route. The table shows the number and amount of "fines" paid by truck drivers — both those who comply and those who do not comply with the weight limit at each station.

It is estimated that the total amount of levies (official and non-official) paid to transport oranges from Kabanjahe to Jakarta ranges from Rp268,500 to Rp1,008,500. Paying the lowest amount would only be possible if the truck complies with its permitted capacity. Nevertheless, even when trucks comply with the regulations, frequently drivers still have to pay levies. As a result, it is common for truck drivers to prefer to carry loads that exceed the trucks' legal capacity. The estimated value of the load of one 8-ton truck of oranges transporting approximately 120 baskets @ 65 kg at the farm-gate price of Rp1,800 for Grade A, B, C, and D oranges is Rp14,400,000. Hence, the total value of the transported goods paid out in taxes and levies is between 2% to 7%.

Table 2.1 Costs Incurred by Truck Drivers at Weighing Stations on the Way from North Sumatra to Jakarta

Province	Number of Stations	Amount of fines	Remarks
1. North Sumatra	4	Rp5,000–10,000 for each ton of excess weight	Per ton of excess weight
2. Riau	2	Rp60,000, paid by all, irrespective of weight trucks.	Fines have to be paid by both complying and non-complying vehicles, plus additional road levies: -Rp2,500 (6-ton truck) -Rp3,500 (8-ton truck)
3. Jambi	2	Rp60,000, paid by all trucks	Plus additional road levies: -Rp2,500 (6-ton truck) -Rp3,500 (8-ton truck)
4. South Sumatra	5	Fine of Rp15,000 for each ton of excess weight	In addition to the possibility of receiving a fine, there are also road levies: -Rp2,500 (6-ton truck) -Rp3,500 (8-ton truck)
5. Lampung	3	Fine of Rp15,000 for each ton of excess weight	In addition to the possibility of receiving a fine, there are also road levies: -Rp2,500 (6-ton truck) -Rp3,500 (8-ton truck)

Table 2.2 Types of official levies on rubber commodities in North Sumatra

Activities	Types of levies	Tariff and location	Remarks/Problems
Production Support	Land and Building Tax	Rp60–130 thousand/ha	Tax valuation too high, annual increases
	Street Lighting Tax	10% of total electricity capacity used, in certain *kabupaten/kota*	Tax base too high. Also applied to electricity generators installed on the premises.
	3. Ground and Surface Water Levies	Rp2–5.4 million/month	
	4. *Hinder Ordonantie* Tax	Rp4.2 million/year in Deli Serdang Rp1.75 million/renewable	
Processing	5. Fees for taking Effluent Samples	Rp450 thousand/sample, 3 samples/month in South Tapanuli	The official charge from the Department of Health Laboratory is only Rp44 thousand/sample.
Marketing	6. Market Levies	Rp6/kg in Asahan Rp20/kg in Langkat Rp3/kg in Deli Serdang	
	7. Compulsory Contributions from Plantation Estates	Rp10/kg in Asahan	
Others	8. Levies on the logging or use of Rubber Timber	Rp300/m^3 in Deli Serdang	
	9. Compulsory Third Party Contributions	Voluntary at provincial level	
	10. Levies from the Department of Manpower		

Source: Gapkindo North Sumatra, 2001.

5)   The management of the North Sulawesi Association of Large Indonesian Pharmacies is to be comprised of members of the organization who originate from within the region.

6)   Apart from the managers, local residents are to be prioritized in the staffing of the Large Pharmacy Branches.

7)   The Large Pharmacy Branches will be encouraged to form partnerships with large local pharmacies in order to distribute their products throughout North Sulawesi.

This situation suggests that there is some justification for emerging concerns regarding policies discriminating against people from outside the region in the interest of 'local sons' at the expense of the consumer as they have to pay higher prices resulting from the less competitive market.

Organized Thugs in West Java.[16]   Until now, the government could not resolve the problem of illegal fees in the streets imposed by both thugs and corrupt police officers. For instance, research in Jonggol and Purwakarta districts shows that the practice of thuggery in the street is very common in which each truck is required to pay Rp300,000 per year to the thugs. These thugs are organized in groups that control specific areas. As evidence that a passing truck has "paid" the fees, usually a sticker that states the codename of the head of the thug groups is posted on the truck's body. Trucks also become targets of illegal fees when they enter the main market in Jakarta. Fees at the terminal also tend to be higher than what is stated in the official rules, with an excuse of covering the salary of part-time/volunteer workers. The rampant thuggery and illegal fees that are illicitly "supported" by the district government and the police shows the weak supremacy of the law and protection of society, especially that of the poor.

Bureaucrats Interests Above that of the Poor in Budget Allocation in West Nusa Tenggara.[17]   Conceptually, public policy of the government of the district of West Lombok in West Nusa Tenggara is focused on increasing the welfare of the poor living in the district. This is done by strengthening the human capital through investment in health and education and improvement of economic conditions of the poor through "the people's economy", which correlates with the purpose of regional autonomy. However in practice, this noble mission is not carried out as planned. This could be seen in the budget allocation that still puts the bureaucrats' interests above others.

Some of the district government's budget allocation policy could be seen in the 2002 district budget (APBD). In 2002, the government of the district of West Lombok allocated Rp2.6 billion for offical car purchases and Rp780 million for official motorbike purchases. In addition, there was a huge increase in the allocation to the district parliament (DPRD) from Rp2 billion (equals to Rp3.8 million per month for each DPRD member) in fiscal year 2000 to Rp3.4 billion (equals to Rp6.4 million per month for each DPRD member) in fiscal year 2002. At the same time, budget allocation for the general public interests that are supposed to be the main priority of the district government tends to be ignored, for instance:

1) The allocation for the village development fund which was Rp10 million in the 2000 budget was not included in the 2001 district budget, with the excuse that the government "forgot" to include it. In the 2002 budget year the fund had been allocated, but up till April it had not been received by the villages.

2) In 2002, the West Lombok district allocated 2.5% of its budget to the health sector, which is much smaller than the amount set on in the agreement made in August 2001 between the Health Ministry and all the district heads/majors in Indonesia. This agreement states that the district/city governments will allocate at least 15% of their budget to the health sector. According to health experts, the budget allocated to the health sector by the district/city governments today has sharply decreased from Rp4–5 billion per year to only Rp2–3 billion per year. This decline is confirmed by the statement of health centre staff that after regional autonomy:

   • Shipment of medicine to the health centres takes longer now than before regional autonomy, additionally the amount shipped is much more limited.

   • The operational fund for the health centres today is only about Rp15 million for each health centre. In the past years, the operational fund for each health centre was Rp50 million, which included programme assistance from the central government.

   • Most of the districts in West Nusa Tenggara are classified as areas prone to malaria and dengue fever endemics. It is very ironic that the district government budget for the health sector does not allocate additional funds to handle the problem of malaria and dengue fever.

4.2.3 Social Safety Net Programme During the Crisis Era

Other examples of how bad governance has made the poor suffer loss can be seen from the implementation of the social safety net programmes. In an attempt to negate the potential negative social impact of the recent economic crisis, in early 1998 the government of Indonesia established social safety net programmes. The programmes were intended to protect both the traditionally poor and newly poor due to the crisis, who may not be able to cope with the impact of the crisis without outside help. The programmes were created based on four strategies: 1) ensuring the availability of food at affordable prices for the poor; 2) supplementing purchasing power among poor households through employment creation; 3) preserving access to critical social services, particularly health and education; and, 4) sustaining local economic activity through regional block grant programmes and extension of small-scale credits.

Unfortunately, however, in many cases the target groups have been largely missed by the programmes, both in terms of low coverage and being only loosely targeted in practice. The programmes were plagued by problems in targeting the beneficiaries and delivering benefits to intended target groups. The programmes suffered from both the problems of low coverage — i.e., there were a large number of the poor who were not covered by the programmes — and leakage, i.e., there was a large proportion of programme benefits which went to the non-poor.[18] Figure 2.2 shows the coverage of various social safety net programmes among the poor and non-poor population.

The leakage of benefits of these programmes to the non-poor is clearly a loss for the poor. Due to this leakage, in some cases the poor received less benefits than they were actually entitled to, while in other cases

Figure 2.2   Coverage of Various Social Safety Net Programmes

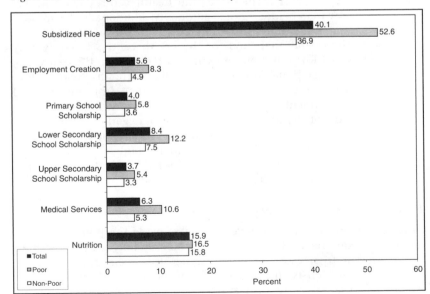

some of the poor were completely left out from receiving the benefits of the programmes. Studies on the implementation on the Indonesian social safety net programmes have pointed out that in many cases the leakage occurred due to bad governance at the lowest distribution points. For example, in the sale of subsidized rice programme, once the rice reached the village level, it was up to the village officials how to distribute the rice to the target group. Even though they have a list of eligible recipients, upon which the rice allocated to the village is based, oftentimes the officials decided to distribute the rice to a much larger number of people, resulting in lower than stipulated rice receipt by each recipient, including the poor.

Another example is the health programme. In this programme, free medical and family planning services were provided for the poor, identified through 'health-cards' which were distributed to eligible households. A health-card given to a household can be used by all members of the household to obtain free services from designated hospitals, clinics, and healthcare centres for medical and family planning purposes, including pregnancy check up and birth delivery. However, in practice, households which owned health-cards did not always use the cards when a household member visited a designated provider.[19] Of all health-card holders who went to public hospitals, only 60% used their health-cards, while for community health centres the proportion was 52%, for village midwives 12%, and for other health facilities 31%. It turns out that the large degree of non-use of health-cards is because some health providers refused to honour the free services for health-card holders. The reason is because the providers were not reimbursed based on the numbers of actual services performed, but instead they received an advance lump sum payment based on a predicted demand for services.[20] This practice certainly hurt the poor who were in need of medical services.

4.3 The Impact on Poverty Reduction: More Systematic Evidence

4.3.1 Methods and Data

Measuring good or bad governance quantitatively is difficult as it has many facets and requires a high degree of subjective judgment.[21] Therefore, the most common method used to measure governance is to survey selected individuals, who are deemed knowledgeable about the situation in a certain country or region, and ask them to rank the governing practices in a country or region on a predetermined scale. The answers of all surveyed individuals in a country or region can then be used as the basis for forming an index of governance in the country or region.

Since the implementation of a wide ranging district level regional autonomy policy in Indonesia, starting in January 2001, there has been growing interest in measuring good governance at the district level. Although the regional autonomy policy is still relatively nascent, there are already some large-scale national-level surveys on measuring district governance. The results of two of these surveys have been made public — they have been discussed in the previous section — and will be used in this study. There have been numerous other similar studies conducted on a smaller scale or in more localized settings.[22]

The first large scale survey was conducted by KPPOD (*Komisi Pemantauan Pelaksanaan Otonomi Daerah* or the Regional Autonomy Implementation Monitoring Committee), a body formed by the Indonesian Chamber of Commerce (KADIN). KPPOD was formed following a growing concern that since the implementation of the regional autonomy policy the district governments have rushed to issue many local regulations (*Perda*) that impose new taxes and levies in order to raise local revenues (PAD).

The business community was among the most adversely affected by this trend, which has negatively influenced the investment climate in the region. In an attempt to counteract this trend, KADIN, through KPPOD, created a ranking of districts based on their friendliness to the business environment and investment climate (KPPOD 2002). A yearly award is presented to the best performing district. It is hoped that the ranking and award will, on the one hand, provide an incentive to the district governments to create an environment favourable to business and, on the other, act as a signal to the business community in locating their investments.

The ranking is based on a composite of district indices on local regulations, security, culture, and infrastructures. There are three indices on local regulations, each looks at the aspects of production, distribution, and others. In each aspect, each district is assessed based on whether it has local regulations which are considered as "highly distortive", "distortive", "acceptable", or "supportive" to the business environment. There are two indices on security, with the first aspect focusing on law and order ("non-existent", "weak", "existent", "good"), while the second aspect focuses on security disorder ("very high", "high", "medium", "low"). The cultural aspects include both society's attitudes and bureaucratic culture, assessing whether they are "disruptive", "less conducive", "conducive", and "very conducive" to the investment climate. Finally, the infrastructure indices include both accessibility ("very difficult", "difficult", "sufficient", "good") as well as quality of infrastructure ("very bad", "bad", "sufficient", "good"). KPPOD calculated these indices for a sample of 90 districts from all over the country.

Among these indices, the one that is most relevant to the measurement of good governance, and hence will be used in this study, is the index on bureaucratic culture. This index is an approximation of a measure on the "quality" of district bureaucracy. Assessing whether the bureaucracy is "disruptive", "less conducive", "conducive", and "very conducive" to the investment climate provides an indication of the overall quality of the bureaucracy. In their report, KPPOD explains that this bureaucratic culture index measures the degree of openness and cultural values adhered to by the district government as stipulated in its development policies, in particular those related to investments. In addition, this index measures the quality of public services from the local government to the business community. In measuring this index, KPPOD used panel judgment and expert choice methods.

The second large-scale survey was conducted by LPEM (*Lembaga Pengkajian Ekonomi and Masyarakat* or the Institute for Social and Economic Research) at the Faculty of Economics, University of Indonesia. As part of a study on the impact of the regional autonomy policy on the costs of doing business, they created six indices on additional costs, regional autonomy, government, infrastructure, pre-crisis security, and post-crisis security aspects (LPEM 2001). The indices scale from 0 to 100, with a higher index number indicating better quality or more favourable conditions for business. From these six indices, they then created a composite of cost of doing business index. LPEM studied the data from 60 districts and used the composite index to rank them based on their friendliness to the business community.

Among these indices, the index on government was the one that most closely related to the measure of good governance and, hence, will be used in this study. Four indicators were used to measure the index on government. Those are: (1) general behaviour/attitude of government and bureaucracy when dealing with the private sector ("disruptive", "neutral", "conducive"); (2) progress toward the relationship between private sector and government bureaucracy ("same", "easier", "harder"); (3) checks and balancing mechanisms within the government bureaucracy ("existent", "non-existent"); and (4) the proportion of senior manager's time spent when dealing with government bureaucracy (less than 15%, between 15% and 25%, between 25% and 50%, and above 50%). The purpose of this government index is to measure business uncertainty due to the behaviour of government.

Since the purpose is to assess the impact of governance on poverty reduction, this study also used data on district level poverty rates, which were obtained from Statistics Indonesia (BPS). The official poverty statistics in Indonesia are calculated in three-year intervals, based on data collected through the National Socio-Economic Survey (SUSENAS). In particular, this study used the 1999 and 2002 data, which covered the periods of both the KPPOD and LPEM studies. The analyses were conducted using two approaches. The first approach uses descriptive analysis, which is meant as an exploration of the relationship between governance and poverty reduction. In the second approach, a multivariate analysis was conducted to confirm the relationship indicated from the descriptive analysis.

4.3.2 Descriptive Analysis

Using the district governance indices from KPPOD and LPEM and district poverty rates from BPS, this section analyzes the impact of governance on poverty reduction. The focus is on the performance of districts in reducing poverty between 1999 and 2002 and how this has varied with different levels of governance, as defined by both KPPOD and LPEM.

Table 2.3 shows the proportional change in poverty reduction from 1999 to 2002 by KPPOD's index of bureaucratic culture. The table shows that none of the districts in the sample has a bureaucratic culture which is considered as disruptive to the business environment. Most of the districts, 61 out of 87, have a bureaucratic culture which is considered as conducive, while the rest are almost evenly divided between those which are less conducive and very conducive.

On average, the districts in the KPPOD sample have a poverty rate in 2002 which is proportionally around 7.8% lower than the poverty rate in 1999. Dissagregated across categories of bureaucratic culture, there is a clear indication that good governance affects districts' performance on poverty reduction. The districts which have a less conducive bureaucratic culture have an average poverty reduction of 3.4% from the original rate, while those districts with conducive bureaucratic culture have an average poverty reduction of around 7%, double the rate of the former group. Further doubling in the rate of poverty reduction was experienced by the districts with a very conducive bureaucratic culture. These districts

Table 2.3   District Level Poverty Reduction Between 1999 and 2002 by KPPOD's Index of Bureaucratic Culture

Index of Bureaucratic Culture	Poverty Reduction (%)		Number of Districts
	Mean	Std. Dev.	
Disruptive	–	–	0
Less conducive	–3.41	31.53	12
Conducive	–6.95	60.66	61
Very conducive	–15.06	56.41	14
Total	–7.76	56.45	87

on average experienced a 15% reduction in their poverty rates during the period.

However, this evidence that districts with better governance experienced higher rates of poverty reduction has to be discounted by the presence of large standard deviations within each category of bureaucratic culture. These large standard deviations make the mean of the poverty reduction rate for each category statistically insignificant from zero. Similarly, the differences in poverty reduction rates across categories are also statistically insignificant.

Table 2.4 shows the same proportional change in poverty reduction from 1999 to 2002 among the districts in the LPEM study on cost of doing business. Since the LPEM index of government is a continuous number ranging from 0 to 100, the districts are grouped into four quartiles of the index.

On average, the 60 districts in the LPEM sample have a poverty rate in 2002 which is proportionally around 7.2% lower than the poverty rate in 1999. The 15 districts with the lowest index of government, the quartile I districts, have an average rate of poverty reduction of 2.7%. Like in the KPPOD sample, the average rate of poverty reduction doubles in the next two quartiles, where the rate of poverty reduction is 5.9% in the quartile II districts and 13.9% in the quartile III districts. However, the average rate of poverty reduction among the 15 districts with the highest index of government, the quartile IV districts, is only around a half of the average rate of quartile III districts.

Furthermore, similar to the KKPOD sample, there are large standard deviations in the rates of poverty reduction within each quartile of index of government. As before, the presence of these large standard deviations make the mean of poverty reduction rate for each quartile not statistically

Table 2.4   District Level Poverty Reduction Between 1999 and 2002 by LPEM Index of Government

Quartile of Index of Government	Poverty Reduction (%)		Number of Districts
	Mean	Std. Dev.	
I (lowest index)	−2.72	66.96	15
II	−5.94	71.53	15
III	−13.88	46.78	15
IV (highest index)	−6.34	40.94	15
Total	−7.22	56.68	60

significant from zero and the differences in poverty reduction rates across quartiles are not statistically significant either.

4.3.3 Multivariate Analysis

The findings in the previous subsection provide indications that governance affects the rate of reduction in poverty at the district level. These results, however, are based on simple descriptive analysis, uncontrolled from possible effects of other variables. In this subsection, a multivariate approach is exercised to control for the effects of other variables. In the KPPOD report, in addition to the various indices used to rank districts, they also publish district level data on Gross Domestic Regional Product (GDRP), routine and development budget, local revenues, and total population.

Based on this data, Table 2.5 shows the regression results of change in poverty rate on two dummy variables of district governance, per capita GDRP, per capita routine and development budgets, and per capita local revenues. The sign of all coefficients of these variables makes sense, but only the coefficient of the dummy variable on conducive bureaucratic culture which is statistically significant. It should be noted, however, that the estimation has relatively low coefficient of determination (10%) and F-statistic (1.46). This probably has to do with the presence of noise in the data, and relatively small number of observations.

Nevertheless, the regression results confirm the indications from descriptive analysis that governance affects the rate of reduction in poverty achieved by districts. Districts which have conducive bureaucratic cultures have a reduction in poverty rates which is 6.5% higher than that achieved by districts with less conducive bureaucratic cultures. Similarly, districts with very conducive bureaucratic cultures tend to have higher rate of poverty reduction than districts with less conducive bureaucratic cultures

Table 2.5   Results of District Level Change in Poverty on Government Indicators

Independent Variable	Coefficient	Standard Error
Dummy of conducive bureaucratic culture	–0.0652	0.0273
Dummy of very conducive bureaucratic culture	–0.0444	0.0347
Log of GDRP per capita	–0.0128	0.0139
Log of routine budget per capita	0.0049	0.0251
Log of development budget per capita	0.0176	0.0173
Log of local revenue per capita	0.0075	0.0089
Constant	–0.3272	0.2163
Number of observations	87	
R-squared	0.0986	
F-test	1.46	

but the coefficient is not statistically significant and its magnitude is smaller than the coefficient for districts with conducive bureaucratic cultures.

The coefficients of the other variables indicate that — with a note that these coefficients are not statistically significant — economic growth tends to enhance poverty reduction but government budget tends to stifle it. The coefficient of GDRP per capita has a negative sign, which indicates that districts with higher GDRP per capita tend to experience faster poverty reduction. This also implies that districts which strive for higher economic growth will achieve faster reduction in poverty. On the other hand, the coefficients of government budget (both routine and development) and local revenue variables have positive signs. These indicate that taxes and government spending are counterproductive to the efforts to reduce poverty, or at least they do not contribute to poverty reduction.

5. Conclusion

It is public knowledge that bad governance is a serious problem in Indonesia. For a long time the country has ranked highly on the list of the most corrupt countries in the world. Prior to the onset of the economic crisis in mid 1997, the problem of governance was apparent, but it was mostly ignored. The expanding economy due to the high economic growth was enough for most people to compensate for the losses suffered and inefficiency due to bad governance. The advent of the economic crisis, however, has highlighted the seriousness of the problem. Some initiatives to create clean and good governance in the country have been put forward and tried. These efforts, however, have so far proved difficult and elusive.

This study focuses on the impact of bad governance on the poor as well as on efforts to reduce poverty. As the group of people who are in the weakest position and who are most powerless in influencing decisions that affect their lives, the poor are the most vulnerable to the impact of bad governance. For example, when in the 1980s and 1990s the government decided to create various marketing boards for agricultural commodities, which would only benefit select government cronies to the detriment of the farmers, the poor farmers had no choice but to live with it. Occasional protests fell on deaf ears or, even worse, they were met with suppressions.

There were efforts to reform this with some successes between 1998 and 2000, made possible in particular by the fall of the New Order Government. However, these were short-lived. In 2001, when decentralization and the regional autonomy policy started to be implemented, various forms of market distortions which were detrimental to the poor were reincarnated. The only difference this time is that they were mostly created by the regional governments, rather than by the central government as they were in the past. The adverse effects on the poor, however, remained the same.

By assembling scattered anecdotal evidence on how current and past practices of bad governance in Indonesia has hurt the poor, this study shows that the adverse impact of bad governance on the poor is real, systematically inflicts many people, and undermines efforts to reduce poverty in the country. More systematic analyses on the impact bad governance has on poverty reduction — using both descriptive and multivariate analyses — show some indications that indeed regions that practise good governance experience faster rate of poverty reduction and *vice versa*. However, more efforts are needed to separate noises from signals in the data as well as to collect better data and indicators of good governance to firmly establish the relationship between governance and poverty.

In theory, decentralization can provide the impetus for poverty reduction and good governance, because civil society has the opportunity to monitor the way the government behaves more closely and also to bring the concerns of the poor closer to the government. However, if the decentralization policy is only to be exploited as a means of providing the regions with legitimate tools to increase the burden on the community without the compensation of better public services, the general public will have ample reason to oppose the implementation of the decentralization policy. Signs of such 'opposition' towards local government policy are becoming apparent. If this continues to occur, decentralization may present a serious threat to the development of both national and regional economic and social development.

Therefore, in terms of policy implication, clear guidelines need to be established at the national level to ensure appropriate regulation of markets and good governance by local authorities. This should be followed by incentives (disincentives) and systematic reforms which will encourage (discourage) government apparatus with reward (credible threat), both at the local and central level, in practising good (bad) governance. At the same time the civil society needs to establish a consensus and build a coalition to combat bad governing practices, through for example media-campaigns, class-action, and evidence-based publications.

Notes

The authors would like to thank the participants of the workshop on The Asian Development Experience: Governance in Asia Revisited, organized by The Japan Institute of International Affairs (JIIA), 4–5 May 2003 in Tokyo. We would also like to thank Wenefrida Widyanti for her research assistance, the Regional Autonomy Implementation Monitoring Committee (KPPOD),

The Institute for Economic and Social Research (LPEM – University of Indonesia), and Statistics Indonesia (BPS) for providing access to the data. All errors and omissions are ours.

[1] See Suryahadi, Sumarto, and Pritchett (2003).

[2] See King (2000) and McLeod (2000).

[3] See Hamilton-Hart (2001) and Sherlock (2002).

[4] See Blaxall (2000), Eid (2000), and Gupta, Davoodi, and Alonso-Terne (1998).

[5] See, for example, Woodhouse (2001).

[6] Klitgaard (1998).

[7] This is commonly known as *the grease hypothesis*.

[8] For example by creating new bankruptcy court and the appointment of *ad hoc* judges from outside the bureaucracy.

[9] PGRI (2001).

[10] There are many critiques about this clause because of its ambivalent nature.

[11] Specifically, authorities of the provincial government are regulated under Government Regulation (*Peraturan Pemerintah*) No. 25, 2000 regarding the Authority of the Central and Provincial Governments as Autonomous Regions.

[12] See Pradhan et al. (2000).

[13] Summarized from Usman et al. (2001b).

[14] Summarized from Usman et al. (2001a).

[15] Summarized from Usman et al. (2001a).

[16] Summarized from Usman et al. (2002).

[17] Summarized from Mawardi et al. (2002).

[18] See Sumarto, Suryahadi, and Widyanti (2002).

[19] Even though the health-card was meant only for the poor, only 35% of all the health-cards distributed were given to the poor (Saadah, Pradhan, and Sparrow 2000).

[20] See Saadah, Pradhan, and Sparrow (2000).

[21] See Dethier (1999).

[22] Another large-scale national-level survey has been conducted by the World Bank and Gadjah Mada Univerisity. However, at the time of writing this paper, the results have yet to be made public.

References

Blaxall, John. 2000. "Governance and Poverty". Paper presented at the Joint Workshop on Poverty Reduction Strategies in Mongolia, The World Bank, Ulan Bator, Mongolia, 4 to 6 October . On the web at http://www.worldbank.org/poverty/strategies/events/mongolia/gov.pdf, downloaded on 22 March 2003.

Crook, Richard and Alan Sturia Sverrisson. 2001. "Decentralization and Poverty Alleviation in Developing Countries: A Comparative Analysis or, Is West Bengal Unique?" IDS Working Paper #130, February. Institute for Development Studies, Brighton, England.

Dethier, Jean-Jacques. 1999. "Governance and Economic Performance: A Survey". Discussion Paper on Development Policy #5, April. Center for Development Research, The University of Bonn, Bonn.

Eid, Uschi. 2000. "Good Governance for Poverty Reduction". Paper presented at the Asian Development Bank Seminar on The New Social Policy and Poverty Agenda for Asia and the Pacific, Chiang Mai, Thailand, 5 May. On the web at http://www.uschi-eid.de/docs/000505-poverty.htm, downloaded on 21 March 2003.

Gupta, Sanjeev, Hamid Davoodi, and Erwin Tiongson. 2000. "Corruption and the Provision of Health Care and Education Services". IMF Working Paper No. 00/116, June. International Monetary Fund, Washington, DC.

Gupta, Sanjeev, Hamid Davoodi, and Rosa Alonso-Terne. 1998. "Does Corruption Affect Income Inequality and Poverty?" IMF Working Paper No. 98/76, May. International Monetary Fund, Washington, DC.

Hamilton-Hart, Natasha. 2001. "Anti-Corruption Strategies in Indonesia". *Bulletin of Indonesian Economic Studies*, 37(1), pp. 65–82.

Huther, Jeff and Anwar Shah. 1998. "Applying a Simple Measure of Good Governance to the Debate on Fiscal Decentralization". Policy Research Working Paper No. 1894, March. The World Bank, Washington, DC.

Kaufmann, Daniel, Aart Kraay, and Pablo Zoido-Lobaton. 1999. "Governance Matters". Policy Research Working Paper No. 2196, October. The World Bank, Washington, DC.

King, Dwight. 2000. "Corruption in Indonesia: A Curable Cancer?". *Journal of International Affairs*, 53(2), pp. 603–624.

Kinuthia-Njenga, Cecilia. date unknown. "Good Governance: Common Definitions". United Nations Human Settlement Programme. On the web at http://www.unhabitat.org/HD/hdv5n4/intro2.htm, downloaded on 21 March 2003.

Klitgaard, Robert. 1998. *Controlling Corruption*. University of California Press, Berkeley, CA.

KPPOD. 2002. "Pemeringkatan Daya Tarik Investasi Kabupaten/Kota: Studi Kasus di 90 Kabupaten/Kota di Indonesia" [The Ranking of Investment

Attractiveness across Districts/Cities: A Case Study of 90 Districts/Cities in Indonesia]. Komite Pemantauan Pelaksanaan Otonomi Daerah, Jakarta.

LaPorte, Robert, Jr. 2002. "Governance: A Global Perspective". Paper presented at the South Asia Regional Conference of the Hubert H. Humphrey Fellowship Program, Kathmandu, Nepal, 20 February. On the web at http://www. fulbrightnepal.org.np, downloaded on 21 March 2003.

LPEM. 2001. *Construction of Regional Index of Doing Business*. Laporan Akhir [Final Report], December, Lembaga Penyelidikan Ekonomi dan Masyarakat, Fakultas Ekonomi Universitas Indonesia, Jakarta.

Mawardi, M. Sulton, Syaikhu Usman, Vita Febriany, Rachael Diprose, Nina Toyamah. 2002. "Dampak Desentralisasi dan Otonomi Daerah Atas Kinerja Pelayanan Publik: Kasus Kabupaten Lombok Barat, Nusa Tenggara Barat" [The Impact of Decentralization and Regional Autonomy on Public Services Performance: The Case of West Lombok District, West Nusa Tenggara]. Field Report, June. The SMERU Research Institute, Jakarta.

McLeod, Ross. 2000. "Soeharto's Indonesia: A Better Class of Corruption". *Agenda*, 7(2), pp. 99–112.

Montgomery, Roger, Sudarno Sumarto, Sulton Mawardi, Syaikhu Usman, Nina Toyamah, Vita Vebriary and John Strain. 2002. "Deregulation of Indonesia's Interregional Agricultural Trade". *Bulletin of Indonesian Economic Studies*, 38(1), pp. 93–117.

PGRI. 2001. "A National Survey of Corruption in Indonesia", December. Partnership for Governance Reform in Indonesia, Jakarta. On the web at http://www. partnership.or.id/data/pdf/Indonesia_Final_Report_Dec_2001. pdf, downloaded on 24 March 2003.

Pradhan, Menno, Asep Suryahadi, Sudarno Sumarto, and Lant Pritchett. 2000. "Measurements of Poverty in Indonesia: 1996, 1999, and Beyond". SMERU Working Paper, June, Social Monitoring and Early Response Unit, Jakarta.

Rajkumar, Andrew Sunil, and Vinaya Swaroop. 2002. "Public Spending and Outcomes: Does Governance Matter?" Policy Research Working Paper No. 2840, May. The World Bank, Washington, DC.

Saadah, Fadia, Menno Pradhan, and Robert Sparrow. 2000. "The Effectiveness of the Healthcard as an Instrument to Ensure Access to Medical Care for the Poor During the Crisis". The World Bank, Washington, D.C., mimeo.

Sherlock, Stephen. 2002. "Combating Corruption in Indonesia? The Ombudsman and the Assets Auditing Commission". *Bulletin of Indonesian Economic Studies*, 38(3), pp. 367–83.

Sumarto, Sudarno, Asep Suryahadi, and Wenefrida Widyanti. 2002. "Designs and Implementation of the Indonesian Social Safety Net Programs". *Developing Economies*, 40(1), pp. 3–31.

Suryahadi, Asep, Sudarno Sumarto, and Lant Pritchett. 2003. "The Evolution of Poverty during the Crisis in Indonesia". SMERU Working Paper, March. The SMERU Research Institute, Jakarta.

UNDP. 1997. "Governance for Sustainable Human Development", January. United Nations Development Program. On the web at http:// magnet.undp.org/policy /default.htm, downloaded on 21 March 2003.

Usman, Syaikhu, Ilyas Saad, Nina Toyamah, M. Sulton Mawardi, Vita Febriany, Pamadi Wibowo. 2001a. "Regional Autonomy and the Business Climate: North Sulawesi and Gorontalo". Field Report, September. The SMERU Research Institute, Jakarta.

Usman, Syaikhu, Ilyas Saad, Vita Febriany, Nina Toyamah, M. Sulton Mawardi, Hudi Sartono, Pamadi Wibowo and Sudarno Sumarto. 2001b. "Regional Autonomy and the Business Climate: Three Kabupaten Case Studies from North Sumatra". Field Report, May. The SMERU Research Institute, Jakarta.

Usman, Syaikhu, Nina Toyamah, M. Sulton Mawardi, Vita Febriany and Ilyas Saad. 2002. "Regional Autonomy and the Business Climate: Three Kabupaten Case Studies from West Java". Field Report, June. The SMERU Research Institute, Jakarta.

World Bank. 1992. *Governance and Development*. The World Bank, Washington, DC.

Woodhouse, Andrea. 2001. "Fighting Corruption in KDP". July. The World Bank, Jakarta, mimeo.

3

Local Governance in Indonesia's Decentralization Era: Prospect and Challenges

Tommy A. Legowo

1. Introduction

Good local governance has been the focus of public expectation since the Indonesia's central government (the Government) introduced the new Laws on Decentralization in 1999, i.e., Law 22/1999 on Regional Government and Law 25/1999 on Fiscal Balance between Central and Regional Government. Since then, however, public discussions and debates on whether or not the new laws can bring about effective fundamental changes on the character and way of local processes of governing as to make up good local governance have never ceased. Indeed, this mixed picture means that although the laws provide Indonesia with a strategic chance or opportunity to establish good local governance, there is a strong public doubt concerning the country's institutional as well as societal capacity to develop programmes on establishing good local governance.

This study tries to look at the impact of the prevailing laws on decentralization towards good local governance. First, it maps the principles of good governance that are adopted by the laws. The main question is whether or not the laws introduce the universal principles of good governance. Second, it depicts the central as well as local governments' responses to the necessity of good local governance. Do the different levels of government respond in similar or different ways? Third, it looks at the past four years' experiences of decentralization especially concerning especially the development of local institutions. A relevant question to be addressed is whether or not the prevailing Indonesian local institutions are compatible with the needs and requirements of making good local governance. Finally, it takes some recent studies and cases of local experiences to see perceptions as well as efforts of making good governance at the local level. By taking these case studies, one may confirm or refute the significant impact of the laws on decentralization towards the establishment of good local governance, and what further efforts should be made in order to accelerate the process of establishing local good governance in Indonesia.

This study argues that although the laws on decentralization provide strategic opportunities to develop local good governance, lack of commitment and experience of political elites, be it at the national or local level, on the necessity of good local governance for the future of democratic Indonesia, and the poor setting and capacity of local institutions have resulted in a relatively bad experience of local governance. A national commitment on good governance, at both national and local levels that has to be consistently manifested in programme implementations would be the best approach to make universal principles of good governance work at the local level. In other words, the laws on decentralization would be less significant to the building of good local governance unless there are committed national and local leaderships to make it work.

2. Defining Good Governance

The concept of governance is complex and controversial. Before one can say what good governance is, one has to be clear about what is meant by governance. A good starting point is the UNDP definition, which states that governance is

> the exercise of political, economic and administrative authority in the management of a country's affairs at all levels. It comprises the mechanisms, processes and institutions, through which citizens and groups articulate their interests, exercise their legal rights, meet their obligations and mediate their differences (UNDP 1997, pp. 2–3).

Two aspects of this definition are worth noting. First, governance is not government. Governance as a concept recognizes that power exists inside and outside the formal authority and institutions of government. In many formulations, governance includes government, the private sector and civil society. Second, governance emphasizes processes. It recognizes that decisions are made based on complex relationships between many actors with different priorities.

In a similar fashion, Sofyan Effendi emphasizes that there is an essential difference between government and governance. Government refers to the pattern of executing authority, be it political, economic and administrative authority, by a government. Governance is a picture of how entities of a nation manage that authority fairly and accountably. There are three main forces that constitute the capacity of a nation to maintain good governance: government, civil society and private sector. A fair and accountable process of governing can be only achieved when the execution of political, economic and administrative authority involves the active participation of the three main forces equally and synergically (Sofyan Effendi 2003, pp. 110–112).

Meanwhile, Robert D. Putnam, et al. (1994, p. 9) translates the definition into a simple model of governance: societal demands → political interaction → government → policy choice → implementation. Government receives inputs from their social environment and produce outputs to respond that environment. Working parents seek affordable day care, or merchants worry about shoplifting, or veterans decry the death of patriotism. Political parties and other groups articulate these concerns, and officials consider what, if anything, to do. Eventually, a policy (which may be symbolic) is adopted. Unless that policy is "do nothing", it must then be implemented – creating new nurseries (or encouraging private agencies to do so), putting more cops on the beat, flying flags more often. A high performance democratic institution must be both responsive and effective: sensitive to the demands of its constituents and effective in using limited resources to address these demands.

> Putnam (1994, p. 9) continues to explain that "(C)omplexities abound this domain. To be effective, for example, government must often be foresighted enough to anticipate demands that have not yet been articulated. Debates and deadlocks may stall the process at any point. The effect of government action, even when well designed and effectively implemented, may not be what proponents had hoped. Nevertheless, institutional performance is important because in the end the quality of government matters to people's lives: scholarship awarded, roads paved, children inoculated — or (if government fails) they are not".

Included in the definition as well as in the simple model of governance is the understanding of the praxis that power has to be devolved (not centralized in one person or institution), that public participation is acknowledged and respected, that authority has to be accountable and thereby its practices should be transparent, and that partnership needs to be implemented. If this understanding is to be translated further, the function of good governance has to result in the following characteristics: democracy (included in this category is decentralization on the basis of subsidiarity,[1] participation in every decision-making process at any level of government; efficient and effective government accounted transparently, and cooperation among government institutions and entities of community.

2.1 Decentralization and Local Governance

Decentralization is one of the principles of governance as it would lead any type of government to be much more efficient, accountable and participatory. Decentralization is a manifestation of respect and trust of higher level of government to the existence and capacity of lower level of government. This explains also that decentralization is in fact part of the democratization process. By definition, decentralization is

> the transfer of responsibility for planning, management and resources raising and allocation from the central government and its agencies to: (a) filed units of central government ministries or agencies; (b) subordinate units or levels of government; (3) semi autonomous public authorities or corporations; (d) area wide, regional or functional authorities; or (e) non-governmental, private, or voluntary organization (Cheema, Rodinelli and Nellis 1983, cited in UNDP 1998, p. 1).

In that respect, decentralization is basically a making of governing process at local levels, which involves and carries out all norms and aspects of democratic government. A successful process of decentralization would result subsequently in the establishment of governance at local levels. In other words, decentralization is a process of making local government. When this process is put in to the framework of democracy, the output of such decentralization would be good local governance. In that sense, local governance can be understood as "the sum of the many ways individuals and institutions, public and private, plan and manage the common affairs of (the) region" (Global Campaign for Good Urban Governance 2000, pp. 6–7).

There is a big question mark, however, whether or not a decentralized government could result instantaneously in maintaining good local governance. Governments decentralize themselves for many reasons and in many different patterns. Decentralization, which aims at establishing good local governance, would involve many aspects and actors. It includes formal institutions as well as informal arrangements and the social capital of citizens. It is also linked inextricably to the welfare of the citizenry. The decentralization programme must enable people to access the benefits of local citizenship.[2] Through such a programme, citizens are provided with the platform, which will allow them to use their talents to the full to improve their social and economic conditions.

In that manner, decentralization needs to implement the following norms and principles. First, it has to balance the social, economic and environmental needs of present and future generations. Therefore, the principle of sustainability has to be applied in all dimensions of local development. Local leaders need to have a long-term, strategic vision of sustainable human development and the ability to reconcile divergent interests for the common good.[3] Second, responsibility for service provision should be allocated on the basis of the principle of subsidiarity,[4] that is, at the lowest appropriate level consistent with efficient and cost-effective delivery of services. This will maximize the potential for inclusion of the citizenry in the process of local governance. Decentralization and local democracy should improve the responsiveness of policies and initiatives to the priorities and needs of citizens. Regions should be empowered with sufficient resources and autonomy to meet their responsibilities.[5]

Third, the sharing of power leads to equity in the access to and use of resources. People must be equally represented, their needs and priorities equally addressed, in all local decision-making and resource allocation processes. Inclusive regions provide everyone with equal access to basic appropriate standards of nutrition, education, employment and livelihood, healthcare, shelter, safe drinking water, sanitation and other basic services.[6] Fourth, efficiency in the delivery of public services and in promoting local economic development would be another principle of local governance. Regions must be financially sound and cost-effective in their management of revenue sources and expenditures, the administration and delivery of services, and in the enablement, based on comparative advantage, of government, the private sector and communities to contribute formally or informally to the local economy. A key element in achieving efficiency is to recognize and enable the specific contribution of women to the local economy.[7]

Two other norms and principles would play a significant role in preserving the conditions for realizing the above mentioned principles. These are transparency and accountability, and civic engagement and citizenship. In this regards, transparency and accountability have to apply for local decision makers and all stakeholders. The accountability of local authorities to their citizens must be a paramount concern; there is no place for corruption in regions. Transparency and accountability are essential in allowing stakeholders to have insight into local government operations and to assess which sectors of society are benefiting from decisions and actions. Universal access to, and the free flow of, information is fundamental to transparent and accountable governance. Laws and public policies should be applied in a transparent and predictable manner. Public officials should adhere to high standards of professional and personal integrity.[8] The norm of civic engagement and citizenship is derived from the basic view that people are the principal wealth of regions; they are both the object and the means of sustainable human development. Civic engagement implies that living together is not a passive exercise: in regions, people must actively contribute to the common good. Citizens, especially women, must be empowered to participate effectively in decision-making processes.[9]

Finally, decentralization for local governance is to guarantee the preservation of security of individuals and their living environment. Every individual has the inalienable right to life, liberty and the security of person. Insecurity has a disproportionate impact in further marginalizing poor communities. Regions must strive to avoid human conflicts and natural disasters by involving all stakeholders in crime and conflict prevention and disaster preparedness. Security also implies freedom from persecution, forced evictions and provides for security of tenure. Regions should also work with social mediation and conflict reduction agencies and encourage the cooperation between enforcement agencies and other social service providers (health, education and housing).[10]

To carry out good local governance, a setting of institutional arrangements that consists of norms, procedures and institutions needs to be established. However, this has to work together with the commitment and capacity of stakeholders that constitute good governance. One could argue, therefore, that first, good (local) governance is a process towards sustaining better quality of managing a process of government; and second, this would be likely a never ending process as the commitment and capacity of stakeholders may change for better or worse over time that could impact on the quality of the setting of institutional arrangements.

3. Indonesia's Local Governance: A New Praxis

Issues of good governance were quite new in Indonesian politics. It went along with the fundamental political reform marked by the downfall of the authoritarian regime of President Soeharto in May 1998. Indonesian politics changed from illiberal to liberal. The system of government was also forced to change from authoritarian to democratic. The public started to talk about the necessity of introducing principles and norms of good governance in order to reform the country's political and government systems.

The immediate results from this unprecedented political change, among others, were the introduction of new laws on decentralization, and a process of constitutional reform. The first refers to Law No. 22/

1999 on Regional Government and Law No. 25/1999 on Fiscal Balance between Central and Regional Government. Both laws were legislated in mid-1999. The latter refers to the process of amending Indonesia's 1945 Constitution that took place from 1999 to 2002. All these have had a clear impact on the nature of governing Indonesia in general and the making of local governance in particular. The question is whether or not these new legal-constitutional foundations provide Indonesia with room and opportunity to initiate establishing good local governance. As pointed out by the Center for Democracy and Governance (2000, pp. 19–20), reform of constitutions and legal codes is one of the necessary conditions for the initial establishment of good governance. For this reason, we need to search for provisions in the new legal-constitutional foundations that may or may not support for the chance to making good local governance. The above criteria of governance are used as standard measurements for this exercise.

The laws on decentralization and Article 18 of the 1945 Constitution reflect clearly or translate directly the first and foremost principle of good governance, that is, "*decentralization* of responsibilities and resources to local (lower level) authorities". However, there is a big question mark as to whether the principle of decentralization adopts the norms of subsidiarity and accountability. There are no clear provisions in both legal-constitutional foundations pointing out these norms. This could also mean that the principle of decentralization adopted by the legal-constitutional foundations is limitedly acknowledged (applied). This is confirmed by the provision of the Law 22/1999 stating that "autonomy is granted to district administration of government". There is no obligation for the district administration to further decentralize its authority to its sub-district administrations and or, on the basis of subsidiarity, to disperse its authority to communities. In brief, the principle of decentralization in the case of Indonesia seems to focus on administrative decentralization. (Legowo 2001) It does not yet touch the true democratic aspect of decentralization that provides community with the opportunity to take responsibility for some public services.

The limited principle of decentralization seems to be in accordance to the principle of participation that the legal-constitutional foundations adopt. Although the principle of participation is taken into account by the foundations as reflected in the objective of decentralization project of Indonesia, it is not elaborated further in the foundations as to how public participation should be arranged and managed so as to involve the public in the design, implementation and monitoring of programmes and policies. The Laws on Decentralization guarantee only that the local process of policymaking, implementation and monitoring (oversight) is controlled by the local executive and parliament, and thus being far away from public (direct) involvement. Even more, among these two government institutions, the local parliament is the most dominant institution grasping all power and authority in all stages of the policy process. The authority of local parliament is far reaching. It does not only hold the authority to formulate local regulations and policies, but also grant the authority to elect as well as to resign the head of local executive in its mid-term of office. There is no obligation for local parliament to consult the public concerning even key local policy issues. Public participation is limited only during the general elections to vote for members of local parliament.

The lack of legal binding that encourages the public's participation in the design, implementation, and monitoring of programs and policies also reduces the opportunity for local stakeholders of governance to using a wide variety of partnerships to achieve common objectives. This problem is clearly reflected in the legal-constitutional foundations in which no provisions in the foundations necessitate the use of partnerships to achieve local common goal. It is likely that Indonesia's decentralization project assumes local government institutions as the main actors that determine and take initiatives of achieving local common objectives.

The presence of all stakeholders of governance is truly acknowledged in the legal-constitutional foundations. These stakeholders include the society, business community, and local government. Part of the society is *adat* (traditional) and village communities. Even more, the *adat* communities are specially treated in which they are granted to enact *adat* laws within their *adat* territories. The village communities also enjoy the same treatment in that villages are allowed to have autonomy. Such acknowledgment might be assumed as the state's commitment to initiate building capacity of stakeholders to contribute fully to decision-making and development processes. However, the legal-constitutional foundations lack the facilities to manage building capacity of other actors or stakeholders in the local governance. The same case is also evident in facilitating networking in all levels of governance. The legal-constitutional foundations do not include any provision that really covers this issue.

The government's lack of will in fostering good governance gives rise to weak legal-constitutional foundations. When this happens, whatever arrangements it makes for, implementing governance will fail since there would not be a clear pattern or mechanism of good governance. In this case, although it can be found the norm of sustainability in the foundations, for example, it is hard to find further elaboration of how the norm of sustainability is to institutionalize. The case is also valid for other norms of good governance, i.e., decentralization, equity, efficiency, transparency and accountability, civic engagement and citizenship, and security.

That critical review of Indonesia's legal-constitutional foundations on governance is to emphasize that although there are many weaknesses of the foundations in directing the making of (good) governance in local practices, the fact that Indonesian politics of reform has succeeded in introducing those foundations has to be considered as a significant progress. One would certainly agree that after more than four decades under authoritarian regimes, Indonesia has no experience at all of maintaining good governance. In other words, if good governance is to apply to Indonesia, this would only materialize through a long process of praxis. Introducing the basic characteristics and norms of good governance in Indonesian politics has been a significant achievement. The current political environment in Indonesia seems to provide more opportunity and change for all stakeholders of governance to develop better and comprehensive legal-constitutional foundations for the enactment of good governance both in national and local practices.

4. Responses to the Necessity of Good Local Governance

The introduction of the Laws on Decentralization has been perceived as a strategic momentum to stimulate reform of local government directing to the establishment of efficient and accountable government. In doing so, it is argued that the application of norms of good governance in local practices is unavoidable. However, it is also believed that there would be a lot of constraints to achieve the objective to apply norms of good governance in local practices. In spite of the lack of institutional arrangements, the pattern of behaviour of national and local elites, as well as the society needs to be fundamentally changed in ways that support the application of the norms of good governance in local practices.

4.1 Lack of Institutional Arrangement

The main problem of the institutional arrangement posing a constraint to the application of the norms of good governance is how to manage public participation in local political processes. The legal-constitutional foundations of local governance seems to focus merely on the decentralization of the government's authority from the central to local government.[11] This is followed by the provision that causes the local administration (executive) to be very much dependent upon the local assembly. Unfortunately, however, there is no direct relation between the local assembly and the local society. This is likely caused by the fact that the legal-constitutional foundations of local governance do not yet touch the decentralization of politics that provide local communities a space to take active part in local political processes. Such arrangement has created a potential of (re-) centralization in the hands of the local assembly. (Hadiz 2003, pp. 122–129)

In that respect, the local assembly holds all power to dominate local political processes. The assembly has the rights, among others, to (a) elect the head as well as deputies of local executive; (b) remove the head of local executive; (c) draft and pass local policies and regulations; (d) draft and pass local budget; (e) exercise control over local executive; (f) give its views to the central government on international agreements that might affect local interests; and (g) aggregate and articulate the aspiration of local people. In addition, to avoid the contempt of parliament at local level, the assembly is also equipped with the right of subpoena in carrying out its functions. Members of the local assembly cannot be sued for any statement they make in an assembly meeting. Equipped with all these rights, it is obvious that the local assembly has immense authority in dominating the course of local political and economic life.

It is hardly found in the legal-constitutional foundations of decentralization and other legal foundations provisions that facilitate local institutions to have the right to balance the immense authority of the local assembly. In other words, the local assembly is constitutionally the highest government institution in local politics. However, as members of the assembly are elected through a proportional representation of general election that gives political parties of their respective affiliation a significant role in determining them as local parliamentarians, only those political parties have potential power to direct as well as to control individual members of the assembly. In this respect, one may argue that in Indonesia's decentralization era, local politics are basically determined by the natures of political parties and the relationship between (local) major parties.

4.2 Agents' Capacity and Pattern of Behaviour

The Indonesian political parties have not been developed and managed under a modern party system. They work only during the very short period of general elections and merely for three relevant election activities: candidacy nomination, election campaign, and inauguration of elected candidates for membership of assemblies. Parties also lack financial as well as human resources to carry out their functions on a daily basis. Not only at the national but also mostly at the local levels political parties are hardly found to manage their political action programmes and activities. Despite failing to absorb people's interests and aspirations, political parties are unable to feed their representatives in the assembly with proper information and policy inputs in order to support them in deliberating issues of policymaking. What is worst about the way Indonesian political parties are managed is that they are very centralized and oriented to their party's central board and or their party's top leader.

As a result, parties lack of alternative policy concepts to be delivered in the policymaking process by their respective representatives at all levels of assembly.

Such nature of Indonesian political parties has resulted in at least three types of party relationships with its respective consequences and impacts on local governance. *First,* local major parties form a coalition. They may work cooperatively to seek the best local policies and regulations for regional development. However, it does not necessarily mean that a party's coalition in local assembly would always be participatory, transparent and accountable to the public. *Second,* local major parties compete with one another over controlling local political power. They are likely to work for their respective political interests. If any coalition of parties exists in such circumstance, it would form only a loose coalition based on a certain selected policy issue considered to benefit their respective interests. In any case, a competitive relationship tends to disadvantage local government practices and development. *Third,* parties' representatives in the local assembly establish "collusion" type of relationships. They misuse the authority of the assembly to take every advantage for individual welfare. The impact of such relationship on local governance is obvious in that local policies and regulations are formulated to cater to the individual welfare of local elites. Principle norms of transparency and accountability are hardly expected to apply in such relationships.

Indonesian political parties are hardly expected to endure the establishment of good local governance. This case also seems to apply to two other entities that in principle should be able to play a similar significant role. These entities are the central government, and local communities. By the legal-constitutional foundations, the central government still has a significant role in directing the course of the decentralization programme. For this role, the laws provide the central government with, among others, the obligations to monitor, supervise and evaluate the implementation programme of decentralization, and to review all local policies and regulations introduced and enacted by local assemblies. Apart from the problem of capacity of the central government in carrying out the obligations, there is a crucial problem of credibility of the government. This is reflected in many cases of local disobedience towards the central government's "warning" and/or even policy decisions. To these many cases, the central government has no power to make local compliances.[12]

There is another problem concerning the efficacy of government regulations aimed at making best practices of local government, considered part of a comprehensive effort to establish good governance at the local levels. The introduction of the Government Regulation 56/2001 on the Reporting of the Working of Local Government, and the Presidential

Decision 74/2001 on the Procedure of Overseeing the Working of Local government, for example, is likely to aim at establishing an institutional mechanism of government monitoring over the workings of local government in implementing the decentralization programme. The problem with these two regulations is how far these regulations can be effectively implemented in was that they have clear and certain implications toward the working (performance) of local government.

In the case of Presidential Decision 74/2001, it is stated, among others, that "Governor, Regent or Major and Speakers of Local Assembly who refuse the overseeing and do not take any follow up actions toward the results of the overseeing are subject to administrative sanctions and or other sanctions in accordance to the available Laws" (Article 21). The Government Regulation 56/2001 also emphasizes, among others, that "The Government may deliver sanctions to the head of local executive". These two different provisions derived from two different regulations, however, do not elaborate further on what kinds of sanction that will be delivered, and what impacts would be accepted by those who are subject to this sanction. Without clear details of sanction, one cannot measure what the implications would be. On the contrary, if there is no implication at all, such regulations would be meaningless.

4.3 Problems of Local Community

Local communities also have no capability to control their local assemblies. First, there is no institutional mechanism that provides local communities access to the assemblies. The relationship between the communities and the assemblies is established formally during the period of general elections, and only in an indirect manner through political parties. Permanent and institutionalized public hearings are never established by law. If there is any public hearing, it could only occur upon the initiative of the local assemblies, and would cover merely specific policy issues that are being delivered by the assemblies. Second, the communities are very weak in terms of lack of initiatives and capacity in organizing their interests and aspirations. Only in big cities where there are more society groups having better education and political consciousness, organizing societal interests and aspirations has more chances to be better managed as political pressures to local policymaking processes. However, these remain as incidental events or activities.

Such conditions of local communities pose two problems (Andi Novi Hendrarto, Dani Wahyu Anggoro 2002, pp. 29–55). The first relates to the availability of political mechanism for public participation during the period in-between two general elections. The problems do not only reflect the lack of laws and regulations at both national and local levels that drive the institutionalization of such political mechanism, but also the weak commitment of national as well as local political elites institutionalizing such mechanism. The lack of laws and regulations on this issue is quite often being used by the elites as an excuse to not take any political initiative to establish the mechanism. The second problem relates to the minimum understanding of the society that in the era of decentralization more chances are open for the public to be more active in voicing and struggling for their aspirations and interests in local policymaking processes. Moreover, local community capacity to manage and organize their aspirations and interests, in the form of interest groups has not been seen and assumed to be effective in influencing the policymaking process.

All the above problems are likely to be the main constraints for establishing good governance at the local level. The current Indonesian Government's decentralization programme has indeed devolved the power and authority of the central government to local governments. However, this programme does not seem to go further beyond the local government, that is, to decentralize local government power and authority to local communities. The decentralization programme seems, therefore, to have resulted in the potential concentration of power and authority in the body of local government.

To look in more detail, the potential concentration of power is likely to mount in and be absorbed by the authority of local assembly. The local assembly controls and dominates political power and processes. With minimum experience and weak commitment over local communities' interests, members of the assembly tend to serve the interests of their respective political parties, and worse, their own (personal) interests. In addition, the weak capacity and capability of local communities to organize their aspirations and interests have brought about the local assembly as an arena for the distribution of power and wealth among members of the assembly, and among their respective political parties.

5. Progress on the Implementation of Local Governance

Some empirical studies and/or cases might help give a much clearer picture of the prospect and challenges of local governance in Indonesia. Apart from the constraints that may impede the establishment of good local governance, significant progress has been achieved in local socio-political development that may be considered as being of fundamental importance to the making of local governance. Although this progress is not systematically carried out under a national framework, it is reflected in individual agents' commitment to work towards establishing good local governance. Some of this progress is indicated by empirical research and by factual initiatives of local community groups.

5.1 Capacity of Local Politics

The CSIS' study on "The Capacity of Local Politics for Regional Autonomy" is interesting. (CSIS 2000) The study was conducted in 2000, covering 27 regencies and cities, aimed at observing the quality of local political process, and public perception of the quality of the processes. The main question of the study was whether or not local politics had performed as a political mechanism being able to accelerate the decentralization programme. This question was raised as the study intended to see whether or not there were significant substantial as well as technical preparations in local politics to respond to the new policy of decentralization. The year 2000 was a preparation period prior to the effective implementation of the decentralization policy (programme) in January 2001. To do this, the study focused on the conditions of local political institutions, and how these institutions worked to prepare the local political process for implementing the programme of regional autonomy. By local political institutions, we refer to local government institutions: the executive and legislature, political parties, interest groups, NGOs, and local mass-media.

The study concluded in some interesting points relating to the issue of local governance. *First*, on the conditions of local political institutions, it resulted, among others, in the following points:

1. During the then pre-implementation of the regional autonomy programme, in many different regions there seemed not only similar "enthusiasm" but also "uncertainty" in responding to the autonomy programme. The enthusiasm was seen in a variety of activities in the preparations of institutional (administrative) reforms, and in many hopes and expectations of the society in general. Meanwhile, the uncertainty was reflected in the general public doubts concerning the process of transferring the authority, personnel, assets, and money from the central to local governments, and the capability of local stakeholders in managing "good and clean government" and in developing local revenue resources necessary for local development.

2. Local political condition of many regions has been inclined to implement, and even has already implemented Law 22/1999, especially concerning the *power relations* between local executives and legislatures (DPRDs). The DPRDs were very confident in taking on the role to control the executives. They did not, however, prove that they were capable of performing other roles especially in fulfilling public interests and needs. Such a political trend, however, did not appear in other non-

government political institutions such as local political parties and interest groups. No real activities of these two types of institutions were shown to be affected by the new programme of regional autonomy.

3. Political parties in the regions did not show any substantial internal reforms merely influenced by the demands of the regional autonomy programme. Several considerations may explain the problem. *First*, political parties at the local level remained subordinate to their respective centrally managed headquarters in the centre (Jakarta). *Second*, there seems to be no management of political parties at the local level. *Third*, they lacked financial as well as human resources. *Fourth*, only local major political parties have conducted activities relating to internal socialization of the regional autonomy programme. Apart from such activities, other parties' activities were moved from local party offices to their respective offices in the DPRDs.

4. Interest groups at the district level also did not show important changes as a result of the new regional autonomy programme. Local business associations, for example, are autonomously managed. But they seemed to be very much dependent on the government's development projects. In some regions, interest groups such as associations of farmer and labour have shown their enthusiasm to develop their capabilities, expand their activities, and try to be more "free" from (local) governments' instructions. Meanwhile, NGOs played different and distinct roles from that of the interest groups. Some NGOs in the regions concentrated more on advocacy activities to empower certain societal groups such as farmer, fisherman, and industrial labour and craftsman. Some other NGOs working on environmental conservation and consumer protection gave their attention to local policy regulations on related issues. And some others, which are more "politically oriented", tried hard to prevent all local political processes from *KKN* (corruption, collusion and nepotism). However, NGOs in many regions remained minor political groupings that had power to drive local society's life.

Second, on the issue of institutionalization of local politics, the study was not really clear whether the national programme of regional autonomy had motivated local political institutions to carry out reform of their performances and attitudes as to contribute to the establishment of local democratic political systems. Apparently, it showed that no performances and attitudes of these institutions reflected a new spirit to seriously attain such a goal. These did not only take place in the bureaucratic circle but also in other local political institutions. In the government bureaucratic circle, for example, there was a general impression that local bureaucrats did not really show serious efforts to maximize public and delivery services. What was seen was "laziness" to work as if there were no necessary tasks to accomplish. Another example is the condition of political parties at the local level. Internal conflicts coloured most major parties at the local level. Meanwhile, there were no party activities that clearly aimed to support the implementation of the regional autonomy programme. Of course, exceptions prevailed for several major parties especially in some rural regions (cities), in which they managed to socialize the new regional autonomy programme for their members down to sub-district level. In general, political parties do their activities merely for the purpose to participate in, if not to win, general elections.

Third, on the issue of optimizing the capacity of local politics, the study emphasizes that given the low quality of political institutions as well as the improper interaction between them, what is necessary in order to respond to the regional autonomy programme is to redefine the roles and functions of the institutions not only in the new setting of local political system but also in the new dynamics of socio-political life of the regions. It is also well realized that the local political system is not yet perfect, not only because of the just mentioned problem but also because of lack of skill and knowledge of local political actors on the authority and functional roles they have to perform. What is exactly needed, although it was not stated explicitly by many groups in the regions, to overcome the uncertain condition mentioned above is the presence of a visionary leadership who has the capacity to consolidate the society and all local potential resources to meet the new demands of regional autonomy. The functional system could play such a leadership. But, local leaders with such leadership qualities could also play that role.

The results of the study is basically explaining that the decentralization programme of Indonesia based on Law 22/1999 and UU 25/1999 has not directly resulted in the immediate establishment of the praxis of local good governance. Even the primary prerequisite of political institutions for local governance had not been available, and thereby, require continuous institutional improvement.

In 2001, CSIS conducted another empirical study on "Capacity Building on Indonesian Local Government". (CSIS 2001) 2001 was the first year of the effective implementation of the regional autonomy programme. The main objective of the study was aimed at observing whether or not there has been significant progress in the capacity of local political institutions since the first study of "the Capacity of Local Politics for Regional Autonomy Program", in 2000. Four of the previous 27 research regions were chosen as samples of the study. These regions were Kabupaten Sukabumi, Kabupaten Sleman, Kota Kupang and Kota Samarinda. In summary, the result of this study shows that no fundamental progress of the conditions of local political institutions as well as local political processes had been achieved. However, the study emphasized that within the bureaucratic circle, the process of institutional reform (adjustment), and the transfer of personnel and government assets had taken place. Another progress noted by the study, was that local communities were more enthusiastic to be able to participate in local political processes. This was seen in societal initiatives to establish "forums of stakeholders" in those regions. These forums consisted of all segments of society and representatives of government's institutions were used as media of communication that could be utilized to understand common problems and to propose ways to solve the problems faced by their local specifics. However, the study did not see that such forums had been effective in influencing or directing local political processes.

No research on a similar theme to that of the CSIS studies has been done in 2002. However, a number of significant cases at the local level might be used to indicate the extent of achievements of good governance which have been prevailing at some local praxis. *First*, on the issue of local political institutions, no evidence has prevailed to show any fundamental change in the institutions' quality. Although always under heavy political pressure from local assemblies, local executives remain playing significant roles in local praxis. Political parties are in status-quo condition, or worse, experiencing internal conflicts. However, there is strong indication in many regions that local communities are more and more eager to take initiative and active participation not only in organizing and managing their interests but also in local political processes. The initiative of Dumai's community to form a "city forum" to partner the local assembly is a clear example of how the society can manage its active political participation.

Second, on the issue of institutionalizing political processes, there seems no indication of progress. The case of electing the head of local executive is a case in point. This reflects basically the all complex problem of governance in Indonesia's local praxis. The case is that many regions seem to have similar problems when they are conducting the process of electing their heads of local executive. The lack of public participation and money politics have always coloured the process (ICW 2002).

5.2 Local Elite's Commitment

Going along with the local institutional problems and development has been the positive signs of local elites to building commitment for pursuing praxis of good local governance. This is reflected by the result of the Asia

Foundation's Indonesia Rapid Decentralization Appraisal (IRDA). This IRDA, conducted from June to November 2002 to cover 30 regions, is a monitoring activity aimed at verifying progress and achievement of the decentralization process of Indonesia. The IRDA 2002 focused on the following issues: district's authority,[13] structure of district administration and district's civil servants, district's revenue and expenditure, district legislature, relation of district administrations, and special issues in Special Autonomous Regions. All findings seem to be relevant to the way local governance is managed by local praxis.

The findings show, among others, that although there remain a lot of problems to establishing the norms of good governance in local praxis,[14] there has been some significant progress in building the commitment of local elites required for the maintenance of good local governance (*The Asia Foundation* 2002, pp. 7, 15–48). This refers to the fact that members of the local legislature are trying to equip themselves with skills that are required to exercise their functions and roles. These efforts covered, among others, participation in training programmes of legal drafting, local budgeting, political education, regional autonomy, and even computer skills, conducted by universities and or non-government organizations. They also are trying to gather information on public aspirations through both formal and informal mechanisms. Formal mechanism includes regular public hearings, and on certain cases, open plenary sessions. Informal mechanism includes site visits, face-to-face communication with members of society, and reading newspapers or other media information.

The more promising evidence of the local elite's building commitment to perform good local governance is the "Joint Agreement for Good Governance" made by four associations of components of local government in October 2001.[15] The Joint Agreement stated, among others, that "the implementation of good governance has become an urgent need and key prerequisite to restoring the faith of the people in the agencies of government", and that "good governance can encourage all relevant stakeholders to exercise their capabilities to the full in order to improve overall conditions of living, therefore there is a need for a joint understanding on good governance as well as the guidelines for its implementations". This Agreement also mentions that the realization of good governance at local praxis should be based and oriented to the 10 principles: participation, rule of law, transparency, equality, responsiveness, vision, accountability, supervision, efficiency and effectiveness and professionalism. Moreover, it was also agreed that to follow up on this agreement, a joint forum between associations to cooperate for the application of good local governance would be established.

The above evidence show clearly that although there are problems in practising good governance at local levels, there is also important progress on the part of local agents that are responsible for developing good local governance. This has created a great chance and opportunity for Indonesia to carry out the programme of regional autonomy. The problem now is the question of the seriousness of all stakeholders of regional autonomy to comprehend and systematize all activities and programmes that may have significant impact on the establishment of good governance at local praxis.

6. Conclusion

The era of decentralization in Indonesia that was marked by the introduction of the new Laws on Decentralization in 1999, has opened new chapter on the praxis of governance at the local level. However, a closed observation might conclude that the legal framework of decentralization seems short of meeting the primary institutional requirements for an immediate establishment of good local governance. Three crucial problems are of significance to that condition.

First, the decentralization programme within the legal framework of Laws 22/1999 and Law 25/1999 has principally provided a momentum for Indonesia to develop the praxis of good local governance. However, the normative principles and/or norms of good governance were unable to be translated in detail and be comprehensive in the prevailing laws. As a result, besides many provisions in the laws that need further elaboration, many other provisions have not had any efficacy supporting not only the society understanding on, but also the developing of, institutional mechanism of good local governance.

Second, the decentralization programme in fact has brought in itself potential factors for re-centralization of power and authority into local assemblies. This trend has closed the chance for the realization of good governance norms susch as transparency and accountability, active and wide public engagement in political processes, efficiency of public services, and equality of societal political rights. In spite of that, this trend also reduces the possibility of dynamic interaction and cooperation among local stakeholders to manage good governance.

Third, pressures over the necessity for enforcing good governance praxis remain very weak. The main constraint seems to derive from the lack of commitment and capacity of the political entities that have significant roles to enforce the praxis of good governance. These entities are political parties, local government institutions and the society. This has caused the likely unavoidable social and political processes which are anti-good governance praxis at the local level.

Notes

[1]   Subsidiarity is a preference that political participation and policymaking proceed first at the local level; if local action proves inadequate, then — and only then — move to a higher level. The principle of subsidiarity suggests that a local government seeking to achieve self-reliance should not rely on the state or federal government. And it should mobilize all its legal powers of investment, purchasing, contracting, hiring, and taxation (Michael H. Schuman 2000, pp. 125, 128).

[2]   Decentralization, based on the principle of local citizenship, affirms that no man, woman or child can be denied access to the necessities of life, including adequate shelter, security of tenure, safe water, sanitation, a clean environment, health, education and nutrition, employment, public safety, and mobility.

[3]   Practical means of realizing this norm include undertaking consultations with stakeholders within communities to agree on a broad-based, long-term strategic vision for the city; engaging in consultative environmental planning and management processes geared to reach agreement on acceptable levels of resource use, applying the precautionary principle in situations where human activity may adversely affect the well-being of present and/or future generations; ensuring financial viability by promoting economic activity through the participation of all citizens in the economic life of the region.

[4]   This principle suggests that local institutions should also implement decentralization. There are a number of advantages embedded in decentralized institutions. First, they are more flexible than centralized institutions; they can respond quickly to changing circumstances and customer's needs. Second, decentralized institutions are more effective. Third, decentralized institutions are far more innovative than centralized institutions. Fourth, decentralized institutions generate higher morale, more commitment, and greater productivity (David Osborne & Ted Gaebler 1992, pp. 252–56).

[5]   Practical means of realizing subsidiarity include: providing clear frameworks for assigning and delegating responsibilities and commensurate resources from the national to the local level and/or from the local level to the neighbourhood level, such as endorsing the World Charter of Local Self-Government; creating transparent and predictable inter-governmental fiscal transfers and central government support for the development of administrative, technical and managerial capacity of regions at the local level; protecting financially weaker local authorities through systems of vertical and horizontal financial equalization agreed to in full consultation with local authorities and all stakeholders.

⁶ Practical means of realizing this norm include, *inter alia*, ensuring that people have equal access to decision-making processes, resources and basic services and that this access is measured through gender disaggregated data; establishing equitable principles for prioritizing infrastructure development and pricing local services.

⁷ Practical means of realizing this norm include, *inter alia*, delivery and regulation of public services through partnerships with the private and civil society sectors; improving the effectiveness and efficiency of local revenue collection; removing unnecessary barriers to secure tenure and to the supply of finance; developing and implementing fair and predictable legal and regulatory frameworks that encourage commerce, minimize transaction costs, protect human rights and legitimize the informal sector; adopting clear objectives and targets for the provision of public services, which maximize the contributions all sectors of society can make to local economic development.

⁸ Practical means of realizing this norm include free and open consultations of citizens on city budgets; transparent tendering and procurement procedures; publishing annual independent audit reports; removing administrative and procedural incentives for corruption; promoting an ethic of service to the public among officials; creating local integrity networks and establishing codes of conduct for public officials; creating public feedback mechanisms such as an ombudsman, "citizen report cards" and procedures for public petitioning and/or public interest litigation; encouraging open, timely and free debate about local issues in the media.

⁹ The civic capital of the poor must be recognized and supported. Practical means of realizing this norm include developing a culture of civic solidarity wherein all stakeholders treat each other on the basis of respect and acceptance of diversity of opinion; establishing the legal authority for civil society to participate effectively; promoting an ethic of civic responsibility among citizens; enabling the equal contribution of men and women and the full participation of citizenry in civic life; making use of mechanisms such as public hearings, town hall meetings, citizens' forums, city consultations and participatory strategy development; undertaking city referenda concerning important local development options.

¹⁰ Practical means of realizing this norm include, *inter alia*, creating a culture of peace and encouraging tolerance of diversity; creating safety and security through consultative processes based on rule of law, solidarity and prevention; developing metropolitan-wide systems of policing as a means of realizing more inclusive regions; raising awareness about the risk of disasters and formulating vulnerability reduction and preparedness plans

for natural and human-made disasters; resisting all forms of abuse against the person, especially abuse against women, children and the family.

[11] Almost all authorities of the central government are devolved to local government, except for the following five: foreign, fiscal and monetary, defence, judiciary and religious affairs. And, among the decentralized authorities, there are 11 authorities that local governments are obliged to carry out. These are the following services: public works, health, education and culture, agriculture, communication, trade and industry, investment, environment, land, co-operation and labour.

[12] This problem is also evident in the dispute between the central government and local authority over sharing revenue from natural resources. The law stipulates that 85% of revenue from oil and gas should go to the central government, while only 15% goes to the local government. The problem arose when the local authority refused to deliver the 85% to the central government (see TA. Legowo 2003, p. 55).

[13] District's authority to be monitored includes the following services: health, education, agriculture, environment and investment.

[14] The following points are examples of problems that remain in local praxis: local legislatures are too late and too slow in initiating regional regulations; almost all drafts of regional regulations are coming from the initiative of local executives. Members of local legislatures lack capacity to exercise their roles as legislators. This is clearly seen in the case of development planning; although local legislatures have the right to legislate the drafts to become regional regulations, they remain left behind in the process of designing and formulating the drafts; there is always tension between local legislature and local executive, especially, in the annual accountability report of the latter. Meanwhile, there is no mechanism of conflict resolution between local executives and legislatives; and local legislatures lack commitment to the interests of their constituencies. Also, there are too few women members in local parliament.

[15] These four associations of components of local government are the Association of District Governments in Indonesia, the Association of City Governments in Indonesia, the Association of District Level Councils in Indonesia, and the Association of City Level Councils in Indonesia.

References

Collongan Jr. and Arellano A. 2003. "What Is Happening on the Ground? The Progress of Decentralization", In *Local Power and Politics in Indonesia,* edited by Edward Aspinall and Greg Fealy. Singapore and Jakarta: ISEAS and CSIS.

CSIS Research Team. 2000. *The Capacity of Local Politics for Regional Autonomy Research Report*. Jakarta: CSIS.

————. 2001. *Capacity Building for Indonesian Local Government*. Jakarta: CSIS.

Effendi, Sofyan. 2003. "Good Governance". In *Memadukan Langkah Membangun Indonesia Masa Depan* (Integrating Movement Developing the Future of Indonesia), edited by Sulastomo & Tommi A. Legowo. Jakarta: Gerakan Jalan Lurus.

Global Campaign on Urban Governance. 2002. *The Global Campaign on Urban Governance*. Concept Paper, 2nd edition. Nairobi: United Nations Settlement Programme. UN-HABITAT.

Hadiz, Vedi R. 2003. "Power and Politics in North Sumatra: The Uncompleted Reformasi". In *Local Power and Politics in Indonesia*, edited by Edward Aspinall and Greg Fealy. Singapore and Jakarta: ISEAS and CSIS.

Hendrarto, Andi Novi, and Munggoro, Dani Wahyu. 2002. *Panduan Menakar Otonomi Komunitas*. Jakarta: Yappika.

Ida, Laode. 2002. *Otonomi Daerah, Demokrasi Lokal dan Clean Government*. Jakarta: Pusat Studi Pengembangan Kawasan, Cetakan II.

Legowo, TA. 2002. "Otonomi Daerah dan Akomodasi Politik". In *Merumuskan Kembali Kebangsaan Indonesia*. Jakarta: CSIS.

————. 2003. "Legal Framework and Problems on the 1999 Decentralization Program in Indonesia". In *Regional Autonomy and Socio-Economy Development in Indonesia – A Multidimensional Analysis*, edited by TA. Legowo and Muneo Takahashi. Japan, Chiba: Institute of Developing Economies Japan External Trade Organization.

Osborne, David and Gaebler, Ted. 1992. *Reinventing Government How the Entrepreneurial Spirit is Transforming the Public Sector*. New York: Pulme.

Peters, B. Guy. 2001. *The Future of Governing*. Kansas: University Press of Kansas, second edition.

Rasyid, M. Ryass. 2002. *Menolak Resentralisasi Pemerintahan*. Jakarta: Millenium Publisher PT. Dyatama Milenia.

Sekretariat Majelis Permusyawaratan Rakyat Republik Indonesia. 2002. *Undang Undang Dasar 1945*. Jakarta: Sekertariat MPR RI.

Sekertariat Negara Republik Indonesia. Undang Undang Nomor 22 Tahun 1999 tentang Pemerintahan Daerah, dan Undang Undang Nomor 25 Tahun 1999 tentang Perimbangan Keuangan antara Pemerintah Pusat dan Pemerintah Daerah.

Shuman, Michael H. 2000. *Going Local Creating Self-Reliant Communities in A Global Age*. New York: Routledge.

United Nations Development Program (UNDP). 1998. *Principles of Good Governance*. Jakarta: UNDP.

The Asia Foundation. 2002. *Indonesia Rapid Decentralization Appraisal (IRDA) Laporan Kedua Juni – November 2002*. Jakarta: The Asia Foundation.

4
Corporate Governance in Indonesia: A Study on Governance of Business Groups

Yuri Sato

1. Introduction

Since the high growth period praised as the "East Asian Miracle" collapsed due to the Asian economic crisis in 1997, good governance has come to be a key issue in the IMF-led reforms in the crisis-hit Asian countries. In these countries, IMF conditionality contained wide-ranging institutional reforms that were, in a word, a reform of governance of the government and corporations. In the case of Indonesia, the long-standing authoritarian regime fell during the crisis, and vigorous public hopes for democracy emphasized a need for institutional reform not only in the political sphere but also in the economic sphere.

One of the key issues in economic reform is corporate governance. After the crisis, a negative view of the governance of Asian firms became widespread. The World Bank (1998) presented its view that the economic crisis could be attributed to the institutional vulnerability of the financial and corporate sectors, stating that "the poor system of corporate governance has contributed to the present financial crisis by shielding the banks, financial companies, and corporations from market discipline" (ibid, p.57). Research by World Bank economists showed that East Asian firms were characterized by high leverage, concentrated ownership, a high level of ultimate control by a few families, and the expropriation of minority shareholders, and argued that these characteristics led to weak corporate governance and impeded legal and regulatory developments.[1] Based on this argument, new institutions of the Anglo-American type, such as independent commissioners/directors, internal auditing/remuneration committees, and protection for minority shareholders, have been introduced for better corporate governance in the crisis-hit Asian countries, including Indonesia.

This chapter deals with the issue of corporate governance in the case of Indonesian business groups. It attempts to examine how failures of corporate governance actually took place, what factors can be attributed to the failures, and what factors affect the structure of corporate governance in the Indonesian institutional setting. It then aims to draw some lessons for improving corporate governance in this country. Section 2 below reviews theoretical and empirical arguments on corporate governance and sets out a framework for the analysis of our cases with the presence of controlling owner-managers. Section 3 constructs hypotheses on what conditions make corporate governance work or fail to work, based on theory as well as insights from observation. Section 4 looks at six case studies of Indonesian business groups and examines characteristics of corporate governance in each one. The last section summarizes major findings of the case studies and discusses the validity of the hypotheses.

2. An Analytical Framework — Corporate Governance with the Presence of Owner-managers

2.1 Recent Evolvement of Analytical Perspectives on Corporate Governance

The problem of corporate governance originally arises from the separation of ownership and management. The standard definition of corporate governance refers to the defence of shareholders' interests against the interests of managers. It deals with the ways in which shareholders control managers so that managers effectively maximize the value of their firm without taking opportunistic actions that hurt shareholders. This is a straightforward agency problem between shareholders as principals and managers as agents. This shareholder-value perspective pre-supposes Berle and Means-type managerial firms, in which ownership is widely dispersed and management is in the hands of salaried professional managers (Berle and Means 1932).

Still on the shareholder-value perspective, Shleifer and Vishny (1997) extend a scope of analysis beyond the pre-supposition of Berle and Means. They define corporate governance as an agency problem between financiers (or investors) and managers. They ask about "the ways in which suppliers of finance to corporations assure themselves of getting a return on their investment", and "how (do) the suppliers of finance get the managers to return some of the profits to them" (ibid., p. 737). Their answer is that legal protection of investor rights can help investors to get their money back. In the case of weak legal protection, financiers can get more effective control rights over managers by being large, that is, in the form of large shareholders, takeovers, and large creditors (ibid., p. 753).

The largeness of financiers can be effective in solving the agency problem, but it may inefficiently redistribute wealth from other minor financiers to the large financiers. This extended framework conforms better to the results of a recent study showing that concentrated ownership with large shareholders is more commonly observed than widely-dispersed ownership.

Recent heated argument over corporate governance shows a trend in moving away from the traditional concept of shareholder value towards the broader concept of the stakeholder society. Managerial decisions do affect investors, but also exert externalities on various other stakeholders of the firm, such as employees, customers, suppliers, communities where the firm is located, potential pollutees, and so forth (Tirole 2001, p. 3).[2] From the stakeholder-society perspective, corporate governance is "the design of institutions that induce or force management to internalize the welfare of stakeholders" (ibid, p.4), and a governance system is "the complex set of conditions that shape the outcome of the *ex post* bargaining over the quasi-rents that are generated in the course of a relationship" (Zingales 1998).

Based on the analytical framework provided by Tirole (2001) on the governance of the stakeholder society, Aoki (2001, Chap. 11) further develops a comprehensive foundation for analyzing a diversity of corporate governance mechanisms. From the viewpoint of the comparative institutional analysis employing game theory, he sees corporate governance as "self-enforcing mechanisms that govern (such) strategic interactions among the players" and defines it as "a set of self-enforceable rules (formal or informal) that regulates the contingent action choices of the stakeholders (investors, workers, and managers) in the corporate organization domain" (ibid., p. 281). Aoki first identifies three major types of corporate organization from the viewpoint of an information processing structure, that is, (i) hierarchical decomposition, (ii) participatory hierarchy, and (iii) horizontal hierarchy. He then analyzes governance mechanisms which conform to three organization types respectively, that is, (i) owner control, (ii) co-determination by managers and workers, and (iii) relational contingent governance, with insider control in the case of higher output level, and with outsider (relational monitor) control in the case of lower output level. Owner control is further classified into (i) owner-manager control over workers (in the Hart-Moore firm[3]) with no debt; (ii) owner-manager control over workers regulated by debt contracts; and (iii) shareholder control over managers. Aoki's framework thus goes beyond the confrontation of shareholder-value and stakeholder-society perspectives, and provides a broader scope of comparative (not normative) analysis on governance mechanisms, connecting the domain of corporate organizations with other domains of financial transactions, labour transactions, political regimes and so forth.

2.2 Key Elements of Corporate Governance in Asia

In the context of corporate governance in Asia, one of the key elements to be taken into account is ownership concentration. Concentrated ownership with large shareholders, compared to the traditional Berle and Means proposition of dispersed ownership with atomistic shareholders, has attracted more interest in recent empirical literature. La Porta, Lopez-de-Silanes and Shleifer (1999) shows that widely-dispersed ownership is not prevalent around the world except in the United States and the United Kingdom; rather, concentrated ownership is a more common organizational form for modern firms in developed countries.[4] The outbreak of the Asian currency crisis in 1997 called attention to corporate ownership structure in Asian developing countries in relation to corporate governance and performance. Researchers, headed by Stjin Claessens of the World Bank, have traced the ultimate owners of East Asian firms and have found that corporate ownership is concentrated in the hands of few families. They provide evidence of the expropriation of minority shareholders with a gap between the control rights and the cash flow rights of controlling shareholders, and suggest that insider-control contributed to the firms' weak performance and risky investment prior to the crisis (Claessens, Djankov and Lang 1999b; Claessens, Djankov, Fan and Lang 1999a). Concentrated ownership and the associated problems of Asian firms have thus become hot issues in the negative sense.

Another key element, which closely relates to ownership concentration but should be distinguished from it, is the coincidence of ownership and management, or the existence of large shareholders who concurrently hold top managerial positions. How can we deal with such owner-manager firms in corporate governance analysis? The traditional shareholder-value perspective pre-supposes separation of ownership and management. The logical consequence is that, if ownership coincides with management, firms have no agency problem, so the self-governance of owner-managers works perfectly. In the Shleifer and Vishny extended framework of financiers and managers, relations between owner-managers and other financiers, such as minority shareholders, general investors through stock markets, creditors, and potential takeovers, and the way in which these financiers make owner-managers assure their return are worth analyzing. The stakeholder-society perspective would provide wider possibilities of analysis; relations between owner-managers and other stakeholders, for example, salaried professional managers, employees, joint venture partners, and the government (or power elite) as licensing authorities or patron. In the Aoki framework, the relevant governance mechanism in this context is (i) and (ii), namely owner-manager's control over workers with or without a threat of liquidation imposed by outside investors/creditors.

There are some empirical studies on owner-manager-led firms in Asia that put forward different views.[5] The World Bank (1998), based on the studies of Claessens group, argues that firms with controlling owners expatriate other investors, pursue personal non-profit-maximizing objectives, and impede the development of professional managers. Yeh, Lee and Woidtke (2001) in their Taiwan study compare firm performance with levels of ownership concentration and representation of the owner family on the managerial board. Their result is that HILO firms (firms with a high level of family ownership and a low level of family board representation) show the highest performance, followed by HIHI and LOLO firms, and LOHI (firms with a low level of family ownership and a high level of family board representation) have the lowest performance. They see this result as consistent with their view that firms have lower agency problems when owner families have higher cash flow rights (decreasing conflict with minority shareholders) and the board is more likely to monitor the controlling family-managers (ibid., pp. 39–45). In contrast to this result, Suehiro (2001), in his Thai study, found that concentrated family ownership as well as the owner family grip on top management do not always result in poor corporate performance, and argues that family ownership management itself is not wrong, but its internal innovation is a relevant key for corporate reform.

While the above studies shed light on the fact that minority shareholders and salaried professional managers are important stakeholders in the owner-manager firms, another key stakeholder to be focused on is the creditor. The Asian economic crisis brought the corporate debt issue into sharp relief, revealing that most large firms heavily depended on borrowing from foreign and domestic creditors. Although corporate insolvency was primarily caused by a sharp drop in currency values; an 80% drop from the pre-crisis value in the case of the Indonesian Rupiah, it is still probable that firms had over-borrowed to finance their excessive investment in the pre-crisis period. It is worth examining whether creditors have been able to effectively monitor the firms' owner-managers to get them to repay debts. Some empirical studies argue that although owner-manager-led corporate governance economizes transaction costs at the initial stage of growth, agency costs increase between owner-managers and external financiers as business expands and requires large amounts of external finance (Khan 1999, p. 22; Lang 2001b, p. 11). For Indonesia, the debt problem is relevant, because corporate debts became a crucial issue in the post-crisis corporate restructuring, and the major debtors of overseas borrowing were large business groups, unlike Thailand where banks or non-bank financial institutions were major debtors.

2.3 Analytical Framework of This Chapter

This chapter deals with the corporate governance of Indonesian business groups. We decided on business groups rather than individual firms as an object of study, for the purpose of observing the ultimate owners who manage multiple firms. A business group is simply defined as a group of firms under the same ownership. The owner can be a single individual, a single family, plural non-family individuals, or plural families.

In most Indonesian business groups, owners coincide with top management of the group. As discussed above, coincidence of ownership and management is contradictory to one of the original concepts of corporate governance that pre-supposes separation of ownership and management. However, recent evolution of analytical frameworks on corporate governance accommodates analysis of owner-manager-led firms, concentrating on the relations between owner-managers and other financiers/stakeholders.

Although one of the prospects of this study is to extend its analytical scope to various related stakeholders in a wide sense, we start this chapter by narrowing the scope down to two key stakeholders. One is creditor as a major outside financier, and another is salaried professional manager as a main inside stakeholder. We look at an example of failure of corporate governance through an incidence of over-borrowing,[6] and examine whether creditors and professional managers can prevent owner-managers from excessively borrowing, and if not, why not. In this context, domestic creditors should be distinguished from foreign creditors, and when talking about domestic creditors we should distinguish between state-owned banks and private banks, as their behaviour and capabilities may be different.[7] Therefore, within this simple framework, the focal point of observation is the relationship between business group owner-managers and creditors, and between owner-managers and professional managers, concerning the problem of controlling excess borrowing.

3. Setting Up Hypothese — Under What Conditions Does Corporate Governance Fail to Work?

Theoretically, debts provide discipline to owner-managers. Discipline is imposed in at least two ways. Debt repayment decreases free cash flow; a part of the net gain of corporate activities that managers can use freely, and therefore restrains managers from spending money on excessive investment. In addition, an owner-manager who performs poorly in debt management would find it difficult to renew debt contracts with creditors, or might even be threatened with liquidation of the firm by creditors. Needless to say, creditors have the motivation to monitor owner-managers of borrower firms in order to have them repay their debts properly.

Nevertheless, how does over-borrowing of firms take place? Why do creditors allow the firms to behave in this way?

One possible reason for the failure of creditors' governance over owner-managers of borrower firms is the asymmetry of information. Owner-managers provide creditors with only good information so as to borrow more, while it costs too much for creditors to gain all the needed information on the firms' management. The asymmetry can be more serious in case of business group management. Thus the first hypothesis is formulated as follows.

[**H-1: information asymmetry hypothesis**]   Governance by creditors fails to work because owner-managers provide creditors with only good information.

Another possible reason for the failure of creditors' governance over owner-managers is the lack of a threat of liquidation or other sanctions. First, this is a matter of incomplete laws and institutions regarding the liquidation of poor-performance firms. The situation is generally true of Indonesia in the pre-crisis period, when a bankruptcy law and commercial courts did not function. Secondly, the lack of a threat of liquidation may relate to collusion with the government. Let us think of collusion between creditors and the government, that is, government back-up to creditors, as could be the case with state-owned banks. The creditors are less motivated to get their money back from borrowers, as they can expect the government to absorb a risk of irrecoverable debts.[8] As a result, creditors' governance loses effect. Similar logic applies to collusion between owner-managers and the government (or power elite), or government back-up to firms. State-owned corporations, business groups run by President Soeharto's family, and those closely linked to political power would be examples of this (Pangestu and Harianto 1998, p. 13). These firms can make use of their advantageous positions to draw more funds from creditors, and the creditors expect the government to assure debt repayment in case the firms become insolvent. Thus creditors' governance fails. The second hypothesis is as follows.

[**H-2: collusion hypothesis**]   Governance by creditors fails to work when either creditors or owner-managers collude with the government (or power elite), because creditors as well as owner-managers expect the government to absorb a risk of governance failure.

An analysis of ownership-management patterns and the economic performance of Indonesian publicly-listed companies in the pre-crisis and post-crisis period in Sato (2004) provides an insight into the corporate governance issue. According to the study, the difference in a firm's profitability (ROA and ROE) and debt dependency (D/E: debt to equity ratio) is not significant by ownership pattern (concentrated or dispersed) or by separation of ownership and management (not separated or separated). Rather, the difference is obvious by affiliation to business groups (group or non-group) and by types of business groups (established group or rapid-growth group).[9]

The result in Table 4.1 shows that, first, firms affiliated to business groups are characterized by high profitability and high debt dependency compared to non-group-affiliated local private firms. Secondly, firms affiliated to nine established business groups showed high profitability and high debt dependency in the pre-crisis period and a relatively high rate of survival of the crisis as seen in their still high shares of sales and assets in total listed companies. Thirdly, firms affiliated to eight rapid-growth business groups showed low profitability and high debt dependency in the pre-crisis period and suffered heavily as a result of the crisis. Although firms belonging to the established groups and those belonging to the rapid-growth groups have an equally high level of debt dependency, the profitability and the degree of survival after the crisis are higher in the established groups than the rapid-growth groups. What factors can this difference in performance be attributed to? What are the possible factors which make the governance structure different between the established and the rapid-growth groups?

The first possibility lies in differences in fund raising behaviour. The established business groups, with their reputations as leading actors on the Indonesian economic stage and business experience of more than two decades, had relatively easy access to overseas sources of funds. Their preference for overseas sources of funds was economically rational, because the cost of foreign funds was at the average interest rate of 9% (from 1987 to 1996), and also the managed Rupiah depreciation was within 4% annually, much lower than the average interest rate of 18% for domestic loans (Husnan 1999, p. 8). On the contrary, rapid-growth business groups with no such reputation depended heavily on domestic sources of funds, especially state-owned bank loans (Sato 2002, pp. 77–85). So the difference is that the firms affiliated to established groups borrow mainly from foreign creditors and those affiliated to rapid-growth groups borrow mainly from domestic creditors. It is likely that foreign creditors have a higher ability to investigate and monitor customer firms than domestic creditors and therefore the firms of the established groups were able to maintain higher profitability and survive the crisis. Thus the third hypothesis is as follows.

[H-3: hypothesis of creditors' ability] Governance by creditors works due to the fact that foreign creditors have a higher ability to investigate and monitor the management of customer firms than domestic creditors.

As Table 4.1 shows, the number of listed companies affiliated to established groups is almost double the number of those affiliated to rapid-growth groups in the pre-crisis as well as the post-crisis periods. This fact indicates a possibility that the more the group firms are publicly listed on the stock exchange markets, the better the governance by outside

Table 4.1 Change of Shares and Performance of Listed Companies in Indonesia by Type of Business Groups

	No.of company		Share in sales		Share in assets		Average ROA		Average ROE		Average D/E	
	1996	2000	1996	2000	1996	2000	1996	2000	1996	2000[d]	1996	2000
Business Group												
Established[a]	20	18	39.9	36.1	35.5	21.9	4.0	-2.9	17.7	-20.1	10.5	-13.2
Rapid-growth[b]	12	9	12.3	6.4	21.8	6.7	3.2	-20.9	10.9	-43.4	5.3	-4.7
Other group	26	17	17.9	13.0	16.1	7.8	4.4	-16.2	12.9	3.8	3.6	0.3
Group total	58	44	70.0	55.5	73.4	36.3	4.0	-11.5	14.3	-14.5	6.3	-6.3
Non-group private	29	27	14.9	15.0	8.9	7.8	4.3	-3.3	11.6	-30.9	2.5	1.9
State	5	16	11.1	22.5	16.3	52.9	10.3	6.4	16.2	-2.1	2.7	7.7
Foreign[c]	8	13	3.9	7.0	1.4	3.0	6.9	10.1	15.4	14.5	1.9	1.6
Total	100	100	100.0	100.0	100.0	100.0	4.8	-3.5	14.2	-11.9	4.7	-0.8

Source: compiled from ECFIN (various years).

Note: a: 9 business groups which satisfy the 3 conditions concurrently; (1) started its core business in the 1970s or before, (2) ranked in the 20 largest groups in the 1980s, and (3) ranked in the 10 largest groups in 1996.

b: 8 business groups which satisfy either of the 2 conditions; (1) started its core business (or its discontinuous spurt) in the 1980s and ranked in the 30 largest groups in 1996, or (2) ranked below the 20th in the 1980s but in the 10 largest groups in 1996.

c: Excludes 4 'apparent foreign companies' owned by Indonesians. Those are treated as domestic private companies.

d: Excludes 23 companies with negative equity due to excess debt (liabilities exceed assets), because ROE becomes extraordinary large value.

List of established business groups
1. Salim
2. Astra
3. Sinar Mas
4. Gudang Garam
5. Lippo
6. Ongko (or Arya Upaya)
7. Bob Hasan
8. Djarum
9. Rodamas
(All are owned by ethnic Chinese businessmen.)

List of rapid-growth business groups
1. Bimantara (owned by the second son of President Soeharto)
2. Gajah Tunggal
3. Nusamba (owned by foundations led by President Soeharto)
4. Barito Pacific
5. Humpuss (owned by the third son of President Soeharto)
6. Danamon
7. Raja Garuda Mas
8. Texmaco (owned by ethnic Indian-Tamil)
(All without notes are owned by ethnic Chinese businessmen.)

financiers works, not only by markets but also by creditors, because the financiers can obtain more information disclosed to the public about the business group. Thus the fourth hypothesis is as follows.

[H-4: hypothesis of public listing effect] Governance by creditors works better, because more group-affiliated firms are publicly listed and more information on the business group is disclosed to the public.

Apart from the creditors' governance over the owner-managers of business groups, the degree of presence of salaried professional managers is another possible factor in distinguishing the performance of established groups from that of rapid-growth groups. Although existing studies do not provide clear evidence, it is likely that the presence of professional managers is higher in the firms in established groups than those in rapid-growth groups, as the former has longer history of organizational development. If so, the hypothesis that a higher presence of professional managers enables a better check on owner-managers would hold true. The findings of Yeh, Lee and Woidtke (2001) that firms with a combination of high levels of family control and low family board representation have the highest relative performance give supporting evidence to this hypothesis. The last hypothesis is as follows.

[H-5: hypothesis of the function of professional managers] Corporate governance works better with a higher presence of salaried professional managers who function as a check on owner-managers.

4. Case Study on the Corporate Governance of Six Business Groups

This section is devoted to a case study on the corporate governance of business groups in Indonesia in order to examine the validity of the above hypotheses. We look into the structure of the corporate governance of six selected business groups in relation to such attributes as (1) ownership and management patterns; (2) levels of debt and main creditors; (3) levels of investment; (4) levels of market disclosure; (5) presence of professional managers; and (6) relations with the government.

The six business groups have been selected bearing the following three points in mind. The first is representation in scale of sales and debts. As Table 4.2 shows, the six groups ranked within the top 30 in annual sales in the pre-crisis period, accounting for 32% of the aggregate amount of sales of the 30 groups. The outstanding foreign and domestic debts of the six groups in total in the post-crisis period account for 41% and 42% respectively of those of the total 30 groups. This means that the six groups are relatively large in sales and heavily indebted.[10] Relatively indebted groups are intentionally selected for the purpose of examining

Table 4.2 Summary of 6 Business Groups (1) : Sales and Debts

Name of business group	Name of owner=manager*		Group sales (1996)		Group debt**		Indicator for over-borrowing	
			(tri. Rp.)	ranking	Foreign (bil.US$)	Domestic (tri.Rp.)	Foreign debt/annual sales	Domestic debt/annual sales
1 Gudang Garam	Rachman Halim	Ch.	9.4	4	negligible	-	0.00	0.00
2 Sinar Mas	Eka Tjipta Widjaja	Ch.	20.2	3	3.8	0.7	0.55	0.03
3 Astra	owner≠manager	-	20.2	2	5.1	0.4	0.74	0.02
4 Gajah Tunggal	Sjamsul Nursalim	Ch.	4.2	7	3.0	1.5	2.08	0.36
5 Texmaco	Marimutu Sinivasan	In.	1.8	26	1.5	17.3	2.43	9.61
6 Humpuss	Hutomo Mandala Putera	Pr.	2.3	18	0.4	5.7	0.51	2.48
Total of 6 groups			58.1		13.8	25.6	0.69	0.44
Share in total of 30 groups (%)			(32.2)		(40.4)	(42.1)	0.98	0.22

Source: Group sales from Warta Economi, 9(27), 24 Nov. 1997 / outstanding foreign debts are estimation by CISI Raya Utama/ domestic debts from IBRA (2001).

Note: * Ch.=ethnic Chinese, In.=ethnic Indian, Pr.=native Malays (pribumi).

** Foreign debts are as of the end of 1997. Domestic debts are the amount of irrecoverable bank loans transferred to IBRA, as of 2001.

Table 4.3 Summary of 6 Business Groups (2): Ownership/Management Pattern, Level of Debt, Disclosure and Investment, and Governance Structure

Group name	Group type	Ownership/management pattern	Debt/creditors	Investment	Major business
Gudang Garam	Established	Ownership=management by founder family	Low	Low/Limited diversification, domestic	Clove cigarette
Sinar Mas	Established	Ownership=management by founder family	High/Foreign	High/ Multi-nationalization, export	Pulp & paper, agribusiness, financial services, property
Astra	Established	Semi-dispersed ownership, semi-separated management after 1992	High/Foreign	Medium/ Less diversification, domestic	Automobile, agribusiness, financial services
Gajah Tunggal	Rapid-growth	Ownership=management by founder family	Very high/ Foreign	High/Diversification, mega projects, export and domestic	Tire, chemical, cable, shrimp farm, financial services, property
Texmaco	Rapid-growth	Ownership=management by a founder (ethnic Indian)	Very high/ Domestic and Foreign	High/Mega projects, export and domestic	Synthetic fiber, machinery
Humpuss	Rapid-growth	Concentrated ownership by a founder (pribumi), semi-separated management	Very high/ Domestic	High/Diversification, domestic	Services, transportation, mining, property, retail trade

Table 4.3 Summary of 6 business groups (2): Ownership/management pattern, level of debt, disclosure and investment, and governance structure *(continued)*

Group name	Market disclosure by publicly listing	Presence of salaried managers	Relation with the government	Structure of corporate governance	Problems
Gudang Garam	Partial disclosure by listing only a core	Low	None	Self-governance by founder family owner-managers	Less rapid growth. Should be take relation with employees into account.
Sinar Mas	Majority disclosure by listing several divisional holding companies	High at the group company level	Out of favor with the Soeharto government	Governance by foreign creditors and markets over owner-managers — failed to work	Eventual debt crisis
Astra	Whole disclosure by listing a group holding company	Highest. Boards of directors are mostly professional management.	Most out of favor with the Soeharto government up to 1992	Management by professional managers of the headquaters, governance by market and creditors — debt crisis, but restructured	Concentration of foreign creditors' lending due to its rare transparancy
Gajah Tunggal	Partial disclosure by listing well-performing companies	High at the group company level	Close to high Army officers in the Soeharto government	Governance by foreign creditors over owner-managers — failed to work	Mechanism of supplying fund raised by listed companies to other group operations
Texmaco	Majority disclosure by listing major companies	Low	Close to the former President Soeharto	Governance by domestic creditors over owner-managers — failed to work	Collusive state-bank loans owing to powerful political backup
Humpuss	Undisclosed. Only one listed company	High	Owned by the President Soeharto's third son	Governance by domestic creditors over owner-managers — failed to work	Collusive state-bank loans owing to powerful political backup

Source: by author.

a corporate governance structure that may allow over-borrowing. The second is a balance of established and rapid-growth groups. The first 3 groups in Table 4.2 are selected from the established and the second 3 are from the rapid-growth. It appears that the rapid-growth groups have large debts in relation to their annual sales. The third is a variety of groups with the attributes raised above. We can see whether or not different attributes affect their borrowing behaviour and governance structure. Table 4.3 provides a summary of the main attributes of the six business groups as examined below.

We use over-borrowing as a measurement of failure of corporate governance. As the state of over-borrowing is not so self-evident, we judge it by combining three kinds of indicators. The first is the amount of debts compared to annual sales (liability to sales) at the business group level, as shown in Table 4.2. When the ratio is above 0.5, or 6 months, the debt level is evaluated as high.[11] Using this standard, all the 6 groups except Gudang Garam are evaluated as high; especially the three rapid-growth groups above 2.0 which are extraordinary high. The second is debt to equity ratio (D/E) at the level of group-affiliated company. Data is only available for listed companies (see Appendix 4.A1a). When the ratio in 1996 is above the average of the largest 100 companies, that is, 4.7 (1.7 for non-financial companies), the debt level can be evaluated as high. Using this, Gudang Garam is low, Gajah Tunggal is just on the average, and others (except Humpuss with no data) are higher than the average. The third is the fact of whether the group actually encountered a debt crisis. The three rapid-growth groups and Astra fell into debt crisis just after the 1997 currency crisis, but Astra succeeded in debt restructuring after a one-year negotiation with creditors. Sinar Mas fell into crisis in 2000.

Putting these results together, the three rapid-growth groups are judged as probably having over-borrowed, and Gudang Garam is judged as obviously not. As for Astra, at least its major listed companies were over-borrowing, but *ex post* governance was successful. On the contrary, Sinar Mas was not so evidently over-borrowing in the pre-crisis period, but after three years obvious over-borrowing was revealed.

4.1 Gudang Garam Group

Gudang Garam Group is the fourth largest business group in Indonesia with Rp.9.4 trillion annual group sales (US$3.9 billion) in 1996 and has long been the largest producer in the Indonesian cigarette industry. The group's core company, PT Gudang Garam, is a publicly listed company on the Jakarta Stock Exchange and the second largest of all listed companies with annual sales of Rp.15.0 trillion (US$1.7 billion) and more than 41,000 employees in 2000. PT Gudang Garam was established as a clove cigarette manufacturer in 1958 in Kediri, East Java, by the late Surya Wonowidjojo (Tjoa Ing Hwie). He was an immigrant from Fujian Province, China, and after his death, his first son, Rachman Halim (Tjoa To Hin), took over the whole business.

Among many Indonesian business groups, the Gudang Garam Group is the most extreme case of exclusive ownership and management by a founder family. Ownership by the family (Rachman Halim, his mother, his brothers and sisters, and his children) accounted for 94% of total shares in 1985 (7 affiliated companies), 80% of shares in 1996 and 76% in 2000 (only PT Gudang Garam).[12] Managerial posts occupied by the family accounted for 64% (1985), 33% (1996), 80% (2000) on the Board of Commissioners (Dewan Komisaris), and 71% (1985), 54% (1996), and 19% (2000) on the Board of Directors (Direksi).[13] Although posts on the Board of Directors were drastically shifted to non-family salaried managers after the crisis (from 46% to 81% for PT Gudang Garam in the period from 1996 to 2000) the owner family's presence on the Board of Commissioners ensures a continuing firm grip on management. The scope of the activities of salaried managers is limited to non-strategic daily management at the single company level.

The group shows high profitability and low debt dependency. PT Gudang Garam is one of the most profitable companies in Indonesia, as shown by an ROA and an ROE of over 20% to 30%, even higher in the post-crisis than in the pre-crisis period. Debt equity ratios were below 1.0 in 1996 as well as in 2000. This is an extremely low level given that the ratio of the established business groups on average was 10.5 in 1996 and fell to negative value in 2000 due to excess of debts to assets.

Such features of the group as exclusive family ownership-management and high profitability with low debt level are closely related to the peculiarity of the group's core business, namely the clove cigarette industry. This industry holds a huge and stably-growing domestic market, the value-added of which constantly accounts for around 10% to 12% of total manufacturing value-added throughout the period from 1980 to 2000. It is said that the production of clove cigarettes (*kretek*) needs a special recipe, which is secretly handed down in the family. This may motivate the family to keep a firm grip on a core part of management. The conservative nature of the group influences its investment and fund-raising behaviour. Since it was founded the group has undertaken no large diversification investment except in related businesses such as cigarette paper, filters, packaging and distribution. Diversification into unrelated businesses is limited to property, plantations and small scale banking. PT Gudang Garam is the only publicly listed company in the group, and other businesses are organized under unlisted family investment companies (see Figure 4.1).

Figure 4.1 Ownership Structure of the Gudang Garam Group

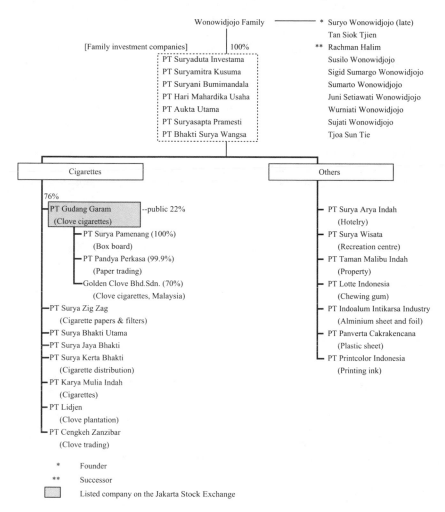

Source: ECFIN (annual), Sukmawaty (2000), CISI Raya Utama (1990, 1999) and other materials.

As for relations with the government, the group has kept some distance from political affairs. When the third son of the then President Soeharto, Hutomo Mandala Putra (Tommy) Soeharto, set up a monopolistic regulatory organ of clove distribution in the early 1990s, the group bravely confronted this manoeuvre, which proved a failure before long.

The structure of the corporate governance of the Gudang Garam Group is almost entirely self-governance by owner-managers, due to the high presence of the founder family in both ownership and management, the limited presence of public investors and salaried managers, and the absence of large creditors. This self-governance seems to work well, as the group avoids excess borrowing and over-investment, keeps high profitability, and keeps a distance from the government. This case provides evidence that concentrated family ownership without the separation of management itself is not a negative factor for corporate governance. Corporate governance by owner-managers can work well on condition that there is no other major stakeholder.[14] As a consequence of low leverage, the growth of the group has not been so rapid, but is still quite stable owing to the profitable nature of the clove cigarette industry. The success of the self-governance of the group is considerably supported by the peculiarity of the core business.

4.2 Sinar Mas Group

The Sinar Mas Group ranked third after the Salim Group and the Astra Group in the ranking of Indonesian business group sales in 1996, with Rp.20.2 trillion annual sales (US$8.5 billion). The Group's core business is in four industries, namely, (i) pulp and paper; (ii) agribusiness and food; (iii) property; and (iv) financial services. The group had 7 listed companies engaged in the four industries in 1996, but the number decreased to 6 in 2000 as the Group's bank, Bank International Indonesia (BII), was subject to capital injection by the government. The Group's development started with the establishment of the first core company, PT Bimoli (Bitung Menado Oil Ltd.), a coconut oil refinery, in 1970 in Manado, North Sulawesi. The founder was Eka Tjipta Widjaja (Oei Ek Tjhong) who emigrated from Fukian, China to Sulawesi. Of his eight children by his first wife, five sons and one daughter are major owner-managers of the group business (see Figure 4.2).

The Sinar Mas Group is also categorized as a typical case of family ownership and management, though it is not as exclusive as the Gudang Garam Group. The founder family accounted for 75% of the ownership of total shares in 1985 (35 affiliated companies), 57% in 1996, and gradually decreased to 45% in 2000 (listed companies in average). The weight of the family in management accounts for 40% (1985), 65% (1996), 47% (2000) in Komisaris, and 39% (1985), 42% (1996), 49% (2000) in Direksi (Appendix 4.A1a and b). The family presence in management increased from the mid-1980s to the mid-1990s, and after the crisis it decreased only in Komisaris. In spite of typical family control of ownership and management, it is also true that the group actively employs competent professional managers, regardless of their nationality. Eka's sons take

Figure 4.2 Ownership Structure of the Sinar Mas Group

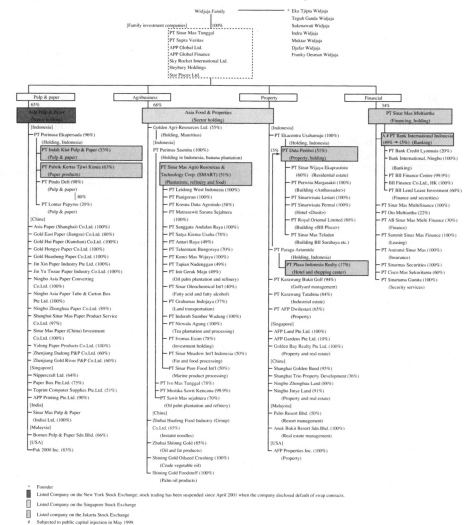

Source: ECFIN (annual), Sukmawaty (2000), Lang (2001a), CISI Raya Utama (1999), APP's homepage (http://www.asiapulppaper.com/) and other materials.

charge of each of four divisions; the eldest son, Teguh Ganda Widjaja (Oei Tjie Goan), of pulp and paper; the third son, Indra Widjaja (Oei Pheng Lian), of financial services; the fourth son, Muktar Widjaja (Oei Siong Lian), of property; and the youngest sixth son, Franky Oesman

Widjaja (Oei Jong Nian), of agribusiness. They are fully supported by a group of professional salaried managers.

The Group's two manufacturing industries, pulp & paper and agribusiness (palm oil refineries and plantations), are resource-based profitable businesses with high export competitiveness. The investment behaviour of the Sinar Mas Group has not been a conglomerate diversification into unrelated business, but a concentration on four core businesses. In addition to the sound foundation of its business lines, the relative transparency of the group ownership structure also contributed to enhancing its reputation. The group has three divisional holding companies; Asia Pulp & Paper (APP) for the pulp and paper division, Asia Food & Properties for the agribusiness and property divisions, and PT Sinar Mas Multiatha for the financial service division, and two sub-divisional holding/operating companies; PT Sinar Mas Agro Resources & Technology Corp. for the agribusiness division and PT Duta Pertiwi for the property division, all of which are listed on the Stock Exchange markets in Jakarta, Singapore or New York and regularly report their consolidated financial statements. Another four companies engaged in key undertakings are also publicly listed. As a result, information on the majority of the group's business activities is disclosed to the public.

Owing to these advantages, the group has attracted investment funds mainly from overseas in the forms of off-shore consortium loans, supplier's credits and corporate bonds, in addition to direct financing from the stock markets. Before the Asian currency crisis, the outstanding external debts of the group were estimated to be US$3.8 billion. The debt equity ratio of seven domestically listed companies was 5.5 on average (for 5 non-financial companies, 1.9) in 1996. This is a subtle level of debt; higher than the average, but not heavily over-borrowing, and it was not considered a serious problem as long as the high profitability of the core business could absorb debt repayment and investment costs. In fact, even after the currency crisis the group successfully kept attracting funds for investment into the multi-nationalization of the pulp, paper and forestry business (China, India, Malaysia and Singapore) and of the property business (Singapore, China, Malaysia and the United States).

With a sharp decline in international market prices of pulp and paper in 2000, the Group's holding company for the pulp and paper division, Asia Pulp & Paper (APP), suffered an insolvency crisis due to huge external debts, which swelled to US$ 20 billion in total at the end of 2000. The group had a series of debt restructuring negotiations with foreign creditors.[15]

The Sinar Mas Group has never had collusive relations with the government, except for some cases of business cooperation between Eka and National Army officers in the early days of development. Rather, the group was out of favour with the Soeharto government. That seems to be one of the reasons why the group's most lucrative business, that of edible oils with its top brand 'Bimoli', was eventually taken over by the Salim Group allied with Tommy Soeharto. The group as an ethnic Chinese conglomerate also often became a target of criticism for nationalistic ministers of the Soeharto government.

The Sinar Mas Group has positive characteristics; a competitive export business, a clear core business strategy, a divisional structure of group ownership, a high degree of information disclosure by listing divisional holding companies, a relatively high presence of professional managers, and a minimum collusive factor. Unlike the Gudang Garam Group, this group has key stakeholders such as foreign creditors, professional managers and public investors, who could have monitored the owner-managers. Nevertheless, over-borrowing took place, followed by the group's debt crisis. This case is evidence that all the above-stated positive attributes, foreign creditors and markets are not sufficient conditions to prevent debt crisis *ex ante*.[16]

4.3 Astra Group

The Astra Group is a leading Indonesian business group ranked second with Rp.20.2 trillion (US$8.5 billion) annual group sales in 1996. The Group's headquarters-cum-holding company, PT Astra International, Inc., is the largest listed company in Indonesia even after it was hit by the crisis, with annual sales of Rp.28.4 trillion (US$3.3 billion) and 91,000 employees as of 2000. PT Astra International (AI), which is also the mother company of the Astra Group, was established in 1957 in Jakarta by Tjia Kian Tie and his friend. Tjia's eldest brother, William Soeryadjaya (Tjia Kian Liong), gradually took the position of major owner-founder, especially after Tjia's death in 1979. William Soeryadjaya is a seventh generation ethnic Chinese born in West Java. The Astra Group started its rapid growth after AI acquired a series of chances to be sole agent and joint venture partner with leading Japanese machinery manufacturers such as Toyota, Daihatsu (automobiles), Honda (motorcycles), Komatsu (heavy equipment) and Nippon Denso (electrical components) in the 1970s. The group is now known as a leading machinery manufacturer in Indonesia.

The Astra Group is a unique example in Indonesia of separation of ownership and management. The separation was a result of a series of unscheduled events. In 1992, when Bank Summa of the Summa Group led by William's eldest son fell insolvent, William and his family were forced to liquidate their shares in AI which had become the collateral for Summa's borrowing. The family shares were transferred to creditors (state-owned underwriters and banks), and then bought by several business groups close to President Soeharto, such as the Barito Pacific, the Bob Hasan, the Salim and the Danamon Groups. Since William was obviously out of favour with President Soeharto, the Soeharto government did not save the Soeryadjaya family from their debt crisis, and went as far to make the well-linked capitalists undergo a substantial take-over. After the 1997 currency crisis, as these business groups faced the repayment of central bank liquidity support loans or state bank loans, they transferred their stakes in AI to IBRA as a repayment, and then IBRA sold 24% of AI shares through tender to a consortium led by Cycle & Carriage of Singapore in 2000. Thus the ownership came to be dispersively held by strategic investors/investment companies unrelated to either the founder family or the government, with the Singapore consortium at the head of the shareholder list with around 30% shareholding (see Figure 4.3). This can be referred to as 'semi-dispersed ownership'.

It is noteworthy that the group's management was not substantially disturbed by the changes in ownership. A group of long-serving top professional managers at the headquarters succeeded in maintaining Astra's unity, identity, quality of management and its reputation after the withdrawal of the founding family. This was possible because the group had long made efforts to institutionalize group management by bringing Astra-bred managers up through the ranks, not only from ethnic Chinese but also from *pribumi* circles, since the early days of group development in the 1970s. At present, the composition of managerial boards is as follows; at AI headquarters, representatives of the semi-dispersed ownership sit on the Komisaris and AI's top professional managers sit on the Direksi; at AI's affiliated company level, AI's directors often occupy some key posts on the Komisaris, and the company's own professional managers occupy the posts of Direksi. In a word, Komisaris represents ownership and Direksi represents pure professional management. We can call this 'semi-separation of ownership and management' which makes good use of the two-tier managerial board system. This structure may become a mode of 'governance through Komisaris' in the institutional framework of Indonesia.

The uniqueness of the Astra Group lies not only in its semi-dispersed ownership with semi-separated management, but also because it is a group holding company which is concurrently publicly listed. In this system, information on the business activities of the group as a whole is disclosed to the public through AI's consolidated financial statement. We can safely say that the degree of information disclosure of the Astra Group is the highest of all Indonesian business

Figure 4.3   Ownership Structure of the Astra Group

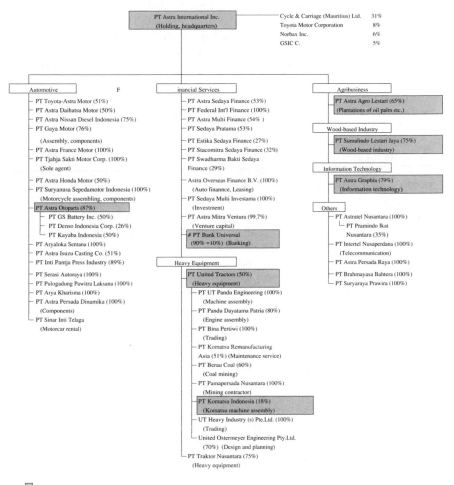

Listed company on the Jakarta Stock Exchange
Subjected to public capital injection in May 1999. Merged with other 4 banks to become Bank Permata in September 2002.

Source: Annual reports and homepage information of PT Astra International Inc. and PT United Tractors, ECFIN (annual), Sukmawaty (2000) and other materials.

groups. In addition to AI, the Group lists six affiliated companies as of 2000 (not including Bank Universal which was recapitalized by the government).

In addition to the Astra Group's close business ties with Japanese manufacturers, which have helped in modernizing the group management system, the high degree of information disclosure constitutes an advantage for the group. In Indonesia, this kind of financial transparency through information disclosure was so scarce that the group won a good reputation with foreign creditors. This resulted in a concentration of foreign creditors' lending to Astra. As of 1996, the outstanding external debts of the group were estimated to have reached US$5.1 billion, the second largest amount after the Salim Group's US$5.5 billion. The debt equity ratio of AI was far above the average level of non-financial companies, at 4.6 in 1996, jumping up after the currency crisis to 15.1 in 2000.

The Astra Group's core business, the machinery industry, which accounts for more than 80% of total group net sales, is domestic-market-oriented with a dependency on imported inputs. The currency crisis in 1997 directly hit the group with sharp rises in import prices, a contraction in domestic demand, and the swelling burdens of dollar-denominated debt repayment. The group soon became unable to service its debts owed to foreign creditors, which amounted to more than US$1.0 billion. Through one-year of hard negotiation between foreign creditors and AI's top professional managers, it eventually managed to win rescheduling (mainly from Japanese creditors) and a cutting down (mainly from Anglo-American creditors) of debt services and started a drastic restructuring of group business in line with a debt rescheduling plan monitored by foreign creditors. The Astra Group is an example which was hardest hit economically, but also successful in restructuring debt and business. The fall of the Soeharto government had no negative impact on the group, as it had no connection to the long-standing president.

The Astra Group is an example of a structure of 'semi-dispersed ownership' with 'semi-separated management', which may become a model of evolved corporate governance through the Komisaris system suited to the Indonesian institutional setting, although it is currently a rare case. The group also has a high degree of transparency due to the fact that it is a group holding company which has gone public. It shows that high exposure to the markets cannot be a sufficient condition for the prevention of excessive borrowing by the group. On the contrary, the high degree of transparency invites an over-concentration of lending by creditors due to the scarcity value of such a group. Regarding governance by creditors, this case shows that even foreign creditors who are regarded as having a higher ability to monitor customer firms were not able to control over-borrowing *ex ante*. But they did impose discipline in the *ex post facto* debt restructuring process.

4.4 Gajah Tunggal Group

The Gajah Tunggal Group is ranked as the seventh largest Indonesian business group with Rp.4.2 trillion (US$1.8 billion) group annual sales as of 1996, although it was not ranked in the 20 largest business groups in 1988, showing the group's rapid growth in the 1990s. The group is not new, but has a long history. The group's mother company, PT Gajah Tunggal, was established in 1951 in Jakarta as a small factory of tires for *becak* and bicycles. In 1970, the present owner of the group, Sjamsul Nursalim (Lim Tek Siong), acquired this company with its brand. After that, he and his wife, Itjih Sjamsul Nursalim (Go Giok Lian), not only developed PT Gajah Tunggal into the largest tire producer in Indonesia, but also formed a highly-diversified business group. He is an ethnic Chinese born in Lampung, at the southern end of Sumatra island in 1942, the son of a primary product trader and rubber refinery owner.

In the 1970s, the Group had already shown its orientation toward diversification into such fields as rubber products, paints, metal cables, sanitary products, and banking. At the end of the 1980s, it went into large-scale investments for diversification into shrimp breeding and fishery, petrochemicals (polyester, nylon filament and synthetic rubber), and fund management services. An example of one of the group's ambitious investment plans in the mid 1990s was the expansion of its integrated shrimp processing farms in Lampung to 70,000 ha., the largest scale in the world. In fact, the Group's old and new core businesses of tire manufacturing and shrimp breeding were resourced-based industries with big markets, and the group's multi-faceted financial business in banking, insurance, financing, securities, fund management and venture capital was highly profitable with no large capital investment. The group seems to make full use of its advantage in competitive business lines to raise more funds for further diversified investment.

The Gajah Tunggal Group had 8 listed companies on the Jakarta Stock Exchange as of 1996. Of these, four were engaged in the financial services sector, three in manufacturing (tire, polyester, and cable), and one in property (Figure 4.4). Unlike Sinar Mas and Astra, these listed companies were not holding companies by nature but pure business undertakings. Therefore their function as a window of information disclosure or as a conduit for investment funds was limited.

Nevertheless, it was found that the group had a mechanism of intra-group lending, where PT Gajah Tunggal played a central role. PT Gajah Tunggal, as the most reputable listed company of the group raised external

Figure 4.4   Ownership Structure of the Gajah Tunggal Group

Nursalim (Lim) Family / Gozali (Go/Kho) Family   ———— *   Sjamsul Nursalim (Lim Tek Siong)

Itjih Sjamsul Nursalim (Go Giok Lian)
Djunaedi Nursalim
Budiman Nursalim
Herman Nursalim
Indrawati Nursalim
Nursalim Cherie
Adhilukito Himawan (Lim Boon Hong)
Gustimego (Gouw Hong Hoe)
Irwan Gozali (Kho Boen Jong)
Fredy Gozali (Kho Bun Fok)
Hamdani Gozali
Kurniawan Gozali
Budiman Gozali
Mulyati Gozali
FX Boyke Gozali
Juliani Gozali
Tetty L Gozali

[Family investment company]

PT Gajah Tunggal Mulia
PT Gajah Tunggal Sakti
PT Gajah Tunggal Abadi
PT Daya Patria Corporation
PT Kembar Madya Utama
PT Arah Guna Sejahtera
PT Dayin Vita Indonesia

[Holding company controlled by IBRA]

PT Tunas Sepadan Investama

Manufacturing

PT Gajah Tunggal (67%)
(Tire)
 # PT Langgeng Baja Pratama (51%)
 (Steel wire)
 # PT Meshindo Alloy Wheel (51%)
 (Aluminuim alloy wheel)
20% # PT GT Petrochem Industries (50%)
 (Polyester, nylon filament, tire cord)
  # PT Filamindo Sakti (93%)
  (Nylon Filament)
5% # PT Sentra Sintetikajaya (95%)
 (Synthetic rubber)
PT GT Kabel Indonesia (69%)
(Cable)
 PT Pirelli Cables Indonesia (50%)
 (High-voltage cable)
PT IRC Inoac Indonesia (49%)
(Polyurethane foam, rubber parts)
PT Gajah Tunggal Prakarsa (99.9%)
(Paint and resin)
PT Bando Indonesia (50%)
(Transformer)
PT Omedata Electronics (73%)
(Semiconductor)
PT Segamas Pertiwi (84%)
(Sport shoes)
PT Softex Indonesia (77%)
(Sanitary napkins)

Financial

PT Bank Dagang Negara Indonesia
(52%) (Banking)
 PT BDNI Finance (98%)
 (Finance)
 PT BDNI Ventura (63%)
 (Venture capital)
 PT Bank Ganesha (97%)
 (Banking)
 PT Bank Dewa Rutji
 (Banking)
 PT BDNI Reksadana (56%)
 (Fund management)
PT BDNI Capital Corporation (66%)
(Fund Management)
PT Asuransi Dayin Mitra (74%)
(General insurance)
 PT Asuransi Binadaya Nusaindah
 (71%) (Life insurance)
 PT Lumbung Sari (80%)
 (Insurance brokerage)
 PT Datindo Entrycom (92%)
 (Share registrar)
 PT BDNI Securities (81%)
 (Securities)

Agrobusiness

PT Dipasena Citra Darmaja (100%)
(Shrimp breeding)
 # PT Wachyuni Mandira (99%)
 (Shrimp breeding)
 # PT Bestari Indoprima (98%)
 (Shrimp feed processing)
 # PT Mesuji Pratama Lines (87%)
 (Vessel facilities)
 # PT Birulaut Khatulistiwa (98%)
 (Shrimp hatcheries)

PT Triwindu Grahamanunggal
(99%) (Shrimp hatcheries)

Properties

PT Indonesia Prima Property
(65%)
(Hotel, apartment, office
and shopping malls)

*   Founder
[ ]   Listed company on the Jakarta Stock Exchange
Controlled by IBRA for asset sales in order to repay Central Bank liquidity support loans.
Liquidated in August 1998.

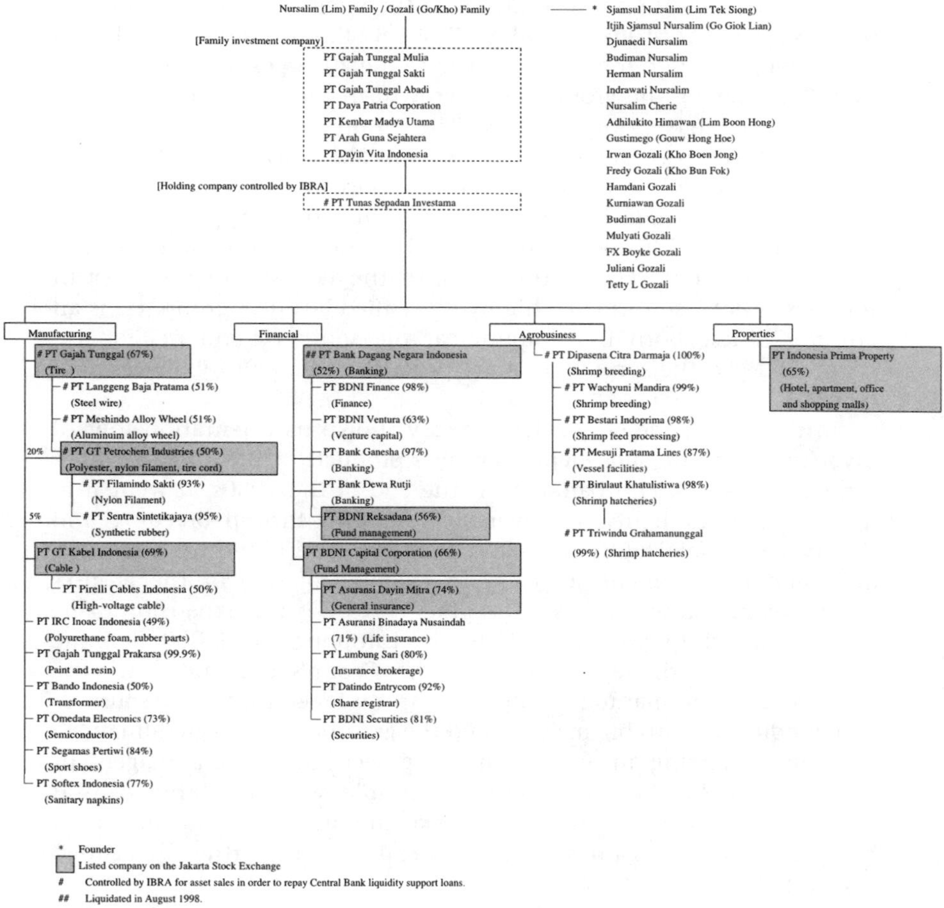

Source: ECFIN (annual), Sukmawaty (2000), CISI Raya Utama (1990, 1999), consolidated financial statements of PT Gajah Tunggal 1996–1997 and other materials.

funds and provided them for group companies by utilizing draft transactions. Figure 4.5 illustrates the flow of funds of the Gajah Tunggal Group as of 1996 and 1997, as observed in the consolidated financial statements of the company. Major flows of funds are (i) net inflow from outside to PT Gajah Tunggal; (ii) net inflow from group banks to PT Gajah Tunggal; and (iii) net outflow from PT Gajah Tunggal to other group companies. Major findings are as follows:

Figure 4.5   Flow of Funds of PT Gajah Tunggal

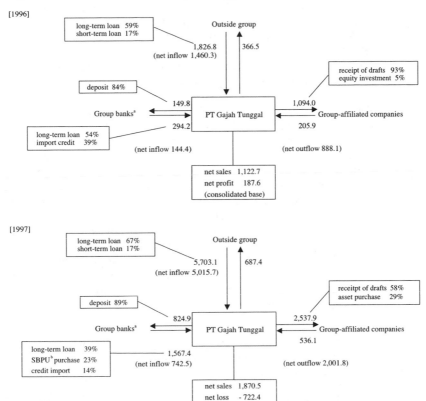

Source: Calculated from consolidated financial statements of PT Gajah Tunggal 1996–1997.
Note: a: BDNI (Bank Dagang Negara Indonesia), Bank Ganesha, and Bank Dewa Rutji.
     b: SBPU (Surat Berharga Pasar Uang) is money market securities, a monetary instrument
     for monetary expansion. It is in the form of promissory notes issued by companies in
     connection with their borrowings from banks or trade bills drawn by companies and
     endorsed by a bank.

1.   Net inflow of external funds to PT Gajah Tunggal amounted
to Rp.1.46 trillion (1996) and Rp.5.02 trillion (1997), which
was much larger than the company's annual consolidated
sales, amounting to Rp.1.12 trillion (1996) and Rp.1.87 trillion
(1997).

2.   A major source of external funds (accounting for 59% to 67% of
gross inflow) was long-term syndicate loans borrowed by the
subsidiaries of PT Gajah Tunggal.

3. Net inflow from group banks to PT Gajah Tunggal amounted to Rp.0.14 trillion (1996) and Rp.0.74 trillion (1997), far smaller than direct inflow of external funds to the company. There was no evidence that intra-group bank lending played an essential role.

4. A major part of inflow from group banks was long-term loans, but PT Gajah Tunggal mostly utilized the group banks as suppliers of import credits and as deposit banks.

5. Net outflow of funds from PT Gajah Tunggal to group companies amounted to Rp.0.89 trillion (1996) and Rp.2.00 trillion (1997), almost on the same scale as the company's consolidated annual sales.

6. A major means of supplying funds to group companies (accounting for 58% to 93% of gross outflow) was that PT Gajah Tunggal allowed the group companies to draw drafts receivable and the company received those drafts.

7. Around 60% of funds supply from PT Gajah Tunggal was allocated to unlisted family holding companies and the remaining 40% was allocated directly to business undertakings. The role of the family holding companies was possibly to pool, coordinate and channel the funds for all the group business, especially for new business that needed fresh funds.

Out of the total net inflow to PT Gajah Tunggal from outside and group banks, the amount of 55% (1996) and 35% (1997) was supplied to group companies, mainly via family holding companies. A long-term overseas bank loan was a major means of fund-raising, while drawing drafts receivable was a dominant means of intra-group fund supply. By this mechanism, the publicly-listed reputable company functioned as an external fund raiser and an internal fund supplier for investment.

Just before the crisis, the total outstanding external debts of the Gajah Tunggal Group as a whole are estimated to have reached US$3.0 billion. Although this amount is less than that of the three largest groups, Salim, Astra and Sinar Mas, the amount is 2.1 times as much as the group's annual sales in 1996, whereas for the three groups the ratios of external debts to sales are 0.3, 0.7, and 0.6 respectively (Table 4.2). It may be safely said that the Gajah Tunggal Group was obviously in a state of over-borrowing. The mechanism as illustrated above is considered to have promoted the group's inclination for over-borrowing and for active diversification investment. From the viewpoint of corporate governance by creditors, the above mechanism widens the asymmetry of information between creditors and owner-managers by disclosing only the well-performing part of the group activities, when actually the creditors' funds are being substantially supplied to other undisclosed parts of the group.

The Gajah Tunggal Group is also a case of family ownership and management. The group's ownership pattern appears to be concentrated ownership by Sjamsul Nursalim and his wife's family, accounting for 62% (1996) and 67% (2000) of listed companies on average (Appendix 1). In management, the weight of family, which was relatively low in 1996 at 46% and 30% in Komisaris and Direksi respectively, further decreased to below 30% after the crisis. It means that the degree of presence of professional managers at the group company level is high. It is also known that management organizations of the group are well structured.

After the crisis in 1997, the Gajah Tunggal Group faced two kinds of debt problems; one was external debt and another was the repayment of central bank liquidity support loans. One of the leading private banks in Indonesia, Bank Dagang Negara Indonesia (BDNI), owned by the group, received emergency loans from the central bank to cope with bank runs amid the crisis, but eventually it was closed by the government. The Sjamsul Nursalim family as owner of the bank was obliged to repay the loans amounting to Rp.28.4 trillion in cash or by sales of assets in four years, so they placed their assets equivalent to the repayment amount under the IBRA's control for sale. These assets included family shareholdings in the group's major businesses, namely, tires, shrimp farming and petrochemicals (marked # in Figure 4.4). As the group's repayment performance was poor, it was criticized by the domestic public, and it was reported that the family tried to gain access to the post-Soeharto governments in order to secure their strategic businesses. On the occasion of formal negotiations with IBRA, Itjih and her niece, Mulyati Gozali, as a top financial director, took charge of the task,[17] showing that the right of final decision making in financial management is still in the hands of the owner family despite the high presence of professional managers. While it seems difficult for the owner family to secure the group's major assets that were heavily debt-burdened, IBRA (substantially the Indonesian government), as well as foreign creditors, had no choice but to accept the low recovery rates of their claims.

The case of the Gajah Tunggal Group demonstrates that partial disclosure of a business group's information can do more harm than good. This is because external financiers can get information relating only to good business, whereas the funds supplied may be utilized in other group businesses, thus widening the asymmetry of information between owner-managers and outside financiers. Another point shown by this case is that a high presence of professional managers does not mean that professional managers can keep owner-managers in check, as the latter has the right of final decision making, at least in financial matters, at the group level.

4.5 Texmaco Group

The Texmaco Group is one of the largest integrated producers of textiles in Indonesia. The Group has expanded its scale of business remarkably in the last decade, raising its rank in the Indonesian business group sales ranking from 99th in 1990 to 26th in 1996, although the Group has a history of more than two decades. The group's mother company, PT Texmaco Djaja (Textile Manufacturing Company Djaja), was established as a weaving factory in 1970 in Pemalang, central Java. The group expanded its scope of business from weaving to polyester filament yarn spinning in the late 1970s, and to garments in the 1980s. One of the group's unique features lay in its strategy of entering textile machinery manufacturing. The group had become the first producer and exporter of Indonesian-made air jet looms by the early 1990s. This success was highly valued by the then President Soeharto. Owing to Soeharto's support, the group pushed on with a further integration of heavy machinery, trucks and trailers, and their component manufacturing. At the same time, it also moved into upstream integration of the synthetic fiber industry, namely, PTA (purified terephthalic acid) production. Expansive investments into these capital-intensive synthetics and machinery industries accelerated in the 1990s. The annual sales of the group in pre-crisis 1996 reached Rp.1.8 trillion (US$0.8 billion) and its estimated assets were Rp.5.5 trillion (US$2.3 billion).

A major founder and owner-manager of the Texmaco Group is Marimutu Sinivasan, a fourth generation ethnic Indian of Tamil descent born in Medan, North Sumatra in 1937. His father, Sinnaja Marimutu, who engaged in *batik* trading with Malaya, moved from Medan to central Java during the Confrontation period with Malaysia in the 1960s. Weaving factories in the early days of the group's development were set up by his father, a friend of his father, Marimutu Sinivasan and his brothers and sisters. However, a discontinuous spurt in the group's operation after the early 1980s was spearheaded by Sinivasan himself, supported by his younger brothers and professional managers. The group publicly listed three major operating companies (Figure 4.6). In 1996, the ratio of concentrated ownership by Marimutu Sinivasan, his brothers, and the group companies was 72% of the total shares of the three listed companies. The weight of Sinivasan and his brothers in management was 35% on the Komisaris and 77% on the Direksi, as Sinivasan gained the position of President Director of all three listed companies. This is a typical case of founder control of ownership and management.

Figure 4.6   Ownership Structure of the Texmaco Group

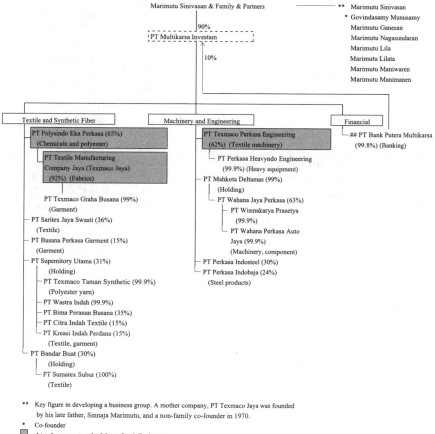

**   Key figure in developing a business group. A mother company, PT Texmaco Jaya was founded
      by his late father, Sinnaja Marimutu, and a non-family co-founder in 1970.
*   Co-founder

▨   Listed company on the Jakarta Stock Exchange
Liquidated in February 2000.

Source: ECFIN (annual), Sukmawaty (2000), CISI Raya Utama (1999), IBRA's press release No.058,
2 July 2002, and other materials.

The Texmaco Group is the most obvious case of over-borrowing in
this case study. Two years after the crisis, it transpired that the Texmaco
Group had been granted special financial facilities in 1997 by the Soeharto
government in order to avoid a corporate default, and that the group
was the largest debtor of irrecoverable loans from domestic banks with
a total amount of Rp.17.3 trillion (as of 2001). This amount is 9.6 times
as much as the group's annual sales in 1996 (Table 4.2). The Group owed
Rp.10 trillion of the debt to the then largest state-owned bank, Bank

Negara Indonesia. As the amount was far in excess of banking regulations on single-customer exposure, the Attorney General stepped in to investigate but dropped the case in the end. Taking into consideration that the group's large-scale capital-goods industry was of 'strategic' importance, the post-Soeharto governments and the IBRA finally decided to take the special step of long-term restructuring for the group. By swapping the bad debt into the IBRA's equity, the IBRA set up a new holding company for the group's indebted affiliated companies and let the holding company issue convertible bonds and repay the debt preferentially to the IBRA.

In Texmaco's case, its remarkably rapid growth with aggressive investment in the last decade was supported by the Soeharto government and by excessive loan disbursement by a state-owned bank. As the state bank loans turned irrecoverable after the crisis, the IBRA took over the claims and accountability for the group's financial restructuring. The government also shouldered the costs of bank restructuring. The case of the Texmaco Group demonstrates that exposure to the market by listing major group companies did not help to control the group's behaviour in pursuing excessive borrowing by colluding with the state bank.

4.6 Humpuss Group

The Humpuss Group is led by Hutomo Mandala Putera Soeharto (commonly called Tommy Soeharto), the third son of the former President Soeharto. 'Humpuss' is an abbreviation of his name. The group started with the establishment of PT Humpuss, the group's holding company, in 1984. Within ten years, the Group was ranked in the top 20 business groups, recorded as the most rapid-growth group along with the Bimantara Group, led by his elder brother, Bambang Trihatmodjo. In 1996, the Humpuss Group ranked 18th with Rp.2.3 trillion annual sales (US$1.0 billion).

60% of PT Humpuss was owned by Tommy and 40% by his eldest brother, Sigit Harjojudanto (Soeharto's first son). Tommy was the President Director, and Sigit was the President Commissioner of this holding company, although Sigit's commitment to management was nominal. Seen as a group, ownership of the Humpuss Group was highly concentrated, while management was semi-separated. In most of the 40 affiliated companies, PT Humpuss owned a majority (51% to 100%) of shareholding (Figure 4.7). All the president directors of the affiliated companies were occupied by salaried professional managers. They were without exception *pribumi* who had high educational and professional careers. Tommy was a decision-maker regarding the top personnel of the affiliated companies, as he had a managerial position in the holding company or on the Komisaris of affiliated companies. The degree of

Figure 4.7   Ownership Structure of the Humpuss Group

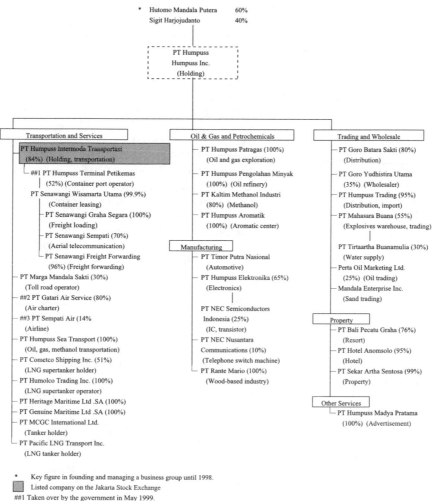

*   Hutomo Mandala Putera   60%
         Sigit Harjojudanto   40%

PT Humpuss
Humpuss Inc.
(Holding)

Transportation and Services
PT Humpuss Intermoda Transportasi
(84%) (Holding, transportation)
  ##1 PT Humpuss Terminal Petikemas
    (52%) (Container port operator)
  PT Senawangi Wisamarta Utama (99.9%)
    (Container leasing)
    PT Senawangi Graha Segara (100%)
    (Freight loading)
    PT Senawangi Sempati (70%)
    (Aerial telecommunication)
    PT Senawangi Freight Forwarding
    (96%) (Freight forwarding)
  PT Marga Mandala Sakti (30%)
  (Toll road operator)
  ##2 PT Gatari Air Service (80%)
  (Air charter)
  ##3 PT Sempati Air (14%
  (Airline)
  PT Humpuss Sea Transport (100%)
  (Oil, gas, methanol transportation)
  PT Cometco Shipping Inc. (51%)
  (LNG supertanker holder)
  PT Humolco Trading Inc. (100%)
  (LNG supertanker operator)
  PT Heritage Maritime Ltd .SA (100%)
  PT Genuine Maritime Ltd .SA (100%)
  PT MCGC International Ltd.
  (Tanker holder)
  PT Pacific LNG Transport Inc.
  (LNG tanker holder)

Oil & Gas and Petrochemicals
PT Humpuss Patragas (100%)
(Oil and gas exploration)
PT Humpuss Pengolahan Minyak
(100%) (Oil refinery)
PT Kaltim Methanol Industri
(80%) (Methanol)
PT Humpuss Aromatik
(100%) (Aromatic center)

Manufacturing
PT Timor Putra Nasional
(Automotive)
PT Humpuss Elektronika (65%)
(Electronics)

PT NEC Semiconductors
Indonesia (25%)
(IC, transistor)
PT NEC Nusantara
Communications (10%)
(Telephone switch machine)
PT Rante Mario (100%)
(Wood-based industry)

Trading and Wholesale
PT Goro Batara Sakti (80%)
(Distribution)
PT Goro Yudhistira Utama
(35%) (Wholesaler)
PT Humpuss Trading (95%)
(Distribution, import)
PT Mahasara Buana (55%)
(Explosives warehouse, trading)

PT Tirtaartha Buanamulia (30%)
(Water supply)
Perta Oil Marketing Ltd.
(25%) (Oil trading)
Mandala Enterprise Inc.
(Sand trading)

Property
PT Bali Pecatu Graha (76%)
(Resort)
PT Hotel Anomsolo (95%)
(Hotel)
PT Sekar Artha Sentosa (99%)
(Property)

Other Services
PT Humpuss Madya Pratama
(100%) (Advertisement)

*   Key figure in founding and managing a business group until 1998.
     Listed company on the Jakarta Stock Exchange
##1 Taken over by the government in May 1999.
##2 Sold by IBRA in 1999.
##3 Went bankrupt in July 1999.

Source: ECFIN (annual), Sukmawaty (2000), Yayasan Humpuss Group (1994) and other materials.

information disclosure of the Humpuss Group was quite low, as the group had only one listed affiliated company. The Group's plan to make PT Humpuss go public was not realized. Instead, the Group published a decennial corporate history, which was not common practice for

Indonesian business groups. With regard to financial data, however, it contained a minimum of information.

Business lines of the Humpuss Group were highly diversified; (1) sea and air transportation and related services such as port and road construction and management; (2) oil and gas excavation and petrochemicals; (3) manufacturing, for example electronic products; (4) trade and wholesale; (5) property; and (6) advertising. There were at least two strategies which contributed to Humpuss's rapid growth. One was the securing of licence or agency businesses: for example, Humpuss became sole marketing agency for methanol and PTA which Pertamina (the state-owned oil and gas company) started to produce in 1987, obtained the sole domestic marketing licence in 1989 for high-graded gasoline 'Premix', got involved in a capital participation in 1989 into a Pertamina spot oil marketing company in Hong Kong, obtained a 20-year licence from Pertamina for LNG marine transportation in LNG exports to Taiwan, and so on. The second strategy was, under the banner of privatization, to become the first local private company entering into fields that had been monopolized by state-owned or foreign companies: for instance, possession of LNG tankers, and oil and gas excavation that had so far completely depended on foreign companies, construction and management of a container terminal, waterworks, and storage and distribution of explosives for industrial use that had been exclusively managed by state-owned enterprises. These strategies explain why the group's business foundation lay in the distribution, transportation, and oil and gas industries, in which acquisition of licences was a matter of great importance. Needless to say, Tommy's direct blood ties with ultimate power enabled him to pursue the strategies.

After the crisis, the IBRA revealed that the Humpuss Group was the third largest debtor of irrecoverable loans from domestic banks, mainly from state banks, with a total debt of Rp.5.7 trillion (as of 2001). This amount is 2.5 times the Group's annual sales in 1996. Of the total irrecoverable debt, more than half was borrowed by PT Timor Putra Nasional, a sole importer-cum-assembler of 'Timor', the national car project, which started in early 1996 under the strong leadership of Tommy and the then President Soeharto. Other large borrowers included the owner of several tankers (Humpuss Inc.), a container terminal project in Jakarta (PT Humpuss Terminal), a domestic aviation service (PT Sempati Air), an oil and gas excavator (PT Humpuss Patragas), and the holding company PT Humpuss. The group's debt was partly repaid to the IBRA in assets and was partly pending in court, while Tommy seceded from the group's ownership and management and was found guilty of crimes that he had committed after the collapse of the Soeharto's rule. While the Humpuss Group lost momentum of expansion as a united business entity, its major businesses survived under the respective professional management.

The Humpuss Group is one of the extreme cases of an owner-manager having a close link to the power centre. Owing to its political backing, the group could draw loans worth more than twice as much as its annual sales. Along with the acquisition of various business licences, this abundant borrowing contributed to the group's remarkably rapid expansion. The group's structure of ownership and management was rather straightforward and modernized. However, as the holding company did not disclose information in the form of consolidated financial statements, there was no way of getting an overall picture of the investment and outstanding debt of the group, which was revealed only after the collapse of the political power.

5. Conclusion

In the last section, our task is to reconstruct findings of the case studies in Section 4 in the light of the hypotheses presented in Section 3, to re-examine their validity, and to draw some implications on better corporate governance in the Indonesian context.

First of all, as for concentrated ownership without separation from management that is often negatively evaluated, the case of the Gudang Garam Group clearly demonstrates that that in itself is not an impediment to good corporate governance. Self-governance by owner-managers can work effectively on condition that there is no other key stakeholder and that there is no collusion with the government. Given no major external financier, the natural consequence should be a slow growth of business. However, the Gudang Garam Group succeeded in developing into one of the largest business groups. This is largely owing to the peculiarity of the profitability and growth of their core business, the clove cigarette industry.

Second, there is at least one good example to support the validity of the first hypothesis that information asymmetry between owner-managers and creditors is a possible cause of governance failure, and that is the case of the Gajah Tunggal Group. In this case, information asymmetry becomes serious when business groups disclose partial information by listing only good-performing businesses. The good-performing listed company functions as a fund-raiser from outside and a fund-supplier to various group businesses, which cannot be monitored by creditors due to the unavailability of information. This mechanism allows owner-managers to pursue over-borrowing for the sake of over-investment.

Third, the second hypothesis of collusion with the government as a possible cause of governance failure is also evidenced as valid by the cases of the Texmaco Group and the Humpuss Group. In both cases, the owner-managers colluded with political power, so that they could successfully draw large-scale loans mainly from state-owned banks. The owner-managers were able to utilize political backing to put pressure to banks to lend to them, while the state banks would not refuse the request at the risk of political punishment and because they knew that their possible losses would be borne by the government as a last resort. In fact, the irrecoverable claims of state banks in the crisis were eventually carried over by government finance (substantially by the Indonesian nationals who were taxpayers). Thus in the Indonesian institutional setting, political collusion was one of the causes of the malfunction of corporate governance by domestic creditors. One of the differences between Texmaco and Humpuss is that the former has publicly-listed companies. However, the outcome is not different, showing that exposure to market does not put the brakes on the behaviour of owner-managers in their collusion with the government.

Fourth, the third hypothesis of foreign creditors' monitoring ability as a possible cause of good governance is proved invalid in every case where there was a dependency on foreign debts, namely, in the Sinar Mas, Astra, and Gajah Tunggal Groups. Even in the Astra case, where the group holding company discloses almost all the group business activities so that information asymmetry is regarded as minimum, over-lending to the holding company by foreign creditors took place. This indicates that when there are obvious profit-making opportunities, even foreign creditors with high monitoring ability will put higher priority on pursuit of profits rather than exerting rigorous discipline over customer firms. The Astra case, however, also shows that, in the *ex post facto* debt restructuring process, negotiations with foreign creditors can give the firms discipline.

Fifth, the fourth hypothesis that the effect of public listing is a positive factor in corporate governance is refuted in two ways. First, as the case of the Gajah Tunggal Group shows, public listing of only good lines of business within the group can do more harm than good, because it leads outside financiers to make mistakes in their evaluation of the activities of the whole group, allowing business groups to pursue over-borrowing. To prevent this, information should be disclosed on not just a limited part but on a major part of business group activities by listing group holding companies or divisional holding companies. Second, we should bear in mind that public listing is not necessarily a panacea. As the Astra case shows, it is not always true that the more the disclosure of information on business groups takes place, the better the governance by outside financiers functions. Astra discloses information on its whole group activities by listing its group holding company, but the consequence is a concentration of financiers supplying funds to the company, resulting in over-borrowing. Thus, public listing does not necessarily ensure financiers' governance with an *ex ante* check on excessive borrowing and investment in any way.

Sixth, the final hypothesis that professional managers' function as a check on owner-managers is a positive factor for governance is evidenced as invalid. Both the Sinar Mas Group as an established group and the Gajah Tunggal Group as a rapid-growth group have a relatively high degree of presence of professional managers in managerial posts. Nevertheless, as far as placing a check on the right of the owner-manager to have the final say in decision making in group management (even without having explicit managerial position), the role of professional manager is severely limited. This result implies that a newly introduced system of independent commissioners (non-owner members in the Komisaris) would also have the same limitations.[18]

The results of this case study on Indonesia demonstrate that self-governance of an owner-manager-led business group can function well if there is no key stakeholder and no collusion with the government. When this is not the case, however, self-governance does not work and governance by key stakeholders, namely, creditors or professional managers, over the owner-manager also has crucial limitations. As far as the ability of the professional manager to check on the owner-manager is concerned, we can see that as long as the controlling owner is the ultimate decision maker in management, any internal governance mechanism will have a certain limitation. For better corporate governance, there is a need for a combination of measures targeting business groups themselves, measures targeting creditors, and measures for preventing collusion. Firstly, business groups need to be encouraged to publicly list their key holding companies, as opposed to their operating companies, in order to expose a larger part of their activities to market discipline. This measure has to be accompanied by a strengthening of the monitoring function of the capital market in Indonesia, as the case study shows that market exposure alone does not ensure efficacy of governance. A key point here may be to establish institutions which can impose a threat of exit from the market on business groups whose owner-managers do not obey market rules. In parallel, institutions which will impose a potential threat of liquidation are necessary to ensure the efficacy of governance by creditors in case owner-managers behave against the creditors' interest. Secondly, on the creditors' side, one of the possible means for better corporate governance will be the public listing of banks; state-owned banks in particular, so that the creditors are also exposed to market evaluation. Thirdly, to prevent governance failure owing to collusion, it is essential to develop systems of checks and balances within the government to control possible collusion between power and business, and to develop watch-dog systems in society to monitor possible triangular alliances between owner-managers of business groups, domestic creditors and the government. Measures for this purpose may include

Appendix 4.A1a Data of Publicly Listed Companies under 6 Business Groups, 1996

Group Name of listed company	Business	Financial indicator			Ownership (%)		Management (%)			
							Komisaris		Direksi	
		ROA (%)	ROE (%)	D/E	Major shareholder*	Public	Shareholder	Non-Shareholder	Shareholder	Non-Shareholder
Gudang Garam										
PT Gudang Garam Tbk.	Cigarettes	15.2	25.7	0.7	79.7	12.6	33.3	66.7	53.8	46.2
Sinar Mas										
PT Sinar Mas Multiartha Tbk.	Financing	1.0	17.0	15.8	71.2	11.8	100.0	0.0	0.0	100.0
PT Bank Internasional Indonesia Tbk.	Banking	1.5	20.8	13.3	49.4	50.6	76.9	23.1	30.0	70.0
PT Indah Kiat Pulp & Paper Corporation Tbk.	Pulp/paper	3.0	8.5	1.8	82.9	16.9	46.7	53.3	33.3	66.7
PT Pabrik Kertas Tjiwi Kimia Tbk.	Pulp/paper	4.5	15.0	2.4	65.0	35.0	55.6	44.4	44.4	55.6
PT SM Agro Resources & Technology Corp. Tbk.	Agro	3.7	10.6	1.9	51.0	49.0	42.9	57.1	56.3	43.8
PT Duta Pertiwi Tbk.	Property	4.6	16.9	2.7	64.9	34.9	73.3	26.7	28.6	71.4
PT Plaza Indonesia Realty Tbk.	Property	5.5	8.5	0.5	17.2	11.5	62.5	37.5	100.0	0.0
Average (mean)		3.4	13.9	5.5	57.4	30.0	65.4	34.6	41.8	58.2
Average (non-financial, mean)				1.9						

Appendix 4.A1a Data of Publicly Listed Companies under 6 Business Groups, 1996 *(continued)*

Group	Name of listed company	Business	Financial indicator			Ownership (%)		Management (%)			
			ROA (%)	ROE (%)	D/E	Major shareholder*	Public	Komisaris		Direksi	
								Shareholder	Non-Shareholder	Shareholder	Non-Shareholder
Astra											
	PT Astra International Tbk.	Automotive	2.8	15.6	4.6	10.7	58.3	75.0	25.0	0.0	100.0
	PT United Tractor Tbk.	Machinery	4.1	16.3	3.0	57.5	41.6	77.8	22.2	27.3	72.7
	PT Astra-Graphia Tbk.	Electronics	1.8	8.4	3.7	79.1	20.9	100.0	0.0	0.0	100.0
	PT Komatsu Indonesia Tbk.	Machinery	16.7	23.2	0.4	0.0	20.7	70.0	30.0	61.5	38.5
	PT Sumalindo Lestari Jaya Tbk.	Wood-based	0.7	1.1	0.6	39.9	19.8	57.1	42.9	44.4	55.6
	Average (non-financial, mean)		5.2	12.9	2.5	46.8	32.3	76.0	24.0	26.7	73.3
Gajah Tunggal											
	PT BDNI Capital Corporation Tbk.	Financing	0.4	6.3	15.9	65.5	34.5	37.5	62.5	0.0	100.0
	PT Bank Dagang Nasional Indonesia Tbk	Banking	1.1	17.7	14.5	60.1	39.9	0.0	100.0	40.0	60.0
	PT Gadjah Tunggal Tbk	Tire	2.7	7.0	1.6	65.0	35.0	42.9	57.1	33.3	66.7
	PT GT Petrochem Industries Tbk.	Polyester	2.6	4.1	0.6	75.0	25.0	80.0	20.0	80.0	20.0

Appendix 4.A1a Data of Publicly Listed Companies under 6 Business Groups, 1996 *(continued)*

Group Name of listed company	Business	Financial indicator			Ownership (%)		Management (%)			
							Komisaris		Direksi	
		ROA (%)	ROE (%)	D/E	Major shareholder*	Public	Shareholder	Non-Shareholder	Shareholder	Non-Shareholder
Gajah Tunggal *(continued)*										
PT Kabelmetal Indonesia Tbk.	Cables	0.9	2.8	2.2	53.4	45.5	42.9	57.1	50.0	50.0
PT Indonesia Prima Property Tbk.	Property	1.7	7.6	2.7	75.6	14.3	77.8	22.2	33.3	66.7
PT Asuransi Dayin Mitra Tbk.	Insurance	15.4	22.7	0.5	73.9	17.9	37.5	62.5	0.0	100.0
PT BDNI Reksadana Tbk.	Mutual fund	12.6	13.7	0.1	30.0	66.7	-	-	0.0	100.0
Average (mean)		4.7	10.2	4.7	62.3	34.8	45.5	54.5	29.6	70.4
Average (non-financial, mean)				1.7						
Texmaco										
PT Polysindo Eka Perkasa Tbk.	Chemical	4.1	11.1	1.7	67.6	32.4	25.0	75.0	66.7	33.3
PT Texmaco Jaya Tbk.	Textile	6.6	19.3	1.9	80.0	20.0	60.0	40.0	80.0	20.0
PT Texmaco Perkasa Engineering Tbk.	Machinery	5.4	14.4	1.7	69.1	31.0	20.0	80.0	83.3	16.7
Average (non-financial, mean)		5.4	14.9	1.8	72.2	27.8	35.0	65.0	76.7	23.3
100 largest listed companies (mean)		4.8	14.2	4.7	37.7	30.3	56.3	43.7	36.2	63.8
(non-financial, mean)				1.7						

Appendix 4.A1b Data of Publicly Listed Companies under 6 Business Groups, 2000

Group	Name of listed company	Business	Financial indicator			Ownership (%)		Management (%)			
								Komisaris		Direksi	
			ROA (%)	ROE (%)	D/E	Major shareholder*	Public	Shareholder	Non-Shareholder	Shareholder	Non-Shareholder
Gudang Garam											
	PT Gudang Garam Tbk.	Cigarettes	20.7	36.7	0.8	75.7	22.2	80.0	20.0	18.8	81.3
Sinar Mas											
	PT Indah Kiat Pulp & Paper Corporation Tbk.	Pulp/paper	-2.5	-5.6	1.2	52.6	38.7	45.5	54.5	60.0	40.0
	PT Pabrik Kertas Tjiwi Kimia Tbk.	Pulp/paper	-15.5	-59.4	2.8	63.4	36.6	55.6	44.4	33.3	66.7
	PT SM Agro Resources & Technology Corp. Tbk.	Agro	-14.1	4441.9	-317.0	51.0	49.0	20.0	80.0	45.5	54.5
	PT Duta Pertiwi Tbk.	Property	2.5	7.6	2.1	50.8	34.7	55.6	44.4	41.7	58.3
	PT Plaza Indonesia Realty Tbk.	Property	-0.4	-0.9	1.4	17.2	8.5	57.1	42.9	62.5	37.5
	PT Sinar Mas Multiartha Tbk.	Financing	-2.4	-20.7	7.5	34.0	13.4	62.5	37.5	0.0	100.0
	Average (mean)		-5.4	727.1	-50.3	44.8	30.2	46.7	50.6	48.6	59.5
	Average (exclude SM Agro mean)		-5.2	-19.2	2.0						

Appendix 4.A1b Data of Publicly Listed Companies under 6 Business Groups, 2000 (*continued*)

Group	Name of listed company	Business	Financial indicator			Ownership (%)		Management (%)			
			ROA (%)	ROE (%)	D/E	Major shareholder*	Public	Komisaris		Direksi	
								Shareholder	Non-Shareholder	Shareholder	Non-Shareholder
Astra											
	PT Astra International Tbk.	Automotive	-0.9	-14.0	15.1	0.0	32.0	50.0	50.0	0.0	100.0
	PT United Tractor Tbk.	Machinery	0.1	1.1	8.6	50.0	36.1	71.4	28.6	0.0	100.0
	PT Astra Otoparts Tbk.	Automotive	6.0	18.9	2.1	87.3	12.7	50.0	50.0	0.0	100.0
	PT Astra Agro Lestari Tbk.	Agro	3.0	6.6	1.2	75.3	15.4	50.0	50.0	0.0	100.0
	PT Komatsu Indonesia Tbk.	Machinery	25.0	27.3	0.1	0.0	26.6	66.7	33.3	53.8	46.2
	PT Sumalindo Lestari Jaya Tbk.	Wood-based	-17.1	-145.0	7.5	75.9	14.6	60.0	40.0	0.0	100.0
	PT Astra-Graphia Tbk.	Electronics	2.4	9.4	2.9	79.1	20.9	100.0	0.0	0.0	100.0
	Average (non-		2.6	-13.7	5.4	73.5	22.6	64.0	36.0	7.7	92.3
Gajah Tunggal	PT Gajah Tunggal Tbk.	Tire	-10.3	259.6	-26.3	67.3	32.5	30.0	70.0	20.0	80.0
	PT GT Petrochem Industries Tbk.	Polyester	-20.0	102.6	-6.1	69.2	30.8	12.5	87.5	37.5	62.5

Appendix 4.A1b Data of Publicly Listed Companies under 6 Business Groups, 2000 (*continued*)

Group Name of listed company	Business	Financial indicator			Ownership (%)			Management (%)			
								Komisaris		Direksi	
		ROA (%)	ROE (%)	D/E	Major shareholder*	Public	Shareholder	Non-Shareholder	Shareholder	Non-Shareholder	
Gajah Tunggal (*continued*)											
PT GT Investama Kapital (BDNI Capital Co)	Financing	−19.1	78.2	−5.1	65.5	34.5	0.0	100.0	16.7	83.3	
PT GT Kabel Indonesia (Kabelmetal Ind.)	Cables	−34.5	110.4	−4.2	68.9	29.0	37.5	62.5	37.5	62.5	
PT Indonesia Prima Property Tbk.	Property	−10.3	91.9	−9.9	65.5	29.7	37.5	62.5	37.5	62.5	
PT Asuransi Dayin Mitra Tbk.	Insurance	7.3	14.1	0.9	73.9	26.1	0.0	100.0	0.0	100.0	
PT Reksadana Perdana (BDNI Reksadana)	Mutual fund	−77.5	−37.8	0.0	55.9	38.3	60.0	40.0	0.0	100.0	
Average (mean)		−23.5	88.4	−7.2	66.5	31.5	25.4	74.6	21.3	78.7	

Appendix 4.A1b Data of Publicly Listed Companies under 6 Business Groups, 2000 (continued)

Group	Name of listed company	Business	Financial indicator			Ownership (%)		Management (%)			
			ROA (%)	ROE (%)	D/E	Major shareholder*	Public	Komisaris		Direksi	
								Shareholder	Non-Shareholder	Shareholder	Non-Shareholder
Texmaco											
	PT Polysindo Eka Perkasa Tbk.	Chemical	-48.0	57.1	-2.2	64.5	35.5	75.0	25.0	50.0	50.0
	PT Texmaco Jaya Tbk.	Textile	-28.3	91.0	-4.2	92.0	8.0	100.0	0.0	60.0	40.0
	PT Texmaco Perkasa Engineering Tbk.	Machinery	-10.2	264.7	-27.1	62.1	22.1	75.0	25.0	50.0	50.0
	Average (mean)		-28.8	137.6	-11.2	72.9	21.9	83.3	16.7	53.3	46.7
Humpuss											
	PT Humpuss Intermoda Transportasi Tbk.	Transport-ation	17.0	110.9	5.5	83.6	16.4	0.0	100.0	0.0	100.0
	100 largest listed companies (mean)		-3.5	-11.9	-0.8	25.9	25.0	47.5	52.5	33.4	66.6

Source: compiled from ECFIN (various years).
Note: * Shareholding of a central shareholder, his family members, and holding companies owned by the shareholder.

governmental and non-governmental systems of accusation against collusive behaviours, independent governmental institutions for supervising banks, judicial systems that enable fair judgments, and a vigorous and neutral mass media.

Notes

[1] See Claessens, Djankov and Lang (1999a, 1999b), Claessens, Djankov, Fan and Lang (1999a, 1999b) for discussions on high leverage, ultimate control by few families, expropriation, and diversification respectively.

[2] Regarding the contrast between the shareholder-value perspective and the stakeholder-society perspective, Tirole (2001) believes it is because the former originated in Anglo-Saxon countries, while the latter is in non-Anglo Saxon countries including France, Germany and Japan. Aoki (2001, Chap. 11) traces back the origin of the confrontation to refutation by Dodd (1932) against Berle (1931). Dodd argues that a manager should be "a trustee" not only for shareholders but also for all other stakeholders who constitute a community of the corporation.

[3] The Hart and Moore (1990) firm here means a firm "in which the hierarchical decomposition of organizational information processing is combined with centralized ownership of physical assets by the manager", namely, "the classic proprietor's firm" (Aoki 2001, p. 123).

[4] See also Demsetz (1983), Shleifer and Vishny (1986), and Morck (2000). Originally, Berle and Means (1932) showed that almost half of large American firms did not have a single shareholder with more than 20% of the stock. This notion of dispersed ownership was supported by the main stream of American corporate studies, e.g., Baumol (1959), Jensen and Meckling (1976), and Grossman and Hart (1980).

[5] Other than studies mentioned here, see also Khan (1999).

[6] Minority shareholders can be a key stakeholder and the associated problem of expropriation can be an evidence of failure of corporate governance, as indicated in the reviews in the previous section. However, these are not focused on in this chapter for the sake of simplifying the framework for analysis.

[7] Major foreign creditors can be roughly divided into Anglo-American and Japanese. It is generally perceived that their behaviour is different; the former tends to be risk-taking with shorter-term contracts and are ready to cut debts (haircut) in case of insolvency, while the latter tends to have longer-term contracts, sticking to debt rescheduling in case of insolvency. Nevertheless, this chapter does not regard the difference as critical in affecting the results of the analysis, so it deals with foreign creditors as a single group.

[8] Zhuang et al. (2000, p. 43) points out that the unsound lending practices of banks with low coverage of collateral generally prevailed in pre-crisis Indonesia.

[9] For definitions of an established group and a rapid-growth group, see Table 4.1 note a. and b.

[10] Although the Salim Group is the largest in sales (Rp.53.1 trillion) and in foreign debts (US$5.5 billion), it is not selected; the Astra Group and the Sinar Mas Group are selected from the top 3. This is firstly because Astra and Sinar Mas contrast well in ownership/management pattern and investment behaviour, while the three are almost the same in the level of indebtedness. Secondly, Salim Group has a peculiarity in its dismantling process caused by the repayment of a huge amount of domestic debts (central bank liquidity support loans to a group bank), which relates more to political factors rather than to a failure of corporate governance. The Salim case may need to be examined separately; for example, see Sato (2003).

[11] In the general textbooks of financial management in Japan, a firm with the level of liability to sales within 4 months, or less than 0.33, is evaluated as good performing.

[12] All the results in 1985 mentioned in Section 4 are from Sato (1993). For 1996 and 2000, results are calculated from a database of publicly listed companies on the Jakarta Stock Exchange based on ECFIN (annual). For details, see Appendix 1.

[13] Percentages of owner family in the managerial boards are calculated by the number of posts occupied by the owner family weighted by 3 for Chairman/ President, 2 for Vice Chairman/Vice President, and 1 for other board members, and divided by the total weighted value of the posts.

[14] In 2003 the workers of PT Gudang Garam went on the first large-scale strike, in line with a rise of labour movements in Indonesia after the fall of the Soeharto regime in 1998. This event shows that workers are no longer a dormant stakeholder but appear as a crucial stakeholder especially in this group that carries out labour-intensive industry. The conclusion here is true only within the framework of this paper; we have to reexamine whether the Gudang Garam's governance is still effective in governing relations with workers.

[15] Although the foreign creditors were major creditors of the Sinar Mas Group, there was also a domestic creditor, namely, IBRA (the Indonesian Bank Restructuring Agency), an Indonesian governmental agency. BII, the group's bank, which received capital injection from the government, had as much as Rp.12 trillion in non-performing loans owing to APP. In order to complete the bank restructuring, the IBRA ordered BII to transfer the non-performing

loans to IBRA. As APP's creditor, the IBRA then ordered the owners of APP, the Widjaja family, to place their group assets equivalent to the loan amount under the IBRA's control for sale.

[16] Lang (2001a) shows that APP's intra-group lending and the pushing of its debt burden down the pyramid of the group played a crucial role in deceiving creditors.

[17] Based on the author's interview (October 2002) with the then deputy chairman in charge of the IBRA.

[18] For the limitations of outside commissioners, see Fitzpatrick (2000).

References

Aoki, Masahiko. 2001. *Towards a Comparative Institutional Analysis*. Cambridge: MIT.

Baumol, William. 1959. *Business Behavior, Value and Growth*. New York: Macmillan.

Bebchuk, Lucian Arye, Reinier Kraakman and George G. Triantis. 2000. "Stock Pyramids, Cross-Ownership, and Dual Class Equity: The Mechanisms and Agency Costs of Separating Control from Cash-Flow Rights". In *Concentrated Corporate Ownership*, edited by R.K. Morck. Chicago: University of Chicago Press.

Berle, A. "Corporate Powers as Powers in Trust". 1931. *Harvard Law Review*, 63, pp. 853–70.

Berle, A. and G. Means. 1932. *The Modern Corporation and Private Property*. New York: Macmillan.

CISI Raya Utama. 1990. *A Study on 300 Prominent Indonesian Businessmen*. Jakarta.

———. 1997. *800 Major Non-Financial Companies in Indonesia 1997/1998*. Jakarta.

———. 1999. *1000 Major Non-Financial Companies in Indonesia 1999/2000*. Jakarta.

Claessens, Stijn, Simeon Djankov, Joseph P. H. Fan and Larry H. P. Lang. 1999a. "Expropriation of Minority Shareholders: Evidence from East Asia". World Bank Policy Research Working Paper no. 2088. Washington DC: World Bank.

———. 1999b. "Corporate Diversification in East Asia: The Role of Ultimate Ownership and Group Affiliation". World Bank Policy Research Working Paper no. 2089. Washington DC: World Bank.

Claessens, Stijn, Simeon Djankov and Larry Lang. 1999a. "Corporate Growth, Financing and Risks in the Decade Before East Asia's Financial Crisis". World Bank Policy Research Working Paper no. 2017. Washington D.C.: World Bank.

Claessens, Stijn, Simeon Djankov and Larry Lang. 1999b. "Who Controls East Asian Corporations?". World Bank Policy Research Working Paper no. 2054. Washington DC: World Bank.

———. 2000. "East Asian Corporations: Heroes or Villains?". World Bank Working Paper no. 409. Washington D.C.: World Bank.

Demsetz, Harold. 1983. "Corporate Control, Insider Trading, and Rates of Return". *American Economic Review*, 86, pp. 313–16.

Dodd, E.M. 1932. "For Whom are Corporate Managers Trustees?" *Harvard Law Review*, 45, pp. 1145–1163.

Ekofin Konsulindo. 2000. "Indonesian Banking Indicator and Financial Performance 31 December 1991 – 31 December 1999" (CD-ROM). Jakarta.

Fitzpatrick, Daniel. 2000. "Indonesian Corporate Governance: Would Outside Directors or Commissioners Help?" In *Indonesia in Transition: Social Aspects of Reformasi and Crisis*, edited by C. Manning and Peter van Diermen, Singapore: ISEAS.

Gajah Tunggal, PT. 1998. "Laporan Keuangan Konsolidasi PT Gajah Tunggal Tbk dan Anak Perusahaan" (Consolidated Financial Statement of PT Gajah Tunggal and Affiliated Companies). Jakarta: PT Gajah Tunggal.

Grossman, Sanford and Oliver Hart. 1980. "The Costs and Benefits of Ownership: A Theory of Vertical and Lateral Integration". *Bell Journal of Economics*, 11, pp. 42–64.

Hart, Oliver and J. Moore. 1990. "Property Rights and the Nature of the Firm". *Journal of Political Economy*, 98, pp. 1119–1158.

Husnan, Suad. 1999. *Indonesian Corporate Governance: Its Impact on Corporate Performance and Finance*. A report for ADB-financed RETA 5802 project on Corporate Governance and Financing in Selected Developing Member Countries.

Indonesian Bank Restructuring Agency (IBRA/BPPN). 1999. *Preliminary Information Memorandum on Holding Companies under IBRA*. Jakarta: IBRA.

———. 2001. *Annual Report 2000*. Jakarta: IBRA.

Indonesian Institute for Corporate Governance (IICG). 2001. *Corporate Governance Perception Index*. Jakarta: IICG.

Institute for Economic and Financial Research (ECFIN) (annual). *Indonesian Capital Market Directory*. Jakarta: ECFIN.

Jensen, Michael and William Meckling. 1976. "Theory of the Firm: Managerial Behavior, Agency Costs, and Ownership Structure". *Journal of Financial Economics*, 3, pp. 305–360.

Khan, Haider A. 1999. "Corporate Governance of Family Businesses in Asia". ADB Institute Working Paper no. 3. Tokyo: ADBI.

Kikuzawa, Kensuke. 1998. *Nichi-Bei-Doku Soshiki no Keizai Bunseki: Shin Seidoha Hikaku Soshikiron* (Economic Analysis of Organizations in Japan, America and Germany: New Institutionalist Comparative Organization Theory). Tokyo: Buntendo.

La Porta, Rafael, Florencio Lopez-de-Silanes, and Andrei Shleifer. 1999. "Corporate Ownership Around the World". *Journal of Finance*, 54, pp. 471–517.

La Porta, Rafael, Florencio Lopez-de-Silanes, Andrei Shleifer, and Robert W. Vishny. 1997. "Legal Determinants of External Finance". *Journal of Finance*, 52, pp. 1131–1150.

———. "Law and Finance". *Journal of Political Economy*, 106, pp. 1113–1155, 1998.

———. "Corporate Valuation Around the World". NBER Working Paper.

Lang, Larry. 2001a. "Case Study of Expropriation: Widjaja Family in Indonesia". Mimeograph, Seminar on Corporate Governance of Family Business in Asia, ADB Institute, Tokyo.

———. 2001b. "Expropriation". Mimeograph, Seminar on Corporate Governance of Family Business in Asia, ADB Institute, Tokyo.

Lang, Larry H. P. and René M. Stulz. 1994. "Tobin's q, Corporate Diversification, and Firm Performance". *Journal of Political Economy*, 102, pp. 1248–1280.

Lang, Larry H. P., Eli Ofek and René M. Stulz. 1996. "Leverage, Investment, and Firm Growth". *Journal of Financial Economics*, 40, pp. 3–29.

Morck, Randall K. 2000. *Concentrated Corporate Ownership*. Chicago: University of Chicago Press.

Pangestu, Mari, and Farid Harianto. 1998. "Corporate Governance in Indonesia: Prognosis and Way Ahead". Paper presented in the symposium Managing Asia's Financial Sector Recovery: the Role of Competition Policy and Corporate Governance, organized by ADB Institute and other institutes, in 9–10 Nov. 1998, Singapore.

Pedro, Alba, Stijn Claessens and Simeon Djankov. 1998. "Thailand's Corporate Financing and Governance Structures". World Bank Policy Research Working Paper no. 2003. Washington DC: World Bank.

Prowse, Stephen. 1998. "Corporate Governance: Emerging Issues and Lessons from East Asia". Mimeograph. Washington DC: World Bank.

Sato, Yuri. 1993. "Indonesia ni okeru Kigyo Gurupu no Shoyu to Keiei: Partnership Gata Kigyo Gurupu wo Chushin ni" (Ownership and Management of Business Groups in Indonesia: with Special Attention to Partnership-Type Business Groups). In *Hatten Tojokoku no Bisinesu Gurupu*, edited by K. Koike and T. Hoshino (Business Groups in Developing Countries). Tokyo: Institute of Developing Economies.

———. 2002. "The Case of Indonesia: Headed for Realignment of the Political Economic System". In *Development Strategies Towards the 21ˢᵗ Century*, edited by I. Yamazawa and N. Amakawa. Chiba: IDE-JETRO.

Sato, Yuri. 2003. "Indonesia no Salimu: Seisho, Kongulomaritto, soshite Kaitai e" (Indonesia's Salim: from Cukong to Conglomerate, and Dissolution). In *Azia no Kigyoka* (Entrepreneurs in Asia), edited by I. Iwasaki. Tokyo: Toyo Keizai Shinposha.

————. Forthcoming. "Corporate Ownership – Management in Indonesia: Does It Change and Does It Relate to Performance?". In *Business in the Reformasi Era: New Challenge, Old Problems,* edited by P. van der Eng and C. Basri. Singapore: ISEAS.

Shleifer, Andrei, and Robert W. Vishny. 1986. "Large Shareholders and Corporate Control". *Journal of Political Economy,* 94(3) pp. 461–88.

————. 1997. "A Survey of Corporate Governance". *The Journal of Finance,* 52(2) pp. 737–83.

Suehiro, Akira. 2001. "Family Business Gone Wrong? :Ownership Patterns and Corporate Performance in Thailand". ADB Institute Working Paper no. 19. Tokyo: ADBI.

Sukmawaty, Alexandra, and Jakarta Research Team. 2000. *Indonesian Connections: A Guide to Conglomerates.* Jakarta: PT UBS Warburg Indonesia.

Tirole, Jean. 2001. "Corporate Governance". *Econometrica,* 69(1) pp. 1–35.

World Bank. 1998. *East Asia: The Road to Recovery.* Washington DC: World Bank.

Yayasan Humpuss Group. 1994. *Humpuss Mengabdi Menggali Potensi Membangun Negeri* (Humpuss Serves to Dig Up Potential for Building the Country). Jakarta.

Yeh, Yin-Hua, Tsun-Siou Lee and Tracie Woidtke. 2001. "Family Control and Corporate Governance: Evidence from Taiwan". *International Review of Finance,* 2(1–2), pp. 21–48.

Zhuang, Juzhong, David Edwards, David Webb and Ma.Virginita A.Capulong. 2000. *Corporate Governance and Finance in East Asia: A Study of Indonesia, Republic of Korea, Malaysia, Philippines, and Thailand.* Manila: Asian Development Bank.

Zingales, L. "Corporate Governance". 1998. In *The New Palgrave Dictionary of Economics and the Law,* edited by P. Newman. London: Macmillan, pp. 497–503.

5

Governance Factors in Indonesian Economic Development

Juichi Inada

This chapter comprises four parts: (1) a summary of the importance and limitations of using the concept of 'governance', (2) an overview of the arguments of governance factors in the Indonesian economy; (3) a case study focusing on the changing role of economic bureaucracy in Indonesia through the 1990s; and (4) another case study focusing on the relationship between governance situations and donors' financial support for Indonesia. The final section, the conclusion, is drawn from my two case studies.

1. Importance and Limits of the Concept of 'Governance'

Before moving on to my case studies on the relationship between governance factors and economic performance in Indonesia, I will briefly review the problems and limitations in conducting research on governance.

1.1 The Emergence of the Concept of "Governance"

The definition of governance is still ambiguous and broad; however, it is a very useful concept to recognize non-economic and institutional factors for development.

In the field of development studies, neo-classical economics has been a dominant academic scheme, but it has some limitations in its relevance, because it usually neglects non-economic factors of development. The word 'governance' emerged as a concept to complement such limitations of neo-classical economics. The concept can explain such important non-economic factors as: (1) institutions; (2) public sector management;

(3) political process; and (4) the role of civil society. By using the concept of governance, we can analyse the non-economic factors of development from a multi-disciplinary standpoint.

Besides, the concept of governance matches the pragmatic necessity of the aid community (especially for the World Bank) to focus and analyse such a multidisciplinary agenda of development.

1.2 Development of the Study of 'Governance'

The study of governance has been evolving over the last ten years. The focus of governance study can be categorized into several types.

1.2.1 Identifying Factors of Governance

The most typical work of governance study is to identify what factors are the governance factors that effect the performance of the economies of developing countries.

One typical example is a report by the World Bank (1992). The report documented such factors as accountability, transparency, predictable legal framework, efficiency of the public sector, etc.[1]

Another example is a report of the DAC on governance (1995). The DAC report raised such issues as participation, civil society, human rights, anti-corruption, democratic political system, rule of law, reduction of excessive military expenditure, etc.[2]

1.2.2 Categorization

The next step in governance study is categorization of several factors of governance. Typical categorization of governance factors is to divide them into political (democratic) factors and administrative factors (public sector management).

One example is a JICA study report (1995), which divides governance factors into a "function of governments which relate to participatory development" and "political system of states which look for democratization".[3]

1.2.3 Making a Governance Index

Of the more systematic research on governance is the effort to make a cross-national governance index. Both of leading international organizations on development, the UN and the World Bank, have been making efforts to elaborate their own cross-national data on governance.

The United Nations University (UNU) has been trying to make a "World Governance Survey" (2001),[4] and the World Bank published its report titled "Governance Indicators" in 1999 and 2002.[5] Indicators of both institutions are different from each other, although some indicators overlap.

In making the governance index, they used a great deal of social and economic data, and in some cases, they made qualitative ratings using social surveys and feedback from experts, especially regarding political and social factors which are difficult to make quantitatively measure.

1.2.4 Analysis on Causal Relations

The next step of governance study is to analyse causal relations between governance factor(s) and economic or efficiency-based performance. This is the most challenging area in an academic sense.

There are two types of analysis. One type is a cross-national analyses. The World Bank has made many kinds of regression analyses. One example is the World Bank report titled Assessing Aid (1998),[6] which analysed the relationship between governance factors of the recipients and the effectiveness of donors' aid. Another type are case studies on a specific country, community, or program, etc, analysing how governance factor(s) affect the economic performance or efficiency of the specific case.

Both types have a common methodology: to define certain non-economic institutional factor(s) as "governance" factor(s); to set the governance factor(s) as independent variable(s); to set the socio–economic performance of the target (country, program, community) as dependent variable(s); to analyse the causal relationship between independent variables (governance factors) and dependent variable (performance) or analyse the impacts of the former (governance factors) to the later (performance).

To do so, various methods are possible, for instance, by an econometrical and statistical method, or in a descriptive way, in which historical development and political processes are analysed.

1.3 Limitations of and criticism against those governance analyses

Although governance has become a popular concept to analyse non–economic factors of development, there are some criticisms against the methodology of governance analysis.

One of the typical criticisms is: what kind of governance factors are picked up (among many possible important non–economic factors) as independent variables? Some say that it depends on an analyst's judgment based on the analyst's personal values.

Another typical argument is a criticism against the ambiguity and difficulty of measurement and index–making of governance factors. Some say that the measurement is more or less arbitrally.

Logically speaking, the governance analysis may neglect other important factor(s). Even if a certain governance factor can be proved to have affected the performance, other factor(s) might still be important (or more important), although it is meaningful to prove the impact of one [governance] factor to the performance. It is possible to reduce the risk of simple causation by making a more comprehensive multi-variants regression analysis, but still 'invisible' (which is difficult to identify as index) factor(s) might be very important for instance, 'social capital', 'initial conditions', or 'political environment'.

There is another trap of causation between governance factor(s) and economic performance. Governance factors themselves may have been changing according to socio-economic performance (economic development, social changes, etc.). This means that governance factors specified in the analysis are not independent variables in reality. We need a "dynamic model" which contains a dynamic relationship among many factors, instead of a simple "static causation model". However, a clear dynamic causation model is very difficult to construct in econometrical methods. Therefore, a descriptive analyses and case studies are very useful and important to supplement the limitations of simple causation models. That is the reason that the two case studies in the following sections are analysed in a descriptive way, and using an interdisciplinary (political economy) approach.

2. Some Focal Points of the Arguments on Governance Factors in Indonesian Economic Development

In this section, focus on governance factors in the Indonesian economy. Firstly, I examine the many conventional arguments on the linkage between governance factors and Indonesian economic performance. Although 'performance' can be defined at different levels and meanings, performance means macroeconomic development in general, typically indexed by GDP growth, in my argument.

2.1 Definitions and Items of Governance

After the Asian financial crisis occurred in 1997, the donor community established the 'partnership for Governance Reform' in Indonesia in 2000. The World Bank and UNDP jointly have been supporting governance reforms in Indonesia. The World Bank has focused on five agenda items: (1) justice sector, (2) governing institutions, (3) regional autonomy, (4) civil service, and (5) civil society strengthening.[7] This agenda has become the focal point of recent reforms in Indonesia.

Since then, the term 'governance' became a very popular word in Indonesian domestic politics. 'Governance' is translated into 'Tata

Pemerintahan' in the Indonesia language. However, the word has different meanings depending on who uses the word. The word has a wide range of meanings, covering different agendas, from political system reforms to corporate governance:[8]

(1) political democratization: election reform, reorganization of political parties, and legislative system reform.
(2) reorganization of police and the military: reforms of the two organizations are closely linked in reality.
(3) problems of KKN (corruption, collusion and nepotism: restructuring the system to prevent KKN.
(4) justice system reform: effective legal procedure, strengthening attorneys groups.
(5) decentralization: decentralization of budget, administrative power, and redistribution of administrators to local governments.
(6) financial management: more effective and transparent procurement procedures are required.
(7) corporate governance: effective and transparent corporate management, fair competitive policies.
(8) state-owned enterprises reforms: improvement of accountability and ownership of those companies.

2.2 Governance Index and Rating

As explained in the former section, several aid and research institutions are elaborating upon a cross-national governance index. Each has used various indices: democracy, administrative capacity, transparency of government, corruption, legal system, or property rights as examples.

How does each organization evaluate the degree of governance of Indonesia? Each organization makes its own rating of Indonesian governance.

The United Nations University (UNU) estimates the degree of Indonesian governance as 80% of a possible total in its 2001 publication. UNU rates each item from 1 to 4 (the higher is better). Indonesia is rated as 4.0 in 'freedom of expression' (average 3.3), and 2.0 in 'administrative capacity' (avarage 2.4).[9] The reason for the relatively good rating of 'freedom of expression' is that the rating was made after the outbreak of the economic crisis.

The OECD made a different rating (1997): Looking at the Indonesian governance indicators, the efficiency of the governance structure of Indonesia is rated as 2.25, the degree of corruption is 1.5, the degree of red tape is 2.75, and the efficiency of the legal system is 2.5 [maximum 10, minimum 0].[10] Almost all governance indicators of Indonesia were rated very bad. The reason seems to be the date when those ratings were made.

Table 5.1　Change of Governance Indicators of Indonesia from 1997 to 2002

Accountability	Much Improved
Political stability	Worsened
Government effectiveness	Almost equal
Quality of regulation	Much Worsened
Rule of law	Almost equal
Corruption	Worsened

(economic performance is much worsened)

The World Bank made different ratings in different years in at least two publications in 2002 and 1997. The World Bank rating is from –2.5 to +2.5, with the lower as the worse. The degree of accountability was rated as –0.4 in 2002 (–1.13 in 1997), political stability was –1.56 in 2002 (–1.29 in 1997), effectiveness of government was –0.50 in 2002 (–0.53 in 1997), quality of regulation was –0.43 in 2002 (+0.12 in 1997) rule of law was –0.87 in 2002 (–0.92 in 1997), and corruption was –1.01 in 2002 (–0.80 in 1997).[11]

The changes in figures for each governance indicator from 1997 to 2002 are not simple. Table 5.1 below is a summary of the changes of those indicators. How to estimate the change from 1997 to 2002? Some of the ratings of Indonesian governance have been improved (accountability), some have worsened (political stability, quality of regulation, corruption), and others are almost equal (government effectiveness, rule of law). Is it possible to find any causal relations between those governance factors and economic performance?

In spite of better accountability, economic performance dropped sharply. It seems that 'bad governance' in terms of political stability, corruption and quality of regulation led the Indonesian economy to bad performance. It means that those governance factors are more important to better performance than accountability, at least in the short-term.

2.3 Case Studies

There are case studies focused on Indonesia and categorized into several types.

One categorization is to divide the research into static analysis which analyses the impacts of certain independent variables on dependent variables (performance), and dynamic analysis which analyzes the mutual relationships among many factors (those factors themselves change with time).

Another categorization is to divide them into econometrical or statistical analysis, and descriptive analysis. We can find many descriptive

Table 5.2 Some Examples of Analyses on the Relationship between Governance Factors and Indonesian Economic Performance

	Static analyses	Dynamic analyses
Statistical or econometrical analyses	• WB, *A Diagnostic Study of Corruption in Indonesia*, 2001 (correlation between management measures of system and degree of corruption) • WB, *Indonesia: Country Assistance Strategy 2001–03* (governance factors which influence base-case and high-case of future economic performance)	
Descriptive analyses	• Kuroiwa, *Asian Financial Crisis and Aid Policies*, 2002 (analysis on the economic influence of "rent" in Indonesia) • WB, *Two Approaches from Indonesia*, 1998 (comparative study between WB approach and UNDP approach on the relationship between participation and sustainability of water supply system)	• Sato, *Indonesia in the Era of Democratization*, 2002 (analysis on interrelationship between Indonesian political system, economic system and state-society relation) • MacIntyre, *Business & Politics in Indonesia*, 1991 (analysis on the influence of business groups to economic policy-making using the concept of 'corporatism')

analyses on specific aspects, of the Indonesian economy or governance, but there are very few that argue the relationship between a specific aspect of governance and economic performance as a whole.

Table 5.2 shows some examples of analyses on the relationship between governance factors and Indonesian economic performance, using the categorizations mentioned above.

An example of statistical analysis is the World Bank's research titled 'A Diagnostic Study of Corruption in Indonesia (2001)', which analysed the correlation between management measures of local government systems and the degree of corruption.[12] In the World Bank report *"Indonesia: Country Assistance Strategy 2001-03,"* governance factors are used as important factors which influence base-case and high-case of future Indonesian economic performance.[13]

An example of descriptive analysis is *Asian Financial Crisis and Aid Policies (Ajia Tsuuka Kiki to Enjo Seisaku)* edited by Kuroiwa (2002), which analyzed the economic influence of 'rent-seeking' activities in Indonesia.[14] Another example of descriptive governance analysis is the World Bank report *Two Approaches from Indonesia* (1998), which made a comparative study between World Bank approach and UNDP approach on the relationship between the method of people's participation and sustainability of water supply systems.[15]

We cannot find any dynamic econometrical model, but can find only descriptive analyses on the relationship among some governance factors and economic performance. One example is *Indonesia in the Era of Democratization (Minshuka Jidai No Indonesia)* written by Sato (2002), which analyzed the interrelationship between Indonesian political system, economic system and state-society relations.[16] Another example is *Business & Politics in Indonesia* written by MacIntyre (1991), which analyzed the influence of business groups to economic policy-making using the concept of "corporatism[17]."

2.4 Necessary and Important Works

What is necessary for further progress in the study on governance. I believe that we need (1) accumulation of concrete case studies, then by assembling anecdotal evidences, we can draw generalizations based on those case studies, and (2) analyses on the changes of institutions or society (focusing on the relationship between governance factors and economic-social change). These are not so simple work that the arguments should be descriptive or conceptual instead of econometrical.

First of all, we should recognize the long-term and recent trends of Indonesian economic performance. Figure 5.1 shows the long-term shift of Indonesian GDP growth rate as economic performance. Figure 5.2 shows recent trend of Indonesian GDP growth since 1997.

In pre-crisis era, Indonesian economy showed good economic performance. During the three decades of Soeharto regime, average GDP growth rate was almost 7%, although there were some fluctuations. However, in the crisis era after 1997, Indonesian economy dropped dramatically, and in post-crisis era after 2000 under Megawati regime, Indonesian economy recovered but still stagnated.

There are already many kinds of arguments on the relationship between Indonesian economic crisis after 1997 and governance factors, such as institutionalized corruption and crony capitalism of the Soeharto family. Table 5.3 shows tentative assumptions on the relationship between governance factors and economic development in Indonesia. Focal points are following.

Figure 5.1   Long-term Shift of GDP Growth (Real) of Indonesia (Five-Year Average)

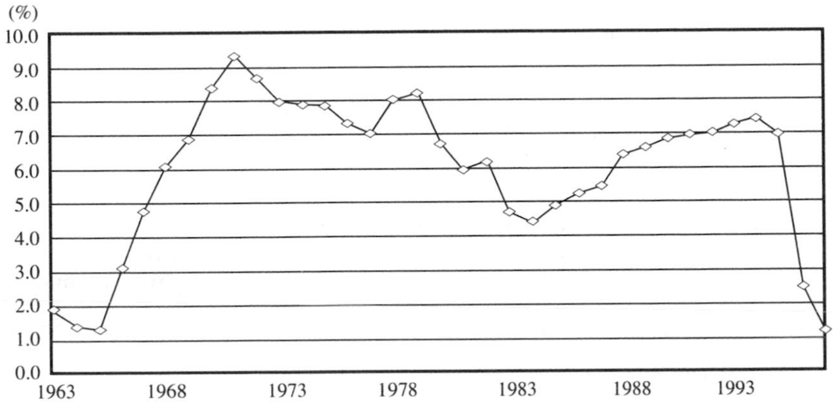

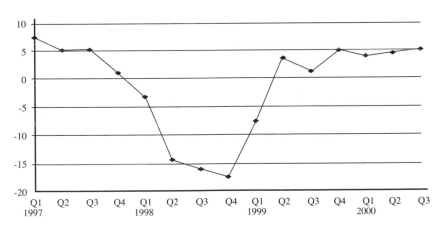

Source: Urata & Kohama, *Sustainable Economic Development in East Asia (Hagashi Ajia no Jizokuteki Keizai Hatten)*, Keisoushobou, 2001, p.38.

Figure 5.2   Recent Trend of GDP Growth of Indonesia

Source: The World Bank, *Indonesia: Country Assistance Strategy FY 2001–2003*, The World Bank, 2001, p.4.

Among many governance factors, which governance factors (have) lead to good economic performance? How is the traditional 'developmental regime' evaluated? What are the very specific governance factors to Indonesia which (have) affect(ed) Indonesian economic performance?

Table 5.3   Tentative Assumptions on the Relationship between Governance Factors and Economic Development in Indonesia

---

(1)   Pre-crisis Era: Economic development after the later half of the 1980s

- governance factors :
  capable economic bureaucrats (Berkeley mafia)- **positive**
  stable political regime- **positive**
  centralized state system (developmental state)- **mixed**

- economic factors:
  increased FDI (especially from Japan)- **positive**
  revenue from natural resources (such as oil)- **mixed or negative**
  economic assistance from abroad (infrastructure building)- **positive (but small?)**

(2)   Crisis Era: Asian Financial Crisis

- governance factors:
  corruption, collusion, nepotism (KKN) - **negative**
  bad corporate governance- **negative**
  lack or failure of financial governance- **negative**
  Soeharto's Autocracy- **mixed**
  limited political freedom- **irrelevant**?
  worsening economic management capability- **negative**

- economic factors:
  dependence on short-term capital from abroad- **negative**
  excessive capital liberalization- **mixed**

(3)   Post-crisis Era: Sustainable development in the future?

- governance factors:
  decentralization- **mixed**
  political reforms and democratization- **mixed**
  legal and legislative system reform- **positive**
  improvement of corporate governance- **positive**
  financial sector reforms- **positive**

There are many hypotheses in this table. I should outline some critical hypotheses regarding the linkage between some governance factors and economic performance. In this argument, performance means macroeconomic growth in general. In this table, 'positive' means the factors which make positive impacts on economic development; 'negative' means those factors which make negative impacts; and 'mixed' means the factors that have both linkages.

Increased FDI (especially from Japan after 1985) and economic assistance from abroad (again mainly from Japan) led to the Indonesian economic growth. It is often said that governance factors such as capable economic bureaucrats (so-called Berkeley Mafia) and stable political regime (of Soeharto) also supported good economic performance.

There are heated debates regarding the causes of the Asian financial crisis. Major Japanese economists argue that excessive dependence on short–term capital from abroad was the main cause of the crisis. On the other hand, such governance factors as KKN (corruption, collusion, nepotism), bad corporate governance, lack or failure of financial control were mentioned as other major causes of the crisis. Some (especially Americans and Europeans) say that Soeharto's autocracy and limited political freedom were other major causes of Indonesian economic and social turmoil, but some criticize such arguments as irrelevant, because those factors have existed for last ten years even in the decades of good economic performance.[18]

In the post-crisis era, those governance factors such as legal and legislative system reforms, improvement of corporate governance, financial sector reforms, political reforms and democratization, and administrative and budgetary decentralization, are regarded as key factors for sustainable development of Indonesia. Almost all agree on the importance of governance factors for future development,[19] but some argue that excessive decentralization and political liberalization might deteriorate the economic performance.

We are still facing many debates on which governance factors are important, which are very positive and which are negative to economic performance. There are some contradictory hypotheses that go against conventional arguments of the international aid community. To get more and better insights on these issues, we need to: (1) analyse the last ten years of experience of the Indonesian economy, and pick up important governance factors, and describe how those factors have affected Indonesian economic performance; and (2) check whether the conclusions can be applicable to the situations of other countries, or whether these are specific factors only to Indonesia, what are the 'universal' important governance factors, and find some lessons for improving governance for development.

I cannot conclude those debates here, but what I can do is to make in–depth case studies focusing on specific issues of governance in Indonesia.

3. Case Study 1: Relationship between Economic Bureaucracy and Economic Performance in Indonesia

In the following section, I will focus on the relationship between capability of economic bureaucracy and economic performance in Indonesia, as one case study. The analytical framework for this case study is as follows:

(1)   To focus on the capability and efficiency of economic bureaucracy of Indonesia as an important governance factor, and analyse the relationship between the change of it and the macroeconomic performance of Indonesia.

(2)   To divide the last ten years into the 'pre-crisis era (before 1997)' 'crisis era (1998–99)' 'post-crisis era (after 2000)', and clarify the differences of the situations of economic bureaucracy and the impacts of the changes on Indonesian economy.

(3)   To analyse the last ten-year experience of the Indonesian economy, and sum up how those factors have affected Indonesian economic performance, and find some lessons for improving governance for Indonesian future development.

In this case study, I propose several concrete questions and identify three crucial factors:

A.   Pre-crisis era: Is it possible to say that a capable economic bureaucracy and liberal macro-economic management were the factors of success in the latter half of 1980s? Focal factors are as follows:

   (1)   appropriate liberal economic management;
   (2)   "Berkeley Mafia" as capable economic technocrats; and
   (3)   relative freedom from political intervention of the President and political parties regarding economic policies.

B.   Crisis Era: Why did the financial crisis occur despite the fact that the "Berkeley Mafia" was still in power? Focal factors are as follows:

   (1)   Failure of economic management
         Hypothesis: Progress of economic liberalization has lead to an increasingly unmanageable area: short–term foreign capital, loss of governance in the financial sector, nepotism between large state-owned companies and core politicians (especially Soeharto family).
   (2)   Decrease of influence of Berkeley Mafia
         Hypothesis: Increasing influence of new technocrats who think much of industrial policy (such as Habibie). Or, loss of coherent economic policies because of unstable political situations.
   (3)   Increasing intervention of the President into economic management.

C.   Post-Crisis Era: What is the situation of the recent economic bureaucracy of Indonesia? What kind of economic bureaucracy is desirable for sustainable growth of the Indonesian economy? Focal points are as follows:

(1) Decrease of power of central government to manage its economy.
(2) Retreat of economic technocrats.
(3) What is the way to reconstruct effective economic management?

3.1 Pre-crisis Era (under Soeharto Regime)

Under the Soeharto regime before the economic crisis, the President had a strong hand in economic policy making. There were three core economic policy decision–making groups in Indonesia, that is, 'technocrats', who had studied economics abroad (most of them received PhDs at UC Berkeley in the U.S. and are usually called the "Berkeley Mafia"), 'technologists' who think much of the governmental supports for industries (headed by Habibie), and the third, "the Soeharto family and rent-seekers".

Technocrats were the core of economic policy decision making. Typical technocrats included Widjojo and Ali Wardhana, and they occupied most of the core positions of economic policy-making (Ministry of Finance, Central Bank, BAPPENAS, Ministry of Economic Coordination, etc.). They adopted liberal economic policies and promoted liberalization of finance, trade and foreign investment. They also tried to be free from political intervention and from domestic political struggles. The president had the ultimate power, but Soeharto had been balancing among the technocrats, technologists and his families, during 1980s (maybe until 1993).

Before the 1990s, basic power structure was technocrats first, technologists next, and the power of the Soeharto family was still not dominant. However, during the 1990s, the power balance had been shifting from technocrats to technologists (after the sixth Soeharto administration in 1993), and next, from those bureaucrats to the Soeharto families (at the final stage of Soeharto regime). Economic policy making began to face more strong political intervention from the Soeharto families, which were deteriorating the efficiency of economic policies.

It cannot be ignored that the power balance between technocrats, technologists and rent-seekers (the Soeharto family) had been changing during the long-lasting regime of Soeharto from 1966 to 1998. Chatib Basri clearly describes the shift of power balance among them from 1966 to 1995.[20] He summarizes the relative power shift among major actors in Table 5.4. He emphasizes the power of rent-seekers, but in my analysis focusing on macro-economic management, technocrats are regarded as a dominant actor.

Table 5.4   The Shift of Roles of Four Major Actors in Policymaking during 1966–1995

	Technocrats	Economic Nationalists	Rent Seekers	Foreign Institutions
1966–72	Strong	Moderate	Strong	Strong
1973–82	Declining	Strong	Strong	Declining
1982–85	Increasing	Declining	Strong	Modest
1985–90	Strong	Declining	Strong	Increasing
1990–95	Declining	Increasing	Strong	Relatively strong

Source: Chatib Basri, "Ideas, Interests and Oil Prices: The Political Economy of Trade Reform during Soeharto's Indonesia," 2003, p.19.

Figure 5.3   Economic Policymaking Structure under Soeharto Regime

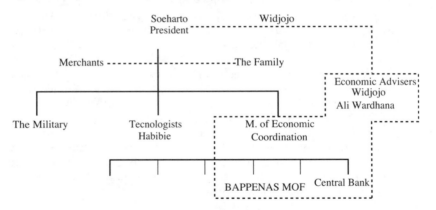

Source: Masaaki Komatsu "Economic Policy-Making Mechanism and Problems of Economic Policy (Keizai Seisaku Kettei Mekanizumu to Keizai Seisaku no Kadai". In *Asian Financial Crisis and Aid Policy (Ajia Tsuuka Kiki to Enjo Seisaku)*, edited by Ikuo Kuroiwa. Institute of Developing Economies, 2002.

Figure 5.3 shows the basic structure of economic policy making under the Soeharto regime in the 1990s. The right-most square shows the technocrats who were at the core of economic policy decisions.

After asking for financial help from the IMF in October 1997, President Soeharto formulated the negotiating team with the IMF, which was known as 'Four Plus Two'. The 'four' were Governor Soedradjad, and Ministers Mar'ie Muhammad, Moerdiono, and Turky Ariwibowo, and the "Two" were economic adviser Professors Widjojo Nitisastro and Ali Wardhana[21]. Most of them were typical technocrats, and adopted the reform policies pushed by the IMF. However, the reform policies faced strong obstacles and the resistance of the Soeharto families and rent-seekers, and could not be implemented.

3.2 Crisis Era (under Habibie and Wahid Regimes)

During the economic crisis, especially under the Habibie regime and the following Wahid regime, the economic policy decision making structure fell into confusion. Some technocrat advisers for economic policy still existed (Widjojo Nitisastro etc.), and they were taking a leading role in the negotiations and cooperation with the IMF and the donor community. However, they didn't have enough power to implement their policy decisions. Political power diffused to many interest groups and political parties, through which many politicians, professors, and NGO leaders began to increase their influence upon many areas of economic policy.

Under the conditions required by the IMF, technocrats must have promoted radical economic reforms, but they had already lost their power, and faced a lot of difficulty coordinating among many actors. The Minister of Economic Coordination also could not coordinate economic policy and sometimes had conflicted with leading politicians and even the Minister of Finance in some cases. BAPPENAS decreased its control over the development budgets, which were decentralized to each of the local provinces, and lost its political and budgetary power. The National Economic Council and National Business Council were established during the Wahid regime, but those councils have not functioned at all as core economic policymaking organs. The Presidents, both Habibie and Wahid, did not provide coherent and strong leadership in making and coordinating economic policies during their regimes.

Thus, Indonesia lost all policy cohesion and credibility of its economic policy decisions, and finally, Indonesia's economy fell into chaos.

Figures 5.4 and 5.5 outline the economic policymaking structure under the Habibie regime and Wahid regime.

The traditional economic team of technocrats (the right-most square of Figure 5.4) still existed (for instance, Widjojo and Ali Wardhana as

Figure 5.4 Economic Policymaking Structure under Habibie Regime

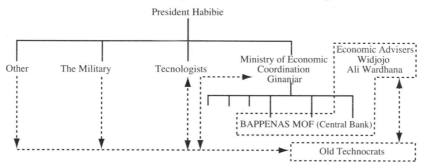

Source: Same as Figure 5.2.

Figure 5.5   Economic Policymaking Structure under Wahid Regime

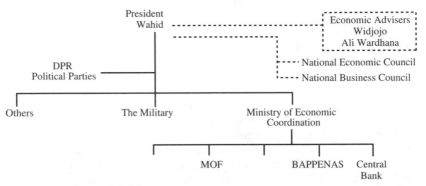

Source: Same as Figures 5.2, 5.3.

economic advisors), but their influence over Indonesian economic policies under Habibie regime had decreased, and the number of such technocrats decreased under the Wahid regime.

Some of the core economic ministerial posts were occupied by people who had different backgrounds. For instance, some were politicians and they were relatively vulnerable to domestic pressures from interest groups. Some capable economists, such as Ginandjar and Boediono, played a key role in negotiations with the IMF and other leading donors, but they were less influential in domestic policymaking, and faced more difficulties in co-ordination among many actors.

3.3 Post-Crisis Era (under Magawati regime)

The Economic policy decision making structure under the Megawati regime has not yet been verified, as there is still some confusion, and still less coordination among the many actors. There are still several traditional technocrat advisers (such as Widjojo), but a different breed of economists and intellectuals (such as Frans Seda, Emile Salim) have emerged as influential economic advisers. Some members of the younger generation also have increased their influence in the core economic policy decision making organs (such as Boediono).

The traditional technocrats, who think much of governmental intervention to industry, seem to have lost their tool in an era of fiscal austerity and budgetary decentralization. On the other hand, inward-looking populist politicians seem to have a greater voice in the trend toward democratization and the increasing power of parliament, and there might be an increased risk of opportunistic pressures for protectionism and governmental interventionism.

Figure 5.6   Economic Policymaking Structure under Megawati Regime

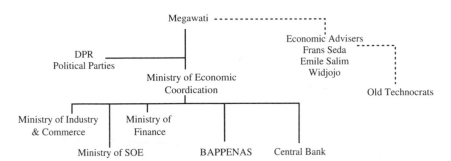

Source: Same as Figures 5.2, 5.3, 5.4.

The decision-making style of new President Megawati is not yet clear and she has shown weak presidential leadership in economic policymaking, depending on economic advisers. There are still many conflicts among many actors. The National Council (DPR) has the right to approve major economic policies, but any single party doesn't have dominant power in it. Figure 5.6 shows an outline of the economic policymaking structure under the Megawati regime.

Old technocrats now seem to have become minor actors in the whole picture. The presidency is weakened, as is the bureaucracy. The power configurations have became more pluralistic and power centres have become vague.

In the case that Indonesia promotes cooperation with the IMF and other donor countries, and make efforts to restructure its economic systems, the Indonesian government must promote consensus building among many domestic actors, including civil society. In such situations, it is a huge task for the new Indonesian government to get a consensus to promote painful reforms.

3.4 Summary of the Arguments

Table 5.5 is a tentative summary of the characteristics of the economic policy decision making system of Indonesia, dividing the stages into three eras. This table sums up the major characteristics of the economic policymaking structure, the core decision makers, and their economic policies and political interventions to them.

In a conclusion, I can say that the effectiveness and the structure economic policy-making are highly related to the economic performance of Indonesia. 'Technocrats-centered decision-making structure with the

Table 5.5   Summary of the Characteristics of Economic Policy Decision-making
            Structure

Era	Major Characteristics	Core Decision Maker(s)	Economic policies / political intervention
Pre-crisis (under Soeharto Regime)	President-centred Balance of some groups (technocrat, technologist, Soeharto family)	President a. Technocrat b. Technologist c. Soeharto family Shift from a/b/c to c/b/a in 1990s.	Technocrats promoted liberal economic policies, tried to be free from political intervention. Increase of political intervention in 1990s.
Under Crisis (under Habibie, Wahid Regimes)	Confusion Some technocrat advisers exist, but no coordination among many actors	Diffusion of power to many interest groups, political parties. Necessity of technocrats for economic reforms, but they lost power.	Co-operation with IMF. Less cohesion, loss of credibility of policies, finally chaos.
Post-crisis (under Megawati Regime)	Confusion and less coordination	Weak Presidential leadership, depending on advisers. Still many conflicts among many actors.	Cooperation with IMF and donor groups, which promote consensus building among many actors (civil society).

appropriate leadership of the President as a power balancer' was one of
the key elements of high economic performance of Indonesia under the
Soeharto regime until the 1990s. The key element has been gradually
lost by the mid-1990s, and completely lost by 1998, at the final stage of
the Soeharto regime. The effectiveness of the economic decision-making
structure has not yet recovered until now.

What is the way to restructure the economic decision-making system
of Indonesia? I expect that there are two key elements.

One will be the revitalization of the economic team, which consists
of senior traditional technocrats and younger new technocrats, and to
improve and strengthen the coordination among those key actors.

Another key factor will be to build a pluralistic political decision-
making structure among many political actors, including many political
parties, pressure groups, and a civil society. The latter has not yet emerged
as functional.

Pluralistic decision-making systems are found in developed countries,
such as Japan, the United States and the European countries. I believe

Indonesia will be shifting gradually to a pluralistic society in accordance with the progress of economic reforms and political liberalization, although it may take some time. I don't know how long it takes to realize the transition, but the international donor community should support transition efforts to achieve the smooth shift of Indonesia to a sound and effective pluralistic society.

4. Case Study 2: Relationship between Governance Situations and the Assistance of Major Donors to Indonesia

The next case study focuses on how the international donor community, especially the IMF and the other two major donors, Japan and the United States (mainly through the IMF/World Bank), responded to the Indonesian crisis, and what relationship we can find between the governance situations of Indonesia and the responses of the donor community.

In the following section, I analyse the political process in detail, especially in the early period of economic crisis.[22] The process can be divided into three stages: (1) the initial stage (under the Soeharto administration) from October 1997 to May 1998; (2) the second stage (under the Habibie administration) from May 1998 to October 1999; and (3) the third stage (under the Wahid administration) from October 1999 to 2001 (until the change of regime to Megawati).

Figure 5.7 shows the change of exchange rate of Indonesian Rupiah in those days, which tells us very clearly the loss of confidence of in the

Figure 5.7   The Change of Exchange Rate of the Indonesian Rupiah

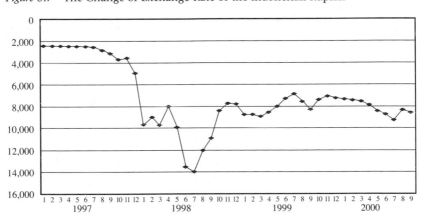

Source: IMF, *International Financial Statistics*.
Note: Rupiah-Dollar rate, spot rate, monthly data

Indonesian economy by the international community during the Asian financial crisis.

4.1 Initial Stage under the Soeharto Regime (from October 1997 to May 1998)

After the Thai financial crisis in the summer of 1997, the pressure to depreciate the Indonesian Rupiah increased, and in October, the Indonesian government requested that the IMF rescue it from its financial difficulties. The decision of the government to call for IMF assistance was based on the recommendation of the economic team of President Soeharto[23]. On 8 October, the IMF and the World Bank pledged to support Indonesia. In November, the IMF, the World Bank and the ADB offered the first line support of US$18 billion, and Japan, the United States and Singapore pledged to offer a second line support of $13 billion to Indonesia. The Japanese offer was for $5 billion, the largest of the bilateral donors, while the U.S. offer was for $3 billion.

In spite of this support program, the Indonesian economic crisis was made worse by the government's failure to sufficiently carry out economic reforms as expected of it by the international community, in addition to the rapid flight of short–term capital of foreign investors as well as speculation of the depreciation of Indonesian Rupiah. Many Japanese companies in Indonesia were forced to stop their production lines in their factories under this economic turmoil.

The FY1998 budget published on 7 January 1998 increased doubts about the government's ability to institute far–reaching reforms.[24] One of the biggest problems of the budget was that expenditures increased 32% over that of the previous year. The reform measures required by the IMF were delayed due to fear by Soeharto and the rent-seekers that instituting reforms would undermine the government's control over the nation.

The rapid monetary flight from the Rupiah occurred, and the IMF very quickly assembled the Second Package of support for Indonesia. The most important feature of this Second IMF package was a major shift in focus to put greater emphasis on structural reforms as the means to restore confidence. After the package was proposed, serious negotiations began regarding the nature of the reforms.

At this time, it was reported that President Soeharto would introduce a Currency Board System (CBS) of monetary management. This made the IMF harden its stance, and the IMF began threatening to suspend its stand-by loan to Indonesia. As disappointment spread rapidly among foreign investors, the Rupiah was sold off on the exchange market, and the Indonesian crisis grew even more serious. The Rupiah declined more than 80% against the U.S. dollar from its level in summer 1997.

The U.S. government was particularly attentive to the Indonesian case, and sent a mission under Deputy Treasury Secretary Lawrence Summers to Jakarta. Defense Secretary William Cohen also visited Indonesia to meet with President Soeharto. The U.S. believed the Indonesian crisis might lead not only to the collapse of the Soeharto regime but also jeopardize the security of the entire Southeast Asia region.[25] President Clinton made a speech saying that the Asian economies must be revitalized because they are vital to American economic and security interests. On the other hand, the United States strongly pushed Soeharto to implement the reforms proposed by the IMF. At that time, the Japanese government also sent its mission to negotiate for additional support to Indonesia, but the mission also found the Indonesian government in extreme confusion and couldn't reach any agreement.[26]

Nevertheless, Soeharto remained in power as president. Soeharto was re-elected in the presidential election on 10 March, and he nominated Bacharuddin Jusuf Habibie as his vice president. At the same time, the donor community began to think that reforms would not be pursued under the Soeharto regime.[27] Technocrats still existed in the economic team, but they seemed to have lost their power.

To prevent the collapse of the Indonesian economy and a loss of confidence in the regime, Japanese Prime Minister Ryutaro Hashimoto visited Indonesia and met President Soeharto on 15 March 1998, requesting that he carry out the agreement with the IMF.[28] This visit illustrated the Japanese intermediary role between the IMF and the Indonesian government, but showed Japanese support for the IMF's conditionality toward Indonesia. The Japanese Ministry of Finance thought the IMF conditionality was necessary to avoid presenting a 'moral hazard' to the recipients, although they did not always have the same stance regarding the IMF prescriptions.[29] Under these pressures, Soeharto accepted the IMF requirements on 21 March, and the Indonesian situation seemed to be easing somewhat.

However, the domestic political situation grew worse. Anti-government rioting broke out when state subsidies were withdrawn and far-reaching price hikes were introduced on gasoline and other commodities, as required by the IMF, (which was now regarded as having proposed the wrong prescriptions). Anger over the price hikes and the collapse of the economy fed popular dissatisfaction with the lack of political freedom in the country. The movements for independence were also intensified in regions such as Ache and East Timor.[30] Pressure to request the resignation of Soeharto increased rapidly both from international donor community and domestic political forces.

The IMF already announced on 6 March that the IMF would not meet to discuss Indonesia before April until changes to the program could be agreed with the new economic team of the in-coming cabinet.[31]

Likewise, the World Bank and ADB (Asian Development Bank) announced that their fast-disbursing adjustment loans had been put on hold.

Faced with widespread domestic rioting and international pressures, President Soeharto was forced to resign in May 1998, and the Habibie administration began to undertake the reform programs.

4.2 Second Stage under the Habibie Regime (from May 1998 to October 1999)

President Habibie tried to tackle economic reforms and show a softer stance with respect to political reforms and the East Timor issue, partly to get support from the international community. He also initiated reforms towards decentralization by signing new laws No.22 and No.25, which defined the transfer of administrative and budgetary authority from the central government to the provinces.

Already in April, the IMF made a change to tranching, which meant that the IMF changed the arrangement to the three disbursements to be released at monthly intervals following satisfactory reviews. In addition, the IMF asked for credible prior action, which took some time before they could be implemented. Therefore, their assistance program was delayed, especially during the period of political turmoil.

As some reforms progressed under the new Habibie regime, the IMF then agreed to the fourth package with Indonesia in June, and the World Bank went ahead with its fast-disbursing assistance in parallel with it. Both institutions offered an additional assistance program for Indonesian economic recovery and structural reforms, and reached a loan agreement with the Indonesian government in July 1998. As the result of that agreement, $6 billion in support ($1.3 billion from the IMF, $1 billion from the World Bank, $1 billion from the ADB, and so on) was pledged.

The IMF, the World Bank and the ADB were basically supportive of Indonesia's new government, but we can find some occasions on which donors suspended their support because of the unstable political situation and lack of governance, even under the new government. For instance, the IMF suspended its financing between June and July of 1998.[32]

Japan was the country most supportive of Indonesia within the donor community, announcing 'the New Miyazawa Initiative' in October 1998 and offering several kinds of assistance to Indonesia. The Export-Import Bank of Japan offered 210 billion Yen in untied loans to Indonesia, through this initiative. Through these efforts from the international donor community, the Indonesian economy seemingly began to show some improvement under the Habibie regime in late 1998 and early 1999.

However, before the general election in June 1999, the political situation deteriorated even further. Since April, there had been heated conflicts between the 'independence faction' and the 'alignment faction' in East Timor. In May, corruption under the Soeharto regime was revealed and widespread rioting broke out, with protestors demanding that Soeharto be prosecuted. On 24 May, the World Bank announced that it would be suspending its financing of $1.1 billion to Indonesia until the end of the general election of June. The IMF made the same decision, and the Japanese government followed these policies.

As the result of the general election held on 7 June, the ruling party Gorukar lost its majority. On 18 June, the vice president of the IMF, Stanley Fisher, met the leaders of five opposition parties, confirmed their commitment to furthering reform efforts in Indonesia, and announced the continuation of IMF support to Indonesia. On 26–27 July, the Consultative Group in Indonesia (CGI) met in Paris. Donors pledged $5.86 billion in assistance to Indonesia, and Japan offered $1.67 billion, nearly one-third of the total. In August, the Paris Club (a lender countries group) agreed to reschedule $2.6 billion of loans to Indonesia.

However, this assistance from the international donor community was suspended after the 'Bali Bank corruption' was revealed. The IMF and the World Bank temporarily suspended their loans until the investigation over the unclear flows of money was complete and concrete measures to prevent a recurrence of such corruption announced. The Japanese government took the same stance as the IMF/World Bank.

Under such pressure and criticism from the international community, the Indonesian government began to investigate corruption under the Soeharto regime,[33] and also accepted the sending of a PKO from the UN to East Timor; the National Council (the supreme decision-making institution in Indonesia) then agreed on 6 October to grant East Timor its independence (this was officially decided on 19 October). In addition, the National Council passed a no-confidence resolution toward Habibie, and decided to hold an election for a new president.

4.3 Third Stage under the Wahid Regime (from October 1999)

On 10 October, Abdurrahman Wahid became the new president by election in the National Council, and he nominated Megawati Soekarnoputri as the vice-president. Wahid showed a willingness to reveal the corruption under the Soeharto regime and to promote political reforms. The international donor community welcomed these political changes and resumed their assistance to Indonesia.

United States President Clinton met Wahid in Washington DC on 13 November, and pledged to continue U.S. assistance to Indonesia. Japanese Prime Minister Obuchi met Wahid in Tokyo on 16 November, and he announced his positive support for assistance to Indonesia. Obuchi visited Jakarta on 27 November, and pledged further assistance from Japan.

The IMF agreed on an additional memorandum (for the implementation of a loan) with the Indonesian government on 23 November. On 9 December, the ADB announced an additional $1–1.5 billion in assistance for medium-sized enterprises in Indonesia, and on 20 January 2000, U.S. Secretary of Treasury Summers visited Jakarta and announced that the United States would continue assistance to Indonesia mainly through international institutions (the IMF/World Bank).

On 25 January, Japan exchanged a note for a 7.19 million yen loan to Indonesia. In February, the CGI (Consulting Group in Indonesia) meeting was held in Jakarta, and donors pledged to offer $4.7 billion of assistance for fiscal year 2000, of which Japan had offered $1.56 billion. In April, the Paris Club approved the rescheduling of official debt amounting to $5.8 billion. The IMF decided to offer a $5 billion three-year loan in February, signed the memorandum in May, and approved another $372 million loan for economic reform assistance.

This story in this paper was over in early 2000. Through the year 2000, the international donor community showed a very clear stance of supporting Indonesian reforms. In 2001, the Wahid regime came to an end and Megawati became a new president, who has been receiving more support from international donor community. Another detailed study would be conducted in the next stage of research.

4.4 Policy Implications

Although my analysis on the process of political and social changes of Indonesia and responses of the donor community ends in 2000 in the early stage of the Wahid regime, by examining the political process and the relationship between donor assistance and the governance situations in Indonesia, we can draw the following conclusions.

First of all, the offering of loans by the IMF and the World Bank was highly linked, in reality, with political issues such as the democratization process and East Timor. The periods during which the IMF and the World Bank suspended their loans were: (1) the period of turmoil at the last stage of the Soeharto administration (from February to April 1998); (2) the period just before the general election under the Habibie administration (from May to June 1999); and (3) the period of turmoil in East Timor and just before the presidential election at the last stage of the Habibie administration (from August 1999 to January 2000).

It can be said that those suspensions of loans were in response to circumstances that made sound economic management impossible, such as political turmoil, corruption and rent-seeking activities. However, those aid suspensions, based on chaotic economic management and the lack of governance served, in fact, as a veto of the legitimacy of the regime facing those political problems.

On the other hand, economic reforms, worsening economic circumstances, and political instability are in fact interrelated.

For instance, in the period from Feburuary to March 1998, Soeharto resisted the reforms requested by the IMF because he wanted to protect his political power base and the interests of his family's companies. The IMF suspension of loans during that period led to a loss of confidence in the Indonesian economy, and worsened the economic situation. Under those circumstances, Soeharto lost political support from the public, and in the end he was compelled to resign.

In the period from August to October 1999, the political turmoil in East Timor and criticism against the corruption of the Soeharto family led to political instability of Habibie regime, and at the same time, a rapid drop in the Indonesian currency. The suspension of loans by the IMF and the World Bank at that time was the final blow to the Habibie administration, and finally Habibie gave up his presidency.

Some have criticized such 'de facto interference' in Indonesian politics by the IMF and the World Bank. On the other hand, if the IMF and the World Bank continued their assistance in spite of the delay of reforms and domestic political turmoil in Indonesia, the assistance would be regarded as political support for the regime, which would constitute another kind of 'de facto interference' in domestic politics. Therefore, it can be said that the IMF and the World Bank had no other choice but to suspend their assistance.

The Japanese government's stance was almost parallel with the policy of the IMF and the World Bank in a practical sense, and was regarded as a passive reaction to political changes and bad governance in Indonesia. In contrast to Japan's stance, the U.S. government seemed to think much more of democratic changes and political reforms in its policy toward Indonesia.[34] We can distinguish between the 'active support' and the 'passive response' to political changes in Indonesia. It can be said that the U.S. policy was an active support, and that the Japanese stance was a passive reaction. In that sense, the difference between Japan's stance and that of the U.S. is relatively clear.

It seems that the economic recovery and political stability of Indonesia were the most important factors in Japanese policy toward Indonesia, and tried to attain those objectives. Japanese aid officials and experts realized how much important the political stability and the effective economic management were for sustainable economic development, through the whole process of the economic crisis of Indonesia.

However, worsening governance situations of Indonesia were almost unmanageable to major donors including Japan. As seen in section 3 of this paper, economic policy-making structure of Indonesia had been gradually losing its effectiveness in mid-1990s, and rapidly been collapsed at the final stage of the Soeharto regime. I believe that the collapse of Indonesian economic management system was not strongly influenced by the responses of outside donor community, but it was an indigenous social movement of Indonesia, although the hard stance of the IMF and the U.S. to the Soeharto regime may have given a final blow to the regime at the final stage of its collapse.

5. Conclusion

In this chapter, firstly, I argued that the concept of 'governance' is very useful for understanding non-economic and institutional factors of economic development, but I also argue that it has some limitations in conducting empirical study. Cross-national regression analyses using econometrical or statistical method are very popular especially among the experts of international organizations such as the World Bank or UN, but those analyses do not always prove causal relations between governance factors and economic performance, especially when we argue the case of specific single country.

In focusing on the Indonesian economy, there are already many kinds of arguments on how governance factors relate to Indonesian economic performance, especially after the outbreak of Asian financial crisis in 1997, but a number of questions remain to be answered.

Is it a dynamic or static argument that governance factors affect the country's economic performance? Is it true that governance factors such as accountability, participation or decentralization have positive impacts to economic performance? Those factors might have negative impacts on economic growth, at least in a short-term. Over what period of time does the positive impact occur? To attain better performance, specific governance factors or elements among many governance factors may be more significant than others, and what are they? Is it possible to apply the proved relationship between certain governance factor and economic performance in one country to other countries? These questions require further verifications.

In this chapter, I didn't answer these questions. Instead, I picked two issues as case studies. One was to analyse the effectiveness of the economic policymaking structure of Indonesia, dividing a decade of 1990s into three eras of pre-crisis, in-crisis and post-crisis. One of the conclusions is that the effective economic policy decision structure has been the key element which have affected Indonesian economic performance in last decade. Capable technocrats, appropriate presidential leadership as power balancers, and consensus-building among many actors are important elements of the effectiveness.

Another case study analyzes the relationship between governance situations and the assistance of major donors to Indonesia during the era of the Asian economic crisis. Major donors, especially the World Bank, IMF and Japan, strongly supported Indonesian economy in response to the Asian economic crisis, but there were occasions of suspension of loans by those donors. I showed that the major reasons for loan suspension were such governance factors as political turmoil, corruption or loss of confidence of economic policies.

I argued that donors' loan suspension worsened the governance situation even more, but on the other hand, donors' policies were basically 'passive responses' to the worsened governance situations. Donors might have had better policies to improve the situations, but I argued that the loss of effective economic management and final collapse of Indonesian regime were the results of indigenous social movements of Indonesia. In any case, I believe this case study shows the importance of political stability and effective economic management as key elements for sustainable economic development among many governance factors.

I also believe that my findings could be applicable to many other developing countries, but we still need to accumulate more lessons from other case studies on other countries, and to examine in detail the factors which affect the effective economic management and 'good governance.'

I hope this chapter and the book as a whole will spur further in-depth studies on the topic of governance in Asia.

Notes

[1]   The World Bank, *Governance and Development*, The World Bank, 1992.

[2]   OECD/DAC, *Orientations on Participatory Development and Good Governance*, OECD (Paris), 1995.

[3]   JICA, *Participatory Development and Good Governance (Sanka Gata Kaihatsu to Yoi Touchi)*, JICA (Tokyo), 1995.

[4]   United Nations University, *World Governance Survey*, UNU (Tokyo)2001.

[5]   Daniel Kaufman, Aart Kraay, Pablo Zoido-Lobaton, *Governance Matters*, Policy Research Working Paper 2196, The World Bank, 1999. &, *Governance Matters II*, Policy Research Working Paper 2772, The World Bank, 2002.

[6]   The World Bank, *Assessing Aid: What Works, What Doesn't, and Why*, The World Bank (Washington DC), 1998.

[7]   Indonesian Brief, *Partnership to Support Governance Reform in Indonesia*, The World Bank (Jakarta), 2000.2.12.

[8]   Based on the hearing to BAPPENAS (February 17, 2000).

[9] UNU, *World Governance Indicators*, UNU (Tokyo), 2001.

[10] Pranab Bardhan (OECD/DAC), *The Role of Governance in Economic Development: A Political Economy Approach*, OECD (Paris), 1997.

[11] The World Bank, *Governance Matters*, 1997, & *Governance Matters II*, 2002.

[12] The World Bank, *A Diagnostic Study of Corruption in Indonesia*, The World Bank (Jakarta), 2001.

[13] The World Bank, *Indonesia: Country Assistance Strategy 2001–03*, The World Bank (Jakarta), 2001.

[14] Ikuo Kroiwa (ed.), *Asian Financial Crisis and Aid Policies (Ajia Tsuuka Kiki to Enjo Seisaku)*, Institute of Developing Economies (Tokyo), 2002.

[15] The World Bank, *Two Approaches from Indonesia*, The World Bank (Jakarta), 1998.

[16] Yuri Sato (ed.), *Indonesia in the Era of Democratization (Minshuka Jidai No Indonesia)*, Institute of Developing Economies (Tokyo), 2002.

[17] Andrew MacIntyre, *Business & Politics in Indonesia*, Allen & Unwin (Sydney), 1991.

[18] See, Ross H. Mcleod, "Soeharto Indonesia: A Better Class of Corruption," *The Indonesian Quarterly*, Vol.XXVIII/2000, No.1.

[19] As an example, Jusuf Wanandi, "Good Governance, Domestic and Regional Stability: Agenda for the Future", *The Indonesian Quarterly*, Vol.XXVI/1998, No.2.

[20] In the paper of Chatib Basri, he categorizes major actors of Indonesian trade policy into 'the technocrats', 'economic nationalists', 'interest groups and rent-seekers', and 'foreign influences'. In my categorization, 'economic nationalists' means 'technologists'. 'Foreign influences'are analysed as an external actor in section 4. Chatib Basri, "Ideas, Interests and Oil Proces: The Polotical Economy of Trade Reform during Soeharto's Indonesia", *World Economy*, 2003 (forthcoming).

[21] Lloyd R. Kenward, *From the Trenches: The First Year of Indonesia's Crisis of 1997/98 As Seen From the World Bank's Office in Jakarta*, Center for Strategic and International Studies (Jakarta), 2002, p. 43.

[22] To get the chronology of policies of the IMF, World Bank and Japan in response to the Indonesian economic crisis, I used the following books and reports. Lloyd R. Kenward, *From the Trenches: The First Year of Indonesia's Crisis of 1997/98 As Seen From the World Bank's Office in Jakarta*, Center for Strategic and International Studies (Jakarta), 2002. JICA, *Report of the Fourth Country Assistance Study on Indonesia*, JICA

(Tokyo), November 2000. Yuri Sato (ed.), *Indonesia Shiryoshu (Documents on Indonesia)*, Institute of Developing Economies (Chiba), 2002. IMF, *IMF-Sopported Programs in Indonesia, Korea, and Thailand: A Preliminary Assessment*, IMF, 1999.

[23] Lloyd R. Kenward, *op.cit.* p. 42.

[24] It is reported that the relationship between Soeharto and the technocrat group of economic ministers and advisors was being heavily strained during this period. (Hadi Soestro & Chatib Basri, "Survey of Recent Developments," *Bulletin of Indonesian Economic Studies*, 34, No.1, 1998.)

[25] Regarding to the US policy toward the Indonesian crisis, see next. John Bresnan, "The United States, the IMF, and the Indonesian Financial Crisis," in Adam Schwarz and Jonathan Paris (eds.), *The Politics of Post-Suharto Indonesia*, Council on Foreign Relations, 1999.

[26] Interview with the official of Japanese MoF (October 2001).

[27] Takashi Shiraishi, *Houkai Indonesia wa Dokoeiku* (Where is Collapsed Indonesia Going), NTT Shuppan, 1999, p. 75.

[28] *Yomiuri Shinbun*, 16 March 1998.

[29] Speech of Eisuke Sakakibara (Ministry of Finance) in Tokyo (Seminar at Tokyo Institute of Technology), 11 July 1998, and interviews with some officials of Ministry of Foreign Affairs, Japanese delegate to the World Bank, and U.S. Treasury official (24 March 1998, 27 March 1998).

[30] The political situations in this period is well described in the next. Takashi Shiraishi, *Houkai Indonesia wa Dokoeiku (Where are Collapsed Indonesia going?)*, NTT Shuppan, 1999, pp. 80–102.

[31] Lloyd R. Kenward, *op. cit.* p. 82.

[32] Lawrence J. Mcquillan and Peter C. Montgomery (eds.), *The International Monetary Fund: Financial Medic to the World*, Hoover Institution Press, 1999, p. 171.

[33] Regarding to the corruptions under Suharto regime, see next. Yoshitaka Murai, *Suharto Family no Chikuzai (Money Seeking of Soeharto Family)*, Commons, 1999.

[34] For instance, see next. Robert B. Zoellick and Philip D. Zelikow (eds.), *America and the East Asian Crisis: Memos to the President*, W.W. Norton & Company, 2000, pp. 58–59.

6

In Search of Endogenous Elements of Good Governance: The Case of the Eastern Seaboard Development Plan in Thailand

Yasutami Shimomura

Part 1: Economic Development and Good Governance Revisited — Attempt at an Alternative View

1. Introduction

The purpose of this chapter is to reconsider the relationship between economic development and good governance and cast light on various aspects that the postulates of mainstream idea have failed to take into account. A consensus is shared broadly among scholars and policymakers about the crucial role of good governance in achieving sustainable development. World leaders have repeatedly asserted in their statements that good governance is an indispensable element for economic development, together with democracy and basic human rights. World Bank President James Wolfensohn has also stressed that "good and clean government" and "an effective legal and justice system" constitute basic prerequisites for sustainable growth and poverty alleviation in his proposed Comprehensive Development Framework.

As a matter of fact, this is a rather new trend. Olav Stokke argues, "It was not until the end of the 1980s that these [political conditionality] issues were brought to the fore of the foreign aid agenda" (Stokke 1995, p. 21).

While the notion of a strong relationship between economic development and good governance is well established, how good (or bad) governance leads to the good (or bad) performance of developing economies and vice versa has not yet been fully analyzed. The aim of this chapter is to argue that the mainstream approach does not pay due attention to some crucial aspects of the relationship between governance and development and to propose an alternative view with an analytical framework for the purpose of improving the "state of the art". In addition, in the second part, the proposed idea is to be applied to a case in Thailand as a kind of "test run".

2. Mainstream Ideas: A Critical Review

2.1 Comprehensiveness of the definition of good governance

Joan Nelson and Stephanie Eglinton point out that there are two definitions of good governance: broad and narrow (Nelson and Eglinton 1993, p. 15). The broad definition, which is adopted by the Organization for Economic Cooperation and Development, stresses democracy as an element of good governance. This is in contrast to the World Bank's narrow definition, focusing on "lack of accountability, transparency, and predictability on the part of politicians and bureaucrats, and the absence of the rule of law". The World Bank (and the International Monetary Fund to a certain extent) does not *explicitly* deal with democracy due to the "non-political vision" of the Bretton Woods system. However, according to Nelson and Eglinton, they tend to *implicitly* assume a specific political regime, namely parliamentary democracy, as a basis of good governance (Nelson and Eglinton 1993, p. 15).

Reviewing the arguments in the international aid community, this chapter adopts the following as the standard definition of good governance:

a) Pluralist democracy: The World Bank and the IMF do not *explicitly* regard this as a component of good governance.
b) Accountability, transparency, predictability, and openness in the manner of exercising power.
c) Rule of law.
d) Effective and efficient public sector management.
e) Prevention of corruption.
f) Prevention of excessive military expenditures.

Apparently this is highly comprehensive and includes everything concerned. Such an encyclopedic definition may have some strength, but it is a handicap as an analytical tool. We will deal with this point in 2.3.

2.2 Explaining high development performance by good governance: the mainstream view

2.2.1 Research testing the mainstream postulate

A lot of research has been conducted in the attempt to show the relationship between development performance and governance. Most of them have been made through regression analysis between macroeconomic figures and governance indicators; the results are at most mixed.

There is a huge amount of literature dealing with the relationship between democracy and development. Many, such as Yi Feng (1997) and Lebrang (1997), claim a strong positive relationship between the two. There are others who do not support that conclusion.

The comprehensive literature survey conducted by Adam Prezworski and Fernando Limongi gives insights toward an overall evaluation of these research findings. According to them, many attempts have been made to find theoretical explanations of the causal relationship between political regime and economic growth. However, none of the quantitative analysis conducted so far has produced any definite conclusion on the relationship between the two variables (Prezworski and Limongi 1993, pp. 51–69; Shimomura 1999, p. 65). A recent work done by the United Nations Development Program shows that there is no automatic link between democracy and human development (UNDP 2002, p. 60).

Beatrice Weder made a comprehensive study of the relationship between five institutional performance indicators (public–private cooperation, bureaucracy, rule of law, corruption, political system and stability) and growth of per capita gross domestic product, respectively. She found that property rights and the rule of law are important for economic performance, but there is only weak support for the proposition that a high level of corruption reduces growth (Weder 1999, pp. 61–62).

A recent World Bank study claims a strong relationship between accountability and the infant mortality rate on the one hand and between rule of law and the level of per capita income on the other (Kaufman et al. 2000, p. 12). However, it is not necessarily advisable to assume that the infant mortality rate and per capita income are indicators of development performance. Unlike the economic growth rate or export growth rate, the infant mortality rate and per capita income are rather reflective of the results of past development attempts.

These empirical studies show at most mixed results. Under the current state of the art, it is not easy to find sufficient evidence of a "causal" relationship between good governance and economic development. This chapter is going to propose an alternative approach in an attempt to overcome the shortcomings of the prevailing approach.

2.2.2 Weakness of the prevailing analytical framework

In order to grasp a clear picture of the causal link between governance and development performance, we need to consider and overcome the weakness of the mainstream approach.

First of all, it is to be emphasized that most analyses deal with a large number of samples, including the United States, Sweden, Papua New Guinea, and Sierra Leone. This means that the mainstream concept of good governance assumes "universality" without paying due attention to the stage of development. In other words, they try to explain sustainable development in such emerging markets as Singapore and Korea as well as sub-Saharan Africa within a single framework. This is not realistic and inevitably limits the applicability, as our real world is highly diversified.

There is a broad consensus among investors and aid officials that getting things done in East Asia is much easier than in sub-Saharan Africa. However, various governance indices do not necessarily show distinct differences between these two regions, particularly when we compare Indonesia/China with Ghana/Kenya (Table 6.1). These indices may be biased against East Asia. If these reflect the reality correctly, it suggests that standard conditions of good governance are not able to fully explain the regional differences between East Asia and sub-Saharan Africa. Paying due attention to endogenous factors, which do not appear in the standard list of good governance, could lead to insights into understanding the reason.

Moreover, the mainstream idea primarily focuses attention on two cases: "better development performance with better governance" and "disappointing development performance with deficiency in governance" (Figure 6.1). Because of this rather simplistic approach,

Table 6.1 Governance Indicators of Selected Countries of East Asia and Sub-Saharan Africa

	Freedom*	Voice and Accountability**	Government Effectiveness***	Corruption****
Thailand	3.3	0.22	0.01	3.2
Indonesia	7.5	−1.13	−0.53	1.9
Malaysia	4.5	−0.09	0.71	4.9
China	7.7	−1.29	0.02	3.5
Ghana	3.3	−0.43	−0.29	3.9
Kenya	6.6	−0.70	−0.90	1.9
Botswana	2.2	0.78	0.22	6.4
Mauritius	1.2	1.01	0.17	4.5

* the lower the freer (1997–98), ** the higher the better (1997–98), *** the higher the better (1997–98), **** the higher the less corrupt (2002)
Sources: * Freedom House, *Freedom in the World Country Ratings 1972–73 to 2001–2002*, ** Kaufmann, D. and Kraay, A. *Growth Without Governance*, World Bank, 2002, *** ibid. **** Transparency International, *Transparency International Corruption Perceptions Index 2002*

Figure 6.1   Governance and Development: Realistic Cases

Mainstream Case	Case 1
High development performance with good governance	High development performance with deficiency in governance
Case 2	**Mainstream Case**
Disappointing development performance with good governance	Disappointing development performance with deficiency in governance

two important and interesting cases in our real world have seldom been examined in detail. These are the following cases:

- Case 1: High development performance despite notable deficiency in governance
- Case 2: Disappointing development performance despite good governance

To get an insight into the causal effects between governance and development, it is essential to include these cases in the analytical framework. Without including these cases, the picture of the world we actually live in is incomplete. Case 1 is particularly important when we consider the experiences of East Asian economies, where persistent growth has been recorded for several decades, while relatively low governance scores have been given by international society (again see Table 6.1).

3. Proposal of an Alternative View: Exploring a Realistic Theory of Governance and Development

Our purpose is to propose a more realistic picture of the function of governance on development by including such variables as stages of development, endogenous elements of good governance, and the above-mentioned two cases. At least we can expect a deeper insight through this attempt.

3.1 Proposal of two hypotheses

For this purpose, we propose the following two hypotheses for further investigation:

Hypothesis 1: What is really required for a developing country to achieve high development performance is to meet a set of crucial governance conditions rather than meeting all (or most) of good governance conditions simultaneously. The crucial conditions to be met are different from one country to another, depending on the development stage. The required conditions might be narrower and less complicated when a developing economy is to initiate its sustained growth. The required conditions are supposed to get broader and more complicated at a higher level of development stage, particularly when a country reaches the level of an emerging market.

It is supposed that a rather limited number of governance conditions were required when Thailand started on its path of sustained growth around 1960, but the requirements became much heavier and more complicated for Thailand to maintain its position as an emerging market in the late 1990s.

Hypothesis 2: While the standard list of good governance conditions proposed by the international aid community claims a universal characteristic, it is not able to explain the reality of Case 1 (or Case 2). Paying due attention to the unique social, economic, cultural, and political features of each socio-economy is expected to cast light on this issue. The purpose is to discover some elements that contribute to strengthening governance, supplementing the standard elements of good governance. These could be labelled as "endogenous good governance elements". Needless to say, these are different from one society to another.

3.2 Proposed Analytical Framework

How can these hypotheses, which are expected to be crucial for understanding the function of good governance on realizing sustainable economic development, be verified?

What is crucial is accumulating a large number of empirical studies, in particular case studies, of success stories as well as disastrous failures in order (i) to identify crucial governance conditions in a specific country in a specific period, or (ii) to identify endogenous elements that are the determinants of high development performance in a specific society in a specific time.

It is expected that we can draw policy implications from individual in-depth case studies. The accumulation of lessons and policy implications could hint at a set of new postulates or a more general picture of the relationship between governance and development.

Having proposed an alternative view and analytical framework, this chapter is going to illustrate how this approach could work. In Part 2, we are going to focus our attention on the second hypothesis, i.e., endogenous good governance elements. To test this hypothesis, the case of the Eastern Seaboard Development Plan, which was a controversial gigantic regional development plan in Thailand in the mid-1980s, is to be studied.

Part 2: The Case of the Eastern Seaboard Development Plan in Thailand

1. A Short History of the Eastern Seaboard Development Plan

1.1 The Mission of the Plan

The Eastern Seaboard Development Plan was a gigantic regional development plan in the southeast of Bangkok. It was composed of two industrial complexes and a wide variety of infrastructures, including two deep seaports. The Laem Chabang was an industrial complex for export-oriented and labour-intensive industries, and the Map Ta Put was basically a heavy and chemical industrial complex based on natural gas reserves in the Gulf of Thailand. The basic idea of the plan was formulated in the late 1970s, and a master plan was completed in 1982.

The task was to tackle two basic problems of the Thai economy. First, one of the central agenda items of the Fourth and Fifth Five-Year Plan, 1977–81 and 1982–86, respectively, was to transform the industrial structure and the composition of leading export goods from agriculture to manufacturing. This had been a long-standing issue, but it became acute with the collapse of primary goods prices in the international commodity market after the two oil crises. Faced with a sharp decline in terms of trade, the Thai government accelerated the promotion of export-oriented industries and utilization of domestic energy resources in an attempt to save foreign reserves and improve the international balance of payments. Owing to the evolution of labour-intensive light industries (garments, apparel, accessories, sport shoes, travel kits, etc.), the share of industry in GDP surpassed that of agriculture, and the share of primary goods (rice, maize, tapioca, rubber, tin, etc.) in exports as a whole persistently declined from two-thirds in 1970 to a half in 1980 and further to one-third in 1985. The Thai government was keen to further accelerate this tendency.

Second, improving the living standard in rural areas had been a central issue since the Third Five-Year Plan (1972–76). In this regard, the Thai government was concerned about the concentration of business activities in the Bangkok Metropolitan area, as this caused widening regional discrepancies and environmental degradation, such as traffic jams and air and water pollution. The discovery of natural gas reserves in the Gulf of Thailand in 1973 led to the idea to construct industrial complexes in the Eastern Seaboard as a means of achieving the decentralization of industrial production and improving the living standard in the rural area.

1.2 Evolution of the Plan

In December 1980 a committee was established under the chairmanship of General Prem Tinsulanonda, who became Prime Minister in March 1980; this committee was reorganized into the Eastern Seaboard Development Committee (ESDC) in June 1981. In March 1981, a report outlining the industrialization strategy in the region (the Anat Report) was submitted to the committee. The Eastern Seaboard Development Plan was adopted in the Fifth Five-Year Plan (1982–86) in October 1981.

Before the launch of the Eastern Seaboard Development Plan in the late 1970s, the Thai government requested the World Bank to finance the plan. The World Bank financed the master plan of Coopers & Lybrand Associates jointly with the British government. When the result was submitted to the Thai government in July 1982, however, the World Bank recommended utilization of the existing Sattahip Port, which is a naval port near the proposed location of Map Ta Put deep seaport, taking into consideration the heavy fiscal burden. According to the master plan, the estimated total investment amount was $4.5 billion (1981 prices).

On the other hand, the Japanese government, the largest donor in Thailand, was very active in its support for the plan. During his visit to Thailand, Prime Minister Zenko Suzuki expressed his willingness to support the plan in January 1981, and in May of that year, Dr. Saburo Okita, former foreign minister, who visited Thailand as the leader of a government mission, initiated a discussion on technical and financial assistance for the Eastern Seaboard Development Plan. Based on Okita's recommendation, the Japan International Cooperation Agency (JICA) of the Japanese government started a feasibility study for Map Ta Pud deep seaport, which was faced with various technical problems, such as strong waves and silting.

In November 1982, the National Fertilizer Corporation Limited (NFC) was established, with equity investment by the International Finance Corporation (IFC) of the World Bank group. The purpose was to construct an integrated fertilizer complex, located near Rayong on the Eastern Seaboard, based on natural gas supplies from the Gulf of Thailand. The Japanese government assured financial assistance to NFC. In October 1985, the Thai government signed loan agreements with the Overseas Economic Cooperation Fund of Japan (OECF) on the construction of major projects, such as Laem Chabang Industrial Complex, Map Ta Put Port, and Map Ta Put Industrial Complex.

1.3 Setback for the Plan and its Background

1.3.1 Movement to Review the Plan

On 13 November 1985, the Thai cabinet approved a surprise resolution to freeze all the Eastern Seaboard Development Plan for 45 days and assigned three ministers to review the whole programme. According to *The Nation*, a Thai newspaper, this was strongly recommended by Dr. Snoh Unakl, who was Secretary-General of the National Economic and Social Development Board and one of the most prominent economists in Thailand in those days, in a note to the Prime Minister dated 1 November 1985 (*The Nation*, 21 November 1985). It was reported that he wrote this letter after being shocked by a Ministry of Finance report on the serious prospects of external debt and stressed the urgent need for regaining fiscal and monetary stability through a belt tightening policy (*The Nation*, 22 November 1985).

This movement was called a "coup by the conservative group", which had tried hard to slow down the implementation of big projects from the viewpoint of fiscal discipline. In order to understand the background further, it is necessary to review the macroeconomic situation in those days.

1.3.2 Macroeconomic Background

While the Thai economy had shown persistent growth for a long time since the late 1950s, it suffered from macroeconomic imbalances under an unfavourable international environment in the first half of 1980s (two oil shocks, stagflation in developed economies, a sharp rise in international interest rates, and a slump in primary goods prices on the international market). As Table 6.2 shows, the investments-savings gap was between 5% and 6%, and the fiscal deficit was around 4%–5% of GDP. In 1983, the current account deficit reached 7.2% of GDP. The largest concern was the rising debt service ratio (from 17% in 1980 to 26% in 1985). There were fears that Thailand could become "another Philippines".

Table 6.2   Macroeconomic Indicators of Thailand in the Early 1980s

(%)

	1980	1981	1982	1983	1984	1985
Economic growth rate	5.8	6.3	4.1	5.8	6.2	4.0
S-I gap	–4.2	–4.1	–2.1	–5.0	–5.8	–4.8
Fiscal deficit/GDP	n.a.	3.2	5.8	4.1	3.8	5.1
Current account deficit/GDP	6.2	7.1	2.7	7.2	5.0	4.0
Export growth rate	23.2	7.0	–1.0	–7.7	16.3	–4.4
Terms of trade	100	87	79	85	84	77
Debt service ratio	17.3	17.4	18.9	22.9	24.8	26.1
Change in consumer price	19.7	12.7	5.2	3.8	0.9	3.3 (Jan–Sep)

Source: World Bank (1986)
Note: 1985 figures are provisional.

In an attempt to overcome the difficulties, the Thai government received the World Bank's Structural Adjustment Loan in June 1983 and adopted austerity measures. It also introduced currency depreciation in 1981 and 1984. While Thailand was highly evaluated afterwards as one of five "top performers" of structural adjustment by the World Bank (World Bank 1990, p. 20), pessimistic views were dominant in the mid-1980s. Under this gloomy perspective, the Thai government diminished the size of external borrowing from $1.6 billion in 1984 to $1 billion in 1985. Such gloomy perspectives inevitably had adverse effects on the Eastern Seaboard Development Plan.

In those days, the potential effect of the Plaza Accord, which was signed in September 1985, was not recognized. The World Bank's country economic report of 1986 does not refer to either the possibility or symptoms of rising foreign investment due to the Plaza Accord.

1.3.3 World Bank Factor

The committee in charge of reviewing the Eastern Seaboard Development Plan comprised three ministers. Suli Mahasandana, the minister attached to the Prime Minister's Office, was Prime Minister Prem's right-hand man and main trouble-shooter. He was a classmate of Prem's around 50 years earlier at a middle school for the sons of lower-ranking public servants (Warren 1997, pp. 25–38); Prem's father was a junior prison officer in Songkla, Southern Thailand. Meechai Ruchupan, another minister attached to the Prime Minister's Office, was a lawyer, and Suthee Singhasaneh, deputy finance minister, was an economic technocrat who had been the head of the Budget Department of the Prime Minister's Office.

While they were beginning the work, it was revealed by Bangkok-based newspapers that the World Bank Bangkok Office had been behind Dr. Snoh when he took the initiative of implementing a review. According to *The Nation*, Mr. Quill Hermans, chief of the World Bank Regional Mission in Bangkok, had sent a letter dated 6 November 1985, to Dr. Snoh. In that letter, Mr. Hermans had suggested that the Thai government eliminate two deep seaport projects (Map Ta Put and Laem Chabang) from the sixth development plan (1986–90) and use Sattahip and Klong Toey (Bangkok) ports as alternatives, in an attempt to cut fiscal expenditures (*The Nation*, 28 November and 2 December 1985). The essential features of this proposal were repeated in a more moderate manner in Chapter 6 of the World Bank's *Country Economic Report*, which was published around seven months later (World Bank 1986, pp. 132–38).

The World Bank report of 1986 claimed "the combined economic rate of return of the (NFC) fertilizer plant and the port (as presently envisaged) is expected to be very low". As the World Bank took the position that the feasibility of the NFC fertilizer plant was acceptable (World Bank 1986, p. 136), this meant that the returns of the two port projects were regarded as very low.

1.4 Outcome of the Review

The Thai cabinet approved the report of the three-minister committee on 24 December 1985. According to a press release, the main points were as follows:

a)   The implementation of the National Fertilizer Project and Map Ta Put Port were approved. While there was no specific condition for NFC, it was stipulated that the implementation of Map Ta Put should be committed only after the signing of a loan agreement on NFC with the Japanese government (NFC was to be constructed in Map Ta Put Industrial Complex).

b)   The implementation of the other projects, including Laem Chabang Port, was postponed for the reason that "conducting the implementation at this moment is not appropriate".

It was made clear that the basic structure of the Eastern Seaboard Development Plan was to be maintained. In other words, the World Bank's proposal to substitute the two deep seaports by existing ports was turned down. When we study the press release carefully, however, it is clear that the implementation of the whole plan was completely postponed. To recognize the intention of the cabinet, we should analyze the following point: Why was NFC, which was the most controversial project in the whole plan, approved without any condition, while implementation of Laem Chabang Port, which was quite promising because of its export-oriented feature, was postponed?

In those days, there was a broad consensus in Bangkok that the economic and political feasibility of NFC was the lowest among all the projects; we will come back to this point later. To introduce a linkage between NFC and Map Ta Put Port was to halt the implementation of the latter. On the other hand, the cabinet did not claim any major shortcomings of Laem Chabang Port and simply declared the postponement without giving any specific reason. Obviously, postponing the whole plan was the central message of the cabinet decision.

1.5 What Occurred after the Cabinet Decision?

Here we will review the fate of the three major components of the Eastern Seaboard Development Plan after the cabinet decision of December 1985.

1.5.1 Laem Chabang Port and Industrial Complex

The Plaza Accord of September 1985 caused a dramatic appreciation of the Yen and fundamental changes in the fate of Laem Chabang.

As shown in Table 6.3, the value of the Yen against the US dollar, which was \249 per dollar at the end of June 1985, rose to \154 at the end of September 1986. Under these circumstances, Japanese manufacturers began to look for alternative plant sites abroad, and they found Thailand and Malaysia to be the most suitable among developing countries. The tidal wave of direct investment from Japan became visible toward the end of 1986, when the Board of Investment of Thailand announced that direct investment from Japan in the first half had increased by around 50% (*JETRO Daily*, 7 February 1989). Stimulated by this movement, investors from Taiwan, Hong Kong, and Korea also began to increase sharply their direct investment in Thailand. Most of this direct investment from East Asia was export-oriented and basically labour-intensive.

As a result of this big wave of direct investment, a lot of new factories were constructed, inevitably leading to serious bottlenecks in infrastructure, such as port facilities, roads, power, telecommunications, and industrial estates. The shortage of port facilities at Klong Toey (Bangkok) was particularly apparent. The volume of containers handled at Klong Toey increased by 20% annually in 1986 and after and exceeded the port capacity in 1988 (*JETRO Daily*, 23 July 1988).

Faced with these serious bottlenecks, the Thai cabinet instructed the Eastern Seaboard Development Committee to resume Laem Chabang Port project on 15 October 1986 (*The Nation*, 16 October 1986).

Table 6.3 Exchange Rate Changes After the Plaza Accord

		Yen per US dollar	Baht per US dollar	Yen per Baht
1985	June	249.0	25.6	9.1
	September	217.0	27.4	8.3
	December	200.5	26.3	7.5
1986	March	179.6	26.7	6.8
	June	165.0	26.5	5.9
	September	153.6	26.3	5.9
	December	159.1	26.1	6.1
1987	March	145.8	26.1	5.6
	June	147.0	25.9	5.7
	September	146.4	25.8	5.7
	December	123.5	25.1	4.9

Source: IMF *International Financial Statistics*, various issues

1.5.2 Map Ta Put Port and Industrial Complex

In comparison with Laem Chabang, the progress at Map Ta Put was not remarkable, mainly because Thai leaders linked this port with NFC, while NFC suffered from various difficulties (see Section 1.5.3). In September 1986, Dr. Snoh of the NESDB told Dr. Okita, leader of a Japanese government delegation, that the necessity of Map Ta Put fully depended on the progress of NFC (*The Nation*, 19 September 1986).

In February 1987, however, Dr. Savit Phothivihok, who was the Secretary-General of the Eastern Seaboard Development Committee and architect of implementation, announced the resumption of international bidding for Map Ta Put Industrial Estate with the reason that the construction of National Petrochemical Corporation (NPC) was in progress (*The Nation*, 28 February 1987).

This announcement could have been a symptom of evolving changes. Finally in January 1988, three years after the cabinet decision, the government officially cancelled the freezing of Map Ta Put Port and Industrial Complex; these projects were completely revived.

1.5.3 National Fertilizer Corporation (NFC)

In the meantime, the NFC fertilizer project had been the subject of much controversy. While its background was highly complicated and sensitive, the following two elements were particularly crucial.

First, most of the leading figures of the Thai private sector were reluctant to cooperate, although the Thai private sector was expected to own more than 30% of the total share amount. It is to be noted that the Bangkok Bank group, the largest business conglomerate in Thailand in those days, had a subsidiary company dominating the business of imported fertilizer distribution. In other words, NFC could threaten the Bangkok Bank group.[1]

Second, and more importantly, the prospect of the return on equity (ROE) or investment (ROI) was quite uncertain. From the beginning, it was recognized that profitability would be highly sensitive to volatile fertilizer prices (IFC 1986, pp. 11–12). In addition, the sharp Yen appreciation after the Plaza Accord damaged the project, because an international bidding had already been made in July 1984, and the bid amounts of two successful Japanese bidders were stated in Yen. It is to be noted that the Baht remarkably depreciated against the Yen (Table 6.3), because of the de facto pegging to the US dollar; the Baht was officially pegged to a currency basket in those days.

The retirement of Finance Minister Sommai Hoontarakool, who had tried hard to realize the NFC project, turned the tide.[2] The Eastern Seaboard Development Committee announced that the NFC was not an issue of the government but of the private sector (*The Nation*, 16 October

1986). In other words, the government washed its hands of the NFC business.

In spite of persistent support by the World Bank and the Japanese government, the NFC project was postponed for a long time and faded away.

2. Assessment of the Positions of the Three Major Players: the Thai Government, World Bank, and Japanese Government

In this section, we will assess the decision made by the Thai government on the management of this gigantic development plan, which was also an important macroeconomic management issue, in comparison with the positions of the World Bank and the Japanese government. The purpose is to cast light on the institutional capacity of the Thai government in those days.

2.1 Structure of the problem

Figure 6.2 illustrates the essential features of the problem that the Thai government faced in the mid-1980s. The government had to make a decision whether (i) to drastically cut the budget for the plan; or (ii) to implement the plan in accordance with the original schedule.

We should pay due attention here to the fact that the prospects of the external environment were highly uncertain in those days. Like other

Figure 6.2 Choices the Thai Government Faced in 1985

	Economic stagnation (Probability?)	Recovery of growth (Probability?)
Execute ESDP as planned (Alternative 1)	Increase in fiscal burden and external borrowings (the second Philippines)	Realization of internationally competitive industrial area Increase in FDI Modernization of economic structure
Postpone the implementation of ESDP (Alternative 2)	Reduction in fiscal burden and external borrowing	Deteriorating bottleneck of infrastructure Deterioration of living, and environmental conditions in Bangkok Deterioration of investment environment

developing countries, Thailand was severely hit by deteriorating terms of trade, declining export volume due to stagflation in developed economies, and rising interest rates on the international capital market. In 1985 particularly, Thailand experienced a huge balance of payment deficit equivalent to 17% of GDP. In view of this disappointment, it was understandable that most Thai policymakers and businessmen were pessimistic, and the World Bank was also very cautious (World Bank 1986, Chapter 2).

Theoretically there were two possibilities regarding the external environment. In the case of an adverse environment, huge fiscal expenditure could lead to unsustainable fiscal and external conditions. The drastic postponement of the Eastern Seaboard Development Plan could be the answer to cope with such risks. On the other hand, in the scenario of an improving external environment, the conservative fiscal policy could worsen the infrastructure bottlenecks and undermine investors' confidence. Constructing modern industrial complexes with deep seaports and strengthening the competitiveness of the Thai economy could be the answer to overcome such problems.

Reflecting its cautious view on the prospects of the Thai economy, the World Bank recommended eliminating two ports from the budget

Table 6.4 Simulation on the Profitability of NFC (US$ million)

	Revenue	Profit before tax	New investment	Investment after depreciation
1987			15.8	
1988			202.3	
1989			410.0	
1990			154.8	
1991	170.6	−33.2	42.5	787.9
1992	183.6	−33.4		750.4
1993	162.7	−676.6		712.9
1994	263.6	36.0		675.4
1995	316.3	91.4		637.9
1996	265.9	43.6		600.4
1997	149.0	−70.6		675.4

Profit before tax (average): −4.8
Investment after depreciation (average): 675.4
POI = (−4.8/675.4) × 100 = −0.71%
Notes: Start of construction: 1987
       Start of commercial production: 1991
       Based on the assumption of F/S except exchange rate and fertilizer price

Table 6.5 Trends of Foreign Exchange Rate and International
Fertilizer Price

(US dollar)

	Yen per US dollar (average)	International price of urea fertilizer*
1987	144.6	100
1988	128.2	132
1989	138.0	88
1990	144.8	158
1991	134.7	152
1992	126.7	145
1993	111.2	115
1994	102.2	187
1995	94.1	225
1996	108.8	189
1997	121.0	106

Sources: Economic Planning Agency of Japan, *ERTECON*
* End of year, bulk, per ton

(see Section 1.3.3). On the other hand, the Japanese government stressed
the importance of enhancing competitiveness from a long-term viewpoint
and recommended the implementation of the Eastern Seaboard
Development Plan. There were a lot of disputes in Thailand, too.

2.2 National Fertilizer Corporation

There was a distinction between the Thai government and the main
donors, i.e., the World Bank and the Japanese government, on the NFC
issue. As we saw, the project was never realized despite the commitment
of equity investment (12% of total share capital) by the International
Finance Corporation of the World Bank group and the Japanese
government's financial assistance through a Yen loan by the Overseas
Economic Cooperation Fund.

In order to assess the decision by the Thai government, a counterfactual
analysis of the rate of return on this controversial project was made in
accordance with the assumption of the feasibility study: green light in
October 1986, starting construction in 1987, commercial production in
1991. The profitability of this fertilizer plant depended on two external
factors, i.e., the exchange rate and world fertilizer prices. Table 6.4 above
shows the results of simulation using the actual figures of the exchange
rate and international price of urea fertilizer (Table 6.5 above).

If the government had given the green light in October 1986, NFC
would suffer a negative rate of return on investment (ROI), due to the
Yen's appreciation and volatile fertilizer prices. Although it is to be

admitted that this simulation is based on various conditions, what this result suggests is the low profitability of the NFC project. In other words, the position of the Thai government was more advisable than that of the World Bank and the Japanese government.

2.3 Construction of Two Ports

2.3.1 Laem Chabang

It had been already confirmed that Thailand suffered heavily from a shortage of port facilities in the late 1980s, especially in the Bangkok Metropolitan area. It is apparent, therefore, that if the World Bank's suggestion to utilize Klong Toey instead of Laem Chabang had been adopted, the results could have been far more disastrous. However, one could argue that this was simply due to the Plaza Accord and the following high wave of foreign investment, which was unpredictable and occurred by chance. As a matter of fact, the necessity of a new port was recognized even before the effects of the Plaza Accord became visible.

The volume of containers handled at the Klong Toey port increased persistently at a rate of 16%–17% annually during the first half of the 1980s, in spite of the stagnant economic situation. A think tank report forecast that even under the conservative estimate of 12% growth rate, the Klong Toey port could suffer from a shortage of container yard capacity (*Far Eastern Economic Review*, 30 October 1986). It is to be stressed that this forecast was made in 1985, at a time of highly pessimistic prospects for the Thai economy. Taking into account the structural deficiency of Klong Toey as a river port (lack of space and limit of depth due to siltation), the Laem Chabang port was indispensable even without the Plaza Accord effects.

2.3.2 Map Ta Put

The central issue of dispute between the World Bank and the Thai government was whether the Sattahip port could take over the function of the Map Ta Put. Utilizing Satttahip as an alternative does not seem to have been a feasible idea, considering the fundamental feature of Sattahip. As it was a naval base, access was limited, and there was not enough space for widening the route connecting it with petrochemical plants to be located around the Map Ta Put area, such as National Petrochemical Corporation (NPC) and Thai Petrochemical Industry (TPE). Accordingly, there was a broad consensus in Bangkok that Sattahip could not be a realistic alternative from a technical viewpoint.[3]

Due to the acceleration of economic growth (in 1986: 9.5%, in 1987: 13.3%) and a sharp increase in foreign direct investment, the number of plants operating at the Map Ta Put industrial estate increased from 14 in

Table 6.6 Trends of Fiscal Balance and Debt Indicator
(%)

	Fiscal balance/GDP	Debt service/export
1986	–4.2	25.4
1987	–2.2	17.1
1988	0.7	13.7
1989	2.9	1.4
1990	4.6	9.8

Sources: Economic Planning Agency of Japan; Warr, P. and Bhanupong N. (1996) *Thailand's Macroeconomic Miracle: Stable Adjustment and Sustained Growth*, Kuala Lumpur, Oxford University Press

1991 to 48 in 1998; most of them were petrochemical plants. In addition, many companies constructed plants in private industrial estates in the Map Ta Put area. While the World Bank claimed "the needs of the fertilizer plant are the major justification for the port" (World Bank 1986, p. 137), there were much wider needs for an industrial estate in this region. This implies that the concept of "general cargo port" envisaged by the Thai government was more realistic than the World Bank's "port for the NFC fertilizer plant" concept.

Our conclusion is that the position taken by the Thai government was more supportable than that of the World Bank.

2.3.3 Balance Sheet of Postponement

Advocates of postponement of the Eastern Seaboard Development Plan emphasized the merits of diminishing fiscal deficit and external debt. However, the scale of these effects was exaggerated.

The World Bank (World Bank 1986, p. 135) claimed that the planned budget appropriation for Laem Chabang and Map Ta Put was 15.1 billion Baht in total in the fiscal years of 1987 and 1988, equal to 7%–8% of total public investment and 20% of external borrowing. Eliminating this fiscal expenditure could contribute to fiscal reconstruction, according to the World Bank. However, this argument did not properly reflect the actual magnitude of public expenditure.

As most of this amount was financed through official development assistance (ODA) loans, the actual fiscal burden for the Thai government could be minimized. Also, the effect on the capital account was to emerge 10 years later only when principal repayment would begin after a grace period. The arguments in those days tended to focus on the nominal figures. As a matter of fact, the fiscal deficit turned into a big surplus and the debt service ratio dramatically declined during the late 1980s (Table 6.6 above).

On the other hand, the postponement was accompanied by the huge cost of infrastructure bottlenecks, which could have been reduced if Laem Cahabang port had been completed in 1990 according to the original schedule; the actual completion was at the end of 1991. The overloaded Klong Toey, together with serious road congestion in the Bangkok Metropolitan area and sky-rocketing real estate prices, could have been reduced by the introduction of Laem Chabang facilities on time.

When this balance sheet is reviewed, the costs of postponement apparently exceeded the benefits. From this viewpoint, it is difficult to support the position of the Thai government.

However, we should take into consideration the fact that economic prospects in the mid-1980s were very uncertain, as was already reviewed. In other words, the decision maker, Prime Minister Prem, was not able to have sufficient information about probability distribution between two cases: adverse or improving. This was also a highly sensitive political issue, because of bitter disputes among policymakers, economists, businessmen, and major donors. Under the circumstances, it was advisable as well as realistic for him to adopt *minimax regret criteria*: minimizing the cost of the worst case. The result was (i) maintaining the fundamental structure of the whole blueprint; (ii) postponing the implementation; and (iii) flexible change of course in response to the change in environment. This was a course between the positions of the World Bank and the Japanese government.

3. Conclusion and Policy Implication

We have found that the Thai government showed good performance in the management of the gigantic Eastern Seaboard Development Plan through its advisable and realistic response to challenges. It is notable that its position was sometimes not in accordance with the intentions of influential donors, such as the World Bank and the Japanese government. The case of the Eastern Seaboard Development Plan is important as it casts light on ownership and institutional capacity, which could have a crucial role in the high development performance of the Thai economy. The task of this final section is to analyze what kind of elements contributed to the achievements of the Thai government in the mid-1980s, and what kind of endogenous elements are found.

Four aspects are considered to be crucial.

3.1 Checks and Balances *á la Thai*

In the mid-1980s there were five influential groups in Thailand: the army, political parties, technocrats, the business community, and the mass media. It is worthwhile pointing out that it was a multipolar system, and checks and balances among the participants functioned well. We will illustrate representative cases.

There was no doubt that the army was most powerful, but unlike in previous decades, it was not overwhelming, particularly when other actors made up their mind to work together in a coalition. For example, in 1984 the Bank of Thailand depreciated the Baht in spite of strong objections by General Arthit Kamlang-ek, Commander-in-Chief of the army, who was concerned about exchange losses. The bank was able to make this move owing to strong support from Prime Minister Prem, technocrats, and leading business figures.

Although Prime Minister Prem was a former Commander-in-Chief of the army, he did not necessary behave in line with the army's interests. As a result, the relationship between Prem and General Arthit, his successor, was strained. This was an important background factor of the abortive *coup d'etat* in September 1985 by the army, and perhaps the above-mentioned currency depreciation in 1984. After the retirement of General Arthit, the political pressure by the army appeared to decline. But Prem had to watch carefully the movements of the army, as he had already retired and could not directly control the military machine.

In Thailand, no single party acquired a majority in congress until very recently. In those days too, many small parties were in rivalry with each other, and it was not possible to choose their leaders as Prime Minister. Under such circumstances, a coalition of five parties agreed to choose Prem, who did not have a seat in the congress. While political parties were not so influential, it was recognized that any party could threaten the coalition, hinting at the end of co-operation. In order to secure the stability of his administration, Prem had to be careful about his relations with the bosses of political parties to prevent their veto. Moreover, complicated rivalry relations were found among technocrats, economists, and business leaders.

It was argued that such delicate checks and balances *a la Thai* could be a serious handicap for strong leadership to drastically modernize the socioeconomic system. Perhaps that was a correct observation. However, the case of the Eastern Seaboard Development Plan shows that the checks and balances *á la Thai* enabled a thorough scrutiny of crucial policy agenda.

Many developed countries have introduced the separation of the three powers, i.e., administration, legislation, and judiciary, for the purpose of functional checks and balances. While Thailand in the mid-1980s had not fully established such a separation, it had an alternative and endogenous system, which led to advisable responses to the challenges of the Eastern Seaboard Development Plan.

3.2 Transparency and Openness in the Policymaking Process through the Role of the Mass Media

This section refers to a lot of newspaper articles of those days. Needless to say, it is very unique to see detailed inside information on public expenditure issues in developing countries. Apparently, most of these newspaper articles were based on "leaks" from high-ranking officials. A typical case was the Hermans Note submitted to Dr. Snoh that triggered the movement to revise the Eastern Seaboard Development Plan.

It is to be admitted that many newspaper articles were not correct (certainly this is not unique to Thailand) and were used as tools of manipulation by each camp. For example, the contents of the Hermans Note were leaked to the press in an attempt to prevent the campaign of the belt-tightening policy camp. Nevertheless, many articles did contribute to transparency and openness, as details of the policymaking process were made known to the public. It is to be pointed out that leaks were usual in Thailand in those days. Despite a wide variety of negative effects, at least it effectively prevented "back-door decision making" by political bosses and barons, which are common in developing (as well as developed) countries. Richard Doner and Anek Laothamatas argue that one of the unique features of the Prem administration was that it allowed a free press (Doner and Laothamatas 1994, p. 412). We would like to emphasize this characteristic as an element of good governance under the Prem regime.

3.3. Technocrats with Certain Competence are Insulated from Pressure Groups

The World Bank report on *The East Asian Miracle* stressed the importance of "technocratic insulation" in East Asia (World Bank 1993, pp.167–174). Perhaps Thailand in the mid-1980s was a representative case of "economic technocrats with a minimum of lobbying for special favours from political and interest group".

The tradition of independent bureaucracy has a source in the pre-modern Siam court. This tradition was strengthened by Field Marshal Sarit Thanarat when he became Prime Minister through a *coup d'etat* in 1958 and delegated power over macroeconomic management to a group of young elites trained abroad; the leader of that group was Puey Ungphakorn, governor of the central bank (Siamwalla 1997, pp. 6–9). A lot of young technocrats were appointed to posts in four organizations — the Ministry of Finance, the National Economic and Social Development Board, the Bank of Thailand, and the Budget Department of the Prime Minister's Office — which have formed the core of Thai technocracy since then. Dr. Snoh Unakle and Mr. Sommai Hoontrakool, who played important roles in the policymaking on the Eastern Seaboard

Development Plan, were among them. They had been promoted to leading technocrats and were regarded as experienced and well-balanced policymakers.

As shown in the case of currency depreciation in 1984, Thai technocrats were effectively insulated from pressure groups, such as the army and political parties, under Prem's "umbrella". Reflecting such insulation, the disputes on the Eastern Seaboard Development Plan were basically among technocrats, and the roles of politicians and generals were limited. This implies that disputes were made with a certain degree of rationality. This is considered to have been an important factor leading to a well- balanced policymaking process.

3.4 Role of Experienced "Balancer"

Prime Minister Prem was born in 1920. He was one year older than Soeharto, three years older than Lee Kuan Yew, and five years older than Mahathir Mohamad. Like these Southeast Asian leaders who belong to the same generation, he was a leader of a developmental state.[4]

As he stated in his farewell address of August 1988, Prem attempted to claim the legitimacy of his contribution not through political or diplomatic achievements but through economic development, more specifically poverty reduction among the rural people (Warren 1997, pp. 18–20). In order to attain this goal, he delegated the power of macroeconomic management to experienced technocrats and protected them from pressure groups. These are typical characteristics of developmental state leaders. Unlike the other three Southeast Asian leaders of the same generation, and unlike Sarit, his great mentor, however, Prem was not a man of charisma but an experienced "balancer". According to Doner and Anek, Prem skillfully played the army and political parties against each other and allowed free elections and a free press while he was outside congress (Donar and Laothamatas 1994, pp. 411–13, 427–29).

Prem functioned effectively as a balancer throughout the Eastern Seaboard Development Plan disputes. One former high-ranking official of NESDB recalled the Prime Minister's patience in listening to different opinions. In his view, such patience finally led to a well-balanced judgment and reasonable solution in the end.[5]

The experiences of the Eastern Seaboard Development Plan show the fact that various aspects that were unique to Thailand in those days played important roles in securing an advisable decision. This implies the importance of paying due attention to the endogenous elements of good governance that might be embedded in every developing society. This is the lesson we can draw from the saga of the Eastern Seaboard Development Plan.

Notes

[1] Interview with Dr. Ammar Siamwalla of Thai Development Research Institute on 10 November 1998. Also *Nihon Keizai Shimbun*, 8 September 1987.

[2] Interview with Mr. Manas Leevirapan, former director, Fiscal Policy Office, Finance Ministry, on 10 November 1998.

[3] Interview with Mr. Paisal Sricharatchanya, editor of *the Bangkok Post*, on 4 November 1998, and also Paisal Sricharatchaya "At last beginning, Bangkok finally commits to ESB Projects", *Far Eastern Economic Review*, 30 October 1986.

[4] A developmental state is a kind of authoritarian regime. Unlike ordinary authoritarian regimes, a developmental state (a) stresses economic growth and poverty reduction as the central policy agenda items and the measure of sustaining legitimacy; and (b) delegate power of macroeconomic management to technocrats.

[5] Interview with Dr. Bunyaraks Ninsananda, former director, Overall Planning Division, NESDB, on 3 November 1998.

References

Doner, R. and Laothamatas, A. 1994. "Thailand: Economic and Political Gradualism". In *Voting for Reform Democracy, Political Liberalization, and Economic Adjustment*, edited by S. Haggard and S. Webb. Oxford: Oxford University.

Feng, Yi. "Democracy, Political Stability and Economic Growth". 1997. *British Journal of Political Science*, no. 2.

IFC. 1986. *Proposed Investment in National Fertilizer Corporation Limited Thailand.*

Kaufman, D., A. Kraay, and P. Zoido-Lobatan. 2000. "Governance Matters From Measurement to Action". *Finance and Development*, Vol. 37, no. 2.

Lebrang, D. "Political Democracy and Economic Growth: Pooled Cross-Sectional and Time-Series Evidence". 1997. *British Journal of Political Science*, Vol. 27.

Nelson, J. and S. Eglinton. 1993. *Global Goals, Contentious Means: Issue of Multiple Aid Conditionality*. Washington D.C.: Overseas Development Council.

Prezworski, A. and F. Limongi. 1993. "Political Regimes and Economic Growth". *Journal of Economic Perspectives*, Vol. 7, no. 3.

Shimomura, Y. "Governance, Economic Development, and Aid: In Pursuit of Functional Policies". 1999. *OECF Journal of Development Assistance*, Vol. 5, no. 1.

Siamwalla, A. 1997. "The Thai Economy: Fifty Years of Expansion". In TDRI Collected Papers, *Thailand's Boom and Bust*. Bangkok: Thailand Development Research Institute.

Stokke, O. 1995. "Aid and Political Conditionality: Core Issues and State of the Art". In *Aid and Political Conditionality*, edited by O. Stokke. London: Frank Cass.

UNDP. 2002. *Human Development Report 2002: Deepening democracy in a fragmented world*. Oxford: Oxford University Press.

Warren, W. 1997. *Prem Tinsulanonda: Soldier & Statesman*. Bangkok: M.L. Tridosyuth Devakul.

Weder, B. 1999. *Model, Myth, or Miracle?* Tokyo: United Nations University Pres.

World Bank. 1986. *Thailand: Growth with Stability: A Challenge for the Sixth Plan Period: A Country Economic Report*. Washington D.C.: The World Bank, Volume I.

————. 1990. *Adjustment Lending Policies for Sustainable Growth*. Washington D.C.: The World Bank.

————. 1993. *The East Asian Miracle: Economic Growth and Public Policy*. Oxford: Oxford University Press.

7

Health Sector Management and Governance in Thailand

Kyoko Kuwajima

1. Introduction

1.1 Decentralization in Developing Countries

It is estimated that more than 80% of developing countries have been experiencing some form of decentralization in recent years (Manor 1999, viii). This trend has become more intense since the 1980s when decentralization was mostly motivated by political concerns.[1] It should be noted, on the other hand, that decentralization in the developing world is not "simply happening" as the World Bank has depicted[2] but has mainly been encouraged by conditionality attached to development assistance. During the last decade, administrative decentralization has become one of the major instruments in public sector reform programmes supported by major donors to improve inefficient, ineffective and non-accountable public sector performance.

Among countries that have articulated decentralization policies, Thailand has been demonstrating a unique development in their actual application. As in neighbouring countries, the decentralization that took place in Thailand in the late 1990s was the result of a political movement calling for more pluralistic governance structures at local levels. Segmented and duplicate public responsibilities have also been addressed in discussions about rearranging tasks among different levels of governments. The situation, however, was not as pressing as in Indonesia where the government recognized the threat to national integrity and had to take decisive measures for local accommodation, on the one hand.[3] Public distrust in and grievances about government functions were not as strong as in the Philippines on the other hand.[4] IMF loans have been encouraging fiscal decentralization of the recipient countries and Thailand was not an exception especially when she sought financial assistance from the IMF at the start of the currency crisis in 1997. Nevertheless, it was certainly Thailand's own decision to stipulate a new constitution in 1997 delineating a clear orientation toward decentralization.

Despite the legal and institutional settings articulated in the Decentralization Act in 1999, decentralization in Thailand has not progressed as drastically and sweepingly as in Indonesia and the Philippines. While the decentralization policy has seen some resistance from central ministries as illustrated in the later sections, the picture in Thailand is not as simple as the mere suspension of decentralization. In the Thai public sector, for example, the health sector clearly addresses its adherence to competitiveness, local initiatives, efficiency, and quality of services in its health plan.[5] The health sector apparently is pursuing another form of "decentralization" by transferring more freedom in decision making to the provincial and district levels.[6] It seems that Thailand has chosen a realistic but gradual approach to improving public management in the context of its long history of a parallel government system with well-experienced local administration by the field units of central government and the immature local would-be autonomous entities, which absolutely lack in management and technical skills.

In the following section, the trend of decentralization in the developing world will be overviewed especially in terms of donor interventions in improving governance and reforming public sector performance. Section 2 will analyze the specific features of the administrative structure, historical development and significance of the decentralization policy in Thailand. Then Section 3 will examine the problems of the health sector in the 1990s and investigate the reform initiatives of the Ministry of Public Health, giving special attention to the "Universal Coverage" policy enforced by the Thaksin administration, which exerts considerable influence on the health care management system at local levels. Section 3 will include an illustration of the case in Khon Kaen Province to see the actual picture and consequences in the field. Section 4 will highlight the major findings and the implications of decentralization and governance issues in developing countries.

1.2 Decentralization and Governance

As mentioned in the previous section, decentralization in the developing world was often motivated by political concerns especially in the 1980s when democratization movements were flourishing worldwide. In the political dimension, decentralization is considered as a form of democracy in which local autonomy is allowed and locally elected governments are held to be more accountable to local residents. At the same time, administrative decentralization has been increasingly viewed as an important dimension of good governance at the local level. Administrative decentralization is expected to help alleviate disillusionment with central planning and control of important economic and social activities. Since the problem of accountability often affects effectiveness and efficiency of public provision of goods and services, decentralization has become one of the relatively high profile components in public sector reform and on the democratic governance agenda.[7]

1.2.1 *Types and Forms of Decentralization*

Decentralization refers to the attempts to transfer authority and responsibility for public functions from the central government to local government or to other sub-national levels including quasi-government organizations and/or the private sector. The rationale behind decentralization is generally two-fold. Decentralization is expected to bring about an improved resource allocation through a better matching of public services to local needs since local governments are closer to the people and more responsive to variations in demand (improved "*allocative efficiency*"). It is also anticipated that decentralization will increase the accountability of local governments to citizens, enhance consciousness of local cost and reduce bureaucratic procedures, since citizens tend to be more aware of the actions of local governments and put more pressure on them to provide public services more efficiently (improved "*productive efficiency*" and *accountability*) (Azfar et al. 2001, pp. 6–7).

Decentralization is a complex process and embraces a variety of concepts. It is often categorized into political, administrative and fiscal aspects. In the economic sense, the market is also regarded as the ultimate form of decentralization where the consumer can acquire a product from a choice of suppliers. In actual application, however, there are considerable overlaps between the above-mentioned aspects, and different forms of decentralization often happen in combination.[8]

With emphasis placed on the administrative aspect, there are three areas that should be distinguished: deconcentration, delegation, and devolution. The Development Assistance Committee (DAC) defines the areas as follows:

Deconcentration involves the transfer of function within the central government hierarchy through shifting the workload from central ministries to field units.

Delegation involves transfer of responsibility for implementing sector duties to regional or functional development authorities, parastatals and other semi-autonomous agencies that operate independently of central *government control. This usually occurs in sectors with a relatively sound income-generating basis.*

Devolution *involves transfer of authority to legally constituted local governments such as states, provinces, districts or municipalities. In devolved systems, the local governments have authority over a wide range of sectoral operations, limited only by broadly defined national policy guidelines. Local level staff are responsible to locally elected officials rather than to sector ministries.* (DAC 1997a, p. 57)

These three types of decentralization are not mutually exclusive. However, they suggest some sort of normative criteria for identifying whether some form of decentralization is desirable or not. Usually, delegation is regarded as an underpinning of political and financial decentralization in which local governments have clear and legally recognized geographical boundaries over which they exercise authority for decision making, finance, and management and within which they perform public functions (World Bank, Decentralization NET).

In reality, experience with decentralization is mixed. It is known that different types of decentralization in different institutional settings will result in different outcomes. It is also commonly known that not all government services need to be decentralized in the same way and to the same degree, and as a concept, a combination of deconcentration and even privatization can co-exist. It seems there is not yet enough evidence to identify actual conditions for the design of successful decentralization.[9]

1.2.2 Decentralization and Public Sector Reform

Decentralization is often undertaken as a component of public sector reform. The World Bank redefined the role of state as a provider of fundamental public services such as property rights, law and order, roads, basic education and health services, and stressed that the public sector should be improved through regulations and restraint, public participation, and competition (World Bank 1997). As the role of the state is reemphasized, public sector reform has become more prominent as one of the conditions for streamlining development management in developing countries.

The fundamental tasks of the state can be defined as the planning and enforcement of economic policies, the assurance of legal institutions, and service delivery of public goods and services, ensuring accountability for the use of public resources. Therefore, the objectives of public sector reform are to achieve improved efficiency, accountability and legitimacy, predictable legal systems, and transparency of the sector (World Bank, PREM website). Among major components for enhancing reform are public financing reform including tax collection, public expenditure management, state enterprise reform, privatization, civil service reform, and decentralization.

As shown in the rationales of decentralization, it is generally assumed that devolving more responsibilities to elected local governments would facilitate holding the public sector more responsive and accountable to local needs and opinions. Thus decentralization is regarded as a focal point of public sector reform and good governance in that increased political responsiveness and local participation induce better decisions for the use of public resources and a more equitable and accountable service delivery.

The remaining and persistent question to pose is how we can actually improve public service delivery, in what form of decentralization, and in what kind of institutional environment. Deliberate and cautious designing of decentralization is required based on political, social and economic conditions, type of services and type of sector in each country.[10] It is ironic that decentralization policies are spreading over such developing countries that often suffer from weak capacity, cannot carry out meticulous designing, or are not actually able to manage appropriate types and forms of decentralization.

In the next section, the case of decentralization in Thailand will be examined as an indigenous process of its government system.

2. The Government System and Decentralization in Thailand

In this section, first the centralized government system and the three-tier administrative structure in Thailand are illustrated. Then the decentralization policy strongly advanced by the adoption of the new constitution of 1997 is analyzed and the process of legislation and its retarded enforcement are examined.

2.1 Government Structure and Central–Local Relations in Thailand[11]

Thailand has a notable centralized government system with a wide spread of local administration wings whose basis can be traced back to the era of King Chulalongkorn in the 19th century. As seen below, the prevailing concept is "deconcentration", however, the search for types of autonomous government has been observed since the 1950s.

2.1.1 The Administrative Structure of Thailand

According to the Thai Administration Act of 1991, the government is composed of three tiers: Central Administration, Regional/Provincial Administration, and Local Administration.[12] (see Figure 7.1)

Figure 7.1 Three-tier Administrative Structure of Thailand

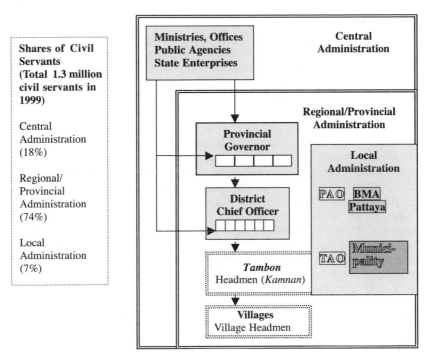

Note: Arrows indicate administrative and budgetary flows
Source: provided by the author based on Nagai (2001, 2003), and Noranit (2002).

2.1.1.1 Central Administration
Central administration includes the Office of the Prime Minister, and other offices; line ministries, departments, independent public agencies and state enterprises, all of which are located in Bangkok.

2.1.1.2 Regional/Provincial Administration
Regional/Provincial Administration refers to the 75 provincial offices, 795 district offices and 81 district branch offices where government power is exercised on behalf of the central government. Each province is categorized into one of the four regions: northern, northeast, central and south. The Governor, Vice Governor and Assistant Governors of a province and the District Chief Officer are high ranking officials of the Department of Local Administration of the Ministry of Interior. Provincial departments and district departments are the administrative arms of the central line ministries and each ministry assigns their officials as heads and staff of

the local departments. Therefore, until now all officers working at central, provincial, and district levels are civil servants directly controlled by the central government.

The provincial administrations are responsible for direct provisions of certain public services such as police, healthcare, and irrigation that require resources that cannot be afforded by local government administration mentioned below. The Provincial Governor is authorized to promote or transfer certain government officials within the province. (Noranit 2002, pp. 1–8)

Under a district administrative structure there are *tambon*[13] headmen, called *kamnan* in Thai, and village headmen. Neither *kamnan* nor village headmen are civil servants but they undertake delegated functions such as law and order, infectious diseases control, resident registration and development planning, under the supervision of district chief officers. Residents elect village headmen including *kamnan*. The Provincial Governor authorizes both *kamnan* and village headmen. Usually both *tambon* and village headmen are the only way for village people to interface with the Governor or the District Chief officer (Nagai 2003, p. 2). Since they undertake delegated tasks and are paid monthly allowances by district chief officers, they also form a part of the Regional/ Provincial Administration.

2.1.1.3 Local Administration

Local Administration is considered to be a form of self-government in Thailand. Local Administration is currently composed of five entities: 75 Provincial Administrative Organizations (PAO); 1,129 Municipalities; 6,746 Sub-district (*tambon*) Administrative Organizations (TAO); and the Bangkok Metropolitan Administration (BMA) and Pattaya City.

Among the above five forms of entities, the BMA and Pattaya City are special forms of local government. The BMA was created in 1972. With outstanding uniqueness in terms of area coverage, population, and fiscal level, a 1985 law granted the BMA exceptional autonomous status compared to the other areas.[14] The BMA functions as a provincial and municipal assembly as well as an administrative body. Pattaya City was established in 1978 and had a system of separating legislative and executive functions until 1999. A city manager had been employed under contract to the elected mayor of Pattaya to undertake a managerial role for the city until the new act came into force in 1999. Currently both the governor of the BMA and the mayor of Pattaya and their council members are directly elected by residents and can exercise autonomous authority over the affairs of each city. Importantly, the Minister of the Interior still has the power to dismiss governors with Cabinet approval.

The decentralization policy of 1999 transferred more authority to the local administrations known as PAO, Municipalities and TAO. There had been previous organizational developments since the 1950s.[15]

PAO were established in 1955 and have been placed in every province to deal with tasks that are not covered by Municipalities and TAO. In 1997, new legislation defined the tasks of PAO as coordination between local authorities such as Municipalities and TAO inside the provincial boundary. Under the new law, PAO are mainly responsible for enactment of provincial ordinances, formulating provincial development plans, support and allocation of the PAO budget to sub-district councils and other local government units and so forth. Provincial governors used to be assigned as PAO chief officers before the legislation came into force in 1997. Now the PAO chief officer is selected from PAO council members who are directly elected by residents.

Municipalities have their predecessor, Sanitary Districts, which were founded in 1907 mainly for community sanitation in urban areas and whose activities were run using fees collected from residential fees. Municipalities were established in 1953 incorporating *tessaban*, which was formed from the integration of former Sanitation Districts in 1935. Municipalities fall into three categories depending on the size of the community and the level of revenue. Municipal territories are small and do not cover all the urbanized areas. Each Municipality is composed of an elected municipal council and a municipal executive committee. The council reviews and approves the annual budget and passes municipal ordinances for activities closely related to community livelihood. Members of the council are elected from residents and their numbers vary according to the municipality category mentioned above. Since 2000, mayors of the largest two categories of Municipalities have started to be directly elected by residents.

TAO were founded in 1994 under the Chuan administration whose aim was to delegate more central authority to rural areas. TAO have their predecessors, which were established in 1956, but there were only 44 in number, and they were not recognized as a juristic entity (Nagai 2003, p.3). TAO were abolished in 1972 and *tambon* councils were formed instead, whose function was development planning and implementation, which was not usually very effective. In 1994, *tambon* councils that met the level of revenue defined in the new legislation became TAO. TAO falls into five categories depending on level of revenue. According to the legislation of 1994, each TAO has a council composed of two villagers elected from respective village as well as an executive committee with selected council members. Former *kamnan* and village headmen who used to hold the posts of council members and executive committee members could continue to keep their seats for four years during the transition period.

2.1.2 Central–Local Government Relations

As seen above, aside from the central government, there exists two parallel types of local government in Thailand: the local administration of the central government (Regional/Provincial Administration) and local self-government organizations (Local Administration).

Regional/Provincial Administration is a form of "deconcentration" which maintains a strong vertical relationship with the central government. The Ministry of the Interior is responsible for direct control and supervision over Regional/Provincial Administration in terms of exercising authority over financial and personnel management. On the other hand, central line ministries, such as the Ministry of Education, the Ministry of Public Health, the Ministry of Agriculture and Cooperatives and others, exercise control over provincial and district departments in implementing policies and providing public services in their specific jurisdiction. It is often pointed out that provincial and district administration is fragmented by the vertical directive lines of central ministries and that the governors and district chief officers lack enough power to preside.

In local administration, the trend towards self-government is regarded as similar to decentralization. However, in reality, local councils of PAO, Municipalities and TAO have to obtain approval for annual and five-year budget appropriations either from provincial governors or from district chief officers before they can be put into effect. With scarce revenue resources and lack of capacity, the local administration is obliged to depend on grants and subsidies from central government except in the cases of BMA and Pattaya City. In substance local administration is subject to the governing and supervisory authority of central government based on the rules and regulations of the Ministry of Interior (Boolert 1997, pp. 5 and 9). Duplication and redundancy of functions among different levels of government also remain (ADB 1999, p. 28).

In the following section, the decentralization mandated in the new constitution and the consequences of the Decentralization Act will be analysed.

2.2 Progress of Decentralization in Thailand[16]

2.2.1 The Democracy Movement and the New Constitution of 1997

In Thailand, decentralization has been actively debated since the 1992 general election when Prime Minister Chuan democratically took office after a series of political upheavals during 1991 and 1992. There was an argument that an elected provincial governor should replace a centrally appointed governor. Because the latter is not currently entitled to exert unitary authority over sectorally segmented provincial departments. The re-establishment of TAO in 1994, as seen in the previous section, was a way of coming to a political compromise in the heated debate.[17] The new constitution promulgated in 1997 furthered this movement by clarifying the principles of decentralization to local government organizations (PAO, Municipalities and TAO) in eight sections (see Box 1). Specific arrangements and the preparatory process to be followed were not addressed in detail and left in the hands of the legislation.

Box 1
Sections concerned with decentralization in the New Constitution in 1997

Section 78: The state shall decentralize powers to local government organizations. The state should promote self-government at the provincial level where people are willing for it.

Section 283: Localities are entitled to formulate local government organizations.

Section 284: Measures to ensure new decentralization system and intergovernmental relations are as follows:

(1) Local government organizations shall have autonomous power in policy formulation, administration, finance, and personnel management

(2) A decentralization act shall be declared to clarify a distinction of functions and responsibilities, and tax collection between the state and local authorities as well as those among localities

(3) A decentralization committee shall be established to prepare decentralization plan, review and monitor and provide policy recommendation to the Cabinet.

Section 285: Local government organizations should consist of a locally elected council and executive bodies with four-year terms.

Section 286 and 287: Voters have right to request election organizations to set up a voting session for recalling local elected members in case of not trustworthiness.

Section 288: Local personnel service committee should be established comprised of equal members of representatives from local government organizations, central government agencies, and qualified persons. Personnel management should be administered based on local needs and approval as well as legal bound. Local civil service law shall be formulated in consistent with the principles.

Section 289 and 290: Local government organizations should carry out additional functions such as preservation of local arts, heritage and culture, education and training service delivery, conservation and management of natural resources, the environment, sanitation and community.

Source: Office of Decentralization to Local Government Organization Committee (date unknown), Nagai 2001.

Based on the orientation delineated in the constitution, the preparatory committee was established to undertake the drafting of new laws for considering such issues as transforming the remaining Sanitary Districts into *tessaban* (municipalities), formulating decentralization plans and procedures, establishing local service committees, and defining structures of local government organizations. Thus within two years of the promulgation of the new constitution, consecutive laws related to decentralization came into force (see Table 7.1).

2.2.2 The Decentralization Act of 1999

In line with the articulated orientation toward decentralization by the new constitution, the Decentralization Act[18] came into force in November 1999. By defining the specific authorities, responsibilities and principles for the allocation of taxes and revenues, the Act is intended to further accelerate the decentralization process. The measures to be taken as stipulated in the Act are summarized as follows:

(1) Establishing a National Decentralization Committee[19] composed of 36 members representing local authorities, government officials, and qualified officials in the areas of government affairs, public law, economics and local politics.
(2) Enumerating the functions and the local services responsibilities of Pattaya City, Municipalities and TAO as well as those of PAO.

Table 7.1 Laws Relating to Decentralization in Thailand

Title of the related laws	Date of enactment
Tessaban Act of 1953 (Revised Version 10 in 1999)	February 1953
Tambon Councils and *tambon* Administrative Organization Act (Revised Version 3 in 1999)	November 1994
Provincial Administrative Organization Act	October 1997
The New Constitution of 1997	October 1997
Act on Elevation of Sanitary Districts to the status of *tessaban* (Municipalities)	February 1999
Act on Signing Bills by Local Government Organizations	October 1999
Act on Voting for Recall of Local Council Members and Local Executive Committee Members	November 1999
Act on Determining Plan and Process of Decentralization	November 1999
Act on Local Personnel Service	November 1999
Act on Government Organization of Pattaya City	November 1999
Municipality Administration Act	May 2000

Source: Office of Decentralization to Local Government Organization Committee (date unknown), Nagai (2001, p.49) and Noranit (2002)

(3) Articulating the allocation of taxes and local revenues to local authorities, and debt financing.

(4) Outlining a decentralization plan including its 10-year timeframe, categorization of pubic services to be devolved and most importantly a bench mark for financial decentralization.

(5) Outlining the necessary measures for a transitional period.

As for (1) above, the National Decentralization Committee was established, chaired by the Prime Minister or the Deputy Prime Minister and authorized by the Prime Minister. The mandate of the Committee is to make strategic and action plans on decentralization, which have to be approved by the Cabinet and reported to Parliament for acknowledgement. The Committee has to set out criteria and procedures to facilitate the transfer of functions and personnel to local government organizations and to ensure the targeted tax and revenue ratio.

Concerning (2) above, the roles and functions to be transferred to local government organizations are redefined by the type of organization: *tessaban* (Municipalities), TAO and Pattaya City are grouped as the first type of local government organization; PAO is a second type of supra-organization whose responsibility covers the provincial boundary; and BMA is a special type of organization undertaking both the roles and functions of the first and second types (see Table 7.2). Six categories of authorities and responsibilities are assigned to local government organizations: Planning on Investment, Commercial and Tourism Promotion; Infrastructure Construction and Maintenance; Promotion of Quality of Life; Community and Social Orders and Security; Management and Conservation of Natural Resources and the Environment; and Local Art, Culture, Tradition and Knowledge.

Among the issues, the most notable is Item (3) that sets out the benchmark ratio of local revenue to the total to be achieved by 2006. As seen in the previous section, the local collection of revenues was less than 10% of the total in the 1990s. Including the grants to be allocated to localities, the local share of total national revenues was around 12% in 2000. The Decentralization Act declares that local revenues shall account for at least 20% and 35% of the government revenues in the fiscal years of 2001 and 2006 respectively.

Item (4) mentioned above explains that the National Decentralization Committee will review the roles and responsibilities enumerated in Table 7.2 every five years to expedite the appropriate decentralization process. It is stated that the timeframe for the transfer of function and personnel to local government organizations may be differently set according to their capabilities and readiness, by taking into consideration the level of revenues, personnel, population, expenditures and quality of service provision. It is stated that the process should be completed by 2010.

Table 7.2 Role and Functions of Local Government Organization in accordance with the Decentralization Act of 1999

Public Functions to be Transferred to Local Government Organizations	Role and Functions of *tessaban* (Municipalities), *tambon* Administrative Organization (TAO) and Pattaya City	Role and Functions of Provincial Administrative Organization (PAO)	Role and Functions of Bangkok Metropolitan Administration (BMA)
Planning on Investment, Commercial and Tourism Promotion	1) Making Local Development Plan	1) Making Local Development Plan and Coordination of Making Provincial Plan as Directed by the Cabinet 2) Support to other Local Government Organizations in Local Development 3) Coordination and Collaboration on Activities of Other Local Government Organizations 4) Budget Allocation for other Local Government Organizations 24) Other activities that are in the authorities of other local government organizations within its boundaries, and those activities should be implemented by the collaboration of other local government organizations or by the PAO as directed by the Committee 25) Support or Assistance to Government Organizations or other Local Government Organizations in Local Development 26) Provision of Services to Private Sector, Government Organizations State Enterprises or other Local Government Organizations 15) Trade and Investment Promotion 14) Tourism Promotion	Combination of *tessaban* and PAO
	7) Trade and Investment Promotion 8) Tourism Promotion		

Table 7.2   Role and Functions of Local Government Organization in accordance with the Decentralization Act of 1999   (*continued*)

Public Functions to be Transferred to Local Government Organizations	Role and Functions of *tessaban* (Municipalities), *tambon* Administrative Organization (TAO) and Pattaya City	Role and Functions of Provincial Administrative Organization (PAO)	Role and Functions of Bangkok Metropolitan Administration (BMA)
Infrastructure, Communication Transportation, Public Works and Building Control, etc.	2) Establishment and Maintenance of Land, Waterway and Drainage 3) Management and Control of Market, Pier, Ferry and Parking Lot 4) Public Utilities and other Constructions 5) Public Works 25) Town Planning 26) Transportation and Traffic Engineering 27) Maintenance of Public Land 28) Building Control	13) Management of Land and Water Transportation Terminals 16) Construction and Maintenance of Land and Waterway Linking Local Areas Combination of Tessaban and PAO 17) Establishment and Management of Central Market 21) Mass Transportation and Traffic Engineering	Combination of *tessaban* and PAO

Table 7.2 Role and Functions of Local Government Organization in accordance with the Decentralization Act of 1999 *(continued)*

Public Functions to be Transferred to Local Government Organizations	Role and Functions of *tessaban* (Municipalities), *tambon* Administrative Organization (TAO) and Pattaya City	Role and Functions of Provincial Administrative Organization (PAO)	Role and Functions of Bangkok Metropolitan Administration (BMA)
Promotion of Quality of Life	9) Education Management 6) Promotion, Training and Occupation 10) Social Welfare and Life Quality Development for Children, Women, the Elderly and the Disabilities 12) Improvement of Slums and Housing Management 13) Establishment and Maintenance of Recreation Areas 18) Garbage Disposal and Wastewater Treatment 19) Public Health, Household Sanitation and Medical Treatment 20) Cemeteries and Crematoria Management 21) Animal Control 22) Operation and Regulation of Slaughter Houses	6) Education Management 9) Promotion of Appropriate Technological Development 27) Social Welfare and Life Quality Development for Children, Women, the Elderly and the Disabilities 10) Establishment of Waste Water Treatment System 11) Solid Waste and Garbage Disposal 19) Establishment of Provincial Hospital and Medical Treatment, and Infectious Disease Prevention and Control	Combination of *tessaban* and PAO

Table 7.2 Role and Functions of Local Government Organization in accordance with the Decentralization Act of 1999 (continued)

Public Functions to be Transferred to Local Government Organizations	Role and Functions of *tessaban* (Municipalities), *tambon* Administrative Organization (TAO) and Pattaya City	Role and Functions of Provincial Administrative Organization (PAO)	Role and Functions of Bangkok Metropolitan Administration (BMA)
Community and Social Orders and Security	15) Promotion of Democracy, Equity, Public Right and Freedom 16) Promotion of Public Participation in Local Development 17) Assurance of Cleanliness and Orderliness 23) Assurance of Security, Orderliness and Sanitation in Theatres and other Public Places 29) Prevention and Alleviation of Public Hazards 30) Assurances of Orderliness, Promotion and Support on Protection and Preservation of Security in Life and Property	7) Promotion of Democracy, Equity, Public Right and Freedom 8) Promotion of Public Participation in Local Development 23) Establishment of Provincial Orderliness System 22) Prevention and Alleviation of Public Hazards	

Table 7.2 Role and Functions of Local Government Organization in accordance with the Decentralization Act of 1999 (continued)

Public Functions to be Transferred to Local Government Organizations	Role and Functions of tessaban (Municipalities), tambon Administrative Organization (TAO) and Pattaya City	Role and Functions of Provincial Administrative Organization (PAO)	Role and Functions of Bangkok Metropolitan Administration (BMA)
Management and Conservation of Natural Resources and the Environment	24) Management, Preservation and Utilization of Forest, Land, Natural Resources and the Environment	5) Protection and Preservation of Forest, Land, Natural Resources and the Environment 12) Environment and Pollution Management	Combination of tessaban and PAO
Local Art, Culture, Tradition and Knowledge	11) Preservation and Maintenance of Art, Custom, Local Wisdom and Culture 14) Sports Promotion 31) Other activities beneficial to local people as directed by the Committee	20) Establishment of Museums and Chronicle Local History 18) Promotion of Sports, Custom and Culture 27) Other activities that are in authorities of the PAO as regulated by the Act or other laws and regulations 28) Other activities beneficial to local people as directed by the Committee	Combination of tessaban and PAO

Source: Office of Decentralization to Local Government Organization Committee (date unknown), Nagai (2001, pp.83 and 84)

2.3 The Progress of Decentralization and Recent Trends

With the legal enactment of decentralization principles and process, the Master Plan of Decentralization was formulated by the National Decentralization Committee and approved by the Cabinet in 2000. In February 2002, the Parliament approved the Action Plan of Decentralization that defines six areas of responsibilities, including 245 items of public services to be devolved to local administrative organizations, either on a mandatory or voluntary basis, by fiscal 2004.

The results of the actual transfer of authority, financial resources and personnel are mixed. There are fundamental structural problems inherent to the current decentralization policy on the one hand, such as the lack of capacity and revenue base of local organizations. The Ministry of Interior who had strongly promoted the decentralization process seems to persist in holding onto its vested power over the local government. For example, the Ministry of Interior imposes a regulation that the personnel cost of local government administration should not exceed 40% of total revenues, and also opposed the direct election of TAO chief officers saying that the people were not ready (Nagai 2003, p. 3, Nora 2002 and *Bangkok Post*, 29 August 2002).

On the other hand, there is the strong political leadership of Thaksin who took office as Prime Minister in February 2001. While he emphasizes tackling the inefficiency and sectionalism of the public sector, he pays more attention to bureaucratic reform than decentralization.

2.3.1 Progress and Constraints of Decentralization

As Nagai pointed out (2001, p. 101) the Master Plan and Action Plan address ways of increasing the share of local revenues by increasing grants, raising the existing tax rate and introducing new tax. Since fiscal 2001, local government organizations have gained a new source of revenue from "grants with transfer of responsibility" allocated by the Ministry of Agriculture and Cooperatives, the Ministry of Public Health and the Civil Engineering Department of the Ministry of Interior (World Bank 2001b, p. 64).[20] The standardized allocation ratio of "general grants" from the Department of Local Development of the Ministry of Interior was also reviewed to set out a more differentiated formula taking into account the size of population, density and levels of revenue (Nagai 2001, p. 103). With increased grants for transferred responsibility, small-scale civic construction work, garbage collection, provision of school meals and some other services are currently being undertaken by local government organizations.

As a result, in fiscal 2001, the share of local revenues received by the government reached 22%. However, locally raised taxes did not increase.[21] The power to raise local taxes is still vested in the central government.

Central government used to collect more than 92% of government revenues on average in the 1990s (World Bank 2003, p. 29). Furthermore, over 70% of TAO are small and rural communities with populations of less than 5,000 people. Most TAO have three to four officials and 80% of municipality offices have around 10 officials.

More importantly, the transfer of personnel has been negligible so far. By fiscal 2002, only 3,600 persons had been added to local government organizations from nearly 1.3 million civil servants. It can be seen in Thailand that the Regional/Provincial Administration is well developed to undertake local affairs with a large proportion of human resources. The percentage of personnel working in Central, Regional/ Provincial and Local Administration was 18.3%, 74.8% and 7.0% respectively in 1999 (Nagai 2003, p. 1). This proportion is unlikely to change because of the lack of incentives for existing civil servants to work in local organizations.[22]

In addition there are currently 6,746 TAO and 1,129 Municipalities. It is actually difficult for PAO and other government organizations to monitor and provide appropriate support individually (Nagai 2001).

2.3.2 From Decentralization to Public Sector Reform?

Decentralization in Thailand was furthered by the new constitution of 1997 and the decentralization act stipulated in 1999. However, there are contradictory moves away from decentralization. Since Thaksin took office in February 2001, he has been advocating more public sector reform rather than decentralization, through his strong leadership, paying special attention to reducing inefficient duplication and to the sectionalism of bureaucracy.[23]

In 2002, the Thaksin government put into action the thorough restructuring of the central ministries.[24] In order to specify the role and functions of each department and ministry with the principle of "one ministry one mission", the numbers of bureaus and ministries were increased. Thaksin stressed that the aim of major bureaucratic reform was to provide faster services for the people by changing the role of the public sector from ruler or controller to director and facilitator (Thaksin 2002). Behind this concept is a new form of public management in which each minister is obliged to identify the mission, strategy, master plan and annual action plan of his/her ministry to the Prime Minister in order to obtain the necessary budget, and by which his/her performance is evaluated.[25]

Thaksin also initiated the "CEO governor" pilot project in 2002 in which six provincial governors are given supra-departmental authority in the province to take unitary leadership in an otherwise segmented provincial administration (Nagai 2002).

Thaksin apparently does not promote the decentralization policy as it is defined in the Decentralization Act. In fact, the National Decentralization Committee appears to have ceased its activities since 2002.[26] Under the concept of participatory democracy and economic competition, Thaksin has stressed that the way to reform central and regional/provincial bureaucracies is to make public services more efficient and more accessible to the poorer strata of people (Thaksin 2002).

There are different approaches to decentralization amongst the central ministries. For example, the Ministry of Education has an "education area" plan to delegate more responsibilities to district education offices to promote basic education reform. The Ministry of Public Health has a plan to establish "area health boards" at provincial level in order to promote greater involvement of PAO, Municipalities and TAO in policy setting, budget allocation and resource management.[27] Both ministries are concerned with delegating more authority to local levels so that they can adjust pubic services to suit the local situation and reduce unnecessary expenditure by streamlining administrative structures for more efficient decision making. However, due to a lack of professional ability in local government organizations, they are reluctant to directly devolve their responsibilities to those organizations. Rather the two ministries insist on choosing more deliberate and differentiated criteria to decide which roles and functions of public services should be decentralized, bearing in mind the situation of each local government organization.[28]

In the next section, health sector reform and the induced different forms of decentralization in Thailand will be examined.

3. Health Sector Management and Sector Reform in Thailand

In this section, the health sector is examined as a case in which decentralization policy has been discussed from a different perspective and in which the health service management system has been changed in the context of health sector reform. Among a series of health sector reform initiatives by the Ministry of Public Health, the most notable is the universal coverage of healthcare scheme, the so-called "30 Baht scheme (to cure every disease)". The introduction of the 30 Baht scheme has altered the relations between provincial health offices, district health offices, health centres, and, to a certain extent, sub-district administrative organizations such as *Tambon* Administrative Organizations (TAO).

3.1 Health Sector Administration in Thailand

3.1.1   Specific Features of the Health Sector in Thailand

The public health sector is the largest in the Thai government system. In October 2002 after the restructuring of the central government, the Ministry of Public Health (MOPH) still maintains a gigantic share of civil servants that amounts to 161,719 (41% of the total government officials) compared to the second largest ministry, the Ministry of Interior with 46,876 (12% of the total). While the Ministry of Interior reduced its number of officials by 16,683, the MOPH on the other hand increased its staff by 159 in number in 2002.[29] In 1998, 93% of civil servants of the MOPH were working in rural areas (MOPH 2000). This indicates that the MOPH is equipped with professionals mostly working at provincial, district and *tambon* levels.

As the main task of the MOPH is to provide preventive and curative services to people, its administrative arms have been well developed throughout the provincial, district, and *tambon* levels. A great deal of development took place during the 1970s when the Third Social and Economic Development Plan (1972–1976) addressed the improvement of social justice and the expansion of community development by launching a primary healthcare programme for the poor. The subsequent Fourth Social and Economic Development Plan (1977–1981) stressed the reduction of income disparities and the improvement of the living standards of low-income groups including farmers and labourers. In order to deliver social services to the general public, particularly in rural areas, district hospitals and health centres were built/established, one in each district and *tambon* respectively during this period (MOPH 2000).[30] At the same time, the Fourth National Health Plan (1977–1982) stated that executive power should be more decentralized to provincial administration as health services were expanded at the provincial level. Thus provincial chief medical officers obtained considerable flexibility in making their own decisions in solving local problems. (Boolert 1997, pp. 4 and 5)

During the decade 1978 to 1988 the MOPH had established systems for more efficient and equitable health delivery services. In order to deal with the rather harsh economic situation which had arisen due to the oil crisis, more targeted development programmes such as district hospitals construction and manpower development were implemented (MOPH 2000). The health status of Thai people improved significantly during this period. Maternal mortality rate had fallen from 1.3 per 1,000 live births in 1977 to only 0.3 in 1987: The infant mortality rate dropped from 50 per 1,000 to 32.

3.1.2 The Administrative Structure of the Health Sector in Thailand

The administrative structure of the MOPH is typically centralized but somewhat unique in that the Provincial Chief Medical Officer (PCMO) undertakes almost all functions for provincial health administration under the supervision of the Permanent Secretary for Public Health. The PCMO is the head of the Provincial Public Health Office (PPHO) appointed by the MOPH. The PCMO is granted full authority in the management of health services in the province and in coordinating the work of the offices of all public health departments located within the provincial boundary (Boolert 1997, p. 6) (see Figure 7.2).

The Thai health sector has gone through a series of organizational developments during the past 30 years. At the centre, efforts were focused on a more unified integration of the functions for public health care administration by merging departments for health and medical services and enhancing the jurisdiction of the Permanent Secretary. At the field level, efforts were geared to developing provincial and district administrative arms. In the process, deconcentration of the health management system had long been enhanced, rather than decentralization of functions and responsibilities to local government administration.

There are three layers of provincial health administration: the provincial public health office (PPHO) (75 provinces), district/sub-district health offices (795/81 offices), and health centres (9,738 centres). The PPHO, which undertakes all health activities in the province, directly reports to the provincial governor but is supervised and logistically supported by the Office of the Permanent Secretary and other related technical departments of the MOPH as mentioned above. District health offices are responsible for management, support, promotion, monitoring and evaluation of activities implemented by health centres. District/sub-district health officers who head the district/sub-district health office have to report to the district chief officer but are supervised and technically supported by the PCMO. Health centres located in each *tambon* are front-line health service units under the jurisdiction of the district health office. Health centres provide integrated healthcare services at *tambon* or village level (MOPH 2000) (see Figure 7.2).

The public healthcare service systems in Thailand are classified into four levels in each province: primary healthcare level for communities, primary care level at health centres, secondary care level at district hospitals, and tertiary care level at general hospitals or regional hospitals. At the community level, Village Health Volunteers (VHVs) are selected from each village and assigned to health centres after one to two weeks of training. VHVs take charge of primary care services such as the prescription of drugs, the registration of births or deaths of villagers at health centres, and the provision of basic public health information to

Figure 7.2   The Structure of Provincial Health Service Management
(Until the Introduction of Universal Coverage Scheme)

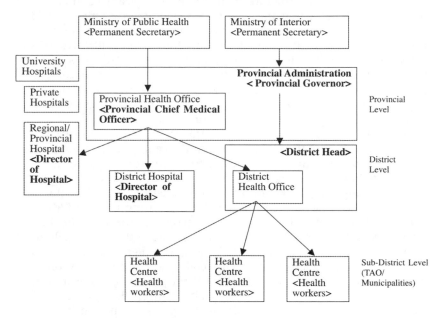

Note: Arrows indicate the direction of administrative supervision and budget flow
Source: formulated by the author

the people. VHVs were not granted any allowances except health cards
to exempt them from medical fees (JICA 1996, p. 12).

At the primary care level, health workers, midwives and technical
nurses at health centres, who are civil servants of the MOPH, provide
integrated health services such as health promotion, disease prevention,
and curative care to people in rural areas. In municipality health centres
outpatient care is also provided by assigned medical doctors. Health
centres are technically supported by district hospitals.

At the secondary care level, there are district hospitals at district or
sub-district level with 10 to 150 inpatient beds. Medical doctors and
nurses put more emphasis on curative care than on primary level care.
General hospitals or regional hospitals located in the capital of each
province or region with 200 to 500 beds may also provide secondary
level care.

At the tertiary level, general hospitals and regional hospitals supervised
by the PCMO as well as university hospitals under the jurisdiction of the
Ministry of University Affairs provide specialized care services (MOPH

2000). These levels are designed to be linked with each other for referral when patients are found to be in need of more specialized or a higher level of services.

Under the health service systems in the current health administration, district hospitals are supervised by the provincial public health office but cannot exercise direct supervisory authority over health centres. This remaining fragmented structure weakens referral links and sometimes causes information gaps between primary healthcare units (health centres) and district hospitals. Whether coordination and links are smooth or not often depends on the relationship between the director of a district hospital and the district health officer.[31]

Integration of public care services and the development of a fully fledged provincial public health administration had led to the betterment of health performance in Thailand as seen in 3.1.1. However, efficiency and equity problems have come to the fore. These problems were especially apparent at the time of the economic crisis.

3.2 Health Sector Reform Initiatives and Decentralization in Thailand

3.2.1 The Social Sector Crisis in the 1990s

The social sector in Thailand in the 1990s exhibited serious problems in delivery of services in terms of quality, equity, and cost effectiveness. The problems became more apparent especially after the economic downturn caused by the financial crisis in 1997.

From 1988 to 1997, Thailand had enjoyed double-digit growth and its health budget had increased from 4.2% of the national budget in 1987 to 7.7% in 1998. Despite positive results from investments in building hospitals, improving equipment and developing more health professionals, health expenditure had expanded at the rate of over 10% annually, similar to the rate of GDP growth. In the second half of the period, the growth rate had become even greater than the GDP growth (MOPH 2000).

Such a rapid rise in expenditure can be attributed to the extravagant use of drugs and technologies and to the bubble growth of the private health sector that expanded by double digits in terms of the number of beds and doctors during that decade.[32] During the crisis, the cost of healthcare had increased further due to the Baht float or devaluation. The rise in expenditure and the rapid expansion of the private sector had not led to better health service delivery but rather to "high cost but less health". As the Health Research Systems Institute (HRSI), a government-run think tank noted, "the health service system is inefficient since it continues to increasingly misuse national resources as overhead expenditures".[33]

Considerable increase in health expenditure per capita in Thailand from 544.90 Baht in 1980 to 4,662.83 Baht (approximately $112US) in 1998 was a serious problem.[34] Thais have to pay up to 200 billion Baht per annum for healthcare services, while about 20 million (39% of the total 60 million) of the population remain without any appropriate treatment especially in an emergency. The consequences for the poor are significant because the spending of the poor in relation to income was five to six times as high as that of the rich. Moreover, two out of three of those who hold low-income health cards cannot access the benefits they are entitled to (MOPH 2000).

Dissatisfaction of patients with low quality and inconvenient public health services had become prevalent by the middle of the 1990s, while prices, skills and morality were criticized in the private sector (MOPH 2000). There was a pressing need for Thailand to have a well-established system to make the quality of hospitals more viable and budget allocation and service delivery more rational and equitable.

3.2.2 Reform Initiatives of the Ministry of Public Health

Reform of health service management had been discussed by the MOPH since the end of the 1990s. The core concept for reform is "good health at low cost" (Preeda 2003). Major policies include initiatives for health system reform, health decentralization, and universal coverage of healthcare in Thailand. Behind these health reform initiatives, there is a theoretical or policy background exhibited in a series of public and political government reforms in the late 1990s.

First, Section 52 of the new constitution of 1997 states that "All Thai people have an equal right to access to quality health services" and defined the concept of decentralization of local government organizations to be put into force. Second, the Decentralization Act of 1999 clarified the timeframe and the mechanism for transferring authorities and social services functions to localities. Third, pubic sector reform for restructuring and result-based management of public services had been planned and enforced since 1999.

MOPH's strategy for dealing with the problems has been formulated reflecting the above government reform policies.

3.2.2.1 Health System Reform Initiative of the Ministry of Public Health

The focal concept of the Health Systems Reform is "to achieve a desirable national health system in which 'health promotion' takes a more precedent role than its 'curative counterpart', and is based on the concept of 'sufficient health' inviting the people to take part in being an active partner in their health system for sustainable health" (Preeda 2003). Based on the idea of health as a basic right of the people as articulated in the new constitution of 1997, the value of equity, efficiency, participation and equity was advocated as a key in reforming the way of thinking of the Thai people on health. The discussion culminated in the drafting of the National Health Act to be enacted by June 2003 as a crossover philosophy for overall health development in Thailand. [35]

3.2.2.2 The Decentralization Act, the Consecutive Master Plan and the Operational Plan and their Consequences in the Health Sector

As seen in Section 2, the Decentralization Act of 1999 and the Master Plan authorized by the Cabinet in 2000 specified the types of services and authorities to be devolved to local administrative organizations such as PAO, TAO and Municipalities. Of the 103 items of services listed for quality of life in the master plan, most public health services are assigned to local administrative organizations, i.e., sub-district governments such as TAO and Municipalities (see Table 7.2).[36]

According to Nagai (2002, p. 41), in 2000 MOPH established a joint committee with the National Decentralization Committee to discuss criteria on how and over what timeframe the decentralization of authority and financial and human resources should take place. The MOPH presented an operational plan for the period 2001 to 2010 in which the concept and the timeframe of "Health Decentralization" was described (Preeda 2003). [37]

The main thrust of "Health Decentralization" is to transfer decision-making authority and coordination functions for basic public health services to the Area Health Board (AHB), a newly established mechanism at provincial level. The aim of the AHB, which is administratively independent from the provincial administration is to formulate a health services network to promote multi-level participation of government and the public and to take responsibility for local health.

The AHB mechanism is currently partly applied in the implementation of the Universal Health Coverage Scheme, which is intended to enhance both coverage and accessibility of healthcare services. This is analyzed in detail in the next section.

Thus the way towards devolution to sub-district levels as outlined in the new constitution of 1997 and the Decentralization Act of 1999 was somewhat reoriented in the health sector. The MOPH has recognized the problems of effectiveness, efficiency and equity of its health service system and has delineated measures to improve the health service system by delegating more authority to the local level. Nevertheless the health sector has delegated more powers to the provincial and district levels with concerns and fears about the lack of local capacity and the efficiency of sub-district government organizations, as well as about increased fragmentation and uncoordinated health service systems.

3.2.2.3 Public Sector Reform and its Consequences in Health Sector Management

There are two specific directions in health sector reform in Thailand: one is more autonomy for hospitals, and the other is the adoption of performance-based budgeting. Public sector reform has been enhanced since 1998 when the Cabinet established the Permanent Public Service Reform Commission of the Office of the Public Service Reform Commission in the Office of the Civil Service Commission (OCSC) under the Chuan Administration. Public functions were scrutinized and categorized into six groups: those that could be performed by government agencies, by state enterprises, by public organizations, by the private sector, by local administrative agencies, and by people's organizations. The restructuring efforts led to the enactment of the Autonomous Public Organization Act of 1999 (OCSC).

The Thai health sector also re-examined its functions and organizations. The MOPH recognized that its role had changed from being a service provider, to being a policymaker or a regulator for all public and private health facilities (MOPH 2000). The ultimate model chosen by the MOPH is the establishment of "autonomous hospitals" which can provide management efficiency and quality services. In the action plan, seven autonomous hospitals were to be allowed more autonomy in managing their financial and manpower resources (MOPH 2002, p. 430).[38]

In 2000, the first state-run autonomous hospital launched its operation in Samut Sakorn, Bangkok, Samutsakhon Province. Banphaeo Hospital, previously a district hospital with 120 beds, pioneered an independent and efficient form of organization, controlled by the board of directors comprised of representatives from the government sector (the MOPH, the District Chief Officer, and the PCMO in Bangkok, the Provincial CEO or the Governor and the PPHO of the province), health or financial specialists, and citizen representatives from TAO local NGOs. This hospital is not under the jurisdiction of the MOPH but is supervised by the board and has to report to the cabinet directly. Members of hospital staff are no longer civil servants and half of the current staff comes from outside organizations.

The success of the hospital is certain with regard to its fiscal sustainability, its increased responsiveness to the community through participation from TAO in decision making, and above all due to the strong leadership of the director of the Board of Directors.[39] However, the lack of the second autonomous hospital following Banphaeo Hospital to date may be due to the fact that public health personnel fear losing their pension privileges and other state benefits and to precarious support from politicians.

Since the Thaksin administration took office in 2001, public sector reform has been accelerated in the direction of reforming the bureaucratic system. As mentioned in Section 2.3.2, each ministry is currently obliged to clarify its missions, strategies, plans and indicators for the assessment of its service delivery in order to obtain the necessary budget allocation. The Prime Minister will make a service agreement with each minister to ensure the realization of committed policies and achievement of expected results (Thaksin 2002). The reorganization of the central ministries in 2002 pushed public sector reform forward by introducing performance based budgeting and by scheduling personnel management reform to be applied from the fiscal year 2004.

The MOPH has come under more pressure to improve its performance and efficiency. Thus, the MOPH recognizes the period from 2001 to 2003 as "an important transition of the Ministry" (MOPH 2002, p. 366).

3.2.3 Universal Health Coverage Policy and its Consequences on the Health Service System in Thailand

3.2.3.1 Problems of the Thai Health Security System
The overall trend in the health services has been a steady improvement in the number of people covered by some sort of health insurance scheme[40] and this coverage was actually expanded by creating a safety net for the poor during the economic crisis of the late 1990s. However, in 2001, approximately 30% of the population were not covered by any scheme (MOPH 2002, p. 351).

There are four heath insurance schemes: 1) a medical welfare scheme for the poor and socially underprivileged groups; 2) the Civil Servant Medical Benefit Scheme; 3) a security scheme for employees in the formal sector; and 4) the Health Card Scheme which is run on a basis of voluntary application. Each scheme has a different benefit package and is managed by different ministries and this results in a variety of provider payment mechanisms and levels of subsidy, and hence different quality in levels of care (Health Insurance Office 2002). As a result, there is inequity in healthcare access and in financial resource allocation. There are still many people without any eligible insurance.

Given the rising cost of healthcare as mentioned previously, effective targeting, equitable financing and good quality services should be provided to eligible people appropriately and sustainably. The MOPH has recognized the need for a universal healthcare coverage scheme which ensures equal sharing and efficient use of health resources as well as providing quality choices of services to people, with a stronger emphasis on health promotion and prevention (Nutta and Kaemthong 2001, p. 2).

3.2.3.2 Universal Healthcare Coverage Policy: Approaches and Principles[41]

Several attempts have been made in the past to achieve the goal of an equitable, efficient and quality service delivery but these failed to be accepted as a national policy because of inadequate policy support. In 2001, the Thai Rak Thai party won a landslide victory using the universal healthcare coverage policy, namely the "30 Baht Policy", as one of its major policy commitments. The idea is to make healthcare more available at a fixed co-payment of 30 Baht per visit to those who are not currently covered by other government health insurance schemes. The ultimate objectives of the policy are to ensure equal access to quality care for the entire population and to minimize differences in benefit packages and quality provided by existing schemes (Health Insurance Office 2002).[42]

This policy is phased over a three-year period starting in 2001. The policy has been developed through initial pilot programmes based on the following principles:

(1) *Emphasis on Health Promotion and the Use of Primary Healthcare Unit as a Gatekeeper*

The "primary care provider" is designated as a key player in the healthcare system to provide care for the registered population. Usually the primary care providers are district hospitals and health centres that should be designated by the AHB. The primary care provider is also expected to act as a gatekeeper to identify whether a critically ill patient should be referred to a secondary level of medical treatment. Better use of primary care providers is expected to improve "allocative efficiency" and to improve the coverage and quality of care provided.

(2) *Developing Standardized Provider Payment Mechanisms which Promote a Cost Containment System*

Appropriate provider payment mechanisms will be developed in order to increase provider productivity (performance-based payment) without increasing unnecessary cost (a cost containment system).

Tentatively, a capitation system is applied. This is the system of budget allocation to the primary care provider based on unit cost per person and the registered number of the population. It applies the following principles: the minimum essential budget for implementing the Universal Coverage Scheme is estimated at 1,202.40 Baht per capita by taking into consideration a population of approximately 46 million people without any insurance coverage. The breakdown of the unit cost is shown in Table 7.3. Out of 1,202.40 Baht, 150.40 Baht specified for high cost care, accident and emergency care and the capital investment budget is earmarked by the Area Health Board (AHB) for the provincial level to manage the scheme. Usually 10% of

Table 7.3 Budget for Universal Coverage Scheme (Unit cost per Capita)
Unit: Baht

	Minimum Essential Budget per capita per year	Amount	Amount allocated to health facilities
1	**Budget for medical care**		
	• Out-patient care cost	574	574
	• In-patient care cost	303	303
	• High cost care	32	(Ear-marked for the Area Health Board: AHB)
	• Accident and emergency care	25	(Ear-marked for the Area Health Board: AHB)
	Sub-total	934	877
2	**Budget for health promotion and prevention**	175	175
3	Capital Investment Budget	93.40	(Ear-marked for the Area Health Board: AHB)
	Total	1,202.40	1,052

Source: Health Insurance Office, 2002

the capital investment budget should be allocated for fund management including system development and personnel training. Another 10% of the capital investment budget should be allocated for a contingency fund for inventing security and improving the efficiency of the scheme. Thus the amount actually allocated to each province is 1,052 Baht per person per year.

The AHB can prescribe adjusted capitation to reward the extra efforts of the health facilities based on utilization rate, the type of health services, consumer satisfaction and health promotion innovation. This is dealt with in more detail in a later section.

(3) *Consumer Choice and the Co-payment System*

People who are eligible to join the scheme are those who are not covered by any insurance scheme. Eligible people are provided with a so-called "gold card" which entitles them to receive care services from health facilities with a co-payment of 30 Baht per visit. Community leaders (*kamnan* and village headmen) and volunteer health workers, monks, and veterans, as well as the elderly, the socially underprivileged and low-income groups are exempted from co-payment.

In theory, those eligible have freedom to choose any health facilities that are accredited as primary care providers. However, because of the incomplete development of the registration information system, a specific provider is usually assigned to the registered population according to its geographical situation and transportation availability during the transition period.

In addition, in order to ensure the standardized quality of service delivery, a hospital accreditation system is under development.

(4) *Benefit Package Including Health Promotion and Prevention, and Approved Alternative Care*

One of the unique features of the scheme is that the benefit package may include community based activities such as home visits and the use of traditional medicine on an approved basis.

3.2.3.3 Management and Operation Systems for the Universal Coverage Scheme

Starting in April 2001, pilot projects have been conducted with hospitals under the jurisdiction of the MOPH in six provinces.[43] Since June 2001, the scheme has been expanded to fifteen other provinces covering certain university hospitals and private hospitals. The principle, and the management and operation systems have been developed through the pilot experiences. Since October 2001, the Universal Coverage Scheme has been officially extended throughout the provinces. The management system and capitation arrangement are still in the process of learning by doing. However, the scheme has a much more locally-oriented design in its application of the concept of "health decentralization" and also due to the fact that the role of the MOPH is more that of policymaker or regulator for all public and private health facilities than that of service provider. The scheme achieves more cost effectiveness by changing the financing mechanism and flows.

First, the Area Health Board (AHB) established at the provincial level is designated to undertake the overall management of the scheme.[44] The main function of the AHB is to formulate health policy and plans for the province, to allocate resources, to set standardized healthcare services, and to monitor and evaluate performance in the area. The Ministry of Public Health (MOPH) provides a broad policy direction to the provincial public health office. The AHB in each province has freedom to adjust the budget it is allocated per capitation from the MOPH. Similarly, human resource management is subject to coordination by the AHB. In theory, the AHB is composed of representatives from local government organizations such as PAO, Municipalities and TAO; experts in health and representatives from the public; representatives from healthcare providers such as provincial hospitals, district hospitals and health centres; and the Provincial Chief Medical Officer (Preeda 2003).

Second, a contracting unit system is applied. The Contracting Unit for Primary Care (CUP) refers to an organization such as a district hospital which provides curative, promotion, preventive and emergency services and sometimes extends primary healthcare services as an in-hospital PCU. The CUP makes contracts with PCUs and procures primary care services from each PCU by paying the necessary cost by capitation. It is significant that the CUP system forms an integrated network of health services by linking health centres that are under the jurisdiction of the district health offices with district hospitals, as well as by involving private hospitals and hospitals under other ministries (see Figure 7.3).

Through the contracting unit system, referral services are to be strengthened. In addition to the CUP, a Contracting Unit for Secondary Care (CUS) is created at hospital level which can provide general care in in-patient services. The CUS is responsible for those patients referred from primary care unit as in-patients. The CUS may include such organizations as district hospitals, regional hospitals, general hospitals, and other public hospitals outside the MOPH as well as private hospitals. The Contracting Unit for Tertiary Care (CUT) is also formed at hospital level, and this can provide specialized care with high technology at high cost. The CUT is usually a regional hospital, a university hospital or a specialized health institution. Thus, it is anticipated that people who do not have serious medical problems will be more likely to utilize health centres first instead of seeking the services of hospitals, in the expectation that this new network will make the referral system more effective and that allocative efficiency will rise.

Figure 7.3   The Structure of Provincial Health Service Management
Focused on the Mechanism of Contracting Unit for Primary Healthcare (CUP)
(After the Introduction of the Universal Coverage Scheme)

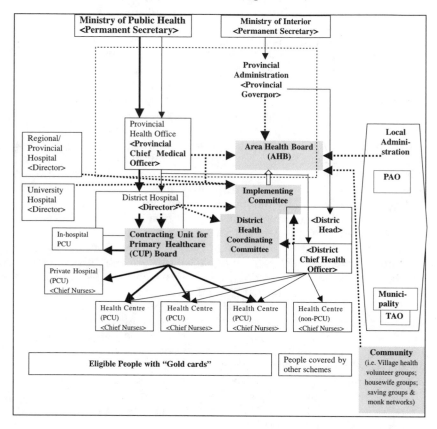

Source: prepared by the author
Note: Arrows ——▶ indicate administrative supervision and budget flow
      Arrows ——▶ indicate budget flow under the CUP mechanism
      Arrows ·····▶ indicate membership of the board (committees)

We have observed that the introduction of the Universal Coverage
Scheme intends to bring about considerable changes in health service
management systems and financial mechanisms. In the next section,
there follows an examination of cases in Khon Kaen Province to see if
improved responsiveness and local participation induce better decisions
for the use of public resources and a more equitable and accountable
service delivery.

3.3 Actual Implementation of Universal Coverage Scheme in Khon Kaen Province[45]

3.3.1 General Background to Khon Kaen Province

Khon Kaen Province is located in the heart of the Northeast region. The capital of the province, Khon Kaen, is 450 km northeast of Bangkok. It covers an area of 10,886 km^2 or about 6.5% of the Northeast region. About 7.8% of Khon Kaen consists of forested areas, and 61% of the region consists of utilizable agricultural areas. The population of Khon Kaen as of February 2003 is 876,223 males and 880,772 females making a total of 1,756,995 inhabitants and 422,643 households. The majority of people are engaged in the agricultural sector such as rice, corn, and sugar cane cultivation. Per capita income is 40,985 Baht/year. The figure

Figure 7.4 Map of Khon Kaen Province and its Districts

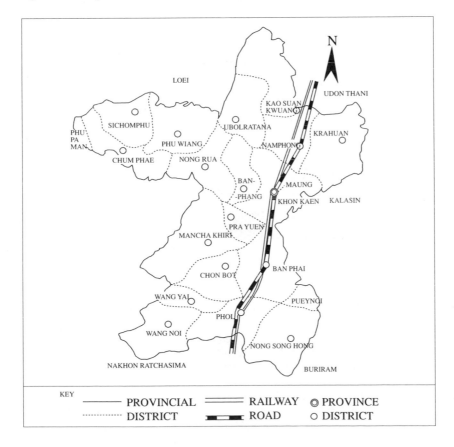

KEY

———— PROVINCIAL   ══════ RAILWAY   ◎ PROVINCE
·············· DISTRICT   ▰▰▰▰ ROAD   ○ DISTRICT

Table 7.4   Health Facilities in Khon Kaen Province

Facilities	Numbers	Characteristics
Public Health Offices	1	Provincial Public Health Office
	2	District public health offices
Regional hospitals	1	714-bed regional/provincial hospital
District hospitals	1	120-bed district hospital
	2	90-bed district hospitals
	3	60-bed district hospitals
	14	30-bed district hospitals
Primary Care Unit for Universal Healthcare Programme	144	Primary care units
Health Centres	247	Health centres
	4	Municipality health posts
Other facilities under the MOPH	1	150-bed Maternal and child health hospital
	1	60-bed Maternal and child health hospital
	1	140-bed Drugs addiction rehabilitation
	1	250-bed Communicable disease control hospital
	1	372-bed Psychiatric hospital
Other facilities under other Ministries	1	777-bed university hospital
	1	30-bed army hospital
Private facilities	3	Private hospitals (one 100-bed and one 250-bed)
	217	Private clinics
	33	Dental clinics
	125	Midwifery clinics
	6	Laboratories
Traditional facilities	5	Traditional medicine clinics

Source: Wongsa and Pattara (2003) originally from the Khon Kaen Public Health Office

is slightly higher than average for the Northeast region but lower than the national average.

The regional/provincial administration of Khon Kaen has 31 regional and provincial government offices and is divided into 20 districts (*Amphou*) and 5 would-be districts (*Ging Amphou*), 198 sub-districts and 2,249 villages. For local administration, it has one provincial administrative organization (PAO), 194 sub-district administration organizations (TAO) and 31 municipalities.

The distribution of health resources such as doctors, nurses, and beds by region (population to resource ratios) shows the unfavourable status of the Northeast region compared to the national average and especially compared to Bangkok and the Central region. For example, the ratio of doctors and professional nurses to population was 1: 8,311 and 1:1,702 respectively in the Northeast region in 2000. These figures are disparate from those in Bangkok by 10.5 and 5.5-fold (MOPH 2003, p. 337). The health facilities in Khon Kaen Province is shown in Table 7.4 above.

On the other hand, at the end of 2002, current forms of health insurance in Khon Kaen covered about 95% of people, a rather high figure compared to the national average of 70% in 2001. Out of the people insured in Khon Kaen, 76.89% had 30 Baht gold cards.[46] The coverage is as high in the two case districts analyzed below (see Table 7.6). It suggests that in Khon Kaen the 30-Baht healthcare programme has been introduced swiftly since October 2001 and more people have become gold card holders than the national average.

3.3.2 Actual Implementation in Khon Kaen Province[47]

A rough sketch of the actual application of the scheme and its consequences is drawn from case studies of two districts: Chum Phae

---

Box 2
General Overview of Chum Phae District

Location: It is located 82km west of Khon Kaen. It has provincial borders next to two other provinces: Loei Province to the north and Chaiyaphum Province to the south.

Provincial and Local Administration: There are 12 sub-districts (*tambon*) and 124 villages. As local administrative organizations, there are 3 municipalities and 12 sub-district administration organizations (TAO). The total population is 126,255 out of which 63,063 are male and 63,192 were female. Majority of the people are farmers. The major crops are rice, bean, corn, sugarcane and cassava. Some others are engaged in factories or services industries.

Health facilities: Public health facilities are composed of a 120-bed district hospital, a district health office, 17 health centres (including 1 primary care unit) and 2 municipality health posts (including 1 primary care unit) Private health facilities include 17 private clinics, 2 dental clinics, 10 midwifery clinics, and 15 pharmacies. Under the Universal Coverage Scheme there are 2 Primary Care Units.

Health statistics:
Crude birth rate: 6.73/1,000 mid year population
Crude death rate: 4.10/1,000 mid year population
Population growth rate: 1.2
Infant mortality rate: 58/1,000 live birth
Children under 5 mortality rate: 116/1,000 live birth
Maternal mortality rate: 0.9/100,000 live birth

Box 3
General Overview of Nam Phong District

Location: Nam Phong District is located 43km northeast of the city of Khon Kaen. Other four districts of the province surround it.

Provincial and Local Administration: There are 12 sub-districts (*tambon*) and 167 villages. As local administrative organizations, there are 2 municipalities and 12 Sub-district administrations organizations (TAO). The total population is 108,215 out of which 54,124 are male and 54,091 are female. Most of its population is engaged in agriculture. The major crops are rice and sugarcane.

Health facilities: Public health facilities are composed of a 60-bed hospital, (including an in-hospital primary care unit), and 18 health centres (including 5 primary care units). Private health facilities include 6 private clinics, 4 pharmacies. In total 1576 village health volunteers are in service for the villagers. Under the Universal Coverage Scheme there are 6 Primary Care Units.

Health Statistics:
Crude birth rate: 12.8/1,000 mid year population
Crude death rate: 3.9/1,000 mid year population

Source: Wongsa and Pattara (2003) originally from Khon Kaen Province (data is mostly those of 2002)

District with a total population of 126,255 sharing its border with two other provinces; and Num Phong District with a total population of 108,215 near Khon Kaen city. Compared to other districts, both districts have a rather larger number of *tambon* and villages where the majority of people are farmers. An overview of the two districts is shown in Box 2 and Box 3 respectively.

3.3.2.1 Management and Operation Systems for the Universal Coverage System
Management and operation systems for the scheme may vary by province. In Khon Kaen Province, there are three levels of committees for regulating, implementing and coordinating the Universal Coverage scheme: the "Khon Kaen Board" chaired by the provincial governor; the Implementing Committee chaired by the PCMO and the District Health Coordinating Committees chaired by directors of district hospitals; and the CUP Board chaired by directors of district hospitals (see Figure 7.5).

(1) The Khon Kaen Board for the Universal Coverage Scheme
In Khon Kaen Province, the Area Health Board mentioned in the previous section was not established. Instead, the Kohn Kaen Board was formed to administer overall operation of the 30-Baht scheme at the provincial level.

Figure 7.5   The Structure of Provincial Health Service Management in Khon Kaen
Province (After the Introduction of the Universal Coverage Scheme)

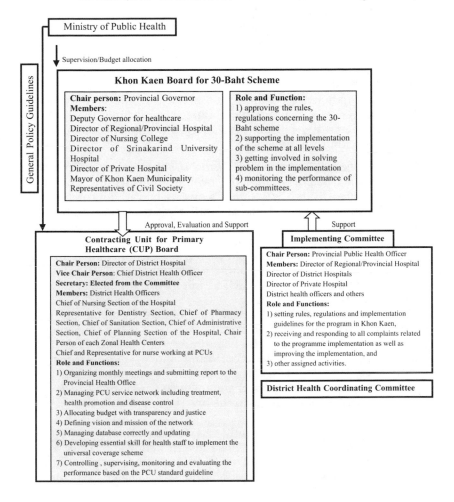

Source: prepared by the author based on Wongsa and Pattara (2003)

This board is chaired by the Provincial Governor, and the Provincial Chief
Medical Officer (PCMO) serves as secretary as well as being a member of
the board. Other members include representatives of the provincial
administration such as the Deputy Governor for healthcare, and directors
of various public facilities such as the regional/general hospital, district

hospitals, the nursing college, the university hospital, and private hospitals. Notably, the board also invites representatives of local administrative organizations such as the Mayor of Khon Kaen City and of public organizations such as the village health volunteer network, the monk network and so forth.

This board is responsible for 1) approving the rules and regulations concerning the 30-Baht Scheme; 2) supporting the implementation of the scheme at all levels; 3) getting involved in solving problems and in the implementations of solutions; 4) monitoring the performance of sub-committees. The above responsibilities clearly show the Universal Coverage Scheme has full authority over the implementation of the programme within the province.

(2) The Implementing Committee and District Health Coordinating Committees
The Khon Kaen Board is supported by the Implementing Committee which is chaired by the PCMO and consists of the directors of each hospital, district health officers, and other related health staff in the province and does not invite representatives from local governments or from civil society. The committee is responsible for 1) setting rules, regulations and implementation guidelines for the programme in Khon Kaen; 2) receiving and responding to all complaints related to the programme implementation as well as improving the implementation; and 3) other assigned activities.

In turn, there are the District Health Coordinating Committees, which operate as district information centres: supporting the Implementing Committee in formulating health plans in response to local problems, in implementing plans, and in monitoring and evaluating their own performance. The District Health Coordinating Committee is chaired by the director of the district hospital and includes the District Chief Health Officer, district health officers, and the head of each major section of the hospital.

The two committees already existed as the administrative instruments for developing provincial health policy and plans, as well as monitoring, advising on and evaluating healthcare services in the province, even before the Universal Coverage Scheme was adopted. Since the scheme has been put into full application, the existing committees provide forums for the communication, discussion, and sharing of all healthcare related issues of the scheme between healthcare purchasers (the MOPH or the provicial administration) and providers (the CUP board mentioned below).[48]

(3) The Contracting Unit for Primary Care (CUP) Board
The CUP Board is a newly established mechanism for the implementation of the scheme through coordination between hospitals and health centres. The CUP Board is chaired by the director of a

district hospital. The board is composed of the District Chief Health Officer, other staff of the District Health Office, the chiefs of major sections of the hospital, representatives of each zonal health centre, representatives from nurses working at PCUs, and the Chief of Primacy Care Units.

The role of the CUP Board is to manage the PCU service network, to allocate budgets with transparency and justice, to develop essential skills for health personnel, and to supervise, monitor and evaluate the performance of PCUs according to the guidelines and standards set by the Khon Kaen Board. Thus the director of a district hospital who manages the CUP Board obtains more authority over budget allocation to health centres. On the contrary, the district health office has now only a minimal budget.

Five working committees are attached to the CUP Board to solve problems and to enhance improvement in its operation: 1) a working committee for receiving and dealing with customer complaints; 2) a working committee for developing a health service network; 3) a working committee for finance; 4) a working committee for referral systems; and 5) a working committee to create a database of universal healthcare coverage in the health service. Each working committee is composed of representatives of district health offices and hospitals, heads of PCUs, and nurses working at PCUs respectively.

The Universal Coverage Scheme allows people to voice their concerns and opinions about the programme. There is a "Working Committee for Receiving and Solving Customer Complaints". This is because the CUP acknowledges that practitioners engaged in healthcare services cannot always deal successfully with complaints themselves. Thus, a cyclical network of receiving and dealing with customer complaints is formed. All complaints are recorded to get feedback within the CUP.

As part of the referral network of the CUP, a contracting unit for secondary care (CUS) and a contracting unit for tertiary care (CUT) are designated in the province.

The overall picture of the management of the service illustrates the movement of the MOPH towards delegating more authority to the provincial level so that all health facilities in the boundary are administered by the mechanism of the Khon Kaen Board. At the same time, the MOPH separates the role of service provider from that of policymaker/regulator and induces the PCMO to delegate more financial authority to the director of the district hospital who heads the CUP board.

3.3.2.2 Financial Management Systems for the Universal Coverage Scheme
There is considerable flexibility in budget allocation at a provincial level.

In 2002, there were about 130,000 people registered for the scheme in the province: its total budget amounted to 1,200 million Baht. The provincial health office first retained 15% of the budget appropriated by the centre. Out of 1,200 million Baht, the province further subtracts

Figure 7.6   Financial Management Flow of the Universal Coverage Scheme in Khon Kaen Province

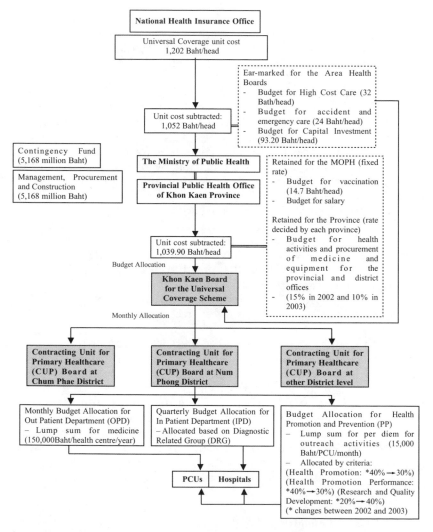

Source: prepared by the author based on Wongsa and Pattara (2003)

salary and 14.7 Baht per capita for vaccines before making monthly allocations to each CUP. The retained budget at provincial level is used for health activities and procurement of medicine and equipment at the provincial health office or district health offices. This ratio decreased to 10% in 2003. It appears that the province is more concerned with pressing budget needs at CUP level.

Resources allocated to each CUP are divided into three categories depending on purpose: out-patient department (OPD), in-patient department (IPD) and promotion and prevention (PP). As for the financial flow see Figure 7.6

The budget appropriated from central level before deductions at provincial level is 574 Baht, 303 Baht and 175 Baht for OPD, IPD and PP respectively. The budget allocated for each CUP can be computed proportionately. The budget for OPD is allotted monthly to each CUP. The budget for medicine in each health centre is in a lump sum: 150,000 Baht per year per health centre. For IPD the budget for each CUP is allocated quarterly, and the amount calculated is based on "diagnostic related group (DRG)".[49]

For health promotion and prevention (PP), a lump sum of 15,000 Baht per month is provided for per diem payment of PCU staff for outreach activities.[50] The rest of the appropriated budget for PP is allocated to each CUP based on the following criteria with fixed proportion: 40% for patient capitation, 40% for health promotion performances and 20% for research and quality development in the CUP network. In 2003, the allocation criteria were changed to 30%, 30% and 40% respectively. The increased focus on research and quality development is related to the increased motivation of the staff for further training and pilot activities. In addition, in 2003, the source of per diem payment is no longer solely the PP budget; half is now taken from the PP budget and the other half from the OPD budget.

It is clear that financial management for the scheme has already been delegated to the provincial and district level. At the provincial level in Khon Kaen the regulations for budget allocation mentioned above have been determined and adjusted by the Khon Kaen Board in which most of the public and private stakeholders participate in decision making. At the district or CUP level, the formula of budget allocation seems to be almost similar for every CUP in Khon Kaen. However, the adoption of performance-based criteria and an increased budget for research and development give more flexibility and motivation in effective use of the budget.

3.3.2.3 Personnel Management for the Universal Coverage Scheme
To realize "good health at low cost", the scheme focuses more on health promotion and prevention than curative care. Furthermore, the MOPH recognizes that the role of regulator should be clearly split from that of a

Table 7.5 Changes of Staff Allocation in PCUs of Chum Phae and Num Phong
Districts *(After the adoption of the Universal Coverage Scheme)*

Location of PCUs	Change in the number of Health Personnel[1]	Proportion of Health Personnel/ persons registered in the covered area	Level of PCUs[3]
Chum Phae District			
- In-District Hospital PCU	12 (rotate)	1:1000	3
- Sri Prasert[2]	3 +(1)	1:2000	2
Num Phong District			
- Ban Sumphan	3 + 0	1:1404	2
- Nong Kanae	5 + 0	1:1500	2
- Bue Ngoen	3 + 1	1:1700	2
- Ban Kham	3 + 1	1:1800	2
- Kaen Kumkoon	2 + 1	1:1200	2
- Moung wan	2 + 0	1:2700	2

[1] For example, "3+ 1" means that the original number of staff was three, and one additional nurse is assigned to help working in the PCU
[2] One additional nurse to Sri Prasert PCU still belongs to a district hospital.
[3] There are three levels of PCUs:
  First Level: only public health workers providing service
  Second Level: at least one registered nurse who provides service
  Third Level: at least one medical doctor providing service
Source: Wongsa and Pattara (2003)

service provider and that the role of the centre and the provincial
administration should be shifted from the latter to the former.
Consequently, organizational restructuring has been conducted at all levels.
A considerable number of health personnel who had mainly functioned
as administrators, managers, and technical support were transferred to
service units such as hospitals and PCUs. The budget is allocated on a
capitation basis, including the allocation for staff salary. This clearly shows
that the province has to maximize use of its human resources.[51,52]

In Num Phong District, human resource allocation was changed in
response to the new policy and additional tasks. After the adoption of the
scheme, registered nurses were newly assigned to healthcare services with
one in every PCU except in the one which already had their own registered
nurse working full-time: The in-hospital PCU has a doctor, nurses, a
pharmacist and a dentist who rotate from normal activities in the hospital
to provide service in the PCU. Monthly supervision is also carried out at
the PCU by joint delegates from Num Phong hospital and the District
Health Office in order to improve and ensure the quality of healthcare
services.

On the contrary, after one year of implementation in the Chum Phae District, there were no doctors or other health personal transferred to PCUs. The staff at a PCU in Chum Phae felt that relocation of human resources to his/her PCU was not particularly necessary whether part-time or full-time. The difference to date, however, is that they have had regular support through supervision from the hospital which is quite useful. Problems that the staff have encountered are that they have to struggle with new forms, records and financial processes which all take time. Furthermore, during the initial stage, the process was still not clearly established and was unstable. For most staff, time was spent on meetings, training and filling in forms.

Changes in staff allocation in both districts are compared in Table 7.5.

3.3.2.4 Public Participation in Decision Making and Implementation
The degree of participation of the people in implementation of the programme is minimal. At the provincial level, only the Mayor of Khon Kaen City and representatives of health volunteers and monk networks are appointed as board members, but they are seldom influential in decision making. It is worse at the CUP level; there are no representatives from the community.

At daily operation levels, people such as village health volunteers contribute to the scheme by carrying out surveys during the registration process and by distributing 30-Baht gold cards. As mentioned earlier, "The Working Committee for Receiving and Solving Customer Complaints" at the CUP level deals with any complaints, and ensures feedback within the CUP. The administrative structure for the scheme adopts certain mechanisms so as to be more responsive to the public.

The sub-district administrative organization (TAO) and Municipalities are not involved either. Links between the CUP network and local government organizations should be strengthened, since the participation of TAO and municipalities can contribute not only to more responsiveness to local public opinion but also to the coordinated use of the local budget. The CUP board of Chum Phae realizes this problem and in 2003 they decided to invite representatives of TAO and municipalities as board members. Normally, the sub-district organisations have an AIDS programme budget (20,000 Baht per sub-district per year). Therefore, the district hospital hopes to get more participation from the local authority in terms of additional fiscal resources for the Universal Coverage Scheme.

In Num Phong District, communication with the public has been strengthened through public health networks such as village health volunteer networks, monk networks and so on, since 1997. Through these networks, public information and health issues and concerns are shared when the hospital staff, and the Director of Num Phong District

Hospital in particular attends the monthly meetings of the networks. This is an indirect means of obtaining contribution and participation from community organizations. TAO also taps some budget to support health prevention activities. In 2002, the Num Phong CUP received 1.68 million Baht from TAO for health activities in the CUP. In 2003, it is expected to obtain more budget allocations from TAO.

3.3.2.5 Performance of the Health Service under the Universal Coverage Scheme[53]

Although very preliminary, the performance of the Universal Coverage Scheme in the two districts is analyzed from the following three aspects: the *equity* aspect, in terms of widened coverage of the people who get insured under the scheme; the *efficiency* aspect by reviewing the behavioural change of the service users; and the *quality* aspect by measuring the level of customer satisfaction.

(1) Equity

As seen in 3.3.1, current systems of health insurance in Khon Kaen covered about 95% of people by the end of 2002, a rather high figure in comparison with the national average of 70% in 2001. Since the implementation of the Universal Coverage Scheme, in Num Phong District, all of its inhabitants are covered by at least one type of health insurance. About 80% of the people in this district are covered by the Universal Coverage Scheme, out of whom about 45% have obtained 30-Baht gold cards and 35% have received free service 30-Baht gold cards (See Table 7.6).

In Chum Phae District, the figure combining the two types of 30-Baht gold cards indicates that 80% of people are covered by the Universal Coverage Scheme. However about 6% of people are still identified as not having a clear insurance scheme (see Table 7.6) This is mostly caused by the rejection of gold card applications in such cases where applicants used to have social security insurance, but have not been deleted from the Social Security Scheme since retiring. These cases cause some financial burden to the CUP which provides services without the capitation budget allocation until the insurance schemes for these people have been clarified. In addition there are 45 foreigners who are not eligible to join the scheme. The CUP has to take care of them without any budget appropriation when they need medical treatment from the hospital.

To sum up, people in both Num Phong and Chum Phae Districts benefit from improved equity in terms of the right to get access to resources. The new holders of 30-Baht gold cards are those who had not held any insurance or bought a health card before the adoption of the Universal Coverage Scheme.[54] In comparison with the health card scheme, the application for the 30-Baht Scheme does not require any voluntarism: rather any Thai who does not have insurance is eligible and can register

Table 7.6 Types and Coverage of Health Insurance in Khon Kaen

Type of Health Insurance	Number of people (its proportion)			
	National Total[*1]	Khon Kaen Province	Num Phong District	Chum Phae District
Civil Servants Medical Benefit Scheme	(8.5%)	109,568 (6.36%)	5,429 (4.8%)	5,409 (4.3%)
Social Security Scheme	(7.2%)	202,117 (11.79%)	5,968 (5.3%)	12,622 (10.0)
30-Baht gold card	(0.9%)	1,324,436 (76.86%)	50,899 (44.9%)	100,292 (79.4%)
Free 30-Baht gold card[*2]			41,144 (35%)	
Others[*3]	(54.4)	—	—	—
Total **People with health insurance**	(71%)	**1,722,543** (95%)	**113,440** (100%)	**126,284** (93.7%)
People without health insurance Not registered for gold card/have more than 3 scheme health insurance/ registered in other province	**(29%)**	**86,422** (5%)	**0** (0%)	**7,961** (6.3%)

Remarks: [*1]: National data are of 2001. Data within the Khon Kaen Province is of 2002.
  [*2]: Except in Num Phong District data of gold cardholders and free gold cardholders is not distinguished.
  [*3]: In 2001 there existed several other welfare schemes that were banned in 2002: medical welfare for the low-income group (12.7%), voluntary health insurance (health card by the MOPH and private insurance) (22.1%), and Others (0.8%)

Source: National data from MOPH (2002) and data of Khon Kaen Province from Wongsa and Pattara (2003) originally from the Khon Kaen Public Health Office, Num Phong District Health Office, and Chum Phae District Health Office

Table 7.7   Interview Results: Health-Seeking Behaviours of Clients in Chum Phae
and Num Phong Districts before and after Implementing 30-Baht Scheme

Type of services and facilities utilized	Before Number of respondents (%)	After Number of respondents (%)
Self-prescription	3 (2.9)	0(0)
Drug store	3 (2.9)	2 (2.0)
PCU	36 (35.3)	49 (48.0)
Private clinic	7 (6.9)	5 (4.9)
Hospital	53 (52.0)	41 (40.2)
Others	3 (2.9)	2 (2.0)
Total	102 (100)	102 (100)

Source: Interviews by Wongsa and Pattara (2003)

with the scheme. Ironically, the Chum Phae CUP has to bear the cost of
health services to people who are identified as having unclear insurance
information.

(2) Efficiency[55]

The interview results indicate that an increasing number of people in the
two districts are using PCU more, and hospitals or private clinics less
than before. Of the total 102 respondents, utilization of PCU after
implementing the 30-Baht Scheme was increased from 35.3% to 48.0%
whereas the percentage of clients attending hospital was reduced from
52.0% to 40.2% (See Table 7.7).

It is known that PCU or health centres provide primary healthcare
services whose unit cost is usually smaller than that of hospitals. In Num
Phong District, as seen in *3.3.2.3*, district hospital nurses are assigned to
help work in the PCU. The Universal Coverage Scheme has given an
indication of its efficiency as far as resources allocation is concerned.

Table 7.8   Interview Results: Type of Health Services Sought from the CUPs
in Chum Phae and Num Phong Districts

Type of Services utilized	Number of respondents (%)		
	Total	Num Phong	Chum Phae
Health promotion (antenatal care (ANC), postnatal care (PNC), and vaccination)	15 (14.7)	15 (22.1)	0 (0)
Acute diseases	71 (69.6)	38 (55.9)	33 (97.0)
Chronic diseases	16 (15.7)	15 (22.0)	1 (3.0)

Source: Interviews by Wongsa and Pattara (2003)

Survey results related to the types of health services, however, show that curative care is preferred over health promotion activities. Most services provided by healthcare providers in the two districts are curative care of which 69.6% is for acute care, followed by 15.7% for chronic care (see Table 7.8). The lowest proportion of services provided are in health promotion. This may be a reflection that the essential policy stressing health promotion in health facilities has still not reached its goal. In other words health promotion activities should be encouraged in proactive ways, not in hospitals or health centres but in the household or community.

From the above results, it would be legitimate to assume that the scheme shows signs of greater cost-effectiveness and allocative efficiency with emphasis on primary care services in PCUs, while health promotion activities that have been advocated to tackle skyrocketing health costs have not been prevalent in PCUs as expected.

Table 7.9   Interview Results: Satisfaction of the Clients Attending PCUs in Chum Phae and Num Phong Districts

Item	Level of Satisfaction				
	Very little	Little	Fair	Much	Very much
Waiting time	0	0	44 (43.1%)	32 (31.4%)	26 (25.5%)
Place/infrastructure	1 (1.0%)	2 (2.0%)	20 (19.6%)	48 (47.1%)	31 (30.4%)
Care services	0	5 (4.9%)	24 (23.5%)	44 (43.1%)	29 (28.4%)
Behaviours of health personnel	0	3 (2.9%)	13 (12.8%)	51 (50.0%)	35 (34.3%)
Overall	0	1 (1.0%)	18 (17.6%)	47 (46.1%)	36 (35.3%)

Source: Interviews by Wongsa and Pattara (2003)

(3) Quality[56]

Can people enjoy good services with only a 30-Baht co-payment? In the survey, more than 81% of clients are satisfied or very satisfied with overall services including the behaviour of health personnel and the infrastructure of facilities. However, satisfaction with treatment/services and time taken is ranked lower by a few clients at 71% and 56% respectively. In general, it could be said that the quality of services under the scheme is appreciated by clients (see Table 7.9).

There is slight difference in the quality of personnel between the two districts. As seen in Table 7.5, in Chum Phae district has more qualified staff because most of them are rotated from a district hospital.

The proportion of staff per registered persons is also quite good. They may perform better because they do not suffer much from personnel constraint.

3.3.3 Preliminary Results of the Universal Coverage Scheme

Khon Kaen Province has had only one and a half years experience of the Universal Coverage Scheme since its adoption in October 2001. Although the results of the scheme are still partial, it has shown some positive effects as we have seen above.

- The formation of the Khon Kaen Board that corresponds to the Area Health Board (AHB) has helped the integration of more health facilities, both private and public, including non-MOPH public hospitals into the unitary referral system, as shown by the fact that more people visit the PCU first for primary care rather than costly secondary hospitals or private hospitals.
- The MOPH provides very general policy guidelines for the administration of the Universal Coverage Scheme. The formation of the Khon Kaen Board for the Scheme chaired by the Provincial Governor, and the support mechanism for policymaking by the implementation committee chaired by the Provincial Chief Medical Officer indicate that more authority in applying and adjusting the rules and regulations was transferred to the provincial level.
- Under the CUP scheme and the formation of the CUP Board, the Director of District Hospitals chairs the board and obtains substantial authority over budget allocation to the PCU.
- Although local government organizations such as TAO and municipalities were not involved in the Khon Kaen Board or the CUP Board, in the case of both districts, the CUP boards have realized the need for their involvement so as to have more communication with localities as well as for the coordinated utilization of the budget for health service activities allocated to local organizations.
- Performance in the service delivery of the scheme cannot be easily assessed with only one and a half years of operation. However, the health insurance coverage of the non-covered population was certainly enhanced by the scheme. The interview survey indicates that an inducement of cost-effectiveness and allocative efficiency as well as of quality of services can be seen, although to a limited extent. More people use the PCU than before instead of visiting private hospitals and private clinics, but clients need curative treatment services rather than health promotion services such as vaccination or maternal healthcare. People are quite satisfied with the service quality of the PCU in terms of the behaviour of health personnel and facilities available.

On the other hand, the consequences to the service delivery as far as its responsiveness to needs and flexibility are concerned are not clearly known. Aside from operational trials and errors, there are also generic problems inherent to the scheme. For example, grievances on the rigidity of the applied ratio of capitation have been heard from district hospitals. This problem stems from the information system and applied formula for aggregation of the capitation mechanism. This leads to the debate over the financial sustainability of the Universal Coverage Scheme.

- The information system for estimating and registering accurately the number of eligible people and for monitoring client information may not be sufficient for reflecting on service contents.
- Some district hospitals that have many beds and cost more to maintain suffer from financial difficulties because of the inflexible adjustment of the capitation formula. One district hospital director complained that the rigidity of the fix capitation ratio for medical care meant that any leftover funds from health promotion and prevention could not be put towards more cost-consuming medical care. The decision to apply a higher budget allocation to primary care in fiscal 2004 might increase the number of grievances from district hospitals.
- Coordinated actions remain inflexible unless health centres come under the jurisdiction of district hospitals.

Evidence to date indicates that more authority was given to the provincial and district levels to manage the scheme and service delivery on the one hand. It is unique that the central government, the provincial administration (including the district levels), and beneficiaries are defined as "purchaser", "provider" and "consumer" in operating the scheme. On the other hand, the capitation system that allocates the necessary budget by unit cost per person per year to district hospitals and PCUs may contain extravagant use of the budget and may lead to incentives to use money more efficiently and effectively. However, concrete evidence of the effect of such financing reform should be identified. The financial and operational sustainability of the Universal Coverage Scheme itself should be reviewed and monitored. We must continue to observe whether the new management mechanism has incentives to encourage more localities to be more responsive to local opinion and to monitor and improve their own performance.

4. Implications and Conclusion

In this chapter, the evolution of and a different approach to decentralization in Thailand has been examined over the years with a focus on specific features of the administrative structures and the characteristics of the policy environment that induced the reform. What is the implication identified from the Thai experience?

Now, more than 80% of developing countries have been experiencing some form of decentralization in recent years, and decentralization is often considered a form of democracy in which local autonomy is granted and locally elected governments are held more accountable to local residents. Administrative decentralization has been increasingly viewed as an important dimension of good governance since accountability of the government often affects the effectiveness and efficiency of public provision of goods and services and the decentralized form of government often makes service delivery more responsive to local needs.

The prevailing concept in Thailand has been "deconcentration". Although the search for types of autonomous government was initiated in the 1950s, local administration had been subject to the governing and supervisory authority of the central government until the new constitution of 1997 clarified its orientation toward decentralization. It should be noted that the agenda for strengthening local autonomous organizations was argued in parallel to the well-developed structure of Regional/ Provincial Administration that is in fact the field functions of central government.

Ministries such as the MOPH have developed their administrative arms in Regional/Provincial Administration up to each *tambon* level to make primary healthcare services accessible to the poor in a standardized way over the years. The health sector, which is the largest public sector in Thailand, addresses decentralization from its unique perspective. Considering insufficient professional capacity in local administration as well as fearing from possible fragmentation and uncoordinated health service systems, the MOPH seems to look for a more realistic approach to formulating an area network at the provincial level for the delegation of more financial power to the district level. It is notable that the MOPH is trying to adopt a new management mechanism in pursuit of such values which provides equitable, efficient and effective public services at the same time.

A new approach to health sector management seems to have taken shape in the adoption of the Universal Coverage Scheme in 2001. The idea is to make healthcare available at a fixed cost of 30 Baht per visit to families. Though it is not yet known whether the Universal Coverage Scheme is financially and operationally sustainable, it has brought about substantial changes to healthcare management systems. The new management systems seem to be an alternative to the devolution to subdistrict levels, considering their low level of local capacity, and also a way of avoiding functional fragmentation and local political capture.

In sum, healthcare management reform in Thailand is pursuing the efficacy of decentralization but in a modified way. Two aspects of efficacy have been examined, namely "allocative efficiency" and "productive efficiency".[57] It can be said that allocative efficiency has been enhanced by the responsibility given to the provincial levels and more financial freedom granted to the district hospitals by the capitation system despite the emergent problems of financial sustainability and inflexible capitation criteria which need to be resolved. As for "productive efficiency", improvement can be expected. For example, the establishment of an independent board such as the Area Health Board (AHB) to manage the scheme at the provincial level is a preliminary effort to mitigate the fragmented decision-making processes and to coordinate health service networks through increased participation of multi-levels of government, the private sector and the public in the province. The CUP Board, chaired by the director of district hospitals may not involve TAO and Municipalities at the moment. However, more involvement from sub-district governments is expected, so that their local budget can be utilized in a more coordinated way for health promotion and prevention activities and hence to improve services delivery in line with local public preferences.

Thailand's experience in the health sector gives us an example of a gradual and realistic approach to decentralization; redefining the role of each level of government, delegating more authority to such mechanisms as the Area Heath Board (AHB) at the provincial level, and granting a freer financial hand to district hospitals. Such gradual approach may not be applied to every country nor every sector unconditionally. The Khon Kaen case indicates that the delegation of more financial powers to directors of district hospitals could be linked to strengthening local networks with various community groups through increased invitation to several committees and through the introduction of built-in mechanisms to feedback complaints from beneficiaries. The basic stance of the frontline service deliverer and the top-down policy direction, which induces more local orientation, may matter significantly to create positive links of deconcentration to improved efficacy of service provision. The whole process is a pragmatic evolution based on the well-developed provincial structure of administration as well as on a government policy which stresses value commitment to efficiency, effectiveness and equity of service delivery.

Notes

[1] In Latin America, decentralization has been introduced under new constitutions as newly elected governments replace autocratic central regimes. In Africa, a sudden move to multi-party political systems was followed by increasing demand for articulating local voices in a formal political realm. In some post-conflict countries such as Uganda and

Mozambique, all former warrior factions were allowed more political participation at local levels (World Bank, Decentralization NET).

[2] See World Bank, Decentralization NET.

[3] In Indonesia, the transfer of administrative authority and officials to district/municipal levels has been sweeping and since 1999 has exhibited a drastic departure from the previous centralized system. After the collapse of the 30-year Soeharto regime, the Habibie government took the drive towards decentralization seriously in order to accommodate intensifying separatist movements such as those in Acheh or Irian Jaya. With more than 2.5 million civil servants and their responsibilities devolved to the local levels in a rushed schedule, it is often pointed out that lack of local capacity and financial resources as well as continuing religious conflicts and increasing local corruption could lead to further political instability and regional imbalances if not well managed (JICA 2000, 2001).

[4] In the Philippines, vigorous NGOs justify their role as complementing government services. Under a decentralized system it is still reported that inadequate inter-governmental task coordination and insufficient resources make local officials, especially at *barangay* (village) levels, unable to adjust services to local demands (JICA 2001, Azfar et al. 2001).

[5] For example, as advocated in the National Health Plan of the Thai Ministry of Public Health and in drafting the National Health Act (HSRO homepage retrieved from http://www.hsro.or.th/background_EngV.html).

[6] As discussed in a later section, the approach of the health sector is often defined as "deconcentration" meaning that more authority is transferred to the field units of the central government.

[7] As for the World Bank experience in developing a public sector reform programme, see PREM website http://www1.worldbank.org/publicsector/overview.htm#2

[8] The "Decentralization NET" of World Bank provides common knowledge on the experience of various forms of decentralization in developing countries.

[9] Azfar et al. (2001), Cohen et al. (1999) and many other studies endeavour to identify an analytical framework for successful decentralization. The World Bank notes that successful decentralization requires at least the following conditions, despite the complexity in reality: financing following clear assignment of functions; informed decision making; adherence to local priorities; and accountability (World Bank, Decentralization NET).

[10] It is pointed out that decentralization may increase regional disparities and inequalities. In Vietnam and some other countries, for example, the central government was more effective than local governments in targeting

poorer areas (Van de Walle 2001 and World Bank 2001b). It is also argued that decentralization may undermine high-level policy objectives and tend to lead to irrational policymaking and more corruption because of the local government's vulnerability to abuse authority and lack of capacity to manage effectively, in addition to people's sluggish attention to local elections (Azfar et al. 2001).

[11] The information and data concerning decentralization in this section is mostly from Charas (2002), Nagai (2001) and Noranit (2002) if not otherwise mentioned.

[12] The Thai Administration Act was first legislated in 1933 when Thailand shifted from an absolute to a constitutional monarchy. The act brought about the creation of the three-tier government structure that is composed of Central Administration, Regional/Provincial Administration, and Local Administration (Municipalities: *tessaban*). Until the current Act was stipulated in 1999, the basic structure had not been changed much since 1933 (Nagai 2001, p.55).

[13] A *tambon* is usually composed of about ten villages.

[14] For example, healthcare services are not the responsibility of the Ministry of Public Health but that of the public health office of the BMA.

[15] The initial form of local administration can be traced back to the 1950s. Both PAO and TAO were created under laws in the 1950s. TAO was abrogated in 1972 when the military government took power. However, strengthening the role of local government became a policy agenda in the 1970s when the Third Social and Economic Development Plan (1972–1976) addressed the improvement of social justice and the expansion of community development.

[16] The information and data used in the section are mostly from Nagai (2001, 2002, and 2003(1), (2) and (3)) if not otherwise specified.

[17] Although in the general election of 1999, pro-democracy political parties had promised the election of provincial governors, there was a variety of opposition to it. For example, the Ministry of Interior resisted the move toward direct election of provincial governors for fear of losing control over the provincial administration. It was a political compromise to establish TAO and Municipalities as the sub-district level self-government (Nagai 2001).

[18] In an official document of the government of Thailand, the act is called "the Act on Determining Plan and Process of Decentralization" (Office of Decentralization to Local Government Organization Committee, date unknown). In this chapter, the act is referred as "the Decentralization Act of 1999" in brief.

[19] In official documents of the government of Thailand, the Committee is called "the Decentralization to Local Government Organization Committee" (Office of Decentralization to Local Government Organization Committee, date unknown). In this chapter, the committee is referred as "the National Decentralization Committee" in brief.

[20] From fiscal 2003, general and specific grants from the Ministry of Interior and grants for the transfer of responsibility from various ministries were replaced by sectoral block grants which allow local governments more autonomy (World Bank 2001b).

[21] According to the Decentralization Act, TAO, Pattaya City, municipalities and PAO are entitled to collect value-added tax and duties on selected businesses, including alcohol and tobacco, and gambling. In fiscal 2000, however, 43% of local government revenue comes from shared taxes with central government, 44% from grants and only 13% from locally collected taxes (World Bank 2003, p. 29).

[22] For example, a TAO under-secretary is a C-4 level official, while a school principal or a resident nurse of a district hospital are C-7 to C-9 level officials (*Bangkok Post*, 10 September 2000).

[23] Public Sector Reform in Thailand has its theoretical foundation in the Cabinet Resolution on Public Service Reform of 1998 and the Public Organization Act of 1999 promulgated under the Chuan Administration. This resolution and act aim to improve the bureaucratic system by decentralizing functions to local administrative units, eliminating the duplication of public sector activities, improving the quality of government officials and services, creating an incentive system for civil servants, and developing the means to prevent misconduct and corruption (OCSC 2002).

[24] Bureaucratic reform with the aim of restructuring government agencies in October 2002 is the culmination of his emphasis on public sector reform (Thaksin 2002).

[25] The public service agreement has been applied to major responsible ministers to ensure outcomes and service quality as well as efficiency of service delivery. This information is based on OCSC (2000) and on interviews with Thai officials and researchers from the Thailand Development Research Institute (TDRI) and the Health Systems Research Institute (HRSI) in February 2003.

[26] This is based on the findings of Thai officials and researchers in February 2003.

[27] The concept of "health decentralization" of the Ministry of Public Health will be described in section *3.2.2.2.*

[28] According to Nagai (2002) joint committees were established in 2001 among the National Decentralization Committee and the two ministries respectively. Ministry of Public Health officials report that the discussion on health decentralization has been suspended since 2002.

[29] Figures were provided by Nagai in a study meeting in Tokyo in April 2003.

[30] Currently, every *tambon* is covered by one or more health centres, amounting to 9,738 in total. There are 720 district hospitals which cover 90.6% of all districts. In addition, there are 214 municipal health centres (MOPH 2003, p. 279).

[31] This is based on interviews carried out in Khon Kaen in March 2003.

[32] It is notable that CT scanners in Bangkok hospitals in the 1990s were more abundant than those in Great Britain. Twenty two percent of doctors resigned to work for the private sector and as a result 21 district hospitals suffered from the absence of doctors in 1997 (MOPH 2000).

[33] "Thai Health and Health Care" retrieved from http://eng.moph.go.th/TechResearch/hsri/hsri web.htm#

[34] In comparison, per capita health expenditure in Thailand is more than double that of Indonesia or the Philippines, while less than one third that of Malaysia in the late 1990s. However, the percentage of health expenditure in relation to GDP is much less in Malaysia than in Thailand: 2.4% in Malaysia and 6.21% in Thailand (MOPH 2000).

[35] The National Health Systems Reform Committee was established under the chairmanship of the Prime Minister in 2000. The mandate of the committee is to outline the structure of the new health systems in line with the philosophy of the new constitution ("Health Systems Reform: What – Why – How?" retrieved from http://hsro.or.th/EnglishVersion).

[36] If simply transferring health service facilities and manpower to local governments as stipulated, about 80% of the MOPH annual budget and 90% of its staff would be shifted to local administrative organizations (MOPH 2002, p. 456).

[37] A series of research projects and studies were sponsored by the MOPH to analyze alternative models for decentralization. For example, the following criteria and objectives had been examined for viability of application: equity, efficiency, service referral, good governance, direct control by local administrative organizations, responsiveness, resistance from health personnel, and smooth transition. The MOPH stresses that health performance, resource mobilization, and quality of service were emphasized in the final policy decision (MOPH 2002, p. 462).

[38] The ADB pushed the move toward autonomous hospitals forward by offering a social sector reform loan (SSRL) to the government of Thailand. The SSRL was designed to promote reforms in the major social sectors such as education, labour and health (MOPH 2002, p. 453).

[39] Interview by the author with Dr. Witit Artavatkun, Director of Banphaeo Hospital in March 2003.

[40] The health insurance coverage rate improved from 32.9% in 1991 to 80.3% in 1998 (MOPH 2000).

[41] The information in this section is basically drawn from the Health Insurance Office (2002) and the report of Wongsa and Pattara (2003) on the Universal Coverage Policy.

[42] The idea of an integrated national health insurance system has also been addressed as an ultimate goal. To this end, the Office of Health Insurance was established under the Prime Minister's Office in 2001. The National Health Security Act that aims to integrate the existing three types of insurance scheme (the health card system having been disbanded in 2001) was passed by Parliament in August 2002. However, Prime Minister Thaksin decided to suspend the enforcement in January 2003 due to mounting criticism on unpreparedness for the implementation. The start of the Universal Coverage Policy with the co-existence of the three different types of insurance schemes was a result of the realistic decision of the Thai government.

[43] The provinces which undertook the pilot projects include: Nakhonsawan, Phayaom, Patum Thani, Samut Sakhon, Yasothron and Yala Provinces (Nutta and Kaemthong 2001).

[44] Currently 51 out of 76 provinces (including the Bangkok Metropolitan Administration) have established a special board for Universal Coverage Scheme (interview with MOPH official).

[45] For the case study of the Universal Coverage Scheme in Khon Kaen, the author mainly draws information and data from the contributions of Dr. Wongsa Laohasiriwong, Associate Professor and Associate Dean for International Relations, and Dr. Pattara Sanchaisuriya, Associate Professor of Nutrition, Faculty of Public Health, Khon Kaen University. In this section all data is from Wongsa and Pattara (2003) unless otherwise mentioned.

[46] In Khon Kaen Province study projects on Universal Coverage were initiated during 1997 and 2000 following the Healthcare Reform of the MOPH. In Khon Kaen Num Phong District, a pilot project on financing and healthcare reform was undertaken (Interview with the district health officer by the author).

[47] Dr. Wongsa and Pattara undertook a descriptive cross-sectional case study in March and April 2003. Both qualitative and quantitative methods were applied for data collection by reviewing documents and interviewing related personnel both at district and provincial levels.

[48] In fact, the CUP Board mentioned below seems to have evolved from the District Health Coordinating Committee for coordinating the Universal Coverage Scheme. The members of the CUP Board include representatives of PCUs in addition to the original members of the Committee.

[49] Under the Universal Coverage Scheme, the budget for IPD is allocated based on DRG. In DRG, diseases are classified into groups according to necessary medical cost through statistical analyses.

[50] Usually the catchment's area of a PCU covers around 10,000 persons.

[51] Sometimes health personnel who were originally assigned to the district hospitals work temporarily at the provincial office (Wongsa and Pattara 2003).

[52] There were alternative choices by each province to include or exclude staff salary from capitation before 2001. Given flexibility, some large-scale hospitals dispatch health personnel to smaller ones. However, from 2002 all the provinces have to exclude staff salary from its budget allocation to CUP boards (Information gathered from the MOPH by the author).

[53] In addition to document review and interviews with provincial and district level officials concerning the Universal Coverage Scheme, Wongsa and Pattara conducted a one-day survey at two PCUs in Chum Phae District and five PCUs in Num Phong District from March to April 2003. A questionnaire interview was given to 102 people who utilize services either for treatment or health promotion (Wongsa and Pattara 2003).

[54] As mentioned in *3.2.3.1*, the Health Card Scheme is one of the four social security programmes that the government offered until 2001. The MOPH provided health cards to those who voluntarily apply for at a cost of 500 Baht/card/year. Health card holders were able to receive free medical treatment at public health facilities.

[55] In this chapter, the study does not involve any comprehensive unit-cost analysis or community survey for expenditure for healthcare of the people. Rather, it will try to search for increased efficiency by investigating the behavioural changes of people getting services more from primary care units and health centres.

[56] To evaluate the quality of services, client opinion was sought through interviews with 102 respondents (Wongsa and Pattara 2003).

[57] Allocative efficiency is improved through a better matching of public services to local preferences. Productive efficiency is promoted through the increased accountability of local governments to citizens, fewer levels of bureaucracy, and better knowledge of local needs. See 1.2.1 (World Bank 2001a).

References

Asian Development Bank. 1999. *Governance in Thailand: Challenges, Issues and Prospects*. Manila: Asian Development Bank.

Azfar, O., Kahkohen, S. and Meagher, P. 2001. "Conditions for Effective Decentralized Governance: A synthesis of Research Findings" IRIS Center, University of Maryland, and World Bank.

Boolert, Leoprapai. 1997. "Social Sector Decentralization: The Case of Thailand". IDRC-Supported Project, Social Decentralization South East Asia – Phase 2. Ottawa: International Development Research Center.

Charas S. 2002. "The Classification of Local Authorities in Thailand". In *Thailand Japan Joint Research Project on Capacity Building of Thai Local Authorities*. Department of Local Administration of Ministry of Interior and JICA, [Japan International Cooperation Agency].

Chartchai N.C. 2002. "Assistance to Constitutional Reform Implementation Support Network: Decentralization and People's Participation". Country paper of Municipal Reform of Asian Research Center for Decentralization, Manila. Retrieved from http://www.decentralization.ws/icd2/papers/decent_thailand.htm.

Cohen, J.M and Peterson B.S. 1999. *Administrative Decentralization: Strategies for developing countries*. Connecticut: Kumarian Press.

DAC. 1997a. *Final Report of the Ad Hoc Working Group on Participatory Development and Good Governance* Part I and Part II. Paris: OECD.

————. 1997b. *Evaluation of Programs Promoting Participatory Development and Good Governance – Synthesis Report*. DAC Expert Group on Aid Evaluation. Paris: OECD.

Health Insurance Office, Ministry of Public Health. 2002. "Universal Coverage of Health Care Policy in Thailand: Introduction, Budget, Health Service Systems, Information System, National Health Assurance, and Benefit". Retrieved from http://www.hinso.moph.go.th/30baht English/health%20insurance%20Office.

JBIC. 2002. *"Tai okoku ni okeru shakai hosho seido ni kansuru chosa hokokusho"* (Report of the study on Social Security System in Thailand). Tokyo: Japan Bank for International Cooperation (JBIC)].

JICA. 1993. *"Tai ookoku kooshuueisei purojekuto junkai shido chosadan hokokusho* (Report of the study mission for the Public Health Project in Thailand)". Tokyo: Japan International Cooperation Agency (JICA).

JICA. 2001. *Local Government and Decentralization*. Tokyo: JICA.

————. 2003. *Road to Democracy and Governance*. Tokyo: JICA.

Manor J. 1999. "The Political Economy of Democratic Decentralization". *Directions in Development*. Washington DC: World Bank.

Ministry of Public Health of Thailand. 2000. *Thailand Health Profile 1997– 1998*. Bangkok: Ministry of Public Health.

————. *Thailand Health Profile 1999–2000*. 2002. Bangkok: Ministry of Public Health.

Nagai, F. 2001. "Current Situation of decentralization in developing countries: a case study on Thailand". In *Local Government and Decentralization*. Tokyo, JICA.

————. 2002. *Magarikado ni kita Tai no Chiho bunkenka* (Decentralization in Thailand at a turning point). In *Aji-ken World Trend* no.85, October 2002.

————. 2003. *Tai no Chiho jichi* (1) – (3) (Local autonomy in Thailand). In *Nihonjin Shoko Kaigisho Ho* (Monthly magazine of Japanese Chamber of Commerce and Industry, Bangkok). January to March 2003.

The National Health Reform Committee (NHRC). 2002. "Appendix to the Draft National Health Act" for the Reading of the Draft National Health Act 24 September 2002 by the Sub-committee for the Drafting of National Health Act, Ministry of Public Health.

Noranit S. 2002. "Introduction". In *Thailand Japan Joint Research Project on Capacity Building of Thai Local Authorities*. Department of Local Administration of Ministry of Interior and JICA. Japan International Cooperation Agency.

Nutta S. and Kaemthong I. 2001. "The Universal Coverage Policy of Thailand: An Introduction". A paper prepared for Asia-Pacific Health Economics Network (AHEN), 19th July 2001.

Office of Decentralization to Local Government Organization Committee. "Decentralization to Local Government Organization". The Office of the Permanent Secretary, The Prime Minister's Office, Thailand, date unknown.

Peerasit K., Supawatanakorn W., Bryant, J., and Prohnno A. 2000. "An Assessment of the Thai Government's Health Services for the Aged". *Asia-Pacific Population Journal*, March 2000.

Preeda T. 2003. "Decentralization and Health Systems Reform Challenged in Rural Public Health System Development in Thailand". A PowerPoint material of 12 March, 2003, Ministry of Public Health, Thailand.

Silverman, J. M. 1992. "Public Sector Decentralization: Economic Policy and Sector Investment Programs". World Bank, African Technical Department, Technical Paper No.188. Washington, D.C.: World Bank.

Thailand Innovative Administration Consultancy Institute. 1999. "The Project on Public Health Services Policy Analysis and Development of

Decentralization of Administration to Provincial and Local Governments in Thailand" (Summary Report). Bangkok: Health Systems Research Institute (HSRI).

UNDP. 1997a. "Reconceptualising Governance". Discussion paper 2. UNDP.

———. 1997b. "Governance for Sustainable Human Development". UNDP Policy Document.

———. 1998. "UNDP and Governance: Experiences and Lessons Learned". *Management Development and Governance Division Lessons-Learned Series No.1.* UNDP.

Van de Walle, D. 2001. *The Static and Dynamic Incidence of Vietnam's Public Safety Nets.* Washington, D.C.: World Bank.

Viroj N. and Anchana N. 2001. "Social Protection in Health for the Poor in Thailand: From Welfare to Universal Coverage" Executive Summary. Bangkok: Thailand Development Research Institute (TDRI).

Wipit, P. "Alliance and Research Coordination Network for Evidence-based Health System Reform in Thailand". Thailand: Health Systems Research Institute (HSRI), date unknown.

Wongsa, L. and Pattara S. 2003. "Report on the Universal Coverage Scheme in Khon Kaen Province". Prepared for the case study for the author.

Woothisarn T. 2002. "Decentralization in Thailand – Issues of Government Policy Formulation Towards Decentralization". Country paper of Municipal Reform of Asian Research Center for Decentralization, Manila. Retrieved from http://www.decentralization.ws/icd2/papers/decent_thailand.htm.

World Bank. 1992. *Governance and Development.* Washington, D.C.: World Bank.

———. 1994. *Governance: the World Bank's Experience.* Washington, D.C.: World Bank.

———. 1997. *World Development Report 1997.* Washington, D.C.: World Bank.

———. 2000. *Reforming Public Institutions and Strengthening Governance: A World Bank Strategy.* Washington, D.C.: World Bank.

———. 2001a. "Decentralization and governance: does decentralization improve public service delivery?". *PREM notes* June 2001 no.55, World Bank.

———. 2001b. *Social Monitor: Poverty and Public Policy.* Washington, D.C.: World Bank.

———. Decentralization NET of World Bank Decentralization Thematic Group, retrieved from http://www1.worldbank.org/publicsector/decentralization.

———. PREM Network website, World Bank Public Sector Group of the Poverty Reduction and Economic Management Network, retrieved from http://www1.worldbank.org/publicsector/overview.htm#2.

Newspaper Articles
<Decentralization>
"Local rule proves to be a flop". *Bangkok Post,* 10 January 1999.
"Public Health: TAOs ill-prepared to take over services". *Bangkok Post,* 1 November 1999.
"Decentralization hits schools snag". *Bangkok Post,* 2 December 2000.
"Power to the people". *Bangkok Post,* 3 September 2000.
"Central govt sincerely doubted". *Bangkok Post,* 7 January 2001.
"Government votes down *tambon* bill". *Bangkok Post,* 29 August 2002.

<30-Baht healthcare scheme>
"The Bt30 health care programme: sadly, it's still way below par' *The Nation,* 2 January 2002.
"30-baht scheme extended to cover anti-retroviral drugs: Pledge comes on eve of World Aids Day' *Bangkok Post,* by Anjira A., 1 December 2001.
"Foreign workers to be included in plan'. *Bangkok Post,* by Aphaluck B., 9 May 2001.
"Abhisit airs concern on fund merger' *Bangkok Post,* by Anjira A., 10 February 2002.
"Thailand's cheap health plan fails to deliver' *BBC News,* by Ingram S., 9 April 2002.
"Thailand's Cheap Health Plan Fails to Deliver,' *Geocities,* by Phairath K., 16 April 2002.
"Top doctor slams 30-baht scheme blamed for drop in hospital standards,' *Thai Labor Campaign,* by Anjira A., 17 July 2002.
"Ten hospitals quit 30-baht scheme' *Bangkok Post,* by Aphaluck B., 21 January 2003.
"Call for freedom of choice in B30 scheme'. *Bangkok Post,* by Charoen K., 15 March 2003.
"Landmark may find flaws in govt's B30 scheme'. *Bangkok Post,* by Aphaluck B., 29 March 2003.
"Dean: Bt30 health plan a 'time bomb'". *The Nation* (date unknown) (on the web of the Ministry of Public Health).
"Has its benefits Care at 30 baht?" (source unknown) 2001 (on the web of the Ministry of Public Health).

Documents in Thai
Num Phong District Health Coordinating Committee. 2003. "Summary Health Report of Num Phong" according to monitoring and supervision presented to Khon Kaen Provincial Health Office, March 18th 2003.
Chum Pae Hospital. 2003. *Annual Health Report in 2002. Khon Kaen: Chum Pae Hospital.*

Khon Kaen Provincial Health Office. 2003. "Guideline of Universal Healthcare Coverage implementation in Khon Kaen".

Universal Healthcare Coverage Development Working Committee. 2001. "Guideline of Universal Healthcare Coverage in transitional period". A summary of Universal Healthcare Coverage Development Working Committee. Bangkok: Goods and Parcel Delivery Printing.

Hospital Resource Management Development Committee. 2001. "Guideline of financing and health resource management under Universal Health Care Coverage". Ministry of Public Health, Thailand.

8
Economic Viability and Local Governance: The Political Economy of Decentralization in the Philippines

Jorge V. Tigno

1. Introduction

Decentralization has a strong potential to provide the conditions for societal transformation along the path of a more empowered and dynamic local community. A decentralized community is presumed to be one that is able to promote genuine and sustainable development even as it reduces the capacity of traditional power centres (to include state and non-state contenders) to undermine the capacities of sub-national entities. During the 1950s and 1960s, decentralization in the developing areas was more associated with preparing colonies for independence by way of devolving responsibilities for certain programmes to local–national authorities. In the 1980s, decentralization again came to the forefront of the development agenda alongside the renewed global emphasis on governance and human-centred approaches to human development.

Political decentralization shifts decision-making powers to lower levels of government thereby encouraging the participation of its citizens. Political decentralization by way of promoting the capacities of sub-national units for substantive self-governance is desirable for a variety of reasons. Administrative decentralization and the promotion of subsidiarity are desirable due to the political advantages they provide to both the central and local government units (LGUs). These bureaucratic benefits can be in terms of (a) alleviating administrative bottlenecks in the delivery of basic services often caused by highly centralized and inflexible government control and manipulation; (b) increasing government sensitivity to local needs and conditions; (c) broadening the administrative reach and effectiveness of the national government; (d) allowing for the representation and participation of diverse groups in decision making; (e) relieving the national government of routine functions; and (f) assisting the coordination of or complementing national government programmes.

A decentralized bureaucracy is more likely to be efficient and effective in dealing with special local administrative problems and concerns. LGUs know best how to evaluate and address the needs and problems of their constituents. At the same time, decentralized governance can greatly enhance the capacities of local decision-making bodies by making such bodies more representative of the constituents and less prone to manipulation by national government entities and by vested interests. What has not been fully examined in the literature as well as the practice of political decentralization in developing areas is the assumption that local governance is more socially and economically sustainable and viable than a centralized administrative system.

Political and administrative decentralization also has its disadvantages. Not all administrative responsibilities may be efficiently undertaken at the local levels especially if the local units are not adequately provided with the financial resources to perform these functions. Coordination between the national and the local governments especially as regards national programmes and projects can be complicated and cumbersome, leading to a delay in the fulfilment or completion of such programmes and projects. Local government authorities may be more prone to political capture by local elites even as the cooperation between different sectors may be undermined by distrust between competing groups.

But while much can be and is certainly said about the positive (as well as negative) politico-administrative prospects for governance brought about by political decentralization, the main economic justification for it has not yet been fully brought to light. A few studies on the Philippines have sought to examine the economic impact and implications of political decentralization. One notable study is by Manasan, et al. (1999) that sought to specify a set of governance quality indicators at the local level. They argue that "the capacity of LGUs to provide social services is largely determined by their financial resources and their ability to manage such resources vis-à-vis competing demands" (see Manasan et al. 1999).

1.1 Decentralization Principles in the Philippines

The Philippines is one of the first countries in Southeast Asia to embark on a systematic and substantive decentralization programme. In the wake of the previous authoritarian political system under Marcos, the Philippines promulgated a new Local Government Code in 1991 that greatly enhanced the political and administrative capacities of LGUs throughout the country. Also known officially as Republic Act (RA) 7160, the Code specifies a number of principles in the conduct of its decentralization project. These are:

(a) The territorial and political sub-divisions of the State shall enjoy genuine and meaningful local autonomy to enable them to attain their fullest development as self-reliant communities and make them more effective partners in the attainment of national goals. Toward this end, the State shall provide for a more responsive and accountable local government structure instituted through a system of decentralization whereby local government units shall be given more powers, authority, responsibilities, and resources. The process of decentralization shall proceed from the national government to the local government units.

(b) It is also the policy of the State to ensure the accountability of local government units through the institution of effective mechanisms of recall, initiative and referendum.

(c) It is likewise the policy of the State to require all national agencies and offices to conduct periodic consultations with appropriate local government units, non-governmental and people's organizations, and other concerned sectors of the community before any project or programme is implemented in their respective jurisdictions.[1]

Moreover, as specified in RA 7160, the country's decentralization strategy is guided by the following operative principles:

(a) There shall be an effective allocation among the different local government units of their respective powers, functions, responsibilities, and resources;

(b) There shall be established in every local government unit an accountable, efficient, and dynamic organizational structure and operating mechanism that will meet the priority needs and service requirements of its communities;

(c) Subject to civil service law, rules and regulations, local officials and employees paid wholly or mainly from local funds shall be appointed or removed, according to merit and fitness, by the appropriate appointing authority;

(d) The vesting of duty, responsibility, and accountability in local government units shall be accompanied with provision for reasonably adequate resources to discharge their powers and effectively carry out their functions; hence, they shall have the power to create and broaden their own sources of revenue and the right to a just share in national taxes and an equitable share in the proceeds of the utilization and development of the national wealth within their respective areas;

(e)   Provinces with respect to component cities and municipalities, and cities and municipalities with respect to component *barangays*, shall ensure that the acts of their component units are within the scope of their prescribed powers and functions;

(f)   Local government units may group themselves, consolidate or coordinate their efforts, services, and resources for purposes commonly beneficial to them;

(g)   The capabilities of local government units, especially the municipalities and *barangays*, shall be enhanced by providing them with opportunities to participate actively in the implementation of national programmes and projects;

(h)   There shall be a continuing mechanism to enhance local autonomy not only by legislative enabling acts but also by administrative and organizational reforms;

(i)   Local government units shall share with the national government the responsibility in the management and maintenance of ecological balance within their territorial jurisdiction, subject to the provisions of this Code and national policies;

(j)   Effective mechanisms for ensuring the accountability of local government units to their respective constituents shall be strengthened in order to upgrade continually the quality of local leadership;

(k)   The realization of local autonomy shall be facilitated through improved coordination of national government policies and programmes and extension of adequate technical and material assistance to less developed and deserving local government units;

(l)   The participation of the private sector in local governance, particularly in the delivery of basic services, shall be encouraged to ensure the viability of local autonomy as an alternative strategy for sustainable development; and

(m)   The national government shall ensure that decentralization contributes to the continuing improvement of the performance of local government units and the quality of community life.[2]

In the final analysis, RA 7160 is premised on the notion that "self-reliant communities" can attain their "fullest development" through "genuine and meaningful local autonomy".[3]

1.2 Political Decentralization and Economic Viability

As applied in the Philippines, the principle of local governance assumes a political economic property in that it is also argued from the perspective that it will bring about "the continuing improvement of the performance of local government units and the quality of community life". Economic viability and social prosperity are assumed to be one of the outcomes of a decentralized politico-administrative system.

However, while there may be reason to be hopeful about the administrative benefits that can arise from decentralized governance, it might be worthwhile to re-examine its actual socioeconomic implications. At the end of the day, it is these socioeconomic aspects that will affect the administrative effectiveness of any political decentralization programme. Basic social services may not be adequately rendered if the financial as well as physical resources in the community are not enough or cannot be sustainably generated.

From the standpoint of political economy, not all administrative responsibilities may be efficiently and effectively undertaken entirely at the local level. Indeed, it may be more costly for individual LGUs to separately address problems that transcend local boundaries. In such cases, national and regional government units may have a comparative advantage. Moreover, this can be a major problem for LGUs that are not adequately funded or endowed with resources and capacities in dealing with such developmental concerns.

Although RA 7160 does provide for "an equitable share in the proceeds of the utilization and development of the national wealth" as well as the enhancement of "the capabilities of local government units... by providing them with opportunities to participate actively in the implementation of national programs and projects", such sharing is still dependent on how resourceful and resource-rich the national government has or can become. This also implies a heavy dependence on the national–central government and which is inconsistent with the principles of political decentralization. Additionally, local political units may depend more on certain resource-rich groups and sectors making their public officials and policies more prone to elite political capture. This can eventually undermine the level of trust and coordination between the local government units and other competing groups and sectors of the community leading to a reduction in local administrative efficiency and effectiveness.

1.3 A Link Between Economic Viability and Political Decentralization

Although it is a popular public policy strategy in developing areas, little is known or understood about the economics of political decentralization particularly in the Philippines. The arguments that have been raised for the desirability of decentralization in previous sections have been largely from the politico-administrative standpoint. The kind of political decentralization being pursued in the Philippines is one that is characterized by popular empowerment. In this regard, the relationship between popular empowerment and economic sustainability or viability has yet to be empirically established in the available literature. The assumption at this point is that there is a significant link between economic growth and political decentralization. This assumption has been made clear in the study by Manasan et al. (1999).

This chapter raises a few research questions pertaining to the linkage between economic viability and political decentralization. More specifically, these are as follows: Is there a positive correlation between political decentralization beginning with the implementation of RA 7160 and economic viability and growth in the Philippines since then? Can it be said in general that the more autonomous and decentralized that sub-national units become politically and administratively, the more likely that these entities will experience increased economic capacities? Additionally, the study also raises a number of secondary questions, which are as follows:

1.   What is the specific nature and current level of political decentralization in the Philippines?
2.   What are the problems and concerns that can be raised about the political decentralization experience in the Philippines since 1991?
3.   What is the current level of local economic development and growth in the Philippines?
4.   What are the internal political factors that can account for economic growth (or the absence thereof) in the Philippines?
5.   What innovative schemes or mechanisms can be found that would enhance the sustainability of economic growth in the decentralized areas in the country?

Economic viability or sustainability refers to two dimensions of local government capacity. The first is the extent to which LGUs are able to generate revenues from local sources. The second dimension of economic viability pertains to the extent to which LGU officials are able to manage these resources. In both respects, the outcome of economic viability is measured in terms of improvements in the quality of life of the community members.

1.4 Research Objectives

In general, this study re-examines the assumption that decentralized governance can bring about positive economic implications for the communities concerned. It will describe the relationship between political decentralization and economic growth and ascertain the correlation between the two. More specifically, it will pursue the following research objectives:

1. To describe the political decentralization experience in the Philippines beginning in 1991 with the enactment of the Local Government Code (RA 7160);
2. To determine the success (or failure) of political decentralization as measured in terms of economic growth and sustainability;
3. To assess the direction of political decentralization that the Philippines is taking since 1991; and
4. To determine whether or not political decentralization is able to provide a sustainable degree of economic empowerment and prosperity.

The research is important in that it attempts to debunk the notion that decentralization is automatically and absolutely beneficial both administratively and economically. Little is actually known about the relationship between political decentralization and economic growth. And the deductions that can be drawn from whatever studies have been made for the way in which decentralized governance affects economic growth has been largely ambiguous if not contradictory and plagued by methodological problems.[4]

As the number of sectors and stakeholders being accommodated throughout the country's politico-administrative mechanisms and processes increases, there is also a corresponding multiplication in the number of organizational, coordination, and management problems associated with the delivery of basic services. Differences as well as tensions and conflicts between and across sectors and groups become more apparent and can threaten to affect organizational coherence, effectiveness, and efficiency in that it can adversely affect economic viability. These tensions are further aggravated and complicated by varying levels of competencies, sensitivities, and social preparedness of the different sectors and in the different areas. At the same time, there is greater competition over scarce resources especially between and among government agencies.

This research adds to the emergent body of literature that examines the correlation between political decentralization and economic growth in developing areas. Local or decentralized governance is typically associated with increased effectiveness and efficiency of local government services. That much is already known. However, there is still much research to be undertaken in the area of examining the relationship between political decentralization and economic performance as well as ensuring local economic viability. The principal issue under examination in this study is that of the economic viability or sustainability of local governance and political subsidiarity as these are being undertaken in the Philippines since 1991.

1.5 Research and Conceptual Framework

The main assumption behind the objectives of the research is that in order to indicate successful political decentralization (as measured in terms of the indicators of good governance, e.g., greater efficiency, effectiveness, transparency, accountability, etc.), local government entities would need to accomplish some measure of economic viability and sustainability for themselves and for their constituents. Another underlying assumption of the research is that for the most part, successful decentralization cannot be measured simply in terms of political goals but also (perhaps more so) in terms of economic empowerment and prosperity for all the members of the community (especially those previously and historically marginalized groups).

Governance is the system by which public authorities are able to craft, adopt, and implement public policies. For purposes of this study, decentralized governance refers to the extent to which the provisions of the 1991 Local Government Code have been implemented in the Philippines. Economic viability is that condition where the constituents of the community are able to experience a significant degree of economic prosperity that is sustainable. It also refers to the extent to which LGUs are able to sustain and generate financial resources for local development purposes. Moreover, it involves a reduction in the said units' dependence on the resources of the central–national government by way of internal revenue allotments (IRAs) and other national government financial sources. Correspondingly, it involves an increased capacity to generate local resources (e.g., exploitation of local resources, local government borrowings, livelihood projects, build-operate-transfer arrangements, and other local revenue-generating ordinances).

According to the World Bank, there are five conditions that must be met for political decentralization to be economically viable. These are:

1.   The decentralization framework must be able to link local financing and fiscal autonomy with local service provision and responsibilities;
2.   The community must be informed about the costs of services and service delivery options as well as the sources involved;
3.   There must be a mechanism for the members of the community to express their preferences in ways that are binding on the local politicians;
4.   There must be a system of accountability that is based on transparent information to enable the community to monitor the performance of local officials and act accordingly; and
5.   The political objectives of decentralization must be supported by proper institutions and mechanisms. [5]

Economic viability is seen in the above enumeration as a function of (a) a healthy fit between resource generation and allocation by way of fiscal compatibility and efficiency; (b) political transparency and accountability; and (c) the extent of political institutionalization as illustrated below. The viability is expressed in terms of (a) the sustained general of local resources combined with (b) a reduced dependence on national government revenues leading to (c) sustainable economic prosperity for all the members of the local community. These dimensions of the link between economic viability and political decentralization are illustrated in Figure 8.1 below.

Figure 8.1 Economic Viability as a Function of Political Decentralization

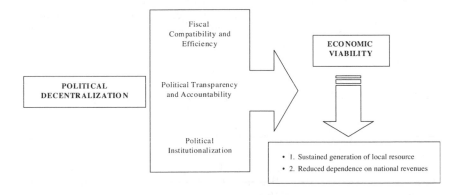

1.6 Research Process and Methodology

In order to illustrate the validity of the framework, the study first identifies the five poorest and richest provinces in the Philippines. These provinces were identified on the basis of their ranking in the Philippine Human Development Report since 1994. This stage is necessary in order to isolate the factor of economic viability. It is therefore assumed in the study that the provinces placed at the top of the human development index are the most economically viable while those at the bottom are the least economically viable.

Second, the study describes the extent to which political decentralization has progressed and been undertaken in these areas (e.g., extent to which national government agencies have been devolved as well as the extent of involvement of civil society groups in local special bodies). This includes a discussion of the major problems and issues encountered and how these were addressed in these areas.

Third, the study examines the extent of dependence of the LGUs on national resources as well as their capacity to generate and utilize local resources. Included in this examination is the manner in which the LGUs have been able to utilize the powers and advantages of political decentralization in order to generate additional resources and increased capacities.

And lastly, the study attempts to establish the extent to which political decentralization has led to economic growth and viability as measured in terms of their movement across the Human Development Report index. It does so by applying the key conditions specified in the research framework. The study relies on statistical information generated from the Philippine Human Development Network as well as the National Statistical Coordination Board (NSCB) and the National Statistics Office (NSO). In determining the decentralization experiences, the study also makes use of existing assessment documents from the Department of Interior and Local Government (DILG) as well as other non-governmental sources.

2. Overview of Decentralization in the Philippines

This overview aims to provide a description of the state of political decentralization in the Philippines. It is divided into two parts. The first part briefly discusses the evolution and development of administrative decentralization and local governance in the country. The second part discusses the major features of the current political decentralization policy in the country as conveyed in two statutes. These are the Organic Act for Muslim Mindanao (RA 6734) creating the Autonomous Region for Muslim Mindanao (ARMM) and the 1991 Local Government Code (RA 7160).

2.1 The Evolution of Philippine Decentralization

Tapales (1995) contends that Philippine history and geography have contributed much to the heavy reliance of local units on the central government. The country is an archipelago of roughly over 7,100 islands. The two largest islands are Luzon in the north and Mindanao in the south. The central part of the country (known as the *Visayas* region) is composed of smaller islands that include Cebu, Samar, and Leyte, among many others (see maps below). Given these physical realities, the historical antecedents of central–local relations in the Philippines are characterized by centralism as the predominant theme in Philippine history (Sosmeña 1995, p. 32). The central government (historically based in Manila) from

The central part of the Philippines including Cebu, Samar and Leyte.

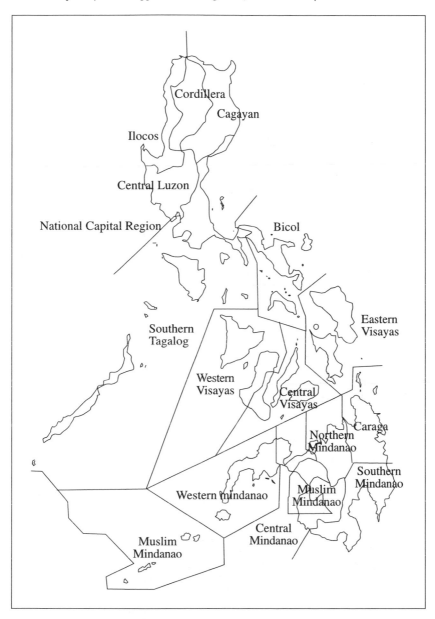

The two largest islands in the Philippines: Luzon in the North and Mindanao in the South.

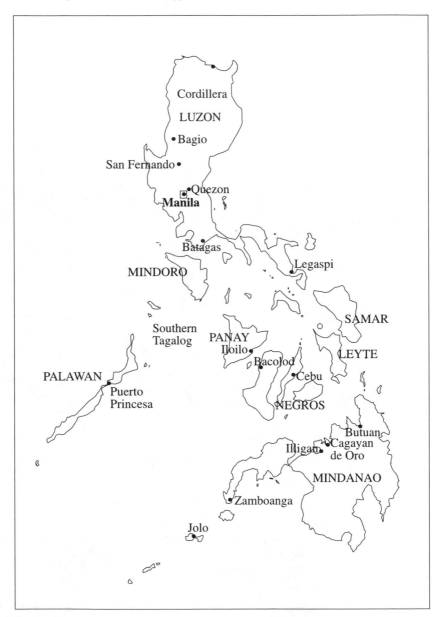

the Spanish regime up to the authoritarian Marcos regime maintained a strong presence and control over local governments. This has led to the popular (and not entirely inaccurate) notion of "imperial Manila".

Sosmeña (1991) referred to five determinants that have primarily influenced the policies formulated by the central government towards the local governments during the various eras of Philippine history: threat to national security; personalities of the Presidents of the Philippines; national integration, national development; and low central government perception on the competence of local government for more responsibilities. He goes on to say that local authorities will continue to get involved in socioeconomic development in an increasingly complex environment. It is in this regard that the central government also continues to raise as an issue the competence of local authorities to manage their own affairs and contribute more solidly to the achievement of national goals (Sosmeña 1991).

2.1.1 The Colonial Period

The *barangay* is the only indigenous local government unit in the Philippines that can be traced to a pre-Spanish institution (see De Guzman 1995). The other major local administrative entities, namely, the province, city, and municipality have their beginnings in the LGUs established during the Spanish regime (De Guzman 1995, p. 103). During the Spanish period, the *barangays* were transformed into *barrios* and the *datus* relegated to the role of tax collectors, known as *cabezas de barangay*. The Maura Law, enacted in 1893, was seen as Spain's belated and half-hearted tribute to Filipino ability in self-government (see Brillantes 1998). The law reorganized town governments in the Philippines by creating the municipal council headed by an appointed captain (*mayor*), with expanded powers for such tasks as revenue-raising, budget preparation, public works supervision by way of conscripted labour, among others. In the context of colonial rule, however, these local powers were still limited.

A democratic system of local government was established during the revolutionary period shortly before the turn of the 19th century (see De Guzman 1995). Sosmeña (1991, p. 32) notes, however, that the first Philippine Republic (lasting only from 1896 to 1898) was too short-lived to be able to contribute anything of significance to the cause of local autonomy. Immediately superseding this short-lived Republic, the Americans also established a democratic system of local government. However, the tradition of centralism was not radically changed in spite of the fact that (during the Commonwealth Period from 1935 to 1946) provinces and municipalities elected their own officials and enacted ordinances since the control of such actions was lodged in Manila (De Guzman 1995, p. 108).

2.1.2 The Pre-Martial Law Period (1946–1972)

Brillantes (1998, p. 104) contends that a trend towards decentralization occurred during the period after the country was granted independence by the United States in 1946. A number of laws giving more autonomy to local governments through the grant of additional powers or through the lessening of national control on local affairs were passed by Congress during this period (see Brillantes 1998). In 1959, two landmark measures on local autonomy were passed — the Local Autonomy Act and the Barrio Charter.

The Local Autonomy Act of 1959 (Republic Act 2264) granted extensive and broader powers to local governments including the authority to impose licence taxes or fees in the exercise of a profession or occupation and in the operation of business enterprises. It also reorganized the provincial government, diminishing national control over both provincial budgeting as well as the planning and implementation of public improvements (Brillantes 1998, p. 111).

The 1959 Barrio Charter (Republic Act 2370 and later amended by Republic Act 3590) recognized the *barrio* or village as a legal entity and empowered its inhabitants to elect their local officials. Later, the Decentralization Act of 1967 (Republic Act 5185) allowed LGUs to supplement the national government's efforts in agricultural extension and health (Tapales 1995, p. 396).

2.1.3 The Martial Law Period (1972–1986)

The imposition of martial law in 1972 was a "great setback for the local autonomy movement" in the Philippines (Brillantes 1998, p. 42). However, this "patrimonial authoritarian" regime was innovative in seeking self-legitimacy (Wurfel 1989, p. 153). For Brillantes (1998, p. 42), the Marcos Constitution of 1973 (at least in rhetoric) committed itself to a policy of local autonomy as it affirms that:

> The State shall guarantee and promote autonomy of local government units, especially the barrio, to ensure their fullest development as self-reliant communities.

Through a series of executive enactments known as presidential decrees (PDs), however, Marcos began the implementation of an Integrated Reorganization Plan (Presidential Decree Number 1) that created the Ministry of Local Government and Community Development (MLGCD and in the post-Marcos period was known as the Department of Interior and Local Government or DILG) and the Metropolitan Manila Commission (MMC and during the post-Marcos period was known as the Metropolitan Manila Development Authority or MMDA), among others (Tapales 1995, p. 396).

Other measures introduced by virtue of these PDs that affected the operations of sub-national agencies and units include the Local Tax Code (PD 231), which laid down the sources of revenues for the local governments; PD 76 which increased the rate of real property assessment; PD 144 that governed the distribution of internal revenue allotments to local units; PD 426 which spelt out national–local fiscal relations; and PD 477 that laid down the rules for local budgeting. These are clearly central government initiatives and interventions at decentralization.

Despite these decentralization measures directed at local government entities, however, the President continued to exercise supervision and control over the local governments (Brillantes 1998, p. 42). The suspension of local elections allowed the President to exercise his broad executive powers to remove and appoint local officials (Brillantes 1998, p. 42).

The serious economic conditions faced by the Marcos administration such as the global economic depression beginning in 1979, the huge capital flight in 1981 that produced a credit crunch and increased distrust of the Philippines in the field of international finance, and the political instability triggered by the assassination of Benigno Aquino in 1983, forced Marcos to consider certain reforms in the authoritarian system. Martial law was lifted in January 1981 and *Batas Pambansa* 337 creating the first Local Government Code for the country was passed in 1983.[6]

2.1.4 The Immediate Post-Martial Law Period: The Aquino Administration (1986–1992)

With the overthrow of the Marcos dictatorship in 1986 by way of a popular uprising came the promulgation of a new constitution. The 1987 Constitution provides for a decentralization policy and mandated Congress to enact a local government code that instituted a system of decentralization in the designation of powers, responsibilities, and duties to LGUs. It also provided the legal bases for the creation of autonomous regions in Mindanao in southern Philippines and in the Cordillera in the north.[7] In general, Valdellon (1999) contends, then-President Corazon Aquino understood "local autonomy as a means to strengthen democracy".

In addition to the attainment of political stability, the challenges faced by the Aquino administration included economic reconstruction and the realization of social equity in the aftermath of at least 14 years of authoritarian rule. It was during her term that the Medium Term Philippine Development Plan (1987–1992) expressly sought to further strengthen political decentralization efforts in the country and increase the participation of local governments and the private sector in development programmes and projects through development administration. Political decentralization was seen as a major contribution in the national reconstruction effort. This plan recognized that effective development administration requires the decentralization of significant and relevant government functions to regional and local institutions in order to encourage more meaningful people participation in the development effort (see Lamberte 1993).

Towards this end, a number of institutional reforms were undertaken by the Aquino administration including the Pilot Decentralization Project (PDP), the coordination and administration of Integrated Area Development (IAD) Projects (by way of Executive Order 363 in 1988), the establishment of the Magna Carta for Countryside and *Barangay* Business Enterprises (CBBE) or *Kalakalan* (literally "Trade") 20 (through Republic Act 6810 of 1989), the Regional Industrial Centers (RIC) in 1987, and other special development areas such as the Cavite, Laguna, Batangas, and Rizal special development projects (CALABAR-SDP).[8] The CALABAR (later CALABARZON) area is composed of provinces just outside of Metropolitan Manila.

Donor institutions also supported the Aquino administration's efforts to promote economic development through decentralization at the regional level. Lamberte (1993) cited some of the lessons learned in the implementation of programmes such as the Central Visayas Regional Project (CVRP) in central Philippines, the Bicol River Basin Development Program (BRBDP) in southern Luzon and the Local Resource Management (LRM) Project. It was noted that the devolution of many decision-making powers and financial control at the site level greatly facilitated the development process in the areas. Moreover, to sustain the process of development, projects should take into account local capability to initiate, identify, decide, plan and implement programmes (see Lamberte 1993).

2.1.4.1 The Pilot Decentralization Project (PDP)

The Presidential Commission on Government Reorganization (PCGR) in 1988 implemented a Pilot Decentralization Project (PDP) in four provinces through Memorandum Circular (MC) No. 63. The same MC No. 63 also created the Cabinet Action Committee on Decentralization (CACD) that was tasked with the responsibility of formulating guidelines and launching decentralization projects in the provinces of Laguna, Tarlac, Negros Occidental and Davao del Norte which are the areas covered by the PDP. The province of Batanes was included as a fifth pilot province in April 1989.

Brillantes and Cuaresma (1991) observed that the CACD failed in its job to ensure that consultations are held not only with relevant regional and provincial officials of affected national line agencies concerned, but more importantly with the five governors and the respective provincial board members in the areas. The minimal achievements during the first PDP indicated the need for a comprehensive framework that will guide similar projects in the future. The need for a framework is emphasized considering the non-uniformity in operationalizing decentralization at the provincial level, human variations in style of leadership, extent of discretion that governors could exercise, and the lack of policies regarding the use of non-government/community organizations and other private organizations (see Brillantes and Cuaresma 1991).

2.1.4.2 The Creation of Autonomous Regions in Mindanao and in the Cordillera

According to Buendia (1995), the intention to create autonomous regions for the Cordilleras and Muslim Mindanao and the adoption of their respective Organic Acts by the Philippine Congress speaks well of the government's recognition of the rights and welfare of the indigenous cultural communities as provided in Section 22, Article II of the 1987 Constitution. In 1987, however, President Aquino enacted Executive Order 220 creating the Cordillera Administrative Region (CAR) composed of the provinces of Benguet, Mt. Province, Ifugao, Abra, Kalinga, and Apayao and the City of Baguio in northern Luzon. Although it was challenged in the Supreme Court for being unconstitutional, the executive order was nevertheless affirmed by way of a decision issued by the SC in January 1990. The principal reason for the affirmation of EO 220 is that it does not violate the Constitution on the establishment of an autonomous region in the Cordilleras. What EO 220 created was an administrative region that coordinated the delivery of services among the different local and national government agencies in the region.

Subsequent to EO 220, Republic Acts 6734 (Organic Acts for the Autonomous Region in Muslim Mindanao) and 6766 (Organic Acts for the Cordillera Autonomous Region) were signed into law in 1989. RA 6734 provides for the holding of a plebiscite in the provinces that are to be affected by the creation of the autonomous regions. Two plebiscites were held, the first in 1990 and the second one in 2001. The result of the first plebiscite held in the 13 provinces and nine cities for the ARMM showed that only the provinces of Lanao del Sur, Maguindanao, Sulu, and Tawi-tawi chose to join the autonomous region arrangement. Not surprisingly, these four provinces are among the poorest in the country. The 2001 plebiscite added the province of Basilan and Marawi City to the areas falling within the jurisdiction of ARMM.

In consonance with RA 6766, a similar plebiscite also was held in January 1990 in the Cordillera region particularly in the provinces of Benguet, Mt. Province, Ifugao, Abra, Kalinga, and Apayao as well as the City of Baguio. The result of the plebiscite showed that only Ifugao province voted for inclusion in the CAR (Buendia 1995, p. 706). Ironically, Ifugao is also one of the poorest provinces in the country. This rejection of RA 6766 led to the re-implementation of EO 220 (establishing the Cordillera Administrative Region) covering the provinces of Abra, Kalinga, Apayao, Benguet, Ifugao, Mountain Province, and Baguio City.

2.1.5 The Ramos Administration (1992–1998)

The most notable achievement of the Ramos Administration was its effort to produce a national consensus for realizing political stability and economic development. As regards economic development, it focused on economic liberalization and democratization, following the policy of its predecessor, and succeeded in establishing laws to implement structural adjustment programme. Its approach to addressing economic development based on political stability thus gained were reflected in its vision "the Philippines 2000", aiming to join the group of newly industrializing economies (NIEs) by the year 2000, and its attempt to forge a national consensus by formulating its Medium Term Philippine Development Plan (1993–1998) and holding an economic summit. It actively utilized the participation of the private sector in the management of the build-operate-transfer (BOT) scheme, and privatization, under the favourable Asian economy and firm business confidence and amid the international trend of reconsidering the role of the public and private sectors.

The Philippine Government adopted the Social Reform Agenda (SRA) in 1994, and it promoted poverty-alleviating projects by selecting 21 provinces and six urban areas, such as the Metropolitan Manila or the National Capital Region (NCR), Baguio City, and Cebu City. The SRA is a series of government efforts aimed at a quality of development that will secure the welfare of the socially disadvantaged. In this agenda, the government indicated priorities of issues in social reform aimed at promoting regional development and alleviating poverty faced by the majority of the population. However, Igaya (1999) pointed out that key components of the SRA were never fully implemented and those that were had a limited effect. The Ramos Administration's apparent success in demonstrating the potential of state capacity through its reform effort lacked the social angle (e.g., social safety nets) in a liberalizing regime.

Republic Act 7916 or the Special Economic Zone Act of 1995 was signed into law on 24 February 1995 to encourage economic growth through the development of economic zones called Ecozones. The same act created the Philippine Economic Zone Authority (PEZA) with its mission to contribute to the national effort of accelerating employment generation, particularly the countryside. The Bases Conversion and Development Act of 1992 also designated areas as Special Economic Zones.

It was during the Ramos Administration that the provisions of the 1991 Local Government Code (RA 7160) were implemented. Tapales (1995) discusses the strategic policy objectives for decentralized governance to (a) promote the efficiency of local development by managing the concentration of power in the national government; (b) reduce regional gaps through the appropriate distribution of resources from the national government to LGUs; and (c) promote development by LGUs' initiative and through local citizen's participation. These are operationalized through the following mechanisms: devolution of five basic services from the national government's regional offices to the local government units; strengthening of people's participation through local governmental mechanisms; increase in revenues for local units by the provision of increased shares in nationally imposed taxes; and in effect strengthening the powers of local executive officials and councils.

2.1.6 *The Estrada Administration (1992–2001)*

Shortly after its inauguration, the Estrada Administration embarked on a Ten Point Action Plan for its first 100 days. This action plan took over the previous administration's policy of promoting the private sector-led economy which was centred on foreign capital and deregulation. However, the action plan did not make any special mention of issues related to decentralization which is an important challenge that the administration had inherited from the Ramos Administration. The short-term goals of the Estrada Action Plan instead focused on poverty alleviation, agricultural promotion, and crime eradication.

In a rapid appraisal of Estrada's *Lingap para sa Mahirap* (Caring for the Poor) Program, Medel (2002) observed that local governments were not harnessed since many of the programmes were conceptualized at the national level though consultations with LGUs were conducted. The very centralized, national-level process contradicted the objective of empowering LGUs.

2.2 The State of Political Decentralization in the Philippines

The Philippines is an archipelago of over 7,100 islands. Administratively, it is divided into several sub-national formations and units. At the top is the national government bureaucracy that functions through a number of executive departments or national government agencies (NGAs) which also have a presence in the different administrative regions. Working in consonance with the NGAs are the LGUs. Coordination across and between these LGUs and the NGAs is undertaken by way of 15 administrative regions (from north to south) composed of 79 provinces, 113 cities, and 1,497 municipalities as shown in Table 8.1 below. With the exception of the Autonomous Region for Muslim Mindanao (ARMM), all the regions are administrative sub-divisions and not actual regional governments (see map below).

Map 3   Philippines: Provinces

1 Ilocos Norte
2 Ilocos Sur
3 Kalinga-Apayao
4 Mountain Province
5 Ifugao
6 Benguet
7 La Union
8 Nueva Vizcaya
9 Quirino
10 Tarlac
11 Nueva Ecija
12 Pampanga
13 Bulacan
14 Rizal
15 Bataan
16 Manila
17 Cavite
18 Batangas
19 Laguna
20 Quezon
21 Occidental Mindoro
22 Oriental Mindoro
23 Marinduque
24 Camarines Norte
25 Camarines Sur
26 Catanduanes
27 Albay
28 Romblon
29 Masbate
30 Sorsogon

31 Northern Samar
32 Eastern Samar
33 Western Samar
34 Leyte
35 Antique
36 Aklan
37 Capiz
38 Iloilo
39 Negros Occidental
40 Negros Oriental
41 Cebu
42 Bohol
43 Siquijor
44 Southern Leyte
45 Misamis Occidental
46 Misamis Oriental
47 Agusan Del Norte
48 Bukidnon
49 Agusan Del Sur
50 Davao Del Norte
51 Lanao Del Norte
52 Lanao Del Sur
53 Maguindanao
54 North Cotabato
55 Sultan Kudarat

Reproduced with permission from UNEP/GRID after the Digital Chart of the World.

Table 8.1   Statistics on Local Government Units (LGUs) in the Philippines

Regions	Provinces	Cities	Municipalities
Ilocos Region	4	7	118
Cagayan Valley	5	3	90
Central Luzon	6	11	111
Southern Tagalog*	11	12	211
Bicol Region	6	7	108
Western Visayas	6	16	117
Central Visayas	4	12	120
Eastern Visayas	6	4	139
Zamboanga Peninsula	3	5	67
Northern Mindanao	5	8	85
Davao Region	4	5	43
SOCCSKSARGEN**	4	5	45
Caraga	4	3	70
ARMM	5	1	93
CAR***	6	1	76
NCR****	0	13	4
16	79	113	1497

Source: Department of Interior and Local Government (DILG) 2002 at http://www.dilg.gov.ph/index.cfm?FuseAction=lgu.statistics.
*   Southern Tagalog is further divided into two sub-regions or growth areas namely the CALABARZON (composed of the provinces of Cavite, Laguna, Batangas, Rizal, and Quezon) and MIMAROPA (composed of the provinces of Occidental and Oriental Mindoro, Marinduque, Romblon, and Palawan).
**   SOCCSKSARGEN is the acronym for the provinces of South Cotabato, North Cotabato, Sultan Kudarat, Saranggani, and General Santos City. These are provinces located on the island of Mindanao in southern Philippines.
*** CAR stands for the Cordillera Administrative Region.
**** NCR is the National Capital Region and actually refers to Metropolitan Manila. It is a special administrative region where the headquarters of NGAs are located.

Regional administrative divisions are actually made for convenience. Only the ARMM has a Regional Governor. The rest of the regions serve as coordinating bodies. The primary political divisions in the country are the provinces. Each province is headed by a governor elected for a three-year term. Each province is in turn comprised of clusters of component cities and municipalities headed by mayors who are also elected for a three-year term. All elected local officials have a three-year term and are subject to a three-term limit. The country's prevailing national and local administrative system is illustrated in Figure 8.2 below.

The most basic and most numerous political unit in the country is the *barangay* (or village) typically composed of about 50 to 100 households. At present there are roughly more than 42,000 *barangays* throughout the country. Each *barangay* is headed by a Chairman. However,

Figure 8.2   Philippine Local Government Units (LGUs)[9]

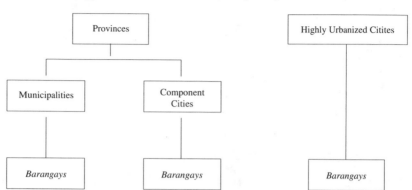

highly urbanized cities (HUCs) are placed on the same level as a province even though these cities are divided directly into *barangays*.

Each political sub-division from the province down has a local legislative assembly or *sanggunian* composed of council members and presided over by the vice-governor (in the case of a province) or vice-mayor (in the case of a municipality or city). Manasan (2002, p. 1) observes that "to a large extent, each level of local government is autonomous although the higher level of government (e.g., province) exercises some degree of supervision over lower level governments (e.g., municipalities and component cities) in terms of budgeting and legislation".

2.2.1 *Decentralization and Economic Viability*

Two major statutes circumscribe the operationalization of political decentralization in the Philippines. The first is the 1989 Organic Act for Muslim Mindanao (RA 6734) creating the Autonomous Region for Muslim Mindanao (ARMM). The second is the 1991 Local Government Code (RA 7160). Also in 1989, the Organic Act for the Cordillera Autonomous Region (RA 6766) was enacted that should have prepared the way for the creation of the Cordillera Autonomous Region (CAR). However, because only one province (Ifugao) opted to be a part of the autonomous region, the implementation of RA 6766 was held in abeyance and the earlier EO 220 creating the Cordillera Administrative Region (CAR) was re-implemented.

EO 220 is different from RA 6766 in that the latter creates an autonomous regional government while the former intends merely:

> to coordinate the planning and implementation of programs and services in the region, particularly, to coordinate with the local government units

as well as with the executive departments of the National Government in the supervision of field offices and in identifying, planning, monitoring, and accepting projects and activities in the region.[10]

RA 6734 determines the extent of powers of the regional government in southern Philippines while RA 7160 establishes the powers, functions, and responsibilities of LGUs that do not belong to the ARMM. In both cases, the powers that are vested were previously held by the central government.

2.2.2 RA 6734 and the Autonomous Region for Muslim Mindanao (ARMM)

The powers and responsibilities of LGUs belonging to the ARMM are different from those non-ARMM LGUs. According to Manasan (2002, p.4), their functions and responsibilities are "slightly broader" in that "the ARMM is charged with the provision of agrarian reform, education, the promotion of employment and workers' welfare and the promotion of trade and industry while non-ARMM LGUs are not". At the same time, Manasan (2002, p. 2) notes that RA 6734:

> also provides for the ARMM's expanded share and automatic retention of national internal revenue taxes collected in the region, significant regional discretion in development planning, and the regional governments' primacy in the delivery of basic services and the utilization and management of natural resources.

Political power is devolved to the Regional Legislative Assembly, the Regional Governor, and the special courts provided for in the law. Also, "the Autonomous Region shall have the power to create its own sources of revenues and to levy taxes, fees and charges, subject to" constitutional limitations.[11] These revenue sources can include (but are not necessarily limited to):

(1) Taxes, except income taxes, imposed by the Regional Government;
(2) Fees and charges imposed by the Regional Government;
(3) Appropriations, internal revenue allotments and other budgetary allotments from the National Government;
(4) Shares in revenues generated from the operations of public utilities within the Autonomous Region; and
(5) Block grants derived from economic agreements or conventions authorized by the Autonomous Region, donations, endowments, foreign assistance, and other forms of aid, subject to the Constitution and national policies.[12]

2.2.3 RA 7160 and Political Decentralization

The current political decentralization policy throughout the rest of the Philippines not falling within the coverage of ARMM and RA 6734 is circumscribed in the 1991 Local Government Code (RA 7160). RA 7160 consists of four books. Book 1 contains the general provisions and guiding principles as well as the definitions of terms and relations in the implementation of political decentralization. Book 2 contains provisions defining the local tax powers of LGUs. Book 3 defines the administrative and political powers, functions, and responsibilities of LGUs while Book 4 contains the miscellaneous and final provisions.

Under RA 7160, economic viability is carried out through political decentralization in several ways. One is through the devolution of bureaucratic services to the LGUs. Another is by way of local fiscal empowerment. Devolution involves the effective transfer of the principal responsibility for basic services delivery from the central government to the LGUs. As specified in RA 7160, the services to be devolved are as follows: agricultural extension and research, social forestry, environmental management and pollution control, primary healthcare, hospital care, social welfare services, repair and maintenance of infrastructure facilities, water supply and communal irrigation, and land use planning. These functions will now be discharged by the LGUs down to the cities and municipalities.

Prior to the implementation of RA 7160, local governments only played a secondary role in providing other services such as agricultural extension, the construction and maintenance of local roads and public buildings, and operation of high schools, hospitals and health centres. It was the NGAs that exercised principal jurisdiction over these services. Devolution affects economic viability because not only are the functions and responsibilities devolved but also the institutions, resources (including budgets that used to go to the NGAs), and personnel. This implies a corresponding reduction in the budgets of NGAs that used to provide such extension services. The affected national agencies are as follows: the Departments of Agrarian Reform (DAR), Agriculture (DA), Budget and Management (DBM), Environment and Natural Resources (DENR), Health (DOH), Public Works and Highways (DPWH), Social Welfare and Development (DSWD), Tourism (DOT), Transportation and Communication (DOTC), and the Philippine Gamefowl Commission (PGF). What this also means is that the appointments of key personnel that used to be one of the central government's responsibilities would now be handled by local chief executives.

In addition to the devolution of NGA functions, RA 7160 also grants LGUs a wider mandate to pursue the development of their respective areas. Prior to RA 7160, the functions of LGUs were limited to imposing and collecting local taxes, the issuance and enforcement of regulations concerning private business activities within their jurisdictions as well as the administration of certain services such as garbage collection, public and markets, and slaughterhouses. As observed by Manasan (2002, p.2), RA 7160 "includes far-reaching provisions affecting the assignment of functions across different levels of government, the revenue sharing between the central and the local governments, the resource generation/ utilization authorities of LGUs and the participation of civil society in various aspects of local governance".

Political decentralization through RA 7160 allowed for an expansion of the tax powers of LGUs. It gave local officials the power to determine the tax base that LGUs can use to determine the levies that can be imposed on products, activities and sectors (like banks and other financial institutions as well as printing offices) that used to be outside the parameters of local taxation. In actual fact, the Department of Finance (DOF) had lost its review function over the schedule of market values of real properties that serves as the tax base of the real property tax. This effectively increased the maximum allowable rates at which most local taxes may be imposed.

Aside from their increased tax powers under RA 7160, grants to local governments were doubled from 20% of internal revenue taxes to 40%. LGUs receive a fixed share of central government tax revenues in the form of the Internal Revenue Allotment (IRA) based on a formula fixed by law. This allotment is actually received by the LGUs as a block grant from the central government for which local government authorities exercise considerable discretion in its utilization. Under RA 7160 IRA appropriations are determined on the basis of population (50%), land area (25%) and equal sharing (25%). Previously, the allocations were determined as follows: 70% on the basis of population, 20% land area, and 10% equal sharing.

Moreover, under RA 7160, provincial legislative councils (*sanggunians*) are now empowered to review the budgets of municipal governments and component cities within their jurisdictions. This function used to be the prerogative of the national DBM.

3. Political Decentralization and Human Development

With the implementation of RA 7160, local government authorities and their constituents are assumed to derive substantial dividends from political and administrative devolution and decentralization by making LGUs better able to provide more appropriate basic services, greater fiscal autonomy, and empowering basic sectors through people's participation in decision making, among many others. Political decentralization is assumed in this study to be a strategic policy undertaken to achieve a strategic objective. This study also assumes that that objective is human development which is achieved through local economic viability / sustainability.

Human development is the process of enlarging people's choices. One way by which human development is measured is through the Human Development Index (HDI). The HDI is actually a simple summary measure of several dimensions of the human development concept. National human development reports build on the analytical framework of the global Human Development Report by examining the most pressing development issues and exploring ways to place human development at the forefront of the national political agenda. Four reports have been generated and published by the Philippine Human Development Network (PHDN) and the United Nations Development Program (UNDP) covering the years 1994, 1997, 2000, and 2002. The reports on the Philippines list provinces according to their HDI rankings that are computed from three types of indicators: the aspect of health or longevity as measured by life expectancy; knowledge as measured by enrolment and literacy rates; and standard of living as measured by the real per capita income (see Appendix for other HDI tabulations).

3.1 The Human Development Ranking of Philippine Provinces

Using the HDI rankings, five provinces from the upper and bottom list were selected. The disparities that exist between provinces in both the upper and lower HDI listing have been observed to be consistent over time in the sense that provinces ranked high in the beginning remain almost at that level for much of the other national human development reports. Tables 8.2 and 8.3 show that over the different periods of reporting, the provinces at the bottom continued to perform poorly in terms of human and social development compared to the rest of the provinces while the top five provinces in the 1994 HDI ranking were seen to perform better compared to those at the bottom.

Based on the Report for 1994, the provinces belonging to the high HDI list are Cavite, Rizal, Batanes, Laguna, and Bulacan while those at the bottom of the list are Sulu, Tawi-tawi, Ifugao, Basilan, and Lanao del Sur (the low list). For those in the high list, however, only Rizal improved during the period from 1994 to 2000; two provinces were unable to maintain their upper ranking in the succeeding periods (Batanes and Laguna) while Cavite dropped to Number 5 in 1997 but managed to pick up again in the rankings by 2000. Bulacan also dropped in 1997 but improved altogether by 2000. All five provinces at the top experienced percentage declines in their respective HDI scores from 1994 to 1997. Despite these drops, however, the provinces for the most part continue to be on the high list.

Table 8.2   Top Five Provinces in HDI, 1994–2000

	1994		1997		2000		Percent Change	
Province	HDI	Rank	HDI	Rank	HDI	Rank	1994–1997	1997–2000
Cavite	0.840	1	0.689	5	0.693	2	(18.0)	0.6
Rizal	0.813	2	0.733	1	0.758	1	(9.8)	3.4
Batanes	0.798	3	0.733	3	0.649	7	(8.1)	(11.5)
Laguna	0.774	4	0.687	6	0.690	9	(11.2)	0.4
Bulacan	0.763	5	0.646	12	0.672	3	(15.3)	4.0

Source: Philippine Human Development Reports (PHDR) 1997, 2000, 2002

Table 8.3   Bottom Five Provinces in HDI, 1994–2000

	1994		1997		2000		Percent Change	
Province	HDI	Rank	HDI	Rank	HDI	Rank	1994–1997	1997–2000
Sulu	0.372	76	0.331	77	0.311	77	(11.0)	(6.0)
Tawi-tawi	0.384	75	0.430	76	0.378	76	12.0	(12.1)
Ifugao	0.409	74	0.539	46	0.512	72	31.8	(5.0)
Basilan**	0.427	73	0.486	68	0.420	74	13.8	(13.6)
Lanao del Sur	0.445	72	0.436	73	0.425	73	(2.0)	(2.5)

Source: Philippine Human Development Reports (PHDR) 1997, 2000, 2002
* The total number of provinces that were ranked in 1994 was 76 while 77 provinces were ranked for the years 1997 and 2000
** Became part of the Autonomous Region for Muslim Mindanao (ARMM) in 2001

Correspondingly, the provinces in the low HDI list remained continually at the bottom of the list up to 2000. Ifugao province went up significantly in the ranking from 74 in 1994 to 46 by 1997 but dropped down to 72 by 2000. The same thing can be said of Basilan which improved somewhat in 1997 to 68 but dropped to 74 by 2000, even lower than its ranking in 1997 (73). The other three provinces (Sulu, Tawi-tawi, and Lanao del Sur) experienced a decline in their overall ranking by 2000.

With the exception of Ifugao province, all of the areas listed in the bottom HDI ranking belong to the ARMM. These ARMM provinces in

Table 8.4 Poverty Incidence by Province
1991–2000

Province	Incidence of Families (in Percent)					Magnitude of Poor Families				
	1991	1994	Inc/Dec (%)	1997	2000	Inc/Dec (%)	1994	1997	2000	Inc/Dec (%)
Cavite	21.8	11.6	-10.2	8.0	10.2	2.10	28,706	22,647	38,084	68.16
Rizal	31.3	18.4	-12.9	8.3	8.0	-0.2	32,088	16,571	27,555	66.29
Batanes	2.9	19.4	16.5	8.7	7.5	-1.20	578	306	249	-18.70
Laguna	25.2	19.4	-5.8	12.3	8.6	-3.7	49,784	40,874	33,412	-18.26
Bulacan	20.4	17.3	-3.1	8.3	5.4	-2.9	53,220	28,512	21,801	-23.54
Sulu	70.6	60.1	-10.5	67.1	63.2	-3.9	50,827	61,266	62,872	2.62
Tawi–tawi	16.6	57.5	40.9	35.0	56.5	21.5	28,295	18,544	27,538	48.51
Ifugao	74.6	72.1	-2.5	57.7	55.6	-2.1	20,013	17,423	18,103	3.90
Basilan	54.9	47.1	-7.8	20.9	26.2	5.3	24,770	11,752	15,866	35.00
Lanao del Sur	43.0	53.0	10.0	55.6	55.0	-0.6	41,355	51,054	66,464	30.18

Sources: PHDR, 1997 (data for 1991 and 1994) and Poverty Estimates 2002, NSO (data for 1997–2000).

the low list perform poorly in all three components of HDI (e.g., life expectancy, literacy, and income). Life expectancy is lowest in this region, reflecting the effects of armed conflicts as well as the loss of political security that can result in the lack of available local health facilities.

Poverty incidence is the measure of the proportion of families with per capita incomes below the prescribed poverty threshold. The poverty threshold is the minimum yearly income required or the expenditure necessary to meet the food requirements and other non-food basic needs of all the members of a household. Table 8.4 above shows that the percentage of poverty incidence among households belonging to provinces in the HDI low list has been substantial (ranging from 26% to as much as 63%) compared to those in the high list (with the highest percentage at 12.3%). Likewise, in terms of the actual number of families falling below the poverty threshold, there appears to be some variance as well. For instance, the number of poor families in Lanao del Sur (66,464) and Sulu (62,872) are the highest among the low list provinces and which would be almost double that of the number in the two provinces (e.g., Laguna and Cavite) in the high list with the largest number of poor families (i.e., 33,412 and 38,084, respectively).

Inasmuch as the poverty incidence in the bottom list provinces are substantial, the rates for the areas did improve over time as shown by their rates in 1991 and 2000 with the exception of Tawi-tawi and Lanao del Sur. For the period 1991–1994, there was a decline in poverty incidence in the provinces under study except for Batanes, Tawi-tawi, and Lanao del Sur. Table 8.4 also shows the alarming increase in the number of poor families in the provinces of Cavite and Rizal for the period 1997 to 2000 at 68% and 66%, respectively, considering their high performance in the HDI during the same period.

3.2 Political Decentralization Factors Affecting HDI Disparities

Immediately, it may be surmised from the above data that the distance between the province and Manila can be a determining factor for the high or low HDI ranking. This may be the effect of the extent of the centralized public administration system that dominated much of the country's political history. Of the five provinces in the top list, four are provinces adjacent to the Metropolitan Manila area (Rizal to the east, Cavite to the southwest, Laguna to the south, and Bulacan to the north) and are considered to be high-growth economic zones even before the start of political decentralization. Indeed, Cavite, Laguna, and Rizal are part of the CALABARZON special development project. Those in the low list, meanwhile, with the exception of Ifugao province (which belongs to the Cordillera Administrative Region or CAR), are

Table 8.5   Per Capita Human Priority Expenditures, 1991–1994

Province	Per Capita Human Priority Expenditures	
	1993	1994
Cavite	6.57	27.64
Rizal	18.48	36.92
Batanes	619.72	923.67
Laguna	23.19	61.33
Bulacan	32.02	9.19
Sulu	6.15	3.69
Tawi-tawi	1.15	nd
Ifugao	1.19	154.60
Basilan	nd	25.34
Lanao del Sur	nd	nd

Source: PHDR, 1997.

provinces belonging to the ARMM in the southernmost part of the Philippines.

Despite its distance from Manila, the high HDI ranking for Batanes province, an island in the northern tip of the Philippines, may be an exception due to its higher levels of life expectancy and functional literacy in relation to its small local population. This is manifested in the larger proportion of per capita public spending on human development priorities for the province as shown in Table 8.5 above. Batanes spent the most in terms of human priority expenditures per capita in 1993 and 1994 than any of the other nine provinces included in the study. Not surprisingly, the provinces with the lower priority expenditures per capita are Sulu and Tawi-tawi.

3.2.1 The Costs of Devolution

Several administrative and political factors and issues can affect the rankings as well as the HDI disparities that exist between provinces over time. One cause of the disparities has to do with issues that are associated with the devolution of personnel and assets. In the course of the implementation of political devolution in the 1990s, certain devolved technical personnel (especially in the health sector) chose to be assigned to provinces near Metro Manila leading to an uneven distribution of skilled staff. LGUs also complained about the quality of assets that were devolved to them by the NGAs arguing that most of them are no longer in good condition.

3.2.2 National Government Assistance

In terms of support from the national government to LGUs, the problems pertain mainly to the lack of technical guidelines that would assist the latter on how to better carry out their new roles in the context of political decentralization. Not all of the LGU officials were able to acquire material and technical resources (e.g., guidebooks on local government organization models and the crafting of new local revenue codes) given by the national government on how best to implement the decentralization strategy for sustained local development purposes. Section 3 of RA 7160 provides that:

> The vesting of duty, responsibility, and accountability in local government units shall be accompanied with provision for reasonably adequate resources to discharge their powers and effectively carry out their functions; hence, they shall have the power to create and broaden their own sources of revenue and the right to a just share in national taxes and an equitable share in the proceeds of the utilization and development of the national wealth within their respective areas.[13]

It may be that those local areas that received such guidelines and technical assistance would be more likely and more inclined to institute effective fiscal policies that allow for the increased generation of local resources than those areas in the country that did not receive such assistance. The effectiveness of certain areas are likely to translate into better HDI performance levels although this could not be shown to be the case that can specifically explain the low and high HDI rankings of the provinces under study.

3.2.3 Fiscal Management and Auditing

Audit reports from the Commission on Audit (COA) on the financial status of LGUs nationwide upon the implementation of RA 7160, for instance, revealed cases of mismanagement of funds and the non-compliance of certain LGUs to existing rules and regulations to the detriment of local residents. Such cases include the illegal use of trust funds, unliquidated cash advances, cash shortages, and failure to conduct the annual physical inventory of supplies and property.

Overspending is a typical problem among many LGUs. Table 8.6 illustrates that at the national level, LGUs had a constant overdraft on their resources that exceeded two billion pesos in 1998. As a consequence, local trust funds including collections of withholding taxes and other taxes for remittance to the Bureau of Internal Revenue and the national government, deductions of government employees for insurance premiums, and Country-wide Development Fund (CDF)

Table 8.6   Cash Overdraft (in Million Pesos), CY 1991–1996

| Year | Amount | Increase (Decrease) Over Previous Year | |
		Amount	Percent
2001	945.65	332.75	(26.03)
2000	1,278.40	104.53	9.00
1999	1,173.87	(918.03)	(43.88)
1998	2,091.90	1,411.50	207.45
1997	680.40	133.85	24.49
1996	546.55	(322.10)	(37.08)
1995	868.65	25.73	3.05
1994	842.92	233.92	38.41
1993	609.00	65.93	12.14
1992	543.07	296.23	120.01
1991	246.84	na	na

Source: COA–Annual Financial Report of Local Governments, 1994 to 2001.

were spent for purposes other than those for which they were entrusted or created that resulted in cash overdraft. This has been the case despite the provision in Section 337 of RA 7160 that states that "no cash overdraft in any local fund shall be incurred at the end of the fiscal year".[5]

Throughout the country, LGUs incurred the most increase in total cash overdraft in 1992 (at the start of the implementation of RA 7160) and again in 1998 (coinciding with the Asian financial crisis). There was a 120% increase in cash overdraft during the first year of implementation of decentralization in 1992 while a remarkable 207% increase was incurred at a time when LGUs were assumed to have built adequate capacities for managing local affairs in 1998. It will be recalled as well that elections were held during these periods. This situation, however, seemed to have improved as shown by the data for the succeeding years. There was a decline of almost 44% in 1999 and 26% by 2001. Still, the 2001 overdraft was a substantial amount (P945.65 million).

Another sign of LGU fiscal mismanagement is in the accumulation of unliquidated cash advances. Table 8.7 shows the substantial amounts of unliquidated cash advances of LGUs nationwide. In 1993, at the beginning of the implementation of decentralization in the country, unliquidated cash advances increased by 90% amounting to P679.64 million. However, by 2001, the increase in unliquidated cash advances went "down" to 17%.

As far as the provinces being studied are concerned, in the Annual Financial Reports of Local Governments (1994–2001) as evaluated by the

Table 8.7 Unliquidated Cash Advances, CY 1987–1996 (in Million Pesos)

Year	Amount	Increase (Decrease) Over Previous Year	
		Amount	Percent
2001	2,704.03	396.19	17
2000	2,307.84	220.94	10.6
1999	2,086.90	–211.72	(9.2)
1998	2,298.62	378.73	20
1997	1,919.89	317.47	20
1996	1,602.42	408.47	34
1995	1,193.95	245.11	26
1994	948.84	269.20	40
1993	679.64	321.40	90
1992	358.24	18.52	5
1991	339.72	109.80	48
1990	229.92	–9.41	(4)
1989	239.33	67.09	39
1988	172.24	60.05	54
1987	112.19	na	na

Source: COA–Annual Financial Report of Local Governments, 1994 to 2001.

COA, it was observed that, in 1996, the provinces of Tawi-tawi and Basilan had the highest amount of unliquidated cash advances (P74.35 million and P66.68 million, respectively) in the country. In 1999, these provinces were again the LGUs with the highest amount of unliquidated cash advances (P131.263 million and P66.312 million, respectively). Sulu was the third highest with P20.578 million in unaccounted cash advances.

However, in 2001, all regions in the country showed an increase in their unliquidated cash advances (with Metropolitan Manila topping the list at P153.45 million) with the exception of the ARMM provinces which by that time had a decline in its unaccounted advances of P27.71 million. This is most likely to be explained by the investigations conducted by the national government on ARMM expenditures eventually leading to the arrest of its principal administrator, Governor Nur Misuari.

According to the COA, the failure to conduct a physical inventory of fixed assets makes it difficult (if not impossible) for LGUs to determine the existence and condition of their resources as well as the validity of its recorded amount in the books of accounts. It also denies the LGU of valuable information necessary for fiscal decision making. In 1995, 1,047 out of 1,683 LGUs (62.21%) failed to conduct the requisite yearly physical inventory of fixed assets and supplies and materials. The numbers improved somewhat in 2001 with only 20.22% or 342 out of 1,691 failing to comply with such requirement.

However, despite these accounting concerns among provinces in the bottom HDI ranking, the individual audit reports for LGUs revealed that provinces with high HDI scores are also not immune from committing the above mentioned violations of existing audit rules and regulations in managing public funds. In 1998, unliquidated cash advances in the provinces of Cavite, Rizal, and Laguna amounted to P3.68 million, P1.19 million, and P10.38 million, respectively. Batanes had P4.95 million in its unliquidated accounts in 1997. It was noted that these provinces did not exert effort to settle these amounts and that cash advances are still being granted to personnel with outstanding advances.

It is also possible that political decentralization can cause changes in the priorities of local officials particularly as regards the management and allocation of funds in the community. For instance, in 1997 the provincial government of Ifugao had placed its trust fund amounting to 69 million in high yield and premium savings accounts for long periods despite the prevalence of unimplemented projects chargeable against the fund. In addition, Calamity Funds totalling P11.93 million intended for restoration and rehabilitation projects were not fully utilized for the purpose but were instead invested in the high yield and premium savings.

Ironically, provinces in the HDI high list do not appear to be immune from these auditing anomalies. The same practice was discovered in Bulacan in 1995 with its placement in time deposit of P9.5 million from its General Fund at a time when the said Fund had a cash deficit resulting in unremitted trust liabilities of P15.63 million. In 1997, the auditor rendered an adverse opinion on the financial statement of the provincial government of Batanes with its overstatement of Payable Accounts totalling P4.1 million which were found to be non-existent and without valid claims. In 1996, the provincial government of Laguna failed to get the most advantageous price in the procurement of generic drugs and medicines intended for its constituents by procuring from supposedly exclusive distributors. The same was observed in 1998 in Bulacan prompting the COA to observe that certain purchases done at the local government level did not provide an advantage to the people of the community due to the absence of proper validation procedures such as pre-qualification of contractors and the evaluation of bids.

3.2.4 Resource Mobilization

In general, decentralization through RA 7160 augmented local taxing powers and devolved tax policymaking authority to the local legislative councils (the *sanggunian*) such as the setting of values on real property. Decentralization in the country expanded the tax base of LGUs to include activities and sectors that used to be outside the reach of local taxation, such as banks and financial institutions, agricultural and forest products, mining operations, and mineral production. Local development financing sources available to LGUs now include not just national allotments such as the internal revenue allotment (IRA) but can also include local tax revenues; loans; the Municipal Development Fund (MDF); bonds flotation; build-operate-transfer (BOT) arrangements; and official development assistance (ODA) from overseas sources.

Manasan (1995), however, argued that the tax powers granted to LGUs by RA 7160 do not automatically translate into substantial local revenue increases from local sources. This kind of outcome would also depend on the extent to which local government authorities are able to effectively and creatively exercise such powers by way of changes in the statutory rates and legal tax bases, and the growth and composition of their taxes, which significantly vary from one LGU to the next.

In 2000, the COA reported that the expansion of the revenue raising powers of LGUs mandated in RA 7160 did not contribute to the improvement of the LGUs' revenue collection from local sources. Revenue data for the period 1996–2000 showed that local sources of income collected by LGUs nationwide contributed only an average of 32.77% as compared to 46.92% for 1988–1992 or an actual net decline of 13.65% (COA–AFR 2000, p. 67) as shown in Table 8.8 below. Clearly, a significant amount of revenues for the LGUs is still derived from non-local (i.e., national) sources. Even more significantly shown in the table, local income collection declined by the same proportion as the increase in national income sources (i.e., by 13.65%). This means that what was lost in terms of local income was gained through revenues from the national government.

The ten provinces in the study indicate essentially the same trends. This is shown in Table 8.9 below. Incomes from local sources continue to lag behind income derived from the national government mainly in the form of the IRA. In the case of Tawi-tawi province, for every peso generated locally, around P683 is derived from IRA on average from 1994 to 1999. However, Table 8.9 would also indicate that those provinces ranking high on HDI tend to have a lower IRA to local income sources ratio than those on the low list. In the case of Rizal province, the ratio is actually P0.54 of IRA for every P1.00 of local income indicating that income derived from local sources is actually larger than income by way of IRA.

However, taken together, the income derived from local sources by provinces in the high list appears to be substantially higher (with the

Table 8.8   Comparative Income Collected by LGUs Nationwide from Local Sources, CYs 1988–1992 and CYs 1996–2000 (in %)

Type of Income Source	1988–1992 %	1996–2000 %	%Increase/(Decrease)
Real Property Taxes	18.51	12.77	–5.74
Taxes on Goods and Services	9.19	9.58	0.39
Operating and Service Income	12.27	2.67	–9.6
Income from Public Enterprise	0.54	0.18	–0.36
Residence Taxes	1.07	0.56	–0.51
Amusement Taxes	1.81	0.66	–1.15
Sand and Gravel Taxes	0.07	0.12	0.05
Capital Revenues	1.54	0.28	–1.26
Others	1.92	6.45	4.53
Locally Generated Income	**46.92**	**33.27**	**–13.65**
Non-locally Generated Income	**53.08**	**66.73**	**13.65**
Total	100	100	

Source: COA–AFR of LGUs, 2000, p.67.

Table 8.9   Average Ratio of IRA to Local Income Sources, 1994–1998

Cavite	Rizal	Batanes	Laguna	Bulacan
1.47	0.54	10.01	0.93	1.62
Sulu	Tawi-tawi	Ifugao	Basilan	Lanao del Sur
13.42	683.59	17.75	7.04	16.80

Source: Commission on Audit as computed by the author.

exception of Batanes) than the low list provinces as shown in Table 8.10 below. At the same time, when compared with their IRA allocations, the high HDI provinces appear to have a significant advantage over their low list counterparts.

Table 8.10   Budget Operation Statement (Incomes and Expenditures) Average, 1994–1999

Income	Cavite	Rizal	Batanes	Laguna	Bulacan	Sulu	Tawi-tawi	Ifugao	Basilan	Lanao del Sur
					Average (1994–1998)					
Local Sources	174,548,316	386,200,351	5,565,604	318,333,187	199,450,322	8,995,610	116,027	5,913,117	13,226,41	711,690,466
Revenue from Taxation	146,171,390	135,898,327	514,222	257,134,738	161,906,297	659,156	115,641	1,453,033	667,410	4,770,994
Real Property Tax	84,875,750	96,396,529	479,060	178,429,642	121,626,475	471,180	8,295	1,141,661	308,879	414,082
Bus/Local Taxes	61,295,640	39,501,798	39,162	78,639,096	40,279,822	187,976	107,346	311,371	358,531	4,356,912
Non-tax Revenues	28,376,926	250,302,024	5,047,382	60,998,448	37,544,025	8,336,454	386	4,460,084	12,559,007	6,919,472
Receipts from Eco Ent.	17,381	8,354,790	159,076	3,765,358	13,259,196	526,438	0	721,685	1,228,820	0
Fees/Charges	3,545,069	7,682,823	622,176	22,729,434	15,737,149	53,273	386	1,004,105	98,744	32,810
Loans and Borrowings	1,000,000	59,108,000	0	10,000,000	0		0	0	5,535,053	0
Other receipts	23,814,475	175,156,411	2,663,060	22,965,657	8,547,680	7,277,366	0	2,075,029	5,696,389	6,886,662
Aids and Allotments	263,683,790	213,184,505	55,721,088	299,511,947	325,473,935	121,068,740	79,881,459	105,259,073	93,722,367	197,034,592
IRA	256,941,041	207,872,600	55,721,088	294,582,746	323,277,558	120,685,651	79,314,815	104,947,936	93,107,875	196,402,897
Other National Aids	6,480,000	5,311,905	0	0	1,805,000	200,000	566,644	77,696	614,492	0
National Wealth	262,748	0	0	4,929,201	391,377	183,089	0	233,440	0	631,695
Total Income	438,232,106	599,384,856	61,286,692	617,645,134	524,924,256	130,064,350	79,997,486	111,172,190	106,948,783	208,725,057

Source: Commission on Audit.

Table 8.11   Average Per Capita IRA,
1991–2001

Province	Average
Cavite	175.471
Batanes	3981.12
Rizal	159.458
Bulacan	184.619
Laguna	191.695
Sulu	251.715
Tawi-tawi	394.492
Ifugao	704.011
Basilan	208.112
Lanao del Sur	332.643

Source: Commission on Audit.

The average per capita IRA data for all ten provinces from 1991–2001 reveals a bit of a pattern in the sense that provinces in the high HDI list (with the exception of Batanes) have a lower average than their low HDI counterparts. This is shown in Table 8.11 above. This is indicative of a lesser degree of dependence on such national allotments.

However, looking at Table 8.12 below, provinces over time tend to increase their per capita IRA (and consequently their dependence on this national allotment) regardless of whether they are in the high or low HDI list. All the provinces in the study show that their per capita IRA increased by an average of more than 1,000% with the lowest (Rizal) at 221% and the highest (Batanes and Ifugao) at more than 6,400% and 1,100% respectively since the start of the implementation of RA 7160.

This increasing dependence on national allocations by way of RA 7160 is also validated at the national level. Aside from the NSO, the National Statistical Coordinating Board (NSCB), the country's highest policymaking and coordinating body on statistical concerns noted that, on a nationwide level, the IRA grants comprised about two-thirds of LGU resources. From 1992 to 1999, the proportions of local tax resources to total LGU receipts had not even reached 25% as shown in Table 8.13 below.

The same report reveals that the total IRA disbursed to the LGUs grew about four times from 1992 to 1999 (i.e., from P19.71 billion to P85.22 billion). On the average, the IRA has been growing each year at 23.3% faster than local taxation income at 20.3% and non-tax revenues at 17.1%. On a per capita basis, the IRA has been increasing at an annual growth rate of 20.6%, more than ten times that of the annual population growth rate of 1.9%.

Table 8.12 Per Capita IRA of Provinces (1991–2001)

Province	1991	1993	1994	1995	1996	1997	1998	1999	2000	2001
Cavite	38.42	114.26	154.89	127.21	134.06	196.26	194.57	243.15	296.89	255
Batanes	314.79	1,871.39	2,628.92	3,335.47	3,569.45	4,618.70	4,833.82	5,669.73	6,488.93	6,480
Rizal	42.30	108.21	109.98	130.70	134.93	183.31	186.75	218.40	258.00	222
Bulacan	42.65	101.49	139.49	149.59	158.12	214.22	220.88	261.25	276.50	282
Laguna	38.09	112.11	153.47	147.72	157.57	208.79	225.17	255.26	302.77	316
Sulu	54.70	156.92	181.36	193.62	212.97	259.92	280.86	345.30	420.50	411
Tawi-tawi	61.93	222.25	480.46	254.50	385.04	388.58	406.33	525.26	600.57	620
Ifugao	93.43	354.43	503.45	587.33	625.45	796.96	835.27	974.23	1,154.56	1,115
Basilan	69.49	nd	nd	291.21	344.37	424.36	417.05	534.64	nd	nd
Lanao del Sur	52.42	nd	nd	263.47	338.75	441.13	418.87	571.79	632	608

Per Capita IRA

Note: Per Capita IRA for 1991,1993,1994 was sourced from the 1997 PHDR while data for 1995–2001 was computed using the COA and DOF data on IRA and the NSO Census-based Population Projections for 1995–2001.

Table 8.13   Percentage of Tax, Non-Tax, and
IRA to Total LGU Receipts,
1992–1999

Year	Tax	Non-Tax	IRA
1992	20.4	18.0	61.6
1993	12.2	12.0	75.8
1994	18.7	12.9	68.4
1995	20.2	11.4	68.4
1996	21.7	11.7	66.6
1997	17.8	16.7	65.5
1998	19.7	16.7	63.7
1999	18.3	13.8	67.5

Source: IRA as a Source of Funds for Local
Governance, NSCB, 2000.

Table 8.14   Average Local Sources and IRA of Provinces, 1994–2001
(in thousand pesos)

Provinces	Total Income	Local Sources	Percentage to Total Income	IRA	Percentage to Total Income
Cavite	578,373	213,695	37	344,860	60
Batanes	74,123	4,123	6	70,000	94
Rizal	604,726	324,814	54	276,593	46
Bulacan	690,986	266,100	39	409,171	59
Laguna	844,855	432,704	51	391,255	46
Sulu	163,835	6,713	4	156,786	96
Tawi-tawi	116,848	126	0.1	111,867	96
Ifugao	140,505	6,974	5	133,425	95
Basilan	127,073	7,096	6	105,942	83
Lanao del Sur	276,798	11,006	4	265,599	96

Source: Computed based on data from COA.

Although Table 8.14 shows that the ten provinces relied heavily on
the IRA, it does indicate that those provinces found in the high list are
more likely to be less dependent than those in the low list. With the
exception of Batanes that had an IRA dependency of 94%, the rest of the
high HDI provinces had a lower dependency (i.e., ranging from 60% to
46%) than those in the low HDI list (with dependency ranging from
83% to as much as 96%).

The extent of dependence on IRA can also be seen to be a function
of the extent to which LGUs are able to generate local revenues mainly

Figure 8.3   Average Collection Efficiency for Basic Real Property Tax Before and After
RA 7160

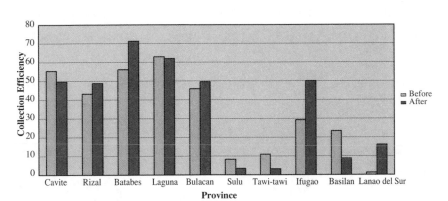

from real property taxes. Figure 8.3 indicates the tax collection efficiency
for basic real property tax in the provinces in the study before and after
the promulgation and implementation of RA 7160. Figure 8.3 shows that
the tax collection efficiency for basic real property tax among the high
HDI provinces has always been impressive both before and after RA
7160. However, the figure also shows that RA 7160 had actually reduced
this collection efficiency among the low HDI provinces (three out of
five) compared to the high HDI provinces (with only two out of five).

3.3 Decentralized Governance in ARMM

The ARMM legislated its own decentralization process with the passage
of the Muslim Mindanao Autonomy Act No. 25 (also known as the Local
Government Code of Muslim Mindanao) in April 1993. This provides for
LGUs within the region with the capacity to exercise powers, functions
and responsibilities necessary for basic services delivery. The Act devolves
to LGUs the direct provision of services like agricultural support, health
and social welfare, infrastructure, and others. Consequently, a Revenue
Code for the ARMM was also crafted with the promulgation of the
Muslim Mindanao Autonomy Act No. 49.

The provisions of Autonomy Act 25 recognize the importance of
LGUs and citizen participation in the attainment of development goals.
One striking feature, however, is the power vested in the Regional
Governor of ARMM. For instance, it is the Regional Governor, instead of
the Provincial Governor, who appoints the Provincial Heads of Offices.
Also, while other provinces receive their IRAs directly from the national
government, the IRA appropriations of the provinces under the ARMM
are released to the Office of the Regional Governor.

Table 8.15 ARMM Collections from Taxes, 1996–2000 (in thousand pesos)

Sources of Collection	1996–97	1997–98	1998–99	1999–2000	Total
30% share of ARMM proper from BIR collections	44,559.88	60,236.34	83,812.99	87,899.68	276,508.89
30% share of ARMM proper from DENR collections	20,101.38	45,013.30	15,481.73	6,185.61	86,872.02
Travel Tax	na	42.23	543.00	837.87	1,423.10
Contractors' Tax	na	na	na	979.10	979.10
Interest Income from deposits	na	na	6,605.15	13,583.98	20,189.13
Others	112.22	238.59	1,053.81	84.26	1,488.88
Total	64,773.48	105,530.46	107,496.68	109,570.50	387,461.12

Source: ARMM–Liason Office.

Section 102 of Autonomy Act 25 states that "the regional autonomous government shall have a comprehensive multi-sectoral development plan to be initiated by the Regional Planning and Development Board (RPDB) and approved by the Regional Legislative Assembly (RLA)". The RPDB is composed of the Regional Governor as ex-officio chairman; all provincial governors and city mayors in the region; seven members of the RLA to be designated by the Speaker of the Assembly; and representatives made up of professionals, youth, and religious clerics.

Autonomy Act 25 also provides that the Regional Government is entitled to a 30% share from the total collections of a province or city from the National Internal Revenue taxes, fees and charges, and taxes imposed on natural resources. Indeed, Table 8.15 shows that there has been a significant increase in total revenue collection in the region from 1996 to 2000 (i.e., from P64.7 million to P109.5 million). However, upon closer scrutiny, this increase is attributed to an increase in the 30% share in internal revenue collections from the national government than to anything else.

In terms of budget expenditures, Table 8.16 shows that 66% of the ARMM's budget from 1991 to 2002 was allotted to personnel services, leaving only 14% and 20% for maintenance, operating expenses and capital outlay, respectively. Roughly, this means that for every P40.00 worth of public goods and services delivered to the provinces in the

Table 8.16 ARMM Expenditures, 1991–2002

Year	Personnel Services	Operating Expenditures Maintenance and Operating Expenses	Capital Outlay	Total
1991	64,295,000	91,403,000	637,114,000	792,812,000
1992	184,279,000	169,223,000	628,453,000	981,955,000
1993	997,138,000	321,397,000	615,078,000	1,933,613,000
1994	1,156,067,000	311,535,000	622,170,000	2,089,772,000
1995	1,362,549,000	405,801,000	716,422,000	2,484,772,000
1996	1,663,620,000	433,691,000	82,964,000	2,180,275,000
1997	2,035,073,000	432,708,000	40,089,000	2,507,870,000
1998	2,848,599,000	540,630,000	1,551,310,000	4,940,539,000
1999	3,072,436,000	752,148,000	545,750,000	4,370,334,000
2000	3,434,827,000	554,602,000	678,379,000	4,667,808,000
2001	3,894,300,000	572,264,000	514,010,000	4,980,574,000
2002	3,997,559,000	708,429,000	696,468,000	5,402,456,000
Grand Total	24,646,447,000	5,202,428,000	6,691,093,000	37,332,780,000
Average %	66.19	14.18	19.63	100

Source: ARMM–Liason Office.

region, P60.00 is required and spent for administrative (i.e., personnel) costs. On average, some P2 billion is spent on personnel compared to only P441 million and P610 million for maintenance and capital outlay expenses respectively.

4. Issues and Concerns in the Implementation of Political Decentralization in the Philippines

In general, Sosmeña (1991) summarized the major decentralization issues and problems confronting the Philippines throughout the history of the country. These include (a) the absence of a common understanding of the definition of decentralization and its application; (b) the absence of evaluation standards useful in the assessment of decentralization consequences and impacts on an integrated manner; (c) perceived weaknesses of the political leadership to initiate and sustain meaningful decentralization efforts; (d) the questionable absorptive capacity of local governments to assume increasing responsibilities resulting from political decentralization; and (e) the non-mobilization of support systems from the national government.

For instance, under RA 7160 and RA 6734, LGUs are given the responsibility of providing efficient and effective basic services in agriculture, health, social services, maintenance of public works and highways, and environmental protection sectors. However, Valdellon (1999) states that decentralized governance also implies the "freedom to fail" on the part of local governments, as well as the freedom of the central government from any responsibility to bail out LGUs failing to perform a devolved function. This flexible condition is more likely to result in the absence of substantive accountability for local executives (see Valdellon 1999). It can, in fact, encourage complacency rather than promote an incentive to do better.

Despite these problems, however, political decentralization in the Philippines has become a celebrated and much-sought after national administrative development. Its positive impact on the bureaucracy has always been the major highlight for its pursuit as a national development strategy from Aquino to Arroyo. Decentralization is favoured as a policy alternative because it empowers grassroots and sub-national entities and units that would allow them to derive solutions to local problems and concerns. As provided for in RA 7160, decentralization in the Philippines is manifested in three aspects — devolution, deconcentration, and debureaucratization.[15]

With these decentralization mantras, however, there is a need to re-examine the impact of political decentralization from an economic standpoint. The imperative to decentralize may not be that desirable when taken in the context of ensuring the economic viability of decentralized units through greater fiscal management efficiency and innovativeness. This is one key aspect of decentralization provided for in RA 7160 and RA 6734, i.e., allowing for greater free play on the part of LGUs to generate and manage their natural, human, and fiscal resources in a sustainable manner for the good of the local communities.

4.1 ARMM and RA 6734

Under the provisions of RA 6734, the Regional Government of the ARMM is given a broad range of powers pertinent to its continued economic survival. One prerogative that the ARMM has under the law is the authority to levy all types of taxes with the exception of the income tax and customs duties that are the sole prerogative of the national government. Article 10 of RA 6734 authorizes the Regional Government to impose and collect taxes, fees, and other charges except the income tax. Such a provision certainly has wide-ranging possibilities compared to LGUs that follow the guidelines set in RA 7160. The ARMM Regional Government appears to be in a better position to increase its internally sourced income.

The experience in many LGUs is that local income is generally sourced from real property taxes and business taxes. However, despite the wide-ranging powers open to it, the Regional Government chose the more traditional route to local income generation. As Manasan (2002, p. 5) observes, "the ARMM has chosen to impose a supplementary rate (i.e., a surcharge) on taxes that are typically levied by LGUs like the real property tax, and the franchise tax". Given the fact that there are not that many businesses in the region to begin with, consequently, its tax rates are 80% to 90% lower than in other LGUs in the rest of the country (Manasan 2002, p. 5).

Another way by which the ARMM's revenue generating capacities are enhanced is through the IRA allocations. Under RA 7160, LGUs are entitled to a fixed share of tax revenues from the national government on the basis of a pre-set formula. The aggregate IRA for the year is set at 40% of internal revenue tax collections of the national government three years prior to the current one.[16] This is then divided up among the different LGUs as follows: 23% to provinces, 23% to cities, 34% to municipalities and 20% to *barangays*. This allocation is transferred as a block grant from the national government to the LGUs and local officials are accorded discretionary powers in its utilization.

Under the terms of RA 6734, LGUs belonging to the ARMM are not only entitled to IRA grants under RA 7160 but they are also given their share as provided for in the Organic Act. Internal revenue tax collections in the ARMM are divided up as follows: 40% goes to the central government; 30% goes to the Regional Government itself; and 30% goes to the ARMM's constituent local governments. This sharing scheme is done at the source. This means that the regional office of the Bureau of Internal Revenue (BIR) automatically remits the share of the Regional Government along with the region's constituent units back to the ARMM.

Unfortunately, as Manasan (2002, p. 6) again points out, "many LGUs have not fully utilized their revenue raising powers even as the IRA distribution formula has been shown to have a disincentive effect on local tax effort". Certainly, the revenue share of the Regional Government from the national government would not be enough to cover the expenditure responsibilities (e.g., devolved agencies and functions) assigned to the ARMM. The tax base in the region is lower than the average for the entire country (Manasan 2002, p. 7).

In addition to its dependence on IRA grants from the national government, the Regional Government is also dependent on the yearly budget appropriations of the central government. Such budget appropriations will depend entirely on the other plans and programmes of the central government. The ARMM has to compete along with other NGAs if only to guarantee the Regional Government's capacity to continue the delivery of basic services.

On the other hand, constituent ARMM LGUs receive appropriations but not the expenditure responsibilities. Manasan (2002, p. 8) observes that "the aggregate inter-governmental transfer accruing to ARMM LGUs is more than 20 times that of the regional government itself". Overall, it may be said that the heavy reliance on IRA grants may have been a disincentive for the ARMM Regional Government to be more innovative and effective in generating local resources.

4.2 Decentralized Governance and RA 7160

To accompany the implementing rules and regulations (IRR), the government came up with a Master Plan (1993–1998) for the Sustained Implementation of the Local Government Code of 1991. This Master Plan provides the framework for the implementation of political decentralization in the country. However, this was adopted only in October 1994 or three years after its enactment. Tapales (1995) also noted the delay in the formulation of standards, indicators, and baseline data that can empirically validate the successful (or failed) implementation of RA 7160.

Under the Master Plan, the implementation of RA 7160 goes through three major phases. The Changeover Phase (1992–1993) involves the transfer of devolved functions to LGUs, with corresponding assets and personnel. The Transitional Phase (1994–1996) covers the period where

NGAs and the LGUs should institutionalize their adjustments to the decentralized schemes introduced by the Code. The Stabilization Phase (1997 onwards) assumes that the LGUs have built adequate capacities in managing local affairs, and the NGAs will provide constant support and technical assistance to LGUs.

4.2.1 The Changeover Phase (1992–1993)

The changeover or devolution of authority that was expected to proceed within six months of the enactment of RA 7160 (i.e., by July 1992) did not proceed as scheduled. This would have consisted mainly of transferring the functions of NGAs to the LGUs including the conversion of Regional Health Offices (RHOs) into technical assistance and monitoring units of such local units and the release of funds for such purposes. Human resource-related issues were among the major concerns during this stage. Eventually, Executive Order (EO) 503, signed by Ramos in 1992, made it mandatory for national government agency personnel to be absorbed by the LGUs giving priority to technical personnel, and assuring that national government personnel not absorbed shall be retained by the national agency concerned.

The objection of health personnel to devolution was capped by a resolution of Congress to recentralize health services. This move placed serious doubts on the wisdom of devolution vis-à-vis decentralization. President Ramos's decision to veto the bill indicates the political will of the executive to follow the devolution process. In her study of three local areas, Bautista (1997) argues that primary healthcare, among other social services, is successfully implemented in areas where there is a close coordination between the LGU, *barangay* health workers (BHW), civil society, and the people (see Bautista 1997). Although these scholars failed to connect health service devolution and the success stories at the local level, it appears that the devolution of health programmes, services, and personnel resulted more in serendipitous outcomes than deliberate policy initiatives.

One major concern in the implementation of decentralization is the new financing sources available to the LGUs, particularly, the Internal Revenue Allotment (IRA). The overall average increment in the shares of the IRA was about P44 million in 1993 or an increase of nearly P30 million over the 1991 overall average. The tax revenues of cities are nearly 5 times as much as that of the provinces and 20 times that of the municipalities in 1993. However, according to Capuno and Solon (1996), the increase in total expenditures of the cities in 1993 was only about P4 million more than their 1991 total expenditure while provinces spent about P27 million more in 1993 than in 1991. While the cities were getting 5 times more than the provinces, they were spending less than the latter was especially on devolved functions and personnel. This fiscal imbalance certainly weighed more on the provinces than on the cities (especially the highly urbanized ones).

Citing a study by the Local Development Assistance Program (LDAP), Rood (1998) noted that in 1993, all cities and municipalities received an increase in the IRA that was larger than the cost of personnel and functions devolved from the national government. In the same year, however, 26 provinces were left with negative net transfers due to the high cost of devolved hospitals, but the deficit was made up for in 1994 except for one province (i.e., South Cotabato).

The study by Capuno and Solon (1996) comparing the health expenditures of 173 LGUs (36 provinces, 20 cities, 117 municipalities) for the years 1991 (before devolution) and 1993 (after devolution) also point to the fact that provinces had lower IRA shares in 1993 compared to cities. Provinces absorbed the bulk of devolved functions, amounting to P41.64 million of which health accounted an average of P33.9 million (see Capuno and Solon 1996). The share of health for the provinces jumped from 2.7% in 1991 to about 25% in 1993 (see Capuno and Solon 1996). The study also noted "deleterious effect of free-riding, which is inherent in a decentralized regime, is most evident in the cross-border use of devolved facilities" and that the "inequities in the devolution of the function of the central tend to generate inefficiencies at the local level" (see Capuno and Solon 1996).

In general, RA 7160 augmented local taxing powers and devolved tax policymaking authority to the local legislative councils such as the setting of values on real property. It expanded the tax base of LGUs to include activities and sectors that used to be outside the reach of local taxation, such as banks and financial institutions, agricultural and forest products, mining operations, and mineral production. Local development financing sources available to LGUs are local taxes; the internal revenue allotment (IRA); loans; the Municipal Development Fund (MDF); bonds flotation; build-operate-transfer (BOT) arrangements; and official development assistance (ODA). Manasan (1995, p. 1), however, argued that the "tax provisions of the 1991 Local Government Code do not guarantee substantial increases in the revenue that LGUs can generate for local sources".

The overall impact of the Code on LGUs' local source revenue will depend on the extent to which LGUs exercise their taxing powers, the changes in the statutory rates and legal tax bases, and the growth and composition of their taxes, which significantly vary from one LGU to the next. IRA has a negative effect on local tax revenue in all levels of local governments in 1992 and 1993 (see Manasan 1995). In terms of expenditures, it was noted that LGU expenditure priorities vary according to the level of government. While municipal government budgets prioritized provision of public services, the majority of provincial spending went to economic services. Meanwhile, the expenditures of cities were more evenly distributed. As a result of devolving the basic services, local government expenditure on social services increased significantly.

The findings of a recent study by Capuno (2001) on estimating the income elasticity of local government revenues and expenditures under decentralization, concurs with previous results that local revenues and total expenditures of either provinces or cities vary positively with the changes in the IRA. Any change in the IRA is likely to have a differential impact across LGU levels or regions. The local revenues of provinces show greater sensitivity to changes in central transfers than cities' revenues. Furthermore, LGUs in the most economically advanced regions are also found to be more susceptible to IRA reforms than others. It was also found that the presence of DOH-retained hospitals has no significant effect on the provinces, but they do have a negative effect on the total expenditures of cities, where most hospitals are located.

Aside from the complaints of governors about the inequitable distribution of the IRA, Bolongaita (1995) also noted the difficulties of the institutionalization of popular participation in local governance through local special bodies since only few local development councils meet regularly.

4.2.2 The Transition Phase (1994–1996)

This phase is identified by the actual implementation of the provisions of RA 8042 and the subsequent change in institutional and administrative arrangements between the NGAs and LGUs. Brilliantes (1996) noted that as decentralization becomes embedded in the country's governance, local leaders are increasingly becoming innovative and creative. He cites the *Galing Pook* awards as a proof that devolution is working. Rood (1998), on the other hand, puts a premium on the role of LGU organizations in studying, measuring and promoting decentralization. He mentions the efforts of the League of Cities at measuring indicators of governance. The group, composed mainly of city officials, came up with "Key Indicators of Local Governance". These efforts, Rood (1998, p. 71) asserts, provide database on local governance that can serve as starting points for possible areas of shareable innovations and experiences.

The *Gantimpalang Pang-Lingkod Pook (Galing Pook* or Service Area Awards)* Program was launched in 1994 to give recognition to LGUs that have demonstrated excellence in local development management and innovations. Jointly undertaken by the Asian Institute of Management (AIM) and the Local Government Academy (LGA) under the Department of Interior and Local Government (DILG), the programme selects outstanding LGU projects based on the following criteria: effectiveness of service delivery; positive socioeconomic or environmental impact; promotion of people empowerment; and creative use of local powers.

In July 1995, President Fidel Ramos issued Executive Order No. 263 which provides for the adoption of community-based forest management (CBFM) as "the national strategy to achieve sustainable development and social justice". The Mining Act of 1995 (RA 7942) which grants the local government units the authority and responsibility, together with the DENR, to approve the issue of quarry permits in their jurisdiction was also passed that same year.

To enable the national government to assist poor LGUs in the financing of local services that have been devolved the Local Government Empowerment Fund (LGEF) was set up in 1996. The fund's objectives were to provide a mechanism for channelling grants and concessional loan funds to LGUs; to rationalize the allocation of funds to priority national projects in support of devolved activities of LGUs over and above their mandated IRA shares; and to effect a more transparent presentation of fund allocations to LGUs in the budget. Two specific facilities were contained in the 1996 LGEF: assistance to the 20 priority provinces identified under the Social Reform Agenda for industrialization, livelihood, and related poverty alleviation projects; and aid to the 20 priority provinces and fifth and sixth class LGUs for agriculture and water supply, sewerage and sanitation wholly or partially by grants or highly concessional loans. The LGEF is a clear expression of the high priority that the Ramos Administration assigned to poverty alleviation efforts and its appreciation of the importance of involving communities and LGUs in the achievement of this objective.

4.2.3 *The Stabilization Phase (1997 Onwards)*

This stage can be described as the attempt of RA 7160 to become an enduring feature of the country's social and political landscape. It is the stage in which decentralization becomes politically institutionalized. One critical factor that affected the implementation of RA 7160 during this phase is the Asian economic crisis. It was also during this period when the mandatory assessment of the implementation of the decentralization under Section 521 of RA 7160 was conducted. Other institutions also continue to formulate indicators of good governance under a decentralized system.

The government continues to favour the implementation of policies at the local level as indicated by the passing of the Agricultural and Fisheries Modernization Act of 1997 and the Fisheries Code of 1998 that have strengthened and supported the provision of RA 7160 regarding fisheries and agriculture. There is also the Clean Air Act of 1999 (RA 8749), which gives the LGUs a share in the responsibility managing and maintaining air quality within their territorial jurisdiction, and the provisions in the Solid Waste Management Act (RA 9003) that mandate the LGUs to segregate, recycle, compost and re-use waste.

Brillantes (1998b) in the five-year assessment of RA 7160 identified factors that have affected its implementation. These include the simultaneous local and national elections in 1992; resistance of certain devolved agencies to devolution (mostly of DOH) and the subsequent moves to recentralize the health sector; unequal distribution of financial resources as a result of not so studied distribution formula among the various levels of local governments; lags in the release of the IRA shares of LGUs; lack of guidelines to the LGUs from the NGAs in operationalizing devolution; the continuing need to define and clarify inter-governmental relations; hesitance among NGOs and POs to participate in local governance; and the general lack of information about the Code among various stakeholders. The assessment was of a "slow but steady progress towards meaningful devolution". It was also noted that the inter-agency Oversight Committee was not active before the 1995 elections and that there was no full-time staff to provide it with technical support and assistance (see Brillantes 1998a).

In a series of surveys conducted by the Politics and Governance Desk of the Policy Forum, Asian Institute of Management (AIM), Bolongaita and Morales (1997) undertook a survey to obtain feedback about how local governments are performing particularly in the four provinces of ARMM: Lanao del Sur, Maguindanao, Sulu, and Tawi-tawi. The survey found that very few ARMM residents visit provincial government offices and that they hardly avail themselves of the services offered by its offices since they felt that nothing can be gained from bringing their concerns to local officials. Residents perceived that no particular office was doing its job well while they were relatively satisfied with the performance of their governors. The reasons given were the governors' association with tangible accomplishments, particularly public works and peace and order and the governors' personal qualities (see Bolongaita and Morales 1997).

The results of the survey also indicate that there is still a significant number of residents in the four provinces identified who are not aware of the existence of the ARMM and the need for the ARMM government to adopt a service delivery improvement programme to enhance the performance of ARMM regional offices.

With the premise that good governance at the LGU level is primarily determined by how well LGUs perform in improving the quality of life of their constituents or how efficient and effective LGUs are in bringing about social and human development, Manasan, et al. (1999) conducted a study that attempts to develop measurable indicators of good governance at the local government level; test how applicable these indicators are in evaluating and monitoring LGU performance; and find out how these indicators can be integrated in a monitoring and evaluation system within the framework of Sustainable Human Development. The governance index that was constructed focused on the three principal elements: capacity of LGU to mobilize and utilize resources; efficiency and effectiveness in the delivery of social services; and presence of mechanisms to ensure accountability. Results of pilot tests (clusters were selected according to their provincial HDI) found that the ranking of the governance quality index derived appears to be consistent with the ranking of the HDI; LGUs which register higher HDIs tend to perform better in terms of the overall governance index particularly at the provincial level; the beneficiaries' net satisfaction rate with social services is largely consistent with the social service delivery effectiveness index when it is measured using administrative data which is a composite of service input adequacy and LGU–NGA cooperation index; and the beneficiaries' participation in NGOs/*barangays* and their perception of the empowerment of NGOs/*barangays* do not correlate well with NGO representation in local special bodies.

In Capuno's (2001) attempt to develop a model of the chief executive's bid to get re-elected, it was found that the threat of competition from local political clans bears pressure on the incumbent governor to adopt development-oriented programmes and projects, even among governors who are members of political clans. An increase in the share of development spending would improve the chances of the incumbent governor to another term but at a declining rate, and it is relatively more difficult for incumbent governors to be re-elected in provinces with mid-level socioeconomic status than for those in provinces with higher socioeconomic status.

5. Conclusions and Recommendations

5.1 Human Development: The Link Between Economic Viability and Political Decentralization

The previous sections have discussed the nature and current level of political decentralization in the Philippines. Political decentralization in the Philippines has been carried out mainly through two statutes – RA 7160 (the 1991 Local Government Code) and RA 6734 creating the Autonomous Region for Muslim Mindanao (ARMM). In addition to pointing out the primary features of decentralized governance in the country, the previous sections were able to describe the current level of local economic development performance. More specifically, provinces were identified on the basis of their listing in the country's human development index since 1994.

This chapter has attempted to illustrate the link that exists between local economic sustainability or viability and political decentralization by exploring the aspect of how RA 7160 and RA 6734 have been able to affect HDI performance. Economic viability, understood in the context of political decentralization, is manifested in the extent to which decentralized and empowered LGUs are able to sustain and generate financial resources for local development purposes by tapping into the provisions of RA 7160 and RA 6734. Viability also involves a reduction in LGU dependence on the resources of the central–national government by way of internal revenue allotments (IRAs) and other national government financial sources. Thus it involves an increased capacity to generate local resources to benefit the local constituents.

Numerous other factors can affect economic viability. History, physical size, extent of urbanization, proximity to the central government, demographic profile, ethnic composition, among many others can all affect the extent to which LGUs are able to achieve economic viability. This chapter does not focus so much on these other factors as it tries to isolate the variables affecting local economic viability in the programme on political decentralization.

An examination of provinces in the high list as well as those listed at the bottom of the HDI rankings yielded certain patterns as far as they relate to the political decentralization project. Most of the provinces in the high list are located next to Metropolitan Manila where the country's capital is located while the provinces in the low list (with the exception of Ifugao) are located in the southernmost part of the Philippines. What the study tried to illustrate is the extent to which political decentralization has contributed to the improvement (or worsening) of the economic viabilities of these LGUs.

What can now be said about the nature of the linkage between the development of political decentralization in the Philippines and economic viability (in terms of HDI performance)? Essentially, the chapter has illustrated that it is possible to use HDI data as indicators for good local governance. Decentralization in the country has always been associated with its political nature more than its socioeconomic and fiscal dimensions. The prevailing literature in the Philippines has indeed been saturated with a political appreciation of governance and decentralized government. In addition to the traditional mantras for good governance (e.g., transparency, accountability, etc.), however, there is a need for a socioeconomic indicator that can gauge the impact of effective governance. This is done by way of associating good governance with genuine human development achieved through effective and efficient local economic performance.

Beyond using HDI data, however, the chapter has sought to provide answers to the question of why certain provinces have only been able to achieve specific levels of human development over time despite political decentralization. On the one hand, the chapter has shown that political decentralization has the potential of revitalizing local government thinking to be more innovative in seeking out new resources and sources of revenues that can bring about genuine and sustainable human development in the local level. On the other hand, the chapter has also shown that in spite of political decentralization through RA 6734 and RA 7160, local governments have actually not manifested enough of an incentive to generate and utilize local resources enough to bring about genuine and sustainable human development.

5.2 The Role of Stakeholders and Players

What is the role played by national and local authorities and institutional arrangements in determining the linkage between political decentralization and economic viability? As discussed in the first section of the chapter, economic viability is measured in terms of the ability of LGUs to sustain themselves by generating and increasing the proportion of local revenue resources as opposed to grants coming from the national government. This reduced dependence on national revenues will most likely lead to sustainable economic prosperity measured in terms of human development.

The study has shown that LGUs have in fact become more dependent on national revenues ironically as a result of the decentralization strategy since 1991. However, there are nuances that can be derived from this broad qualitative assessment. Provinces that are less dependent on IRA grants from the national government are more likely to experience higher HDI levels mainly because of the incentive on the part of local authorities in these areas to sustainably generate local revenues as discussed further below.

5.3 The Role of Institutional Arrangements

While there is the impression that local decision-making bodies (e.g., the *sanggunian*) are now more empowered under RA 7160 to enact relevant local legislation, there is still much to be said about how such bodies are able to utilize their capacities to generate local resources. Local *sanggunians* do not appear to be encouraged to promulgate local tax ordinances that would be to the LGUs' advantage. Additionally, the problem of support from the national government to LGUs also stems from the lack of technical guidelines that would assist the latter on how to better carry out their new roles in the context of political decentralization. Not all of the LGU officials were able to acquire material and technical resources (e.g., guidebooks on local government organization models and the crafting of new local revenue codes) given by the national government on how best to implement the decentralization strategy for sustained local development purposes. It may be said that those local areas that received such guidelines and technical assistance would be more likely and more inclined to institute effective fiscal policies that allow for the increased generation of local resources than those areas in the country that did not receive such assistance.

Cases occur where local officials are accused of funds mismanagement along with the non-compliance of certain LGUs to existing and accepted auditing and accountability rules and regulations to the detriment of local residents. Such cases include the illegal use of trust funds, unliquidated cash advances, cash shortages, and failure to conduct the annual physical inventory of supplies and property. Overdraft is another major problem among decentralized LGUs. As a consequence, local trust funds including collections of withholding taxes and other taxes for remittance to the BIR and the national government, deductions of government employees for insurance premiums, and Country-wide Development Fund (CDF) were spent for purposes other than those for which they were entrusted or created.

In 1996, the provinces of Tawi-tawi and Basilan had the highest amount of unliquidated cash advances (P74.35 million and P66.68 million, respectively) in the country. In 1999, these provinces were again the LGUs with the highest amount of unliquidated cash advances (P131.263 million and P66.312 million, respectively). Sulu was the third highest with P20.578 million in unaccounted cash advances.

It is also possible that political decentralization can cause changes in the priorities of local officials particularly as regards the management and allocation of funds in the community. In 1997, the provincial government of Ifugao had placed its trust fund amounting to 69 million in high yield and premium savings accounts for long periods despite the prevalence of unimplemented projects chargeable against the fund. Provinces in the HDI high list do not appear to be immune from these auditing anomalies either.

5.4 The Role of National Grants-in-Aid

While decentralization allows for more significant tax powers to be exercised by LGUs, these do not seem to be effective in raising local revenues. Paradoxically, in effect, the extent of national revenue grants to LGUs have become a major stumbling block in the attainment of genuine local human development. This stems from the local political complacency that is encouraged in the local authorities that benefit from these national grants-in-aid.

In 2000, the COA reported that the expansion of the revenue raising powers of LGUs through RA 7160 and RA 6734 did not contribute to the improvement of the LGUs' revenue collection from local sources. Indeed, the revenue data for the period 1996–2000 showed that local sources of income contributed only an average of 33.37% as compared to 46.92% for 1988–1992 (before decentralization) or a net decrease of 13.65%. This reduced income that is generated by provinces and city governments cannot even subsidize the expenditures for personnel services devolved by NGA by virtue of RA 7160.

In particular, provinces with low HDI belonging to the ARMM have not exhibited any capacity to improve local revenue generation despite the implementation of RA 6734. Ironically, the "centralized" nature of decentralization in the ARMM has concentrated fiscal and administrative powers on the Regional Governor to the point that provincial authorities become financially dependent on the support of said Governor. This is one good example of the adverse implications of local political capture on sub-national communities even in the context of political decentralization.

5.5 Prospects and Options

Nevertheless, with the implementation of decentralized governance, the national government has substantially helped the provinces increase their available financial resources per capita. This has been achieved mainly through the IRA. However, the resulting impact of IRA on the LGUs is that it has created a heavy reliance on the part of the LGUs on the resources of the national government. This is certainly not consistent with the principles of decentralization as provided for in RA 7160 and RA 6734.

What lies ahead for decentralization in the country? Several issues need to be reviewed and addressed as regards the implementation of decentralized governance in the Philippines. The first step is to address the problem of the lack of baseline data. When RA 7160 was first implemented, either there was little baseline data to rely on or whatever data existed at the time could not be used to validate the success (or failure) of the decentralization programme or that those assigned to monitor its implementation did not know how to process the data they were generating.

Intergovernmental financial flows and transfers (particularly from the national to the local governments) tend to be unpredictable and essentially dependent on the whims of national politicians. If an objective database is available that can guide judgments of policymakers, it would go a long way in effectively assisting LGUs.

The second step is to make sure the national political leadership continues to be sensitive to the strategic needs and interests of LGUs. Appropriate support structures and mechanisms need to be provided to better local officials on how to deal with their powers under RA 7160 and RA 6734. Fiscal management, local tax ordinance making, local finance planning are just some of the aspects where LGUs (including especially the local legislative assemblies or *sanggunians*) would certainly benefit the most in terms of information that they can get, not just from national government agencies but also from non-governmental organizations.

Corollary to this, there is a need for local development efforts to rely on institutional arrangements that encourage the dissemination and utilization of localized information. Such information can then be combined with technical expertise that is in many cases available at the central–national level of government. This balance between local knowledge and technical expertise can be more effective in dealing with local economic sustainability and human development than a purely centralized or totally decentralized institutional arrangement.

A third step to be taken is to strengthen accounting and accountability mechanisms and processes in the local governments so that they do not succumb to the temptations of over-spending and over-dependence on national government resources. For instance, unliquidated cash advances especially among the provinces in the HDI low list ought to be reduced either by way of more relevant financial management systems or through stringent auditing procedures that places a premium on responsive performance and effectiveness.

There is a need to introduce innovations in local governance that can encourage LGUs to be more resourceful in generating income from local sources or at the very least diversify their revenue sources so that they do not become overly dependent on a single revenue source. It is possible to mitigate the problem of undermining local revenue sources by reducing national transfers if some minimum level of local revenue effort is not met. At the same time, local counterpart contributions may also be required for national grants to LGUs.

Lastly, the framework identified at the beginning of this chapter remains a valid assumption. A decentralization framework can be economically relevant when it is able to link local financing and fiscal autonomy with local service provision and responsibilities. Moreover, a system of accountability and public information ought to be instituted in decentralized areas so as to prevent political capture by local elites. Indeed, political decentralization can increase the vulnerability of LGUs to local political capture. Decentralized governance can create certain conditions that could reduce the cohesiveness of certain groups and sectors at the local level leading to the facilitation of local capture by powerful vested interests.

Notes

Research paper presented at the workshop conducted by the "Governance in Asia Revisited" Study Group under *The Asian Development Experience Research Project*, Japan Institute of International Affairs (JIIA) with support from the Japan-ASEAN Solidarity Fund, Tokyo (May 2003). The author is grateful for the research assistance of Ms. Lauren Borja and for the comments and suggestions of those who participated in the Workshop for the Research Project that was held in Tokyo in May 2003. All views and information contained herein are entirely the author's responsibility.

[1]   Section 2, Book 1, RA 7160.

[2]   The *barangay* (village) is the smallest political sub-division in the Philippines. Section 3, Book 1, RA 7160.

[3]   Book 1, Section 2, RA 7160.

[4]   See The World Bank Group, (no date) "Decentralization and Economic Growth", in http://www1.worldbank.org/publicsector/decentralization/growth.htm.

[5]   For details, see The World Bank Group (no date) "Rationale for Decentralization", in http://www1.worldbank.org/publicsector/decentralization/rationale.htm.

[6]   *Batas Pambansa* literally means national law as promulgated by the country's National Assembly at the time.

[7]   See Philippine Constitution (1987), Sec. 10–21, Art. X

[8]   These are provinces adjacent to Metropolitan Manila. Eventually, Quezon province joined in and the acronym became CALABARZON.

[9]   Figure 1, page 2 in Rosario Manasan, "Fiscal Decentralization: The Case of the Philippines", background paper on "Decentralization and Intergovernmental Fiscal Reform in East Asia", World Bank, Bangkok (07 June 2002), p. 2 in http://www.worldbank.org/wbi/publicfinance/decentralization/Bangkok.html.

[10]   Section 5, Executive Order 220 dated 15 July 1987.

[11]   Article 10, Section 1, RA 6734.

[12]   Article 10, Section 4, RA 6734.

[13]   Section 3, RA 7160.

[14]   Section 337, RA 7160.

[15] Devolution refers to the transfer of functions from national government agencies (NGAs) to local government units (LGUs). Deconcentration means the local presence of NGAs (i.e., not devolved to the LGUs). Debureaucratization is that process of allowing non-governmental entities (including the private sector) to perform basic social services delivery functions. It can also include arrangements between the private sector and LGUs (e.g., build-operate-transfer schemes, joint projects, etc.).

[16] Prior to RA 7160, LGUs would only get a maximum of 20% of internal revenue tax collections from the national government.

References

Bautista. V., (ed.). 1997. *A Reader in Philippine Social Development Administration.* Quezon City: UP National College of Public Administration and Governance, UP Press.

Bolongaita, E. 1995. "Rethinking Participatory Local Governance". *AIM Policy Forum* No.2.

Bolongaita, E. and J. Morales. 1997. "A Perilous Peace: The challenges to democratic governance in the Autonomous Region in Muslim Mindanao". AIM Policy Paper, no. 4.

Brillantes, A. 1998a. "Decentralized Democratic Governance Under the Local Government Code". *Journal of Public Administration*, Volume 42, Nos. 1 & 2, pp. 38–57.

————. 1998b. "Five-Year Assessment of the Implementation of Devolution in the Local Government Code". In *Local Government in the Philippines: A Book of Readings (II)*, edited by Tapales, et al. Quezon City: CLRG,UPNCPAG.

————. 1996. "Local Governments in Democratic Polity: Trends and Prospects". Paper presented during the Philippine Political Science Association Conference held in Pangasinan, 9–11 May 1996.

Brillantes, A. and J. Cuaresma. 1991. "Assessment of the Aquino Pilot Decentralization Project". *Journal of Philippine Development*, Volume 35, No. 1, pp. 33–54.

Buendia, R. 1995. "The Cordillera Autonomy and the Quest for Nation-Building: Prospects in the Philippines". In *Local Government in the Philippines: A Book of Readings (I)*, edited by Tapales, et al. Quezon City: CLRG,UPNCPAG.

Capuno, J. and O. Solon. 1996. "The Impact of Devolution on Local Health Expenditures: Anecdotes and Some Estimates from the Philippines". *Philippine Review of Economics and Business*, Volume 33, No. 2, pp. 283–318.

Capuno, J., et al. "Is Local Development Good Politics? Local Development Expenditures and the Re-election of Governors in the Philippines for 1992, 1995, and 1998". UPSE DP 0104.

De Guzman, R., et al. 1995. "The Evolution of Local Government in the Philippines". In *Local Government in the Philippines: A Book of Readings (I)*, edited by Tapales, et al. Quezon City: CLRG,UPNCPAG.

Igaya, L. 1999. "The Political Economy of the Philippine Democratic Transition". In *Transitions to Democracy in East and Southeast Asia*, edited by K. Gaerlan. Quezon City: Institute for Popular Democracy.

Lamberte, M. 1993. *Decentralization and Prospects for Regional Growth*. Quezon City: PIDS.

Manasan, R. 1995. "Fiscal Decentralization: the Early Years of the Code Implementation", *PIDS Development Research News*, Volume 13, No. 4, pp. 1, 10–16.

———. 2002. "Fiscal Decentralization: The Case of the Philippines". In http://www.worldbank.org/wbi/publicfinance/documents/ASEM/manasan.pdf, background paper on "Decentralization and Intergovernmental Fiscal Reform in East Asia". World Bank, Bangkok (6–7 June, 2002).

Manasan, R., et al. 1999. "Indicators of Good Governance: Developing an Index of Governance Quality at the LGU Level". *Journal of Philippine Development* 26, no. 2, pp. 149–212.

Medel, A. 2002. "Rapid Assessment of Anti-Poverty Programs and Projects". In *Developing Good Governance Indicators for Anti-Poverty Program Assessment*, edited by H. Razon-Abad, et al. Manila: UNDP.

Rood, S. 1998. "An Assessment of the State of Knowledge Concerning Decentralized Governance under the Philippines' 1991 Local Government Code". *Philippine Journal of Public Administration*, Volume 42, Nos. 1 & 2, pp. 59–81.

Sosmeña, G. 1991. *Decentralization and Empowerment*. Manila: LOGODEF.

Tapales, P. 1995. "Devolution and Empowerment". In *Public Administration by the Year 2000*, edited by P. Tapales, et al. Quezon City: CLRG, UPNCPAG.

Valdellon, I. 1999. "Decentralized Planning and Financing for Local Development: The Case of the Philipppines". *Regional Development Dialogue*, Volume 20, No. 2, pp. 21–57.

World Bank Group "Decentralization and Economic Growth". Retrieved from entralization/growth.htm" http://www1.worldbank.org/publicsector/decentralization/growth.htm.

World Bank Group "Rationale for Decentralization". Retrieved from http://www1.worldbank.org/publicsector/decentralization/rationale.htm.

Wurfel, D. 1989. *Filipino Politics: Development and Decay*. Quezon City: Ateneo de Manila University.

Appendix: Background on the Human Development Index:

Eastern Seaboard Development Plan — List of Japanese ODA-Loaned Projects

National human development reports build on the analytical framework of the global Human Development Report by examining countries' most pressing development issues and exploring ways to place human development at the forefront of the national political agenda. The HDI estimation in the Philippines was initiated by the Human Development Network (HDN) with assistance from UNDP. In 1994, the first Philippine Human Development Report (PHDR) introduced the use of the HDI as a yardstick of the progress across regions in the Philippines in terms of life expectancy, literacy and educational attainment, and access to resources or income. HDI estimates at the provincial level for the years 1990 and 1994 came out in the 1997 PHDR.

A presidential directive during the Ramos Administration called for the institutionalization of the HDI estimation within the National Statistical Coordination Board (NSCB) which is under the National Statistics Office (NSO). A Memorandum of Understanding between HDN and NSCB was signed in May 1997 to transfer the responsibility for the computation and publication of the HDI from the former to the latter. Thus, the provincial HDI estimates for 1997, together with updates for the 1994 estimates, were prepared by NSCB with technical assistance from the HDN. The *Report on the 1997 Philippine Human Development Index* was released in March 2000. NSCB has recently released the *Report on the 2000 Philippine Human Development Index,* which covers the years 1994, 1997, and 2000.

The HDN, on the other hand, continued with its publication of the PHDR. Four reports have been generated and published by HDN and UNDP covering the years 1994, 1997, 2000, and 2002. These reports discussed different themes. The first report tackled governance issues. The second report focused on gender issues in development and defined benchmarks for determining the commitment to human development at the local government level by analyzing social and human priorities and budget allocation patterns. The third report looked at the state of education in the country. It tackled issues such as the quality of inputs to education and low achievement levels for critical areas of learning, the relevance of learning to the context of living, the increasing gap between public resources and the rising demand of a rapidly growing population, and the unevenness of access and quality among the provinces. The latest report analyzed the state of employment. It aims to trace the complex relationships between growth, employment, poverty and human development.

The HDI scores published by each organization (i.e., the HDN and NSCB) are not exactly the same. However, their differences are slight. This can be attributed to the different methodologies adopted by NSCB and HDN as well as the data used in the computation. The top and bottom five provinces in the HDI rankings of the two organizations are listed below.

Top Five Provinces in HDI (NSCB), 1994*–2000

Province	1994		1997		2000	
	HDI	Rank	HDI	Rank	HDI	Rank
Cavite	0.782	1	0.724	2	0.735	3
Batanes	0.760	2	0.713	3	0.717	5
Rizal	0.730	3	0.693	5	0.733	4
Bulacan	0.727	4	0.702	4	0.760	1
Laguna	0.721	5	0.676	7	0.709	6

Source: Report on The 2000 Philippine Human Development Index NSO–NSCB
* The total number of provinces that were ranked in 1994 was 76 while 77 provinces were ranked for the years 1997 and 2000

Top Five Provinces in HDI (HDN), 1990*–2000

Province	1994		1997		2000	
	HDI	Rank	HDI	Rank	HDI	Rank
Cavite	0.840	1	0.721	1	0.693	2
Batanes	0.798	2	0.709	7	0.649	7
Rizal	0.813	3	0.690	4	0.758	1
Bulacan	0.763	4	0.700	2	0.672	3
Laguna	0.774	5	0.673	6	0.690	9

Source: Philippine Human Development Reports 1997, 2000, 2002

Bottom Five Provinces in HDI (NSCB), 1994–2000

	1994		1997		2000	
Province	HDI	Rank	HDI	Rank	HDI	Rank
Sulu	.357	76	.336	77	.351	77
Tawi-tawi	.387	75	.430	74	.390	76
Ifugao	.406	74	.452	72	.461	74
Basilan**	.423	73	.439	73	.425	75
Lanao del Sur	.442	72	.415	76	.464	72

Source: Report on The 2000 Philippine Human Development Index
** Became part of the ARMM in 2001

Bottom Five Provinces in HDI (HDN), 1990–2000

	1994		1997		2000	
Province	HDI	Rank	HDI	Rank	HDI	Rank
Sulu	0.372	76	0.331	76	0.311	77
Tawi-tawi	0.384	75	0.435	75	0.378	76
Ifugao	0.409	74	0.448	73	0.512	72
Basilan**	0.427	73	0.434	74	0.420	74
Lanao del Sur	0.434	72	0.445	72	0.321	77

Source: Philippine Human Development Reports 1997, 2000, 2002

9

Economic Governance in Malaysia and its Links with the Asian Crisis

Mahani Zainal Abidin

1. Introduction

In the early 1990s, the World Bank gave a strong endorsement to the development approach of East Asian countries, calling them the "Miracle Economies". From the mid-1980s up until 1997, East Asian economies registered a series of impressively high growth rates, and by the end of that time some had almost reached developed country status. East Asia's economic governance through export-oriented industrialization and a cooperative public-private sector relationship were hailed as a model that other countries should emulate. The East Asian countries were also exemplars of good market economies, with a high degree of global integration, serious efforts to liberalize and deregulate, and active private sector participation. Malaysia was one of those countries, and during that period enjoyed its best economic performance since independence in 1957.

The 1997–98 Asian economic crisis, which started with the floating of the Baht on 2 July 1997, came as a surprise to many, including Malaysians. In the beginning, Malaysians did not see any possibility that they would be dragged into the crisis: they believed that the economic fundamentals and governance were strong. The regional contagion effect, which soon spread around East Asia, was a completely new phenomenon. The initial response to the crisis in Thailand did not revive investors' confidence, capital continued to flow out of the region and countries in the region began experiencing economic difficulties. The most drastic and serious effect of the crisis was the sharp depreciation of regional currencies and the collapse of their stock markets.

After the rapid recovery of the Asian economies in 1999, discussion of the causes of the crisis has been centred on the quality of economic governance in these economies. The East Asian economic success was, at one time, a model to be emulated by other developing countries seeking higher economic growth, with policies of setting the prices right, liberalising the economy and the private sector as the engine of growth central to the model. Yet, there have been questions whether governance in these economies contributed to the crisis. Malaysia is an economy that went through the crisis and recovered rapidly, and so presents itself as a good case study. We can analyse the role of economic governance in economic growth, its links to the crisis as well as its part in the recovery process.

To begin, it is important to define economic governance. Governance is a multi-faceted concept, touching all aspects of the exercise of authority both formal and informal, in the management of resources. In other words, governance can be defined as

an exercise of economic power in the management of resource endowment of a country done through mechanisms, processes and institutions through which citizens and groups can articulate their interest, exercise legal rights, meet their obligations and mediate their differences.

The quality of governance is thus determined by the impact of the exercise of power on the economic well-being of the country and its people. For the purpose of this study, the analysis of this impact is done through the examination of policies, institutions and management environment in which the economy operates.

An analysis of the relationship between economic governance and economic performance consists of two components — firstly, the identification of the areas covered under economic governance and secondly, an examination of how the governance is deployed. Economic governance is often studied through its role in the promotion of growth. This is done by setting policies, incentives and institutions that create an environment conducive to sustained stable growth through efficient management of a country's resources. Broadly speaking, good economic governance should aim to produce an outward oriented economy, ensure central bank independence and prudent management of national debt (World Bank 1992).

Many studies have examined the economic governance and growth nexus. Huther and Shah (1998) identified this relationship in a study of six Southeast Asian countries, namely, Indonesia, the Philippines, Thailand, Malaysia, South Korea and Singapore — countries that practised good governance have also enjoyed high growth. However, doubts were raised about the quality of economic governance in these countries when

Indonesia, Malaysia, Thailand and South Korea experienced sharp economic contraction in the crisis. Here are some of the questions that were asked:

- Did the same economic governance that produced high growth also create some weaknesses that rendered the economy vulnerable to external shocks?
- In pursuing a high growth strategy, did economic governance fail to avoid market failures?
- Was crony capitalism, which was alleged to be a contributing factor to the crisis, a result of governance failure?
- Are the conditions for good governance always the same, irrespective of the stage of economic development?

The purpose of this chapter is to examine the economic governance practised by Malaysia in order to determine whether it had, inadvertently, created conditions in which systemic flaws were able to exist without the government and markets fully realizing their significance. For example, did the "de facto" exchange rate policy of these economies encourage un-hedged foreign borrowings by domestic companies? Was the liberalization of the financial sector wrongly sequenced so that domestic financial institutions were not ready for a freer movement of capital? Likewise, could the shift towards a private-sector-led growth, (based on a high-investment policy), have overlooked the resulting higher total debt liability for the economy?

For the purpose of this chapter, which analyzes the linkage between economic governance and the 1997 crisis, the indicators of economic governance are widened to cover areas that can create vulnerabilities.[1] The indicators are macroeconomic management, level of investment, trade regime (openness), financial sector management, exchange rate regime, private sector participation and social development. In analyzing these economic governance indicators, the role of institutions that were tasked with economic decision making is important, as also is the utilization of resources.

Besides studying the link between governance and the causes of the crisis, it is also important to discuss how governance has helped in the recovery. Because the financial sector was the main source of the problems and had the fastest impact, the Malaysian government quickly relieved it of non-performing loans and recapitalised distressed financial institutions. The pace of restoration of the health of the financial sector was seen as a critical factor in the recovery process. But the fact of rapid recovery also fitted the explanation that Malaysia was fundamentally strong in the beginning, with good economic governance. This in turn implies that the crisis was coming regardless of the state of domestic economic governance and thus was influenced entirely by external factors.

To answer the above questions, this research will focus on the Malaysian crisis experience: a country case study to provide a close look at the economic governance prior to and during the crisis period. The first part of the study will examine the links between economic governance and the causes of the 1997–98 crisis in Malaysia. The research work will utilize published data on Malaysian economic management during its high growth period — the late 1980s to 1997. It will cover four broad economic governance areas — macroeconomic management, the external and financial sectors and the exchange rate regime.

The second part of the study will focus on governance during the recovery period. The definition of economic governance is expanded to include management of the recovery process because new institutions were established and a co-ordinated style of governance was introduced to undertake a proactive response to the crisis. It will describe the crisis management body established by the Malaysian government to coordinate Malaysia's response. In the financial and corporate sectors, three institutions were formed to remove non-performing loans from the financial sector, recapitalise troubled financial institutions and restructure corporate debt.

2. Indicators of Economic Governance

For the purpose of this study, the economic governance indictors are more broadly based than the usual ones, namely outward orientation, central bank independence and fiscal position. A wider range of indicators is necessary because the cause and impact of the crisis cover many aspects of the economy. The indicators are:

a) Macroeconomic management — fiscal management, level of government debt, unemployment and inflation
b) Investment — size and trend of foreign and domestic investments, capital flows and allocation of resources
c) Trade regime — trade orientation, export and import performance and balance of payment position
d) Financial sector management — the banking sector and capital market
e) Exchange rate regime
f) Private sector participation — privatisation and corporate governance
g) Social development — income distribution and level of poverty

3. The Malaysian Economy before the Crisis

3.1 Economic Performance from 1970 to 1997

In the early 1970s, Malaysia began its transformation from an agriculture-based to an industrialised economy. In 1970, agriculture contributed 29% of the GDP while the manufacturing sector was only 16%. But by 1996, the contribution of the agriculture sector had declined to 12% while that of the manufacturing sector had jumped to 34%. This was driven by the quest to seek higher economic growth that could generate more employment. In the 1960s, agriculture did not give steady high economic growth because it was very dependent on the export of rubber, which was susceptible to sharp price changes. The drive for industrialisation was led by Foreign Direct Investment (FDI), with the arrival of multinational companies from developed countries such as the US and Japan. The FDI went mainly to textiles, fashion apparel and electronic industries. In the early 1980s, Malaysia made a significant turn in its development path when it embarked on an industrialisation strategy based on heavy industries. Some of the promoted industries were automotive, steel and cement. During that period, high tariff rates were imposed to keep heavy industries viable, and this reversed the earlier trend of reduced import duties introduced in the 1970s. In 1985, Malaysia experienced a recession when its GDP declined by 1%, as a result of twin deficits — namely a government fiscal shortfall and a trade deficit. To overcome this crisis, the government liberalized the economy through a more open trade policy, measures to attract FDI, deregulation of the financial sector and implementing a privatisation policy. This set the stage for a period in which the Malaysian economy experienced its best performance to date. Table 9.1 summarizes Malaysia's economic performance.

The 1986–97 period is fondly remembered as Malaysia's Golden Age: from 1990 to 1996 the economy grew at an average annual rate of 8.5%, the longest period of sustained high growth in Malaysian history. Other economic statistics are equally impressive:

- Exports grew by double digits annually, reaching a high of 26.5% in 1995.
- Unemployment was substantially reduced from 8.3% in 1986 to 2.5% in 1997. In fact, from 1993 to 1997 Malaysia enjoyed full employment.
- Inflation remained below 3.7%, except in 1992 when it was 4.7%.
- FDI in manufacturing grew almost four-fold, from US$1,778 million in 1986 to US$6,561 million in 1995.

The transformation of the Malaysian economy is shown in Table 9.2. It had become more open — in 1985 exports constituted 54.8% of GDP and this increased to 89.7% of GDP in 1997. The export composition

Table 9.1 Malaysia's Key Economic Indicators

	1970	1975	1980	1985	1990	1995	1996	1997	1998
Real GDP growth (%)	6.3	3.5	8.0	-1.0	9.8	9.5	8.6	7.7	-7.4
Manufacturing sector growth (%)	12.3	0.1	11.5	-3.8	17.9	14.5	12.2	10.1	-13.4
Growth in CPI (%)	1.9	4.5	6.7	0.3	3.1	3.4	3.5	2.7	5.2
Balance of trade (US$ mil)	346	280	2359	3671	2608	92	1857	151	8933
Current account balance (US$ mil)	8.1	-157.9	-244	-742	-1686	-7358	-4901	-5100	5100
Export growth (%)	2.2	-9.5	16.4	-1.6	17.4	20.2	6.5	10.8	2.0
Import growth (%)	19.7	-13.7	37.2	-7.6	30	24.6	1.5	10.2	-10.7
External debt service ratio	n.a	n.a	1.8	6.6	3.5	1.4	1.1	0.7	0.9
Unemployment rate (% of labor force)	7.5	6.9	5.3	7.6	6	2.8	2.5	2.6	4.9
Savings (% of GNP)	20.5	21.9	28.3	27.2	29.6	37	38	39	42
Population (million)	10.8	11.9	13.5	15.7	17.7	20.7	21.2	21.7	22.2
Gross fixed capital formation (US$ billion)									
Private	0.4	1.3	3.8	4.5	9.3	26.2	29.3	30.6	15.3
Public	0.3	0.8	2.3	5.1	4.7	10.8	9.5	11.3	8.1
% of GNP	18.6	25.9	27.4	32.2	34.7	45.2	41.3	44.8	34.2

Source: Treasury, Economic Report, various issues.

Table 9.2 Malaysia: Selected Economic Indicators, 1980 and 1985–97

	1980	1985	1986	1987	1988	1989	1990
Per capita income ($)	1723	1850	1607	1793	1933	2053	2037
Real per capita income growth	4.07	−3.55	−1.65	2.71	6.3	6.63	7.21
Unemployment rate	5.6	6.9	8.3	8.2	8.1	6.3	5.1
Inflation rate (CPI–based)	6.7	0.3	0.8	0.2	2.5	2.7	2.8
Money supply (M2) growth (%)	28.4	9.8	11.0	3.8	6.7	15.2	10.6
Average commercial bank deposit rate (%)	6.0	7.5	7.0	4.3	4.3	5.4	7.2
Gross domestic investment (% of GDP)	30.4	27.6	26.0	23.2	25.9	28.4	31.3
Gross domestic saving (% of GDP)	29.3	25.6	25.6	31.3	31.3	29.2	29.2
Fiscal balance (% of GDP)	−6.9	−5.7	−10.5	−7.7	−3.6	−3.3	−3.0
Public debt (% of GDP)	44.0	82.4	103.4	103.5	98.0	87.8	81.4
Foreign debt (% of GDP)	20.7	36.1	38.3	33.5	29.1	26.9	25.7
Export/GDP ratio (%)	51.47	54.85	56.31	63.85	67.61	73.26	76.28
Growth of export (%)	17.1	−7.7	−10.5	30.9	17.4	18.1	16.6
Growth of import (%)	33.6	14.1	10.6	15.8	28.6	31.7	28.4
Current account balance (% of GDP)	−1.1	−1.9	−0.4	8.1	5.4	0.8	−2.1
Total external debt (% of GDP)	28.8	54.8	70.5	63.2	51.7	44.3	39.7
Short–term debt (% of total)	—	—	—	—	5.2	7.4	9.6
Debt service ratio, total (%)	4.3	15.8	18.9	16.4	13.1	9.6	8.3
Debt service ratio, federal government (%)	1.8	6.7	7.2	5.9	6.2	4.4	1.2
Foreign reserves, end of year ($bn)	4.4	4.9	6.0	7.4	6.5	7.8	9.8

Note: — data not available
Source: Compiled from IMF, International Financial Statistics Yearbook 1988 and BNM, Monthly Statistical Bulletin, March 1999.

Table 9.2 Malaysia: Selected Economic Indicators, 1980 and 1985–97 *(continued)*

	1991	1992	1993	1994	1995	1996	1997
Real GDP Growth	8.66	7.79	8.34	8.75	8.94	9.21	9.74
Per capita income ($)	2491	2925	3174	3505	4133	4449	4315
Real per capita income growth	6.15	5.3	4.74	4.41	6.7	5.7	5.5
Unemployment rate	4.3	3.7	3.0	2.9	2.8	2.5	2.5
Inflation rate (CPI-based)	2.6	4.7	3.5	3.7	3.4	3.5	2.7
Money supply (M2) growth (%)	16.9	29.2	26.6	12.7	20.0	23.8	18.9
Average commercial bank deposit rate (%)	8.2	7.8	6.3	6.2	6.9	7.3	8.2
Gross domestic investment (% of GDP)	37.2	33.5	37.8	40.4	43.5	41.5	42.8
Gross domestic saving (% of GDP)	28.4	29.7	33.0	32.6	33.8	37.1	37.2
Fiscal balance (% of GDP)	–2.0	–0.8	0.2	2.3	0.9	0.7	2.4
Public debt (% of GDP)	74.6	65.6	58.0	48.9	41.8	35.9	32.5
Foreign debt (% of GDP)	25.5	21.6	20.2	15.9	14.6	11.7	14.4
Export/GDP ratio (%)	80.84	77.65	81.45	89.82	95.5	92.01	89.76
Growth of export value ($)(%)	17.1	18.1	16.1	23.1	26.5	7.4	0.7
Growth of import value ($)(%)	26.9	10.1	17.8	28.1	30.3	1.9	1.2
Current account balance (% of GDP)	–8.8	–3.8	–4.8	–7.8	–9.7	–4.4	–5.6
Total external debt (% of GDP)	38.5	37.9	41.9	38.7	38.9	39.2	61.6
Short-term debt (% of total)	14.1	23.5	25.0	19.3	19.1	25.7	25.3
Debt service ratio, total (%)	6.9	9.3	6.4	5.5	6.6	6.9	5.5
Debt service ratio, federal government (%)	2.7	4.2	2.8	1.4	1.4	1.1	0.7
Foreign reserves, end of year ($bn)	10.9	17.2	27.2	25.4	23.8	27.0	20.8

Note: — data not available
Source: Compiled from IMF, International Financial Statistics Yearbook 1988 and BNM, Monthly Statistical Bulletin, March 1999.

shifted from a concentration in commodities in 1985 (66.7% of exports) to manufacturing products in 1998 (82.9% of exports).

To ride out the global recession in 1985, the government liberalised the economy, with the emphasis on attracting FDI. In the early 1980s, Malaysia's fiscal position was weak because the public sector had participated actively in heavy industries. However, this changed and the 1998 fiscal surplus was the fifth consecutive one, at 2.4% of GDP, a vast improvement from the 1985 deficit of 5.7% of GDP. Inflation was benign (the annual average for 1993–96 was 3.5%) and Malaysians enjoyed virtually full employment (unemployment in 1996 was 2.5%).

While Malaysia had always received long-term FDI, short-term capital only began to arrive in large volumes in the early 1990s – a product of the newly global scope of capital flow management and the policy of liberalising the capital account. During the period 1990–96, total net flows to Malaysia amounted to over 12% of GDP or US$8.6 billion, compared to 4.2% (US$1.5 billion) in the whole decade of the 1980s. In 1993, the inflow reached its historical high of 17%. International reserves were adequate to service the low level of short-term external debt (outstanding short-term debt level was 16.6% of GNP) and the debt service ratio was a comfortable 6.7%. The banking sector was also in a relatively strong position in 1998, with a risk-weighted capital adequacy ratio of 11.8% at the end of 1998, compared to only 7.5% at the end of 1985.

However, the globalization of international capital flows and the relatively open capital account in the 1990s exposed the economy in a way not done before. During the 1990s, Malaysia's current account recorded higher deficits (in 1985, current account deficit was a low 1.9% of GDP), reaching its most serious position in 1995 when it reached 9.7% of GDP. Growing services account shortfalls and higher imports of goods were mostly to blame for the poor numbers. The situation was precarious in 1997, prior to the implementation of selective capital controls. Current account deficit was still significant at 5.6% of GDP and the savings-investment gap was rather large. Although Malaysia had one of the highest savings rates in the world at 37.2% of GDP in 1997, it was still insufficient to fund the investment activities, which stood at 44.8% of GDP in 1997. Investment financing came largely from the domestic banking sector whose loan to GDP ratio was 156% in 1997. This situation only improved after the imposition of capital controls in 1998, which resulted in a large current account surplus (13.7% of GNP), stabilization of short-term capital flows and hence significant strengthening of the international reserves at US$26.2 billion by the end of 1998.

One of the most admired features of the Malaysian economic transformation was the socioeconomic restructuring, namely reduction

Table 9.3   Malaysia: Incidence of Poverty, 1970–1995

Strata	Total Poor Household (thousand)				
	1970	1976	1984	1989	1995
Pen. Malaysia	791.8	764.4	483.3	448.9	365.6
Rural	705.9	669.6	402.0	371.4	281.8
Urban	85.9	94.9	81.3	77.5	83.8
Strata	Incidence of poverty (%)				
	1970	1976	1984	1989	1995
Pen. Malaysia	49.3	39.6	18.4	15.0	8.7
Rural	58.7	47.8	24.7	19.3	14.9
Urban	21.3	17.9	8.2	7.3	3.6

Source: Ishak, S. and M.Z. Ragayah (1995)

of poverty and income inequality (Table 9.3). The incidence of poverty declined significantly from 49% in 1970 to 8.7% in 1995. Between 1970 and 1995, income inequality, as measured by the Gini coefficient, fell from 0.537 to 0.446, which meant that the higher income from economic growth was enjoyed by all.

3.2 Economic Governance from 1970 to 1997

Just before the crisis, on 17 June 1997, the IMF view of the Malaysian economy drew particular attention to the role of economic governance:

> *Malaysia is a good example of a country where the authorities are well aware of the challenges of managing the pressure that results from high growth and of maintaining a sound financial system amid substantial capital flows and a booming property market. Of course, the life of policymakers is always easier when one starts, as Malaysia does, with a long history of low inflation and an outward-oriented economy. But significant further progress has been made in dealing with new challenges. Over the last year, output growth has moderated to a more sustainable rate, and inflation has remained low. The current account deficit, which is primarily the result of strong investment spending has narrowed substantially. The increase in the fiscal surplus targeted for this year is expected to make an important contribution towards consolidating these achievements. The Malaysian authorities have also emphasised maintaining high standards of bank soundness* (Michael Camdeussus, former Managing Director, IMF).

The examination of the efficacy of economic governance in Malaysia began with the growth strategy introduced in the early 1970s. This was later modified in the light of contemporary domestic and external changes and challenges, and it provides the overall direction of how the economy was managed. The shift to an economy based on industrialisation had produced more sustained and higher growth than the previous agriculture-based economy. Growth then generated job opportunities, and thus higher incomes. Resources flowing from this included physical and human capital development and financial capacity, and these provided the policy flexibility and resources needed to respond to the 1997 crisis. The decision to liberalise the economy and to make the private sector the engine of growth had made the economy more flexible and competitive, and these features together had attracted foreign investment and expanded our export markets. Despite or even because of these achievements by Malaysian economic policy-makers and managers, the economic structure was so closely integrated with the world economy that Malaysia was vulnerable to external vagaries, including sharp changes in market confidence, and these were later proven to partially cause the crisis.

Export-oriented industrialization was implemented when Malaysia opened its doors to foreign multinationals, especially in the electronic and textiles industries, and offered a lower cost operating location. It established free trade zones and licensed manufacturing warehouses that offered tax-free facilities for imported inputs, which enabled these companies to operate at world prices. In addition, Malaysia also introduced a variety of tax incentives such as pioneer status that gave exemption from income tax for qualified companies, (contained in the Promotion of Investment Act 1986). These measures attracted much FDI, particularly from Japan, which had an additional push factor when the Yen appreciated as a result of the Plaza Accord (Plaza pushed for a stronger Yen as a way of reducing the large Japanese trade surplus).

This export-oriented industrialisation both expanded the Malaysian industrial sector and was also a means of entry to export markets. Malaysia's labour-intensive export products were competitive globally, and double-digit export growth was soon achieved. As a broad strategy to attract investment, all types of infrastructure were expanded and the Malaysia Industrial Development Authority was established to act as a one-stop agency in promoting investment in the industrial sector.

Another important part of economic governance in Malaysia was the choice of the private sector to lead the growth, using privatisation. Guidelines on privatisation were introduced in 1985, and the Privatisation Master Plan was adopted in 1991. The starting point was the privatisation of government-owned enterprises such as airlines and telecommunication agencies. Subsequently, privatisation was extended to include new projects proposed by the private sector such as toll roads, ports, utilities (water supply) and energy (power generating plants). The government also took steps to forge closer relations with the private sector through initiatives such as Malaysia Inc. and the Malaysian Business Council.

To assist the private sector to take this leading role, the financial sector was strengthened and deregulated. The banking sector capital base was enhanced: at the end of 1997, the banking system's Risk Weighted Capital Adequacy Ratio was 11.2%, well above the minimum level of 8% set by the Bank of International Settlement. In addition, the level of non-performing loans, another indicator of the health of the banking system, was only 5.5% of the total loans outstanding at the end of 1997. The central bank, the Bank Negara Malaysia (BNM), exercised significant authority derived from the Banking and Financial Institutions Act (1989) to supervise financial institutions under its jurisdiction. Strict prudential requirements and close supervision were also exercised to ensure the stability and adequacy of the banking system.

The growth and vitality of the private sector is very much dependent on the availability of funding. To complement the banking system as a source for financing, the equity and bond markets were also strengthened. The Kuala Lumpur Stock Market (KLSE) became a key source of capital. At its peak in February 1997, the market capitalisation of the KLSE was three times the size of the national GDP. The KLSE was then the third largest stock market in Asia. The Securities Commission was established in 1993 as the regulator of the capital market. Other institutions were also formed to develop the capital market, such as rating agencies and Cagamas, the national mortgage agency.

On the external front, Malaysia enjoyed a healthy balance of payments position, but there was a worm in the bud. The balance of payments had generally been characterised by surpluses in the merchandise account from a strong export performance but with persistent deficits in the services account (Table 9.4). In most years until the late 1980s, the trade surplus out-weighed the services deficit to yield a current account surplus. This pattern changed during the rapid growth phase beginning in 1989. Strong economic growth led to a surge in imports of capital and intermediate goods which, at least in the first instance, reduce the merchandise account surplus. At the same time, the services account remained in deficit, reflecting a large net outflow of profits and dividends primarily by FDI. Consequently, the current account shifted from surplus in the late 1980s to deficit in the 1990s. In most years, the large FDI inflow was sufficient to finance the current account deficit. Effectively, the basic balance (current account balance plus long-term capital flows) was always in surplus during the 1990–96 period, adding to national exchange reserves.

A feature of capital flows that had raised concern was its volatile nature. The large capital inflow since 1993 had exposed Malaysia to the risk of a sudden reversal in that flow. As part of capital account

Table 9.4 Net Balance Of Payments (US$ Million)

Item	1990	1991	1992	1993	1994	1995	1996	1997	1998 Qtr 1	1998 Qtr 2	1998 Qtr 3
Merchandise f.o.b.	2,627.04	526.91	3,376.08	3,177.99	1,702.29	38.65	4,029.37	4,034.52	2,934.95	3,666.33	5,295.15
Balance on services	-3,601.11	-4,798.18	-5,712.94	-6,436.29	-6,490.46	-7,660.96	-7,703.97	-7,755.16	-1,063.27	-1,197.45	-1,429.85
Balance on goods and services	-974.07	-4,271.27	-2,336.86	-3,258.30	-4,788.17	-7,622.31	-3,674.60	-3,720.64	1,881.89	2,468.88	3,865.31
Unrequited transfers	54.44	37.09	132.16	198.07	-849.24	-1,001.99	-1,165.08	-1,316.01	-214.80	-311.73	-284.18
Balance on current account	-919.63	-4,234.18	-2,204.71	-3,060.23	-5,637.40	-8,624.30	-4,839.68	-5,036.65	1,656.89	2,157.14	3,581.12
Official long-term capital	-1,050.37	-241.82	-1,127.84	377.99	328.63	2,449.00	296.83	1,653.02	-348.47	289.80	29.08
Federal Government	-291.48	38.55	-1,243.14	-1,210.04	-1,818.32	-650.60	-864.68	-598.93	-262.50	269.64	-130.10
Market loans	364.07	118.91	-1,121.18	-704.25	-1,651.91	-434.66	-267.86	-248.04	-246.68	0.00	-90.82
Project loans	134.81	-20.00	-72.16	-462.55	-166.41	-215.94	-596.83	-350.89	-15.82	269.64	-39.29
Suppliers' credit	-62.22	-60.36	-49.80	-43.24							
Non-financial Public Enterprises	-764.44	-269.09	152.55	1,651.35	2,198.85	3,094.82	1,128.57	2,265.48	-85.71	-24.74	166.33
Other assets and liabilites	5.56	-11.27	-37.25	-63.32	-51.91	4.78	32.94	-13.52	-0.26	-4.59	-7.14
Private long-term capital	2,336.67	3,998.55	5,178.04	4,974.90	4,121.37	4,168.92	5,070.24	5,111.39	717.35	569.13	-281.12
Balance on long-term capital	1,286.30	3,756.73	4,050.20	5,352.90	4,450.00	6,617.93	5,367.06	6,764.41	368.88	858.93	-252.04
Basic balance	366.67	-477.45	1,845.49	2,292.66	-1,187.40	-2,006.37	527.38	1,727.76	2,025.77	3,016.07	3,329.08
Private short-term capital	502.22	1,867.27	4,689.02	5,378.76	-3,238.17	1,007.57	4,094.05	-4,034.52	-2,358.42	-1,164.03	-1,170.15
Errors and omissions	1,118.15	-143.64	31.76	3,617.76	1,272.14	-755.38	-2,143.25	-1,569.40	-139.54	-1,631.89	3,787.24
Overall balance (surplus +/ deficit −)	-1,987.04	1,246.18	6,566.27	11,289.19	-3,153.44	-1,754.18	2,478.17	-3,876.16	-472.19	232.91	5,946.17
Allocation of Special Drawing Rights	—	—	—	—	—	—	—	—	0.00	0.00	0.00
IMF resources	—	—	—	—	—	—	—	—	0.00	0.00	0.00
Net change in international reserves of Bank Negara Malaysia (increase −/decrease+)	-1,987.04	-1,246.18	-6,566.27	-11,289.19	3,153.44	1,754.18	-2,478.17	3,876.16	472.19	-232.91	-5,946.17
Special Drawing Rights	-26.30	-14.91	107.84	-11.97	-8.78	-16.33	-14.68	-18.15	-1.28	-3.57	-61.73
IMF Reserve Positon	-8.52	-25.82	-58.04	3.47	-70.23	-279.28	-5.95	41.64	0.00	0.00	-177.30
Gold and Foreign Exchange	-1,952.22	-1,205.45	-6,616.08	-11,280.69	3,232.44	2,049.80	-2,457.54	3,852.67	473.47	-229.34	-5,707.14
Bank Negara Malaysia	10,009.26	11,073.45	18,508.24	29,511.58	26,020.23	25,406.37	27,783.73	21,040.21	14,610.20	14,843.11	20,783.93
International reserves, net (Reserves as months of retained imports)	4.1	3.6	5.6	7.8	5.5	4.1	4.4	3.4	3.3	3.7	4.2
(Services balance as % of GNP)	-8.8	-10.5	-10.4	-10.6	-9.4	-9.2	-8.2	-8.3	—	—	—
(Current account as % of GNP)	-2.2	-9.3	-4	-5.1	-8.2	-10.4	-5.1	-5.4	—	—	—

Source: Department of Statistics, Malaysia and Bank Negara Malaysia

liberalisation and to encourage capital inflow, no controls on capital flows were in force, except in 1994 when some measures were imposed for a limited time to mitigate the impact of the surge of short-term capital inflow in late 1993. The large short-term capital inflow was probably encouraged by the de facto peg exchange rate of the Ringgit to the US dollar, which kept the Ringgit exchange rate constant despite a large capital inflow (otherwise the Ringgit would have appreciated). This had given the illusion that there was no risk associated with capital flows.

These specific economic governance initiatives took place against a background of sound management of the economic fundamentals. The strategy had succeeded in accumulating surpluses. The federal government[2] achieved a balanced budget in 1993 and this was maintained until 1997. In the Malaysian budget system, state budget allocations are agreed and controlled by the federal government. In this way, the overall fiscal stance was consistent between the federal and state levels. When we compare the 1986–89 period with 1990–1996, we see the fiscal balance retreating from a deficit of 2.5% of GDP to a surplus of 1.5% between these two periods. With the stronger fiscal position, domestic public debts declined dramatically from 64% of GDP to 39% between 1990 and 1996 while the external public debt fell from 23% of GDP to 6.6% during the same period.

The availability of financial resources had made the nation less dependent on external borrowing. During the period 1990–96, Malaysia's external debt remained between 38% to 42% of GDP (Arthukorala 2001), while the debt-service ratio[3] remained below 10%, remarkably low by developing country standards. Similarly, foreign loans taken by the private sector were low and sufficiently covered by the reserves.

Malaysia also did well in terms of inflation and employment. The low level of inflation was the result of careful balancing of monetary and fiscal policies. Interest rates were adjusted to handle any signs of upward price pressures. A price control system was, and still is, applied to basic food items, the largest item in the budget of low-income households. The high economic growth had produced full employment, and had necessitated the recruitment of unskilled foreign workers.

The crisis also opened a popular debate on the link between politics and business, termed as crony capitalism that had created inefficiencies and misallocation of resources and became a source of vulnerability (Jomo 2001 and Haggard 2000). The New Economic Policy was introduced in 1970 to restructure the Malaysian society and one of its objectives was to increase the share of corporate ownership of the *bumiputra* ethnic group to 30% of the total corporate equity. In the implementation of this policy, the government had intervened, sometimes directly and through the political structure, to create the *bumiputra* business class. For example, the public sector contracts have an allocation for small *bumiputra* businesses. In addition, the strategy to make the private sector as the engine of growth also saw a closer business-government relationship, particularly in establishing a more co-operative business environment and facilitating privatisation projects. This relationship was not limited to the *bumiputra* community but was also extended to the other ethnic groups.

This business-government relationship was regarded as a crucial element for the high growth enjoyed by Malaysia and has an influence on the economic governance through a "balanced" distribution of economic activities. However, this relationship might have resulted in some companies being able to accumulate a large amount of domestic and foreign debt. As a consequence of the crisis, some of these companies had to be restructured, through a change in the management (for example the Renong and Malaysian Resources Corporation Berhad).

The fundamental achievement of this period was the transformation of Malaysia into an economy with strong macroeconomic fundamentals, a vibrant private sector and social cohesion and stability. Yet, the economic governance had also created some vulnerability. The high growth strategy based on high investment had led to excessive and risky lending: during the 1995–1997 period, bank loans expanded by an average annual rate of 24%. The results were a high level of domestic debt (152% of GDP) and booms in the stock market and the property sector. Another vulnerability was that the de facto fixed exchange rate had the effect of obscuring the changes that should have been made when the Ringgit became over-valued. The close links between short-term capital inflow, the stock market and the banking system was another cause for concern. Shares are used as collateral for bank loans and when the stock market was on the upward trend due to additional liquidity from short-term capital inflow, the value of shares as collateral was inflated. Similarly if capital were to flow out suddenly, the value of shares used as collateral will fall, and expose the banks to losses, unless additional collateral is provided.

4. Impact of the 1997 Crisis on the Malaysian Economy

4.1 Economic Performance

The Malaysian economy experienced its deepest recession in 1998, when GDP contracted by 7.5%, after growth of 7.7% in 1997. The crisis was initially felt in the first quarter of 1998 when GDP declined by 3.1%. The severest contraction occurred in the third quarter of 1998 when GDP fell by 10.9%, and was caused by a combination of several factors: the deflationary force of the regional crisis, massive capital outflow, public sector expenditure reduction and tight monetary policy. The massive outflow of short-term foreign capital, particularly from the equity market and the withdrawal of loans by foreign banks had drastically reduced the funds available to companies, forcing many to trim down their business activities.

The sharp contraction of the Malaysian economy in 1998 was caused by a 20.3% collapse in aggregate demand. This had three sources: public consumption, private consumption and investment. Public consumption fell by 7.2% and private consumption by 7.5%. However, the single most important cause was the 50.5% fall in private investment, triggered by the complete absence, (or at best the higher cost) of funds, excess capacity and the expectation of decreasing consumption. Public investment did not help very much, because it grew only by 0.4%.

The following are the specific effects in key areas:

a)   Exchange rate

     At the onset of the crisis, when regional currencies were under pressure to devalue, Malaysia tried to defend the Ringgit but it found this strategy unsustainable and costly. On 14 July, the Ringgit was floated and subsequently it slipped from RM2.50 to US$1 (prior to the crisis) to its lowest level of RM4.88 on 7 January 1998.

b)   Equity market

     The equity market was badly hit: the KLSE lost 80% of its market valuation. From a high of RM917 billion in February 1997 the market valuation sank to RM182 billion on 1 September 1998, when selective capital controls were imposed. In other words the KLSE composite index fell from 1271 points to 262 points.

c)   External sector

     During the initial phase of the crisis, exports had decreased as the troubled East Asian economies (which represented half of Malaysia's export market) slashed their demand for imports. When the Ringgit was pegged (at RM3.80 per US dollar), other regional currencies appreciated, and this increased Malaysia's relative price competitiveness. This allowed Malaysian exporters to take advantage of robust US export demand. In nominal Ringgit terms, total exports grew by 29.8% in 1998, with palm oil registering the highest increase of 64.4%, followed by manufactured goods (32.2%) and crude petroleum (6.2%). The sharp Ringgit depreciation also increased Ringgit export revenue, which contributed to higher domestic liquidity.

     Malaysia's large positive merchandise balance of RM69 billion (or US$18.2 billion) in 1998 was achieved not only from high export growth but also from the collapse of imports. Sharply dampened consumer demand and low investment reduced the demand for imports — total imports only grew by 3%. Due to the strong performance of the merchandise account balance, the balance on goods and services emerged from its chronic deficit of the 1990–1997 period into a surplus of RM46.7 billion in 1998. The merchandise account surplus of RM69 billion was more than sufficient to offset the RM22.3 billion deficit from the services account.

d)   Capital flows
In 1998, RM10.6 billion worth of long-term capital flowed into Malaysia, a reduction of about RM9 billion over the 1997 inflow. Not unexpectedly, the short-term capital account showed a substantial net outflow of RM21.7 billion due to the decline in net external liabilities of the commercial banks and the liquidation of portfolios by foreign investors. The lower net external liabilities of commercial banks followed the stagnation in domestic demand and the unwinding of trade-related hedging activities.

e)   Financial sector
The crisis had created stress on the banking system. High interest rate and the collapse of the stock market brought non-performing loans (NPLs) of financial institutions up to a level that was considered threatening. Prior to the crisis, financial institutions' NPLs were 4% (1997), but they reached 15.8% by August 1998. Higher cost of financing and tighter liquidity discouraged private investment. The cost of funds for investment increased substantially when the base lending rate rose from 10.3 % in June 1997 to 12.3% in July 1998: in some cases the effective interest rate was as high as 20%.

f)   Inflation and unemployment
Unlike the experience of some other crisis-hit economies, in Malaysia the severe economic contraction did not lead to hyperinflation and widespread unemployment. In 1998, inflation rose to 5.3%, double that of 1997, and unemployment climbed to 3.2% from 2.5%. Immigrant workers from nearby countries felt the sharpest edge of the recession, and many quit Malaysia for their home countries. This mitigated the effect of unemployment on the local workforce.

4.2 Economic Governance in Managing the Crisis

The ferocity and speed of the unfolding events clearly required a radical solution. Were the situation to get much worse, all of Malaysia's economic achievements stood to be destroyed. Therefore, a co-ordinated, comprehensive and centralised approach was adopted. This was unlike the crisis management approach of 1985, which was primarily the responsibility of the Ministry of Finance (MoF). In 1985, globalisation was not as pervasive and the Malaysian economy was less integrated with regional and global economies. Therefore the government had more time to react to events, as capital flow was also less volatile then. Unlike in 1998 when the public sector was in surplus, Malaysia in 1985 had deficits both in the fiscal and external payment positions. Hence the fiscal policy adopted by the MoF was different, with the focus on fiscal restraint. The government downsized its role in the economy, through privatisation and other measures.

In 1998, by contrast the private sector was the weak link in the economic chain and this posed a greater problem — if the private sector were to succumb to the crisis, then it would bring down the banking sector in its turn. Fortunately, the public sector was in a stronger position than in 1985, having a smaller share of outstanding external debt, namely 11.4% in 1998, versus 53.6% in 1985. It was thus able to lead the recovery process.

It was very clear that a co-ordinated and hands-on crisis management style was needed, even to the extent of looking at the microlevel, because of the unprecedented speed with which the crisis was unfolding. For this purpose, a new institution called the National Economic Action Council (NEAC) was established in January 1998.

The economic governance process during the crisis, particularly in the key years 1997 and 1998, was the product of an extremely dynamic situation. The Malaysian economy was, in the 1990s, already very much integrated with the global one, and many of its crisis parameters were external. Thus, any policy decisions had to bear in mind the openness of the economy. Policies could not always be reactive: there was a need to be proactive when the opportunity arose.

The idea of forming a crisis institution came from the experience of the 1969 riots,[4] when Malaysia declared a state of emergency, suspended the powers of the executive and established a National Operation Council (NOC). The NOC was given wide powers to govern and this included the economic management of the country. The NOC was very effective because it was allowed to override the separate functions of individual ministries and was therefore was able to minimize any conflict of power and jurisdiction that might delay policy implementation. The NOC provided a broad and integrated approach to policymaking and focused the attention of all relevant parties on the most urgent tasks. The idea was that the NEAC should have a similar approach, which permitted the crisis management team to act with a minimum of bureaucratic delays.

There was, however, a question of ministerial jurisdiction that might hinder the quick and effective implementation of future proposed measures. Before the formation of the NEAC, management of the economy was primarily in the hands of the Treasury, part of the MoF. But the Treasury did not have jurisdiction over the many other parts of the government that are also essential in dealing with the crisis. The government needed a national committee that brought together all the relevant ministries and interest groups to overcome the problem of inter-agency areas of responsibility. This would eventually allow a focused and integrated strategy, applied consistently to all ministries. This council would also mobilize the national institutional capacity in implementing measures and so ensure a quick response to any new challenges thrown up by the crisis.

But public sector representation (ministries) alone in the NEAC was not sufficient — a broader representation, from consumers, industries, employees and the financial sector were essential. This would bring into the process the ideas and perceptions of many sectors, interest groups and the general population.

The need for impartiality of the crisis management team decisions was paramount. They must look beyond any particular inclination or stance of any ministry or central public agency. In the early part of the crisis, the MoF, including BNM, favoured the adoption of IMF-style solutions. But others, particularly the Prime Minister, argued for other counter measures, namely, an easier interest rate and expansionary fiscal policies. This policy impasse was not a good platform from which to develop a crisis response. Ideally of course, Malaysia would be best served by policies flowing from all ministries and public agencies, which also reflected the general sentiment. Such neutrality would ensure that whatever policies were adopted were not perceived by the public and media, as coming solely from one influential group. Also conflicting and overlapping jurisdiction of ministries and public agencies could vitiate the full implementation of the decisions. Unfortunately, with the above division in views becoming more and more evident, the opportunity to develop consensus was diminishing. A quite new policymaking body was needed, one that had credibility and broad bi-partisan support. The NEAC therefore had to be a high-level council with a strong executive implementation mandate.

By virtue of its diverse membership and powerful leadership, the NEAC was well positioned to integrate the diverse functions and jurisdiction of the many ministries and government agencies. This proved to be a key success factor later on in solving the many and complex problems that were to come the NEAC's way. These two strengths — an integrated policy response and the ability to overcome institutional rigidity — came from having the Prime Minister as the chairman of the NEAC.

4.2.1 Relationship with the Cabinet

NEAC was established as a consultative body to the Cabinet, and many questioned the wisdom of it not having an implementation mandate. Moreover, at that time the Treasury was in charge of most economic and financial decisions and so few could imagine that the NEAC was going to lead the crisis management process. As time went on however, NEAC became very influential, primarily because of the mandate derived from its chairman, the Prime Minister.

Although the NOC was the inspiration for the formation of the NEAC, the powers of the two bodies were vastly different. The NOC was given an all encompassing executive power on all matters, because both the Parliament (Dewan Rakyat) and the Upper House (Dewan Negara) were suspended. The NOC then became the sole executive power in the country during the period of emergency. However, the Cabinet did not confer executive power to the NEAC during the 1997–98 crisis. Executive power can only be transferred from the Cabinet to another body after the proclamation of emergency under Articles 150(1) and 150 (2B) of the Federal Constitution.[5] If the NEAC were to be given executive power, there would be two executive bodies – the Cabinet and the NEAC. This would lead to uncertainty as to who was in charge.

However, the NEAC needed a mandate and some clout to implement its decisions: it would not be able to do so as just another consultative body. It was decided while that executive powers would remain with the Cabinet, the NEAC would be its consultative body on economic matters. The control structure of NEAC therefore requires that every important decision made by NEAC be approved or endorsed by the Cabinet, although sometimes there is a time lag when some of the measures have to be implemented immediately. In addition, Parliament must also approve any major new policies or institutional changes.

Objectives of the NEAC are to:

* Restore public and investor confidence with regard to the economy, which suffered from an image problem despite having relatively strong fundamentals;
* Ensure that the shocks from the depreciating Ringgit and falling share values are not transmitted to the real economy, hence avoiding the pitfalls of recession;
* Revive the national economy and make it more attractive globally by enhancing its international competitiveness;
* Strengthen the country's economic fundamentals so that the economy is back on track to achieve the developed country status as stated in the nation's Vision 2020.

Figure 9.1   Structure of the NEAC

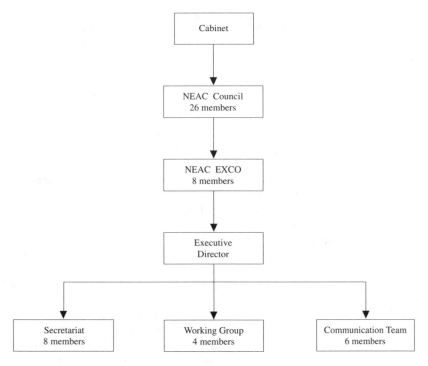

The Cabinet also required that the NEAC held meetings with a wide spectrum of Malaysians, from the private sector, non-government organisations (NGOs), consumer groups, professional associations and political parties, in order to obtain general consensus and support for the recovery measures. The success of the NEAC recovery proposals would in the end require general public understanding of the measures taken and support for their implementation. Thus, in delegating to the NEAC the task of reviving the economy, the public had to understand that the Cabinet was very much aware of the urgency of the crisis and the need for decision-making flexibility. The structure of NEAC is shown in Figure 9.1.

4.2.2 Recovery Measures

The recovery measures have five major thrusts:

• Boosting the domestic economy through fiscal stimulus programmes;

- Easing the monetary stance;
- Stabilisation of the Ringgit;
- Strengthening and restructuring of the financial and corporate sectors; and,
- Corporate governance.

Below are some of the salient measures taken:

- *Fiscal stimulus programmes*
  The budget stance was reversed from a surplus of 3.2% of GNP in 1998 to a deficit of 6% in 1999. Additional development expenditure of US$1.8 billion was allocated to agriculture, low- and medium-cost housing, education, health, infrastructure, rural development and technology upgrading. The fiscal stimulus programmes concentrated on infrastructure projects and an Infrastructure Development Fund (US$1.6 billion) was established to finance essential projects.

- *Easing the monetary stance*
  The statutory reserve requirement for banks was gradually reduced from 13.5% in February 1998 to 8% in July, 6% on 1 September, and 4% on 16 September 1998. The reduction of the SRR meant that an additional RM38.3 billion was injected into the banking system and this increased liquidity. The base lending rate (BLR) was reduced from a high of 12.3% in June 1998 to 6.79% in October 1999.

- *Stabilisation of the Ringgit*
  Malaysia created widespread controversy when it implemented selective capital controls measures on 1 September 1998. These had two inter-related parts: first, the stabilisation of the Ringgit and second, the restriction of outflow of short-term capital. Stability of the currency is guaranteed by pegging the Ringgit to the US dollar at a rate of RM 3.80 to USD 1.00. The capital control measures restricted the transfer of funds among non-residents via non-resident external accounts, import and export of Ringgit by travellers (both resident and non-resident) and investment abroad by Malaysian residents. Similarly, non-residents were restricted from raising credit domestically for purchase of shares. Non-resident portfolio investors were required to hold their investment for at least 12 months in Malaysia.

  However, capital controls did not impede current account transactions (trade in goods and services), repatriation of interest, dividends, fees, commissions and rental income from portfolio investments and other forms of Ringgit assets and FDI inflow and outflow (including income and capital gains).

  The selective capital controls were modified effective 15 February 1999 when the quantitative control (the requirement that proceeds from the sale of Ringgit assets be kept in the country for one year) was replaced by a price-based regulation, the exit levy. The maximum rate was 30% for capital that stayed for seven months and it was less for longer capital stays. Further relaxation was introduced on 21 September 1999, with a flat rate levy of 10% on profits repatriated. It was withdrawn totally on 1 May 2001.

- *Strengthening and restructuring of the financial and corporate sectors*
  - An asset management company (Danaharta) was set up to manage NPLs of financial institutions. Its main objective was to remove the NPLs from the balance sheets of financial institutions at fair market value, and to maximize their recovery value. This will free the banks from the burden of debts that had prevented them from providing loans to their customers.
  - As the capital base of banks had been affected by the decline in share prices and NPLs, these banks needed to be recapitalised. For this purpose a Special Purpose Vehicle (Danamodal) was set up to recapitalize the banking sector, i.e., to inject capital into banks facing difficulties and especially to top-up their capital, which was reduced when the NPLs were taken out by Danaharta. The injection of capital would enhance the resilience of banks, increase their capacity to grant new loans and as a result speed up the economic recovery process.
  - To complement the restructuring of the financial system by Danaharta and Danamodal, the Corporate Debt Restructuring Committee (CDRC) was set up in August 1998 to facilitate debt restructuring of viable companies. The aims were to minimise losses to creditors, shareholders and other stockholders; avoid placing viable companies into liquidation or receivership and enable banking institutions to play a greater role in rehabilitating the corporate sector. The CDRC devised a market-approach debt restructuring plan to enable creditors and debtors to resolve their debts without resorting to legal procedures. It also brought together all interested parties to assist in the process.

- *Corporate governance*
  Although Malaysia had implemented measures for good corporate governance, the crisis highlighted some of the shortfalls of the existing regime. Additional measures were introduced to enhance the governance environment and there were calls for more effective execution. The additional measures were:
  - Improve transparency and disclosure standards.
  - Establish a committee on corporate governance. It produced a comprehensive report on measures to enhance governance.
  - Enhance monitoring and surveillance.

- Enhance accountability of company's directors.
- Protect rights of minority shareholders.
- Review Codes and Acts such as the Securities Industry Act to minimise any weaknesses that can lead to breaches of the Act.
- Change the rules of the KLSE and its clearing and depository system to ensure orderly and transparent trading of securities.

5. Recovery of the Malaysian Economy

The Malaysian economy had a V-shaped recovery. After a deep contraction of 7.5% in 1998, GDP grew by 5.4% in 1999 and by 8.3% in 2000. Other indicators of recovery include:

a. Industrial production recovered strongly after a continuous decline for 12 months. February 1999 marked the turnaround of industrial production when it grew by 3.9% compared to January of the year. By June 1999, the industrial production index had expanded by 8.3%. Industrial revival continued and the index grew 27.5% by October. Within the industrial sector, manufacturing was the driving force with growth of 19.5% in the third quarter of 1999. The construction sector recovery was slower than that of other sectors.

b. The external sector was the engine of recovery. The Malaysian trade surplus in 1998 was RM58.4 billion and in 1999 it rose to an unprecedented surplus of RM72 billion. The strong trade balance helped improve significantly the current account position, and in 1998 the current account surplus was RM34 billion or 13% of GNP. The strong external sector also led to more international reserves. In August 1998, Malaysia had reserves of US20.2 billion, and these had increased to US31.7 billion in July 1999.

c. The interest rate decreased significantly. In October 1999, the base-lending rate was 6.79%, compared to a high of 12.27% in June 1998.

d. Inflation remained mild throughout the crisis. The rise in the consumer price index peaked at 6.2% in June 1998 and then declined to only 2.1% in October 1999.

e. The stock market also rebounded strongly. The key indicator of broadly established confidence, the Kuala Lumpur Composite Index, went from its low of 262 points on 2 September 1998 to 991 points on 10 February 2000.

f. Another important recovery indicator is consumer aggregate demand. This improved, albeit not strongly. Indications of more consumer demand came from increased sales of consumer durables, such as vehicles and houses and higher collection of sales tax.

g.   Financial and Corporate Sector Restructuring

- As at 31 December 2001, Danaharta had successfully carved out a total of RM48.03 billion of NPLs. The level of NPLs in the banking sector has been significantly reduced to 11.4%. The first phase, namely purchase of NPLs, was completed in six months, much faster than the original time target of one year and the average discount rate for NPLs was 55%. The second stage of Danaharta operation was asset management. Danaharta conducted five property tenders, offering to the market 614 properties. Of these, 498 properties (approximately 81%) have been sold, with a value of RM843.52 million.

- Danamodal has injected RM7.6 billion into ten financial institutions, pre-empting any potential systemic risks to the financial sector. As a result, the capital adequacy ratio of the recapitalised financial institutions rose to 11.7%, almost that of the industry overall (12.6%).

  The capital injection was accompanied by the absorption of losses by shareholders through reduced shareholding in the institutions, changes in the composition of the boards of directors and/or changes in management. Danamodal has also appointed their representatives at the recapitalized institutions to ensure that these institutions are managed prudently and efficiently as well as to institute changes that will strengthen these institutions. Most of the recapitalised institutions have repaid Danamodal's capital injection.

- By the middle of 2001, CDRC had taken on 75 cases, representing debts of RM47.3 billion, and had resolved 33 of them, representing RM27.6 billion. Working within a voluntary framework, the CDRC helps companies restructure without government support. CDRC ceased operation in June 2002, when it had resolved almost all the outstanding cases.

6. Economic Governance and the 1997 Crisis

The above analysis has shown that economic governance in Malaysia prior to the crisis was sound, albeit there were areas of weakness. Huther and Shah (1998), using a composite index of economic governance consisting of performance indicators of fiscal policy (debt-GDP ratio), monetary policy (central bank independence) and trade policy (outward orientation), concluded that the Malaysian economy was well managed.

Their index covers selected times during the 1980–1993 period. Gonzalez and Mendoza (2001) when examining the relation between governance and development are of the view that better tax collection, which increased the government financial resources and high priority given to public spending in health and education have been central to poverty reduction in Malaysia.

Indicators of macroeconomic fundamentals are clear evidence that support the point that economic governance in Malaysia has helped make the economy strong and diversified, with the flexibility needed to respond to external changes. Furthermore, economic governance has also coped well with the challenge that a large inflow of short-term capital posed to a small and open economy. It had a robust external sector, the public fiscal position was in surplus, the banking sector was well supervised and had sufficient capital, it was a recipient of foreign capital (both short-term and long-term) and its equity market was the third largest in Asia. In addition, it had full employment and inflation was low.

However, the high growth strategy also brought some shortcomings, namely a savings-investment gap, persistent current account deficits, high domestic debt and rising wages that were not matched by productivity. The current account deficit was not new, and the market had come to terms with it, and it did not appear to have deterred capital inflow. With respect to the savings-investment gap and raising wages, these were regarded as long-term issues and were thought unlikely to cause a sudden reversal in capital flow. Looking beyond the traditional indicators of economic fundamentals, there are also some signs of weakness such as the *de facto* peg exchange rate, asset price bubbles and exposure to a large capital outflow.

Malaysia's relatively strong fiscal and debt management policies allowed it to weather the early effects of the financial crisis – the economic contraction at that stage was not extreme. Besides the reduction of development expenditure, the improvement in the fiscal position was attributed to higher tax revenue collection that came with strong growth, as well as a broader tax base and improvement in efficiency in the tax collection system. Unlike the situation in many other developing countries, the budget deficits were not a source of inflation because they were not financed through borrowing from the central bank. The financing of these deficits came from local sources. Malaysia's budgetary surpluses for the five years before the crisis had also sheltered the social sector from budgetary cuts, sparing the poor from the full impact of the crisis.

The more cautious approach toward capital account liberalisation also helped Malaysia. As part of a prudent and sequenced liberalisation to match domestic capacity, Malaysia limited foreign borrowing by the private sector — it is only allowed for companies that have a natural external hedge. In other words, these companies must have sources of foreign currency to match their foreign borrowing. This ruling is useful, and ensured that Malaysia had a low level of short-term foreign loans with sufficient reserves coverage.

To know whether economic governance had made the economy vulnerable to a crisis, we need to examine the causes of the crisis and to link them with the economic weak points. Was the crisis due to imprudent economic management or due to external factors? Although external factors have been recognized as the key cause of the crisis, domestic shortcomings were also responsible for deepening or aggravating the impact of the crisis. In theory, if market-based economic systems and export-oriented industrialization policies are adopted then the market will also call for a form of economic governance which can respond to market changes and minimize market distortions. However, the crisis has shown that even in such an economy there were weak points, particularly the use of shares as collateral for bank loans that severely exposed the banking sector to a fall in share prices. A liberalised capital account that encouraged a large inflow of short-term capital had made the economy vulnerable to a relentless downward pressure on the exchange rate as a result of a massive reversal of this flow.

It is acknowledged that the crisis was not of a type called "First Generation" which is caused by the mismanagement of economic fundamentals. Many commentators agree that this crisis is more like a "Second Generation" type, in which the source is external — the crisis was spread through the contagion effect, which took little account of domestic fundamentals (Yoshitomi and Shirai 2000). The trigger factor of the crisis was massive capital outflow, aggravated by the loss of market confidence that put severe pressure on the regional exchange rates. The argument that the current account deficit was the root of the crisis is not entirely convincing: the deficit had existed since the early 1990s, and had coincided with the massive capital inflow into Malaysia. Notwithstanding external factors, domestic weak points such as a high level of domestic debt, investment inefficiency, a stock market boom and excess capacity in the property sector had all exacerbated the impact.

Malaysia's own crisis remedies and recovery and the rejection of the IMF's standard crisis solutions open the debate on what is good economic governance. The prevailing economic growth model before the 1997–98 crisis was the so-called "Washington consensus", which was promoted by the IMF and World Bank and advocated a free-market system — open trade regime, liberalized economy and strong role of the private sector in generating economic growth especially thorough privatization. Malaysia and the other crisis economies were good students of the "Washington consensus" school of economic thought yet they were vulnerable to a

Second Generation type of crisis. This raises a more fundamental issue of what is the definition of good economic governance. Certainly, the 1997–98 East Asian experience showed that the economic governance framework as set by the IMF and World Bank has some weaknesses, namely unfettered short-term capital flows, lack of long-term and broader macroeconomic objectives when growth is driven by the private sector and minimal attention given to socioeconomic issues such as income distribution.

The IMF crisis response strategy requires countries to reduce public sector spending, increase interest rates, abolish subsidies and float the exchange rate. These measures did not bring about the desired effects of returning market confidence and stabilising capital outflow. Instead, these economies worsened and they experienced severe economic contraction, large capital outflow, collapse of the stock market and sharp currency depreciation. Malaysia's recovery measures, which were the opposite of that of IMF's addressed the key problems faced: fiscal stimulus was for the expansion of the domestic demand that had contracted because of cutbacks in government expenditure, lowered interest rates to reduce the cost of funds and imposition of capital controls to stabilise the exchange rate and outflow of short-term capital.

The rapid recovery by Malaysia and Korea, which adopted different strategies shows that there are alternative ways to respond to a crisis,[6] implying that there is also no single definition on economic governance. The criticism of the "Washington consensus" as the sole model to be followed in light of the East Asian crisis signals the shift in opinion about economic governance. In fact, since then most countries in East Asia have embarked on measures to boost their domestic market in order to reduce the volatility caused by the fluctuations in global markets and transmitted through the export-oriented strategy.

The recovery also offers another perspective of economic governance. Policy flexibility arising from good economic governance before the crisis, allowed Malaysia to take response measures specially tailored to its needs and situation. First, Malaysia refused to rely on the IMF and instead sought its own path to recovery. Second, Malaysia imposed capital controls instead of liberalising the capital account. Third, it fixed the Ringgit to the U.S. dollar, instead of floating its currency in the way that other crisis countries did. Fourth, Malaysia used both expansionary monetary and fiscal policies, as soon as the capital controls were in place.

The new expansionary macroeconomic stance helped Malaysia recover quickly, but it was only made possible because of capital controls. A policy of high interest rate to perhaps, hopefully, stabilize the exchange rate would have had serious implications in Malaysia because of the large domestic banking debt. Although Malaysia was less vulnerable to external shocks, thanks to a relatively low level of short-term external debt, an expansionary monetary policy could not be effectively implemented without capital controls. In the Malaysian case, its sustainable trade and current account positions were important components in the successful implementation of the controls.

Many reasons were put forward as to why Malaysia was successful in implementing capital controls. Probably the answer is that, for capital controls to be successful, it is crucial that the crisis country is fundamentally strong, both at the macroeconomic and industry level. For example, manufacturing industries must be efficient to take advantage of recovery, the financial system must be well capitalized and supervised, and there must be sufficient domestic sources of funds. In such a situation, a country can choose the measures that best suit domestic conditions, rather than be forced to adopt a set of standard measures. This is because availability of external financing would no longer be the primary consideration.

Malaysia's rapid recovery was due to its strong external sector. The robust export growth propelled the strong recovery of the manufacturing sector, which contributes 33% of GDP. Moreover, the resulting large trade surpluses had boosted international reserves, turning a negative current account balance into a positive one and injecting liquidity into the economy. The balance of payments also had an in-built stabilizer, in that when exports fell, imports fell by even more.

Malaysia has also used the crisis as an opportunity to introduce measures to strengthen corporate governance, the banking system and capital and equity markets.

> Malaysia had one of the most developed capital markets in East Asia in the early 1970s. At first, securities market regulation followed mostly the English system of market self-regulation. Although a comprehensive securities act was enacted in 1973, jurisdiction over market supervision was divided among several state agencies – including the ministry of finance, the registrar of companies, and the capital issues committee.
>
> In 1993, after a decade of rapid market development, controls were unified in a new Securities Commission. Before the financial crisis in 1997, the Commission had determined to replace the detailed merit-based regulations system with a liberalized system based primarily on disclosure. But in the wake of the crisis and with the aim of reducing capital outflows, policymakers adopted selective capital controls.
>
> After an evaluation of the crisis, a series of more substantive institutional changes were introduced in preparation for continued liberalisation. Focused on transparency and governance, these changes included new accounting standards, merger and acquisition rules, capital adequacy rules for stock-broking companies, and broker commission liberalisation.

> The implication for policy makers is clear: if crises expose real vulnerabilities
> in markets, policy makers should take advantage of these times to fix the
> vulnerabilities (World Development Report 2002, p. 25).

7. Conclusion

The rapid pace and spread of globalization pose stiff challenges to economic governance. New criteria and developments may impose a heavier governance burden on the government and economy. One of the biggest challenges is the increasingly volatile international flow of capital that makes economic governance much more difficult: economic fundamentals are not the only factors that determine performance. Global integration also limits the choice of measures that are available to a country in making its response. Yet good governance is essential for sustained economic growth. The challenge is to determine what good governance consists of, under these changing conditions.

For Malaysian economic managers, since the crisis, the bar has been raised. To achieve the nation's Vision 2020, which is to be an industrialised country by the year 2020, the economy must grow by 7% per annum. The fluctuating economic performance of Malaysia since the crisis cruelly reminds us all that it will become more and more difficult to meet the stated growth target. There are also new governance pressures on the public and private sector after the crisis. The level of public debt is increasing and budget deficits will have to be narrowed. At the same time, there is need for higher social spending to improve socioeconomic factors such as better income distribution.

The crisis also uncovered dormant weaknesses; for example an unsatisfactory level of investment efficiency, lacklustre domestic investment, heavy dependence by the private sector on projects given by the public sector, a skewed export structure that depends heavily on electrical and electronic exports and less competitiveness in capturing FDI and export markets. Ever better economic management is called for, to preserve economic resilience and prevent external shocks from turning into crises. Thus, a close and critical evaluation of the new economic governance parameters and institutions is essential.

Notes

[1] Most of the discussion about economic governance focussed on the issue of decentralization (see World Development Report 2000, Huther and Shah 1998). The indicators used were also fewer e.g., debt to GDP, independence of the central bank and outward orientation.

[2] Malaysia is a federated nation of 14 states and federal territories. The federal government comprises by a coalition of 15 parties called the National Front. The dominant partners in the National Front are the United Malay National Organisation, Malaysia Chinese Association and Malaysia Indian Congress parties. Currently, all but two states are ruled by the National Front.

[3] The debt-service ratio is the ratio of debt and interest payments to the country's export earnings.

[4] In 1969, Malaysia experienced a racial riot that rose from an election result that was regarded as unsatisfactory to certain political parties. The Malay majority believed that the election result would diminish their political power as the Chinese opposition party won more seats. The Malays feared that the newly acquired political clout would further enhance the Chinese dominance of the economy.

[5] Under the Article 150 (1) the Yang di-Pertuan Agung (King of Malaysia) may proclaim a state of emergency if he is satisfied that the security, or economic life, or public order in the Federation or any part of it is threatened. Meanwhile, Article 150 (2B) grants the Yang di-Pertuan Agung the power to promulgate any ordinances to take immediate action under two conditions: first, the situation of grave emergency exists, and second, both parliaments are not in session concurrently.

[6] For a more detailed comparison between the Malaysian and Korean experience, see Mahani, Z. A, Shin, K and Wang, Y. 2003, "Macroeconomic Adjustments and the Real Economy in Korea and Malaysia since 1997", Working Paper 03–07, Korea Institute for International Economic Policy, Seoul.

References

Arndt, H. W. and Hill, H., (eds.). 1999. *Southeast Asia's Economic Crisis: Origins, Lessons and the Way Forward*. Singapore: Institute of Southeast Asian Studies.

Athukorala, P. 1998. "Malaysia". In *East Asian in Crisis: From Being A Miracle to a Needing One?* edited by R. H. McLeod and R. Garnaut. London, Routledge, pp. 85–101.

Athukorala, P. 2000. "The Malaysian Experiment". In *Reforms and Recovery in East Asia: The Role of State and Economic Enterprise*, edited by P. Drysdale. London, Routledge, pp. 170–90.

Athukorala, P. 2001. *Crisis and Recovery in Malaysia: The Role of Capital Controls*. Cheltenham: Edward Elgar Publishing.

Bank Negara Malaysia. *BNM Annual Report*. Kuala Lumpur, various issues.

Booth, A. 1999. "The Causes of South East Asia's Economic Crisis: A Sceptical Review of the Debate". Paper presented at ASEASUK Seminar on the South East Asian Crisis, University of North London, June, 1999.

Claessens, S., Bhattacharya, A., Hernandez, L., Alba, and P. Gosh. 1999. "Volatility and Contagion in a Financially Integrated World: Lessons from East Asia's Recent Experience". Working Paper No. 2008, World Bank.

Corbett, J. and D. Vines. 1999. "The Asian Crisis: Lessons from Vulnerability, Crisis and Collapse". *World Economy*, 22(2), pp. 155–77.

Corden, W. M. 1999. *The Asian Crisis: Is There a Way Out?* Singapore: the Institute of Southeast Asian Studies.

Furman, J. and J. E. Stiglitz. 1998. "Economic Crises: Evidence and Insights from East Asia". *Brookings Papers on Economic Activity, 1998:2*. Washington DC: the Brookings Institute, pp. 1–36.

Gonzalez, E.T and Mendoza, L. 2001. "Governance in Southeast Asia: Issues and Options". Mimeo. Philippines: Philippine Institute for Development Studies.

Haggard, S. 2000. *The Political Economy of the Asian Financial Crisis*. Washington DC.: Institute for International Economics.

Huther, J. and A., Shah. 1998. "Applying a Simple Measure of Good Governance to the debate on Fiscal Decentralisation". World Bank Working Paper, Washington D.C.: World Bank.

Jomo, K. S. 1998b. "Malaysian Debacle: Whose Fault". *Cambridge Journal of Economics Special Issues On The Asian Crisis*, Vol. 22, No. 6. Oxford: Oxford University Press.

Jomo, K. S., (ed.). 2001. *Malaysian Eclipse: Economic Crisis and Recovery*. London: Zed Books Ltd, 2001.

Kaplan, E. and D. Rodrik. 2001. "Did the Malaysian Capital Controls Work?" *NBER Working Paper No. w8142*. Cambridge, Massachusetts: National Bureau of Economic Research.

Kaufman, D., Kraay, A., and Zoido-Lobaton, P. 1999. "Aggregating Governance Indicators". *Working Paper No. 2195*. Washington D.C.: World Bank.

Kaufmann, D. and Kraay, A. 2002. "Growth Without Governance". *Working Paper No. 2928*. Washington D.C.: World Bank.

Mahani, Z. A. 2000b. "Malaysia's Alternative Approach to Crisis Management". In Institute of Southeast Asian Studies, *Southeast Asian Affairs 2000*, Singapore, Institute of Southeast Asian Studies, pp. 184–99.

Mahani, Z. A. 2002. *Rewriting the Rules: The Malaysia Crisis Management Model*. Kuala Lumpur: Prentice Hall.

Mahathir, M. 1999. "Why Malaysia's Selective Capital Controls are Necessary and Why They Have Worked". Paper presented at the Symposium of the First Anniversary of Capital Control, 2 September 1999, Kuala Lumpur.

Mahani, Z. A, Shin, K and Wang, Y. 2002. "Macroeconomic Adjustments and the Real Economy in Korea and Malaysia since 1997". Working Paper 03-07, Korea Institute for International Economic Policy, Seoul.

Radelet, S., and J. D. Sachs. 1999. "What Have We Learned So Far, From the Asian Financial Crisis". Mimeo.

World Bank. 1992. *Governance and Development*. Washington, D.C.: the World Bank.

World Bank. 1993. *The East Asian Miracle: Economic Growth and Public Policy*. New York: Oxford University Press for the World Bank.

World Bank. 2002. *World Bank Development Report 2002; Building Institutions for Markets*. Washington D.C.: Oxford University Press for the World Bank.

Yeats, A., and Ng, F. 1999. "Good Governance and Trade Policy: Are They the Keys to Africa's Global Integration and Growth". *Working Paper No. 2038*. Washington D.C.: World Bank.

Yoshitomi, M., and S. Shirai. 2000. *Technical Background Paper for Policy Recommendations for Preventing Another Capital Account Crisis*. Tokyo: Asian Development Bank Institute.

10
State Bureaucrats, Economic Development, and Governance: The Case of Singapore

Ikuo Iwasaki

1. Introduction

Ever since the second half of the 1980s, academic research has been going on, involving many economists and political scientists concerned with the Asian development scene, for factors that were responsible for the growth in East Asian states. The debate has been particularly intense over the prime cause of the growth: whether it was achieved through the active role of the state, including intervention in the market, or, on the contrary, by the proper work of the market — i.e., the adaptation of an export-oriented strategy and good economic fundamentals. In the course of a heated debate between "neo-classical economists" on the market side and "statists" on the state side, the World Bank (1993), one of the influential organizations in the neo-classical camp, partially consented to the importance of the state in a book that analyzed the causes of East Asian development, with mention of the necessity of an "institutional basis for shared growth". This meant that an effective state apparatus and efficient bureaucracy are indispensable and decisive elements for development. Consequently, statists named the East Asian states that were characterized by authoritarian political systems and state-led industrialization as "developmental states" (Woo-Comings 1999) and conceived this type of state as the general type in the region then.

In the 1990s, however, a sort of paradigm shift of the state relating to economic development occurred. After democratization in the third-world countries, whereby many authoritarian developmental states in East Asia have democratized and globalization has become a prevailing phenomenon in the world economy, making states weaker and less competent in the area of economic management than the preceding states, a new paradigm emerged pointing out the importance of governance for any government. Despite the fact that it has not yet sufficiently answered several points, for instance, what the essential elements of governance are, or whether it has any positive linkage with economic development, governance has taken a central place in development thinking in the developed as well as the developing nations.

Apparently, the developmental state equipped with an "institutional basis for growth" in the 1980s and the present state expected to comply with governance in the 1990s are totally unrelated. Nevertheless, it is our hypothesis that since one of the core conditions postulated by governance is efficient state machinery, both "institutional basis" and "governance" have some similarity in content, albeit not the same. Then, it is our conviction that the Singapore state, one of the developmental states instituted in the late 1960s that has continued up to the present day, will provide a suitable case for investigation of the correlation between the state, bureaucracy, and governance in development.

The object of this chapter is two-fold. One is to elucidate the framework of the economic development system created in Singapore over the last 30 years and to shed light upon the system of mobilization of bureaucrats and their way of management, in particular, in order to gain practical evidence for the East Asian development study. The other is, through this investigation, to think about the correlation between the state, bureaucracy, and governance in several aspects. The method employed in this regard is to scrutinize governance from the viewpoint of East Asian states to make it more applicable to the actual situation in the region. However, this chapter does not claim to successfully achieve this task. Rather, it will remain incomplete and be satisfied with pointing out the whereabouts of the issues in question.

The chapter proceeds first with addressing some concepts related to the developmental state and the political and economic characteristics of the Singapore state, especially the close relations between the ruling party and bureaucrats. This is then followed by an analysis of the structure and practice of the Singapore bureaucracy in general and the Economic Development Board in particular. At the end, several aspects of the Singapore state and its bureaucracy will be evaluated in the light of governance.

2. Characteristics of the Singapore State

2.1 State Autonomy in a "Developmental State"

For the developmental state of East Asia that reached its zenith in the 1970s and 1980s, one of the crucial factors was "state autonomy" (Evans 1985). In Western democratic countries, it is accepted as the normal state of affairs that opposition parties, pressure groups, or interest groups freely participate in the policy process and oppose government policy in one way or other, the result being reassessment or abandonment of the initial policy by the government. In the developmental states, however, the situation where opposing forces that may antagonize or criticize the government disappear through ruthless oppression or tight control by the government has become a regular state of affairs. Thus being freed from any political demands or pressure from the public, the government (bureaucrats) obtain a "free hand" in policymaking, and their sole concern in development was "rationality" — whether it brings targeted growth effectively. While statists named this condition as state autonomy, the World Bank (1993, p. 167) called it "technocratic insulation", which meant, "The ability of economic technocrats to formulate and implement policies in keeping with politically formulated national goals with a minimum of lobbying for special favours from politicians and interest groups". South Korea, Taiwan, Indonesia, Malaysia, and Singapore in the 1970s and 1980s came under this type, and these states were considered not as "institutions" but "actors" in development (Evans 1985).

The characteristics of the Singapore state are that it is a city-state with small land and population, no natural resources, and no rural area. From the conventional point of view of the political economy of development, these characteristics are regarded as disadvantageous, especially for economic growth. Yet the degree of political stability and the duration of high economic growth after Singapore became an independent country in 1965 have been remarkable by any standard. Many political scientists and economists have been searching for the secrets of this growth, and the explanations they have submitted are many-sided, reflecting the differences in their disciplines and interests. Yet, on the role of the state, without exception they have come to a similar view, acknowledging that economic development was achieved, among other things, through the system that the Singapore state had purposely created. This system comprised three actors, i.e., the "state", "foreign companies", and "national labourer". Under the skillful, determined guidance of the state, the first two, in particular, collaborated closely for the goal of development.

One of the key elements that underpinned this system is the monopoly of state power by the People's Action Party, or PAP, which has continued right up to the present. The monopoly was epitomized by the outcome of general elections held from 1968 to 1980, where all seats of parliament went to the PAP, leaving not even a single seat for the opposition. This monopoly of parliament then partly provided a solid base for PAP rule and, more critically, state autonomy for the government. Without doubt, the PAP government in Singapore possesses this extraordinary capacity in its development management.

2.2 Dual Functions of Bureaucracy under the PAP Regime

Under the PAP regime, which had consolidated its power by the end of the 1960s through the elimination of rival groups forcefully and skillfully, one of the peculiar features is that bureaucrats have not only afforded administrative support as professionals of economic management but also political support, with many bureaucrats changing over to become members of parliament (MP) of the PAP. The association of the two actually started in 1959 when the PAP took power. Since then, the two have been collaborating closely, and the level and degree of their association reached the utmost limits in the 1970s.

Table 10.1 shows the social careers of PAP MPs. In the early 1960s, when the PAP boasted about being the mass party representing poor people and was actually supported by them, "trade union leaders" (26.8%), "party staff" (21.9%), and "bureaucrats" (19.5%) made up the top three social careers. This changed drastically after 1965. In accordance with the transfiguration of party character from mass party to elite party, solely based on an English-educated elite, the main social careers of fresh MPs from 1968 to 1984 changed to "bureaucrats" (23.9%), "university teachers" (22.9%), "professionals (lawyers, doctors, accountants)" (14.6%), and "company managers" (14.6%), in that order. The phenomenon of bureaucrats occupying the position of leading suppliers of human resource for the PAP had the effect of pushing the whole bureaucracy into near complete fusion with the PAP.

Apart from the political sphere, the roles of bureaucrats in the economic sphere are almost no different from those in other countries.

Table 10.1   Social Background of PAP MPs

	1963 General Election	1968–84 General Elections and By-elections
Bureaucrats	8 (19.5%)	23 (23.9%)
Trade union leaders	11 (26.8%)	12 (12.5%)
University teachers	2 (4.8%)	22 (22.9%)
Journalists	5 (12.2%)	7 (7.3%)
Professionals	3 (7.3%)	14 (14.6%)
Company managers	3 (7.3%)	14 (14.6%)
Military	—	2 (2.1%)
Party staff	9 (21.9%)	2 (2.1%)
Total	41	96

Source: Iwasaki, Ikuo (1988). "Shingaporu no Seiji Shidosha" (Social Background of Political Leaders in Singapore), *Ajia Keizai*, 29(2), p. 14. (in Japanese)

In this area, the PAP requires them, as trained and qualified professionals, to accomplish their utmost in development administration. With much help from the state autonomy provided by the PAP, bureaucrats have been faithfully discharging their duties. As a result, Singapore has achieved sustained growth, although from time to time its economy has been disrupted by depression originating from outside sources beyond its control.

3. States and Economic Development

3.1 Types of Government Economic Agencies in Singapore

Many government agencies have been involved over the last 40 years in development administration in Singapore; nonetheless, they can be divided into three types according to the characteristics of organization, task, and activity. The first type is the "ministry" of the central government, i.e. the Ministry of Finance or Ministry of Trade and Industry. The function of this type of government agency comprises routine administrative work to keep economic and social life orderly. The second type is the "statutory board", i.e., the Economic Development Board or Jurong Town Corporation. This type is established by special law to supplement the activities of the ministries or to undertake a special task in a certain area as a proxy of the ministries. Unlike ministries, which come under the supervision of parliament by law, statutory boards have been provided special privilege free from any supervision by it. This is deliberately done by the government to give them with a free hand and flexibility in order to carry out their duties efficiently. The third type is the "government-linked company" (GLC), or public enterprise, i.e., Singapore Airlines or the Development Bank of Singapore. This type has been incorporated by company law, which applies to private companies, but comes under government ownership.

In 2001 there were 15 ministries, 56 statutory boards, and about 500 GLCs (Ministry of Information and Arts, 2001). Whereas the number of ministries and statutory boards has not changed much in the last 40 years, the number of GLCs has increased from 2 in 1961 to over 500 in the 1990s (Vennewald 1994, p. 24). It should be pointed out, however, that the total number of GLCs includes subsidiary companies or related companies of other GLCs. Thus, after omitting these companies from the counting, the actual number of "independent GLCs" decreases to about a hundred.

The tasks of economic planning, management, and implementation have been shared among these three types of government agencies, and they have been closely interacting with each other. Nonetheless, there is a "division of labour". Interestingly enough, the ministries alone have not been exclusively conducting development administration; rather, the statutory boards in many areas and GLCs in some areas have been sharing tasks with the ministries, and in certain areas ministries have left tasks completely to the statutory boards. In those areas, the statutory boards have been acting as the sole government agency; for instance, from the start of industrialization, the task of inviting foreign companies into the Singapore market has been entrusted to a statutory board, not a ministry, as we will explore later in some detail.

After closely observing the system of allocation of development administration among government agencies and examining at length the activities of key statutory boards, it is not an overexaggeration to conclude that, without the enthusiastic contribution of the statutory boards, the economic condition of Singapore would be considerably different from that of today. The statutory boards, as well as the ministries and GLCs, have been staffed and managed by bureaucrats; it is, therefore, vital to examine the bureaucratic system in Singapore, particularly such topics as recruiting and allocating them to the government machinery.

3.2 The System of Recruitment of Fresh Elite Bureaucrats

The task of recruiting fresh candidates for future elite bureaucrats has been entrusted to the Public Service Commission (PSC), which was originally established in 1951 by the British colonial government and then restructured by the PAP government in 1959. At the beginning, the PSC took charge of recruiting fresh graduates for both ministries and statutory boards, but in the 1970s the system was partially revised, and as a result the PSC recruits only for ministries. The statutory boards and GLCs have launched their own programmes; for instance, the EDB Scholarship for statutory boards and SIA Scholarship for GLCs, as shown in Table 10.2. In the following, we will focus our analysis on PSC programs, because not only has the PSC been the largest agency in this regard, but also the programs of other agencies are more or less copied versions of those of the PSC.

Table 10.2 Scholarship Organization and Programmes

Organization	Subject
Public Service Commission	Ministries
Statutory Board	Statutory Board
Government-linked Companies	GLCs

Source: The Author

The PSC has been entrusted with all matters related to the bureaucracy. In terms of development administration, however, the following two are of utmost importance: i.e., 1) the recruitment of candidates into the administrative service; and 2) the appointment of candidates as chief executive officers of statutory boards, despite the fact that this has not been prescribed as its task in the constitution of Singapore (PSC 2001). We start by examining the first task.

In order to recruit future elite bureaucrats, the PSC introduced several types of "government scholarship", which are awarded to high school students as shown in Table 10.3. The first scholarship started in 1961, but it was in the middle of the 1970s that the present programmes shown in Table 10.3 were completed. Among the various types of scholarships, the "President's Scholarship" (PS), "Singapore Armed Forces Overseas Scholarship" (SAFOS), and "Singapore Police Force Overseas Scholarship" (SPFOS) are intended to honour excellent students and are awarded to less than 10 students, respectively, each year. Thus, from the viewpoint of securing enough students, the "Overseas Merit Scholarship" (OMS) and "Local-Overseas Merit Scholarship" (LOMS), which have been awarded to over 200 students in total each year, are vital and crucial.

How does the PSC approach prospective candidates in high schools? In this regard, the education system in Singapore is greatly supportive of the PSC. As Singapore is a small city-state, it was not too difficult to introduce a unified system of education and examination covering the whole country. Under this system, it is compulsory for every student to sit for a unified examination at the end of each stage of school to proceed to the next higher course; that is, the PSLE (Primary School Leaving Examination) at the end of primary school (six years), the GCE (General Certificate of Education) "O" level at the end of junior high school (four years), and the GCE "A" level at the end of high school (two years).

In the PSC's favour, after the examination a complete list of all students, from top to bottom according to their examination scores, is published. Since the most important criteria in selecting candidates has been their excellent examination scores, as we shall discuss soon, the PSC selects and awards scholarships to those students who have recorded higher scores in the GCE "A" level examinations. In a sense, however, this is merely a formal procedure. According to the PSC officer whom I interviewed in December 2002, actual selection starts two years earlier, when the PSC eyes the top several hundred students who record higher score in the GCE "O" level examination, which is implemented at the end of junior high school. The PSC approaches them through their schoolmasters and requests them to apply for scholarships. This means that the selection process normally takes two years, and this long duration certainly gives the PSC enough time for eyeing and selecting the best candidates or persuading them to apply if they are reluctant.

Table 10.3 Major Scholarship Programmes Provided by the PSC

Type	Number (2001)	Value of Award	Requirements	Bond Period
President's Scholarship	3	#$1,500 p.a. for scholars also awarded Overseas Merit Scholarship		4–6 years
Singapore Armed Forces Overseas Scholarship	8	#Monthly salary for duration of studies		6 years
Singapore Police Forces Overseas Scholarship	3	#Monthly salary for duration of studies		6 years
Overseas Merit Scholarship	122	#Full scholarship allowance #Tuition fees and other approved fees #Return economy class air fair #Book allowance #Clothing allowance #Computer allowance #Settling-in allowance	#Singapore Citizen or PR #Attempted SAT 1 #For GCE A Level Science Stream: 4 A level subjects and 2 S papers #For GCE A Level Arts Stream: 3 A level subjects and 2 AO level subjects and 1 S paper #Possess good CCA record #Strong leadership qualities and potential	English-speaking country: 6 years Non-English-speaking country: 5 years
Local-Overseas Merit Scholarship	131			

Source: PSC (2002)

What is the PSC's criterion in the selection of scholars? This differs slightly according to the different types of scholarship. As we have pointed out, however, the OMS is the most important type, so we will examine this. As shown in Table 10.3, the OMS requires the following qualifications: 1) citizenship (Singaporean or permanent resident); 2) good academic results (they differ according to arts stream and science stream); 3) good co-curricular activities record; and 4) strong leadership qualities and potential. Although formally applicants are required to satisfy all qualifications, in practice, priority is placed on good academic results, and the other qualifications are not strictly questioned unless the results are extremely inferior.

It is said that the final selection process requires applicants who meet the required qualifications mentioned above to go through two stages. First, candidates are required to sit for another paper test to evaluate their IQ, numerical and verbal skills, and second, the PSC interviews candidates twice through two selection boards, comprising two or more PSC members. In 2001, selection boards held a total of 64 interview meetings with candidates, and in the end 253 students were awarded PSC scholarships. Among them, 122 students were sent to overseas universities and 131 students to local universities (PSC 2001). The PSC provides selected OMS scholars with full scholarship allowance, tuition fees, and several other allowances. As explained earlier, the PS, SAFOS, and SPFOS are more privileged awards, so these scholarships provide special bonus or monthly salary on top of the value of awards already provided to them as OMS scholars.

Which overseas universities do PSC scholars choose for their studies? The PSC has been urging OMS scholars to select universities in the United States, United Kingdom, France, Germany, Japan, Canada, Australia, and the People's Republic of China, while SAFOS and SPFOS scholars are restricted to either the United States or United Kingdom. Table 10.4 shows the overseas universities that the most prestigious PSC scholars chose in 1991 and 2001. It is clear that the top-class universities in the United States and the United Kingdom were preferred. This preference for English-speaking Western countries among scholars reflects exactly the social culture of the Singapore elite.

Table 10.4 Overseas Universities Chosen by President's Scholars in 1991 and 2001

	1991	2001
1	University of London, UK	Princeton University, USA
2	University of Cambridge, UK	Oxford University, UK
3	University of Cambridge, UK	University of London, UK
4	University of Cambridge, UK	

Source: PSC (1991, 2001)

Which fields do they study at universities both overseas and in Singapore? Table 10.5 shows the fields they chose in 1991 and 2001. In 2001, of the total of 253 students, engineering (79) and science (79) were the most favoured fields, followed by humanities and social science (57). Of the 79 students who selected science, however, 56 students are expected to join the educational service, such as schoolteachers, upon graduation. Since our purpose here is to examine the designated generalist-type bureaucrats, we exclude them from the counting; then, only 23 students are left as generalist-type. Thus, among the total of 145 students in 2001 who were designated as future elite bureaucrats, engineering was the most favoured field with 78 students, more than half of the total, followed by science (23 students) and economics/ politics (16). It should be noted that this reflects not only the spontaneous choice of students but also the government preference in qualifications for elite bureaucrats.

Table 10.5   Scholarships Awarded By Field of Study in 1991 and 2001

Field of Study	1991	2001
Engineering	–	79 (1)
Engineering Technology & Applied Science	100	–
Science	55 (44)	79 (56)
Humanities & Social Sciences (not including Economics)	70 (40)	57 (48)
Economics / Philosophy, Politics & Economics		19 (3)
Applied Science	7	
Accountancy / Business Administration	8	6
Law	11	4
Education	16 (16)	
Others		2
Total	271 (100)	253 (108)
Overseas	109	122
Local	162	131

Source: PSC (1991, 2001)
Note: Numbers in parentheses are students deemed to serve in educational service.

3.3 Allocation of Elite Bureaucrats

The core of the government scholarships is the regulation that requires scholars to resume government posts for a defined number of years after completing their studies. The "bond system" secures this. The duration of the bond varies, depending upon which type of scholarship students were awarded, from a minimum of four years to a maximum of six years.

In the case of OMS, it requires a maximum of six years. Thus, through government scholarships and particularly by the bond system, over a hundred fresh graduates join the bureaucracy each year.

What is the allocation system for each ministry? For this, a "three-party system" has been created: i.e., fresh graduates, who nominate their preferred ministry but without any guarantee; ministries, which request the type of qualified graduates they need; and the PSC, which participates as a mediator between the two. Under this system, the PSC interviews students on behalf of ministries and allocates them after overall consideration. After fresh graduates join, both the ministries and the PSC treat them as management associates for the first four years. When two years have passed, they are rotated to an entirely unrelated ministry and functional area as part of their career development (PSC n.d.). This means that government scholars have been treated and trained as generalist-type elite bureaucrats from the start.

As we have examined so far, the Singapore state skillfully created a system to insure that the best talents from society are drawn into the bureaucracy through government scholarships. Under this system, about half of the scholars have been attached to top- class universities, especially in English-speaking Western countries, and by the bond system they join the state bureaucracy machinery in the end. It is worthy to note that in recruiting bureaucrats, meritocracy has been the sole principle in Singapore, never nepotism or favouritism. These facts partly explain the secrets of the efficiency of the Singapore bureaucracy, and hence its capacity as a developmental state, which we will address later.

3.4 The Trinity System for Elite Bureaucrats

The other important task of the PSC has been the appointment of candidates as chief executive officers of statutory boards from among the pool of elite bureaucrats. A special committee, headed by a minister with a few members, most of them permanent secretaries from key ministries, undertakes this task. For example, the appointment of chairmen and directors of GLCs has been conducted by the Directorship and Consultancy Appointments Council, founded in 1971, chaired by a minister with several members (Vennewald 1994, p. 35). The peculiar practice in this area is that elite bureaucrats are concurrently entrusted with several executive posts of government agencies, i.e., ministries, statutory boards, and GLCs.

Figure 10.1 shows a part of it. In 1989 there were three permanent secretaries in the Ministry of Finance, and functions were shared among them. One of them, Ngiam Tong Dow, who was considered as one of the most influential bureaucrats then, held several posts almost superhumanly. Despite the fact that he was already entrusted with three permanent

Figure 10.1 The Trinity System of Elite Bureaucrats (1989)

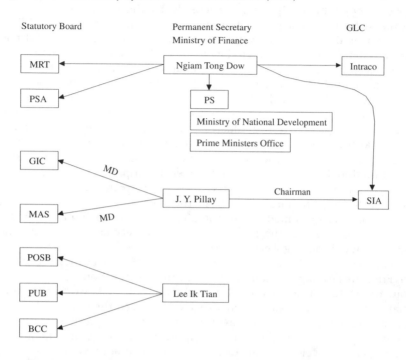

secretary posts, i.e., in the Ministry of National Development, Prime Ministers Office, and Ministry of Finance, he was furthermore allotted the post of vice- chairman of Intraco, a government-owned trading company created to undertake trade with communist countries, and board member of the Mass Rapid Transit and the Port of Singapore Authority, both statutory boards. Then J.Y. Pillay was allotted the additional posts of chairman of Singapore Airlines, one of the excellent GLCs in Singapore (it has been acknowledged by many observers that the growth of SIA into a world-class company in a short period was practically due to his service), and managing director of the Monetary Authority of Singapore, the de facto central bank in Singapore. He was also managing director of the Government of Singapore Investment Corporation, a government investment company for the overseas market and one of the largest investment organizations in the region. And lastly, Lee Ik Tian held four executive posts in statutory boards in addition to the post of Ministry of Finance.

The practice of elite bureaucrats holding key government agency posts concurrently started in the early 1970s. Since then, it has become a common practice of the personnel management of elite bureaucrats. This is called the "trinity system". However unique and characteristic it may be, though, it cannot be claimed that this practice is solely confined to Singapore. It is not uncommon to discover similar practices in other countries, irrespective of the number of bureaucrats involved and the different degree of concurrency by each country. Nevertheless, it may perhaps be safe to note that in Singapore the degree and extent of the trinity system has reached the utmost limits, making the Singapore bureaucracy unique and extraordinary in this regard.

Why did Singapore adopt this singular system, and what is the rationale behind it? The system was introduced with the following conviction and logic of PAP leaders. They are, of course, well aware that, if there are a hundred government agencies, it is definitely desirable that each agency be managed by its own full-time executive officer. Yet they reject this with the reason that Singapore is a very small country with scarce manpower in talented bureaucrats in general and, worse still, in bureaucrats who are qualified enough to take up management posts of all government agencies in particular. Then they came to the conclusion that Singapore cannot afford the "luxury" of appointing a manager to each agency and had to nominate a few qualified bureaucrats concurrently.

The reasoning given by PAP leaders may sound somewhat defensive, or apologetic, for the system, but nonetheless there is a positive reasoning in their judgment, too. They convincingly assumed that if a few selected bureaucrats are allocated and share in the management of government agencies, it would certainly generate coordination, efficiency, and the quick response of government agencies in policymaking and implementation. So the trinity system became a principle in the personnel management of elite bureaucrats and consequently a common practice. According to Vennewald (1994, p. 59), who extensively investigated actual conditions of the trinity system from the 1970s to the early 1990s, on average one elite bureaucrat held 1.7 director posts of government agencies in 1970, and the number increased to 2.3 in the early 1990s. He concluded his research with the comment that "only 47 technocrats control 600 state enterprises and statutory boards".

Generally speaking, any textbook on bureaucracy would teach us that the trinity system practised in Singapore may inevitably lead to corruption and inefficiency among the bureaucracy and result in the dysfunction of all government agencies. As a matter of fact, however, from the inception of the system, corruption, inefficiency, and dysfunction hardly reached serious levels in terms of the number of cases and content, and even when they occurred, they remained relatively minor and exceptional cases. This explains why the trinity system has been the case in Singapore.

So far, the focus of our examination of Singapore bureaucracy has been on the macro structure; in the following, we will turn our focus to the micro performance of a certain agency and its bureaucrats.

4. The Case of the Economic Development Board

4.1 Development Strategy and the Tasks of the EDB

Singapore started industrialization in 1959, and its process over the last 40 years can be divided into four phases according to the differences in the strategies adopted, as shown in Table 10.6. The first phase, from 1959 to 1965, began with "import substitution", a common strategy for developing countries then. This did not bear fruit and did not last long. In 1965, the second phase of "export-oriented" strategy replaced it when Singapore was suddenly forced to separate from Malaysia and accordingly lost the common market, which was vital for Singapore to industrialize. Ironically, it was in this phase that the Singapore economy recorded sustained high growth with the help of massive direct investments from multinational companies in labour-intensive manufacturing industries in developed countries. This strategy continued up to 1979, when Singapore adopted a new strategy because of the limitation of economic resources. Thus, the third phase of "economic restructuring" commenced, in which capital-intensive and skill-intensive industries were promoted to upgrade industrial structure. This strategy was inevitable, as Singapore could not afford labour-intensive industries any longer. Then in the second half of the 1980s, the latest phase of "globalization" commenced, with the government placing priority on encouraging local companies to invest overseas in order to overcome limited conditions in the domestic market.

Thus, over the last 40 years the Singapore state has been pursuing different strategies in accordance with changing conditions and the resources available. Nevertheless, the fundamental policy that foreign manufacturing companies, especially MNCs from developed countries, are the main actors and the engines of growth has never changed through all the phases. This feature of Singapore's development strategy is certainly different from other developing countries, where governments placed priority in fostering local companies. Needless to say, there were, and are, many local companies in Singapore, too, which the government could utilize. However, the government bypassed them on the grounds that they have been engaging entirely in the commerce and finance sectors from colonial days and lack experience in the industrial sector. As a result, Singapore had no other choice but to rely on MNCs, which are endowed with sufficient capital, industrial technology, and export markets, all of which are vital elements for Singapore's industrialization.

Table 10.6 Stages of Development Strategy in Singapore, 1959–2002

	Strategy	Duration	Target	Target industry	Leading industry
1	Import substitution	1959–65	Job creation	Labour-intensive industry (shipbuilding, engineering, chemicals)	Food
2	Export-oriented	1965–78	Job creation	Labour-intensive industry (consumer electronics, electronic components)	Petroleum
3	Industrial restructuring	1979–85	Skill improvement of labour	R & D Higher value-added industry Capital-intensive industry Skill-intensive industry	Electronics
4	Globalization	1986–	Investment to emerging Asian market	Operational Headquarters International Procurement Office	Electronics and financial service

Source: The Author

Because of this strategy, it became imperative for Singapore to invite MNCs both to create employment and exports. It was exactly this particular situation that made the Economic Development Board (EDB) the most important government agency in development, for its task has been to invite foreign companies to Singapore. However, this was not the only task entrusted to the EDB over the last 40 years. First, the most important task has been, as explained above, to invite MNCs into the domestic market, albeit with a change of priority in industries from time to time; for instance, from low-tech, labour-intensive industries in the early stage to capital-intensive and skill-intensive industries in the 1980s.

The second task was closely related to the first, such as the development of industrial estates, industrial finance, and manpower training. The EDB assumed these tasks until 1968, when the government came to assess that the EDB had become too overburdened to be effective and completely restructured the EDB. After the reshuffle, tasks such as factory land development, industrial finance, labour training, and technology development were transferred to other newly established agencies.

The third task is to encourage and assist local companies to advance overseas, especially to newly emerging markets in Asia like China, Vietnam, and India to cope with the short supply of resources and manpower in the domestic market. This task was added at the end of the 1980s, when the government commenced the globalization strategy. Since then the EDB has been spearheading overseas investments.[1]

Figure 10.2   Restructuring of the EDB (1968)

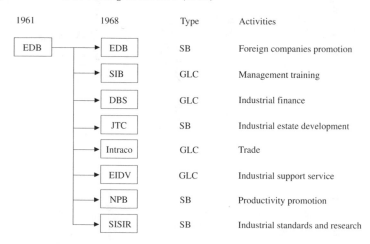

Source: Low (1993, p. 91)
Note: SB = Statutory Board, GLC = Government-linked Company

Currently the EDB has been entrusted with two missions, and the present organizational configuration of the EDB and other government economic agencies was accomplished in 1968, as shown in Figure 10.2. In the following, we will focus on the most important task of the EDB, i.e., inviting foreign companies, and try to examine how the EDB organized its manpower and how EDB officers carried out their task.

4.2 Characteristic of EDB Manpower

Originally the former EDB was established in 1957 by the British colonial government, and in August 1961 it was wholly reshuffled and renamed the EDB as a statutory board under the auspices of the Ministry of Finance. Then in 1979 it was transferred to the Ministry of Trade and Industry. In 1961, with an initial budget of S$100 million (Schein 1996, p.38), the EDB started to undertake any services related to attracting foreign companies. After another reshuffle in 1968, the new EDB was fully equipped, particulary in terms of manpower.

Table 10.7 shows the manpower forces of the EDB from 1961 through 1990. In 1961 it started with only 50 officers, but the number increased to 317 in 1971, more than six times. This is evidence that the government

Table 10.7 Profile of EDB Officers and Headquarters and Overseas Centres, 1961–1990

	1961	1971	1981	1990
No. of officers by level	50	317	197	329
Senior officers	11	94	87	147
Junior Officers	39	223	110	182
Senior-junior officers	1:3.55	1:2.37	1:1.26	1:1.23
Male	43	198	96	143
Female	7	119	101	186
Higher qualification				
Postgraduate	3	12	21	39
University				
Engineering	11	29	47	80
Non-engineering	11	74	41	87
Diploma	2	16	8	11
A level	0	11	7	10
O level	15	139	71	115
Others	11	48	23	26
Total (excluding postgrad)	50	317	197	329
Median age	26	25	32	32
Range	19–62	17–68	15–63	18–60

Source: Low (1993, p. 396)

placed priority on the EDB in the allotment of the scarce manpower resources of the bureaucracy. This special treatment was practised, for at that time the fate of the Singapore state was totally dependent on the success of inviting a sufficient number of foreign companies, so the government injected the best human resources into the EDB.[2] In the 40-years history of the EDB, the 1970s and 1980s were glorious times, and the EDB has two striking characteristics with regard to manpower.

One is the relatively young average age of its officers. As indicated in Table 10.7, in 1961 the average age of EDB officers was 26 years, and this had not changed even 10 years later. On the contrary, the average age actually went down by one year, slightly rose to 32 years in 1981, then surprisingly kept the same level throughout the 1990s. As a rule, it would be natural to expect that as time passed the average age of EDB staff would go up accordingly. This did not happen at the EDB, though. Presumably the reason is either that the rotation of officers was frequent and younger ones replaced predecessors, or the EDB injected fresh young officers in large numbers, or a combination of both. In any case, this fact clearly reveals that during that time the government allocated fresh graduates or young officers to the EDB. Conversely speaking, this means that the task of inviting MNCs was placed on the shoulders of young elite bureaucrats, of whom about half were engineering graduates.

If this is the characteristic of middle-rank officers, what is the characteristic of top officers of the EDB? In the hierarchy of the EDB, the chairman has been the top post since its inception. Table 10.8 shows all the past chairmen from 1961 to the present day. So far seven bureaucrats have assumed the post. They can be categorized into two types according to their character and the task assigned to them.

One type is "manager". For this type, the tasks have been setting up the organization in the first place or restructuring and strengthening it in order to cope with fast-changing circumstances or new missions. The first chairman, Hon Sui Sen (1961–68), the fourth chairman, Ngiam Tong Dow (1975–81), and the sixth chairman, Philip Yeo (1986–2001) correspond to this type. The entrusted tasks for each of them were to erect the foundation (for Hon), to restructure the organization to adjust to new circumstances (for Ngiam), and to tackle the economic downturn of negative growth in 1985, which Singapore faced for the first time since its independence (for Yeo). For these tough tasks, which at the same time were national missions, super bureaucrats, who were regarded by political leaders as the best bureaucrats then, were accordingly spotted from outside the EDB.

The other type is "businessman". The second chairman, I.F. Tang (1968–72), the third chairman, Chan Chin Bock (1972–75), the fifth chairman, P.Y. Hwang (1982–85) and the present chairman, Teo Ming Kian (2001–) correspond to this type. The tasks of this type are completely

Table 10.8 Profile of Past EDB Chairmen

Name	Duration	Former post	After post	Type
1 Hon Sui Sen	1961–1968	Permanent secretary, Ministry of Finance	Minister of Finance	Organizer
2 I. F. Tang	1968–1972	Officer, ECAFE	Officer, Jurong Town Corporation	Businessman
3 Chan Chin Bock	1972–1975	Manager, Ford Motor(S)	Director, New York Office EDB	Businessman
4 Ngiam Tong Dow	1975–1981	Permanent Secretary, Ministry of Trade and Industry	Permanent Secretary, Ministry of Finance	Organizer
5 P. Y. Hwang	1982–1985	Ambassador in Brussels	Vice-Chairman, Temasek Holdings	Businessman
6 Philip Yeo	1986–2001	Permanent Secretary, Ministry of Defense	Chairman, Agency for Science, Technology and Research	Organizer
7 Teo Ming Kian	2001–	Chairman, National Science and Technology Board		Businessman

Source: Chan (2002).

different from the first. They are duly expected to utilize the existing staff force to its maximum, given the assumption that the present structure and manpower are at their best. For this type of chairman, bureaucrats, who have had long working experience with the EDB and have had direct contacts with executives of foreign companies, were promoted from within the EDB.

Whereas the first type of chairman can be described as an "organizer" or "commander" as well as a "manager", the second type can be described as a "salesman" or "deal maker" as well as a "businessman".[3] It is interesting to observe that in the last 40 years the EDB has been managed by two contrasting types of bureaucrats almost alternately, and which type should assume the post of chairman was decided by the circumstances and tasks that the EDB faced then. This certainly verifies the fact that personnel management of the Singapore bureaucracy has been considerably flexible, and never stark and stiff.

4.3 The Way of Doing "Business" — EDB Officers on the Front Line

As explained, the PAP government established the EDB in the early 1960s to invite foreign companies that were indispensable to Singapore's industrialization. Around that time, however, other East Asian countries also established government agencies equivalent to the EDB with a practically similar purpose. It is reasonable to assume that competition among those countries had been considerably intense. If this was the case, what were the weapons and secrets of the EDB in this regard?

Currently, the EDB has opened over a dozen overseas offices to deal with foreign companies directly and effectively. It opened its first offices both in New York and in Hong Kong in 1966–67 and then expanded to Germany, the United Kingdom, Japan, and other major cities in the United States. In inviting foreign companies, the EDB has maintained the official stance that it will welcome any investment from any country; nonetheless, priority has actually been placed on companies from the United States. This was the case because Singapore's "main selling points were English-speaking population and the similarity of our legal infrastructure to that of the UK and the US" (Chan 2002, p. 61). On this, the EDB has formed another informal criterion that targets companies that are top-class MNCs in the world in each industry.

With those informal rules, the task of inviting foreign companies has fallen on the shoulders of young bureaucrats, as we explained earlier, some even in their 20s. From the start, these young officers were thrown out into the field without any working experience and were compelled to deal with seasoned executives of the top-class companies. Gradually, however, they followed manuals accumulated by predecessors. EDB officers who were stationed overseas in the 1970s and 1980s recalled that in carrying out their mission they behaved as if they were salesmen of a private trading company (Schein 1996, p. 71). Certainly they literally sold Singapore to MNCs. As I.F. Tang, one of the former chairmen of the EDB, explains, "We are not selling coffee or tea, we are selling a country". They had the task of convincing the executives of MNCs that it was worthwhile for them to invest in Singapore (Schein 1996. p. 70). Although nearly all of them were graduates from world-renowned universities, as we examined, it would be reasonable to assume that their missions were very tough, especially for young officers from a country with scarce resources, a small domestic market, almost nothing to sell, and totally unknown to the executives of MNCs.

How did they overcome these disadvantages and accomplished their "impossible" mission? They later disclosed that their "secret weapons" were a stable political climate, domiciled labour, a well-prepared infrastructure, and trained skilled labour in general (Chan 2002). As pointed out earlier, these factors were correctly planted and were materialized through the monopoly of state power by the PAP government, state autonomy, and systematic bureaucracy. Armed with these special weapons, young EDB officers eagerly and dutifully carried out their mission. As a result, MNCs committed up to a satisfactory level for Singapore in terms of capital and type of industry.

As explained above, in carrying out their duties, EDB officers behaved as if they were salesmen of a private trading company. By no means did they behave as government officers, who may be inclined more to control investment from foreign companies than to encourage it, hence discouraging their investments. It would be worthy to note that, on the contrary, EDB officers almost always stood by the side of the MNCs when they carried out their mission. Figure 10.3 illustrates the situation. As the figure shows clearly, although they were government officers, they acted as if they were business partners of the MNCs or their representatives in Singapore. Edger Schein (1996, pp. 1 and 10), an American economist who was requested by the EDB to analyze elements of success in the EDB's mission from the outsider's point of view, noted in his book that "the success of the EDB is largely the function of the culture that this organization created." And together with many other researchers who coin the Singapore government "Singapore, Inc.", Schein too describes the EDB and the Singapore government as "Singapore, Inc.", which means they "run the country (EDB) much like a business".

Many former EDB field officers confirmed this peculiar culture of the EDB in the book, which recounted their activities. According to it, when they approached prospective candidates of MNCs, they were ready to adjust their working hours at the convenience of the MNC's candidate

Figure 10.3   Position of EDB Officers

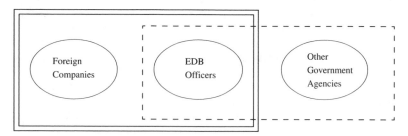

Partner, or Agent of Foreign Companies

or even to attend private requests from their family members (Chan 2002, p. 283). Interestingly, this was practised even in Singapore, too. In dealing with executives from prospective MNCs, EDB officers at the headquarters were ready not only to offer ready-made factory premises, which would conveniently cut the time for them to start operation,[4] but also to offer to arrange a certain number of skilled labour, if requested, by providing enough graduates from EDB-run vocational institutes. They did more than that. If the foreign companies were in need of a local manager for the subsidizing company to be established, they would even lend a helping hand to search for a candidate by using private headhunting companies (Chan 2002, p. 166–72).

Many executives of MNCs that invested in Singapore over the last 30 years appreciated the EDB as a reliable, trustworthy partner in an unfamiliar country and hardly thought of them as government officers with red tape who would more often than not discourage investment and business by the private sector. They concluded by revealing that without the presence and help of the EDB, their decision to invest in Singapore would not have been placed on the table for the selection of overseas investment sites and hence would never have materialized (Chan 2002).[5]

The EDB case that we examined above seems to reveal the following vital facts with regard to the "state bureaucracy and development": i.e., while the Singapore state has been maintaining a rigid system in the political area, it has been very flexible and practical in managing bureaucratic machinery and highly attentive to the needs of foreign companies in the economic area. This sharp distinction between political and economic areas is one of the typical characteristics and aspects not only of the Singapore state but also the developmental state in general.

5. State Bureaucrats and Governance in Singapore and East Asia

5.1 Paradigm Shift in the Role of the State

It would be obvious from the observation of development management in Singapore that the state played an active, decisive role in export-oriented industrialization by creating an efficient bureaucratic machinery to lead development and to guide private companies in the direction it had set. It may perhaps be true to say that without the deep involvement of the state, economic development in Singapore would be considerably different from that of today. Besides the state, of course, the MNCs from developed countries also participated actively in the process and greatly contributed to the development by making the best use of favourable circumstances, or in more concrete terms, by utilizing Singapore as a base for export production. If we consider this as a growth mechanism not only of the Singapore state but also East Asian states, then the Singapore state epitomizes this model.

In development thinking in the 1980s it was widely acknowledged that state played a vital role, as examined in this chapter. It was stressed that one of the decisive elements in the development of developing countries was the state, and the state should be rational, effective, and efficient. With this understanding, the state that was effective and efficient in policymaking and implementation was considered endowed with "state capacity" (Evans 1985). It was advocated by statists that state capacity could be obtained partly through securing state autonomy and partly through creating efficient bureaucracy, as the Singapore state rightly did. At that time, it was conceived that state capacity and state autonomy, i.e., effective and efficient government machinery, were the sole qualifications that the state needed for development.

In the 1990s, however, development thinking with regard to the state in development drastically changed in content, as remarked in the introduction. By the early 1990s, a new school that preaches primacy of the democratic political system coupled with supremacy of the market over an authoritarian political system and state-centreed economy came into command in development thinking. Closely related to this, governance has been stressed as a vital quality that any government should be armed with. According to this school of thought, a state that is merely efficient in the area of policy formulation and implementation cannot be regarded as a good government anymore. In addition, it has been stressed that if a government intends to achieve fair economic performance, good governance is a prerequisite, at least in theory.

Despite the fact that there are several unsettled or unanswered issues relating to governance, such as what factors constitute governance, or why it is necessary for the state in development, it seems interesting and meaningful to irradiate the Singapore state with the notion of governance and to elucidate how the developmental state appears in the light of governance. For this review we define governance by invoking the broad definition provided by the Organization for Economic Cooperation and Development (1995) as, 1) democratic political system; 2) ability of government: i.e. stable political base, good administration, and policy formulation; and 3) the way of using the government power: i.e., accountability, openness, and transparency to the public.

We are aware, of course, that the result is self-evident. Of the three elements of governance cited above, for the developmental state only the element of government ability matters, and the other two elements are totally unknown. Even so, further analysis will reveal two critical points on the theme of "state and governance". One is the fact that whereas there is only a single qualification for a developmental state, governance requires more elements in number as well as in quality. The other is the fact that "state capacity" of the developmental state and "government ability" of governance have much in common in content.

5.2 Why Governance for East Asian States?

Table 10.9 shows the results of the comparison. Of the three factors, it is obvious that the Singapore state lacks the "democratic political system factor", since the monopoly of state power by the PAP and suppression of political opponents are apparent even now. Still, for the "government ability factor", Singapore is satisfactory, since it has been maintaining a stable political base, efficient bureaucracy, and almost no corruption among bureaucrats and politicians. Comparing these two factors, the "use of government power factor" is somewhat ambiguous. While some of them are clear, others are not. We will discuss the latter. As explained, statutory boards and GLCs have been given the privilege of "autonomy" in their activities, free from the control of parliament. Thus, even an MP from the ruling PAP once complained in parliament that "there is no proper accountability in the case of the State-owned company" (Vennewald 1994, p. 56).

We have obtained mixed figures of the Singapore state with regard to governance: i.e., it lacks a democratic political system, for political stability has been rooted in an authoritarian system, fair with bureaucratic machinery, an essence of the developmental state, and vague with accountability, openness, and transparency, elements almost unknown to the developmental state. This is the condition of the present Singapore state; however it may be able to extend this condition to several other present East Asian states.

Table 10.9 Singapore State and Governance

Governance		Assessment	Developmental State
I	Democratic political system	No	Authoritarian political system
II	Ability of government		State capacity
	Stable political base	Fair	State autonomy
	Good administration	Fair	
	Policy formulation	Fair	
III	Way of using government power		–
	Accountability	Vague	
	Openness	Vague	
	Transparency	Vague	

Source: The Author.

Before we proceed to examine the present Singapore state and the East Asian states in terms of governance in some detail, it is necessary to clarify one question. Why does governance matter for the Singapore state and the East Asian states? It is extremely difficult to provide an answer, and particularly to satisfy those who are keenly concerned with this critical theme. Nevertheless, it seems at least the following ground can be presented, albeit not directly related to the elements of governance.

First of all, it is not because, as is widely accepted, in the coming age governance is catching momentum in the world and is placed as a prime condition for development aid from developed countries and international organizations, but because of causes originating from conditions in the region itself. If we assume the sole goal of the third- world state is development or growth, then the developmental state may be a more relevant system than a democratic political system, as the performance of the developmental state in the 1980s clearly manifested. However, it is obvious that development in East Asia has been achieved at the expense of some other elements; for instance, participation of the public in the policy process, or total neglect of "due process". Both are vital and essential elements, together with development, for the public in the region. Therefore, even if the developmental state is more relevant for the task of growth than any other type of state, the state, at the same time, has to realize those other vital elements, which the developmental state cannot provide on its own.

The democratic political system and accountability of the government to the public, for instance, are elements for its own sake, which are valuable and desirable for even East Asian states. Thus, regardless of being considered insufficient as an academic analytical concept in several points, it is no doubt the notion of governance, together with the democratization movement, that has reminded people of the importance of these elements to this region. In this regard, it is vital to examine the specific conditions of present East Asian states with regard to governance. We will investigate the Singapore state as a case study.

5.3 Motivation of the Singapore Bureaucracy

In this chapter, we have arrived at a temporal evaluation that the bureaucratic machinery of the present Singapore state is efficient, albeit not perfect. How does the Singapore state succeed in creating and maintaining a relatively corruption-free, efficient bureaucracy, and what are the motivations of the bureaucrats in maintaining their morale? This is a critical question, and the result will be vital for third-world countries, which are suffering from inefficient bureaucracy.

It may be possible to point out several causes in relation to political, economic, and social elements. Nonetheless, it seems that one of the decisive causes can be attributed to the system of government scholarship. As explained earlier, it was established in full scale in the early 1970s with the aim of securing future elite bureaucrats. Under this programme, over a hundred young students have been dispatched to overseas universities each year to study required subjects, dominantly engineering, and after completion they are destined for government agencies, i.e., ministries, statutory boards, or GLCs. Interestingly enough, this system is very similar to that of Japan, which was introduced in the early Meiji era in order to catch up with Western countries within a short period. At that time, the Meiji government dispatched a few elite persons to Western countries to acquire expert skill or knowledge, and after completing their studies they assumed government posts in various fields. The students sponsored by the Japanese government undertook their mission solely to serve the "developing" Japanese state in its modernization and never for their personal interest or gain.

It may not be irrelevant to assume that the Singapore system too, intentionally or unintentionally, has been successful in instilling into the students' minds the motivation that they are working for the Singapore state to survive in a severe international world, particularly to assist its economic development.[6] Generally speaking, to brew this kind of "devotion to the state" even in the hearts of young elites, let alone common people, is a tremendously difficult undertaking for third-world countries that are geographically diverse and socially segmented by multiethnic groups, languages, and cultures. In this sense, Singapore's small size has an advantage in helping to create a motivated and unified bureaucracy.

Needless to say, this cannot be the sole element responsible for creating an efficient bureaucracy. Certainly it has been assisted by other elements, such as relatively high salary reward, rigid and close surveillance on the misconduct of bureaucrats by the Corrupt Practice Investigation Bureau under the direct control of the Prime Minister, or the system that pertinently eliminates sprawling intervention of politicians through state autonomy (Quah 1990). At any rate, those elements combined have contributed to creating an efficient bureaucracy.

Thus, one of the temporal propositions on the "state and governance" from the Singapore case is that efficient state machinery can be created and economic development can be attained, irrelevant of the political system, i.e., whether it is democratic or authoritarian.

5.4 Two Problems with the EDB Bureaucracy

It may be true that no perfect organization or bureaucracy exists in the man-made world. The Singapore state and bureaucracy, too, is not exceptional in this dictum. We will show two examples from the EDB case, both of which arose from double-edged relationships with MNCs.

First, it is widely acknowledged that EDB officers maintained cordial relationships with MNCs, and this was appreciated as one of the causes that contributed to the success of their mission. However, this is only one side of the coin; there is certainly another other side. It has somehow become common practice among EDB officers, who collaborated closely with MNCs, to quit the EDB later and join the counterpart MNCs as management staff (Chan 2002, pp. 131–33). This practice, of course, is not absent even in the developed countries; for instance, in Japan this became a long-standing custom coined *amakudari*. Thus, generally speaking, there may be no room for criticism against government officers merely because they switched their jobs to responsible positions in counterpart private companies. Nonetheless, in the case of EDB officers, who were evidently given the privilege nurtured during their official position, it will be an unavoidable problem of the "government-business union", whereby the personal gain of bureaucrats is pursued at the expense of impartiality.

Second, Glaxo is a renowned British pharmaceutical company, and when Glaxo invested in Singapore in the early 1980s, EDB officers helped them greatly. Later, the chairman of Glaxo came to perceive that the assistance given by the EDB for its company was tremendous, so he offered to do something for the EDB as a token of appreciation. To this offer, the EDB proposed to start a human resource development programme, and, as a result, Glaxo set up a scholarship fund of S$50 million for Singapore students to study at overseas universities in the early 1990s.[7] Since then, every year 30 scholars have been dispatched to universities in the United States or United Kingdom, and after graduation 10 to 15 of them have been joining the EDB as staff. Consequently, Glaxo scholars have now reached almost 100 among the total staff of the EDB, and they have been specifically given posts in managing overseas operations (Chan 2002, pp. 211, 303 and 304).

Despite the cordial relationship between the EDB and MNCs, it has at the same time resulted in an undesirable union of the government with the private sector, or more concretely, EDB officers with MNCs. This practice would never become a problem in the ethic of the developmental state, but it has surely become a serious point of issue in the light of governance. Although this issue has not yet got much public attention in Singapore, it will be hardly tolerable within the range of acceptable practice of the bureaucracy.

5.5 Two Problems with the Singapore Bureaucracy

The Singapore bureaucracy as a whole also has been facing some serious problems related to governance. For this we cite two issues. One issue is the possibility of "insider trading" among top bureaucrats. As we have pointed out, the PAP government has been relying heavily on the trinity system, in which one bureaucrat manages several public agencies concurrently, as full-time manager for one and part-time manager for the others. Whereas this system has been providing a source of coordination and quick response among government agencies on the one hand, it has been unavoidably providing a chance for undesirable insider trading on the other hand. Any bureaucrat entrusted with additional posts is able to access confidential information in that agency, thus giving rise to the threat of abusing obtained information for personal gain. Vennewald (1994, p. 55) discovered this deficit inherent in the system in his study of the Singapore bureaucracy and plainly pointed out that "the flaw of the Singapore state enterprise system lies in its lack of institutional control mechanisms".

However, not surprisingly the PAP government has been utterly optimistic about this matter. They comfortably assume that elite bureaucrats are so highly motivated and endowed with self-discipline that they will never abuse their power or privilege. Certainly it is not deniable that the behaviour of the bureaucrats hitherto has hardly betrayed this optimistic trust placed upon them, and even when abuse occurred, it remained a minor case and never ended in distorting the bureaucratic efficiency and reliability. Yet the fact that it did not happen in the past does not guarantee that it will not happen in the future.

The other issue is politicization of the bureaucracy. In classical textbooks of political science, it is stressed that bureaucracy should stand by a neutral position against any political parties, and this is a crucial pre-condition for them in gaining reliability from the public. As pointed out earlier, the Singapore bureaucracy has fused with the ruling party to an extreme degree. Although the efficiency of the Singapore bureaucracy has been in part guaranteed by this fusion and state autonomy, at the same time this has led to the questioning of its neutrality and reliability. However, the principle of bureaucracy mentioned above has been partially revised in the 20th century, as fusion of the bureaucracy with the ruling party has become a common feature to some extent in a country where one party successfully maintained long-term dominance, even in Western democratic countries. Thus, there is no room to criticize the Singapore situation merely because the fusion has occurred.[8] The issue is not the fusion itself but the degree. In this regard, the Singapore case is highly questionable, as many bureaucrats have been deeply involved in politics and have been acting as agents of the ruling party.

Currently, under the tight control of the PAP regime, it is nearly impossible for the public as well as opposition parties to express criticism against this practice. However, the present situation of the Singapore bureaucracy that has been pursuing only efficiency at the expense of, or simply ignoring, other elements i.e., neutrality and impartiality, will definitely cast doubts on the relevance of governance.

5.6 Implications for Other Developing Countries

Despite the fact that the Singapore bureaucracy has several shortcomings and problems, it is certain that it has been skillfully keeping motivated, well-qualified, and well-performed bureaucracy over the last 30 years. What kind of implications with regard to the bureaucracy can we obtain from the Singapore case for other developing countries? Some may claim other developing countries should learn, or more directly, imitate or transplant the systems and policies that the Singapore state has employed, if they intend to be another Singapore. For this, it should be reminded that the Singapore state is totally different from other countries by any standard. Efficiency of the bureaucracy has been greatly helped with state autonomy purposely provided by the PAP government and by close association with the ruling party. It must be impossible for other countries, where fundamental political and social conditions are totally different from Singapore, to transplant the Singapore system. More critically, it will certainly be questionable from the viewpoint of governance to emulate such a system.

Nevertheless, there are definitely some qualities that the Singapore state can offer to other countries that are desirable and applicable. One of these is that the Singapore state has aptly utilized every factor available to maximum capacity and consequently skillfully created a system that is exactly suitable and only workable for Singapore. Edgar Schein (1996,

p. 70), who extensively examined the activities of the EDB, concludes his analysis with the remark that "the general lesson rather is that each country must think clearly about its particular situation and develop its own version of strategic pragmatism". This means any government needs to "create" a system which best fits its own country, and certainly this must be the most significant lesson Singapore can offer.

6. Conclusion

In this chapter we have examined the Singapore state and its bureaucracy in the light of both the developmental state and governance. The following remark is presented as a temporal conclusion. Although there is room for further clarification as to the proper elements of governance in the context of East Asian states, and especially whether it is relevant to include the democratic political system into the elements of governance, three elements advanced by governance are certainly relevant and useful to understand the present states in the region. With regard to the three elements, the Singapore state created an effective state apparatus in the 1970s up to a satisfactory level and has been maintaining it to the present day, but for other factors, i.e., using government power and political system, it has room for improvement. The Singapore state needs to incorporate such factors as accountability, openness, and a more democratic political system into its efficient bureaucratic machinery.

If we extend this Singapore situation into a broader perspective in the region, it is said that one of the current tasks for the East Asian states on hand is to convert state capacity of the developmental state to comply with governance. However, this is not an easy task for the East Asian states, for state capacity of the developmental state is deeply rooted in an authoritarian political system, as if both are a "seamless web". It is nearly impossible to cut and take state capacity out of the latter. The situation of the Indonesian developmental state clearly testifies to this, where, with the collapse of the authoritarian Soeharto regime in 1998, somehow the systematic bureaucracy collapsed together. Thus, the East Asian states are in need not only of a partial overhaul of the state system and apparatus but a total overhaul. In the context of the present situation in the region, it is necessary either to transform the present regime of the developmental state to a regime that complies with governance while keeping the continuity of the regime, or change it completely with another regime, which satisfies the requirements of governance.

These are prescriptions for the present task that the East Asian states are facing in relation to governance. How to tackle and achieve this task, while keeping the original character of the society in the region on the one hand, and adjusting some aspects of the state to that of international standard on the other hand, is certainly a critical and interesting challenge for the East Asian states in the 21st century. Yet, this is another practical issue more related to the theme of democratization or political reform that is beyond the purpose and scope of this chapter.

Notes

[1] Major overseas projects that have been undertaken by government initiative are "Batamindo Industrial Park" and "Bintan Beach International Resort", both in Indonesia, "Vietnam Singapore Industrial Park" in Vietnam, "Suzhou Industrial Park" in China, and "International Tech Park in Bangalore" in India.

[2] S. Dhanabalan, who joined the EDB in the early 1960s and later became foreign minister, once observed, "EDB always took the cream of all Public Service scholars as Dr. Goh made economic development the national priority"; in Chan (2002, p. 31)

[3] Chan Chin Bock, former management staff of Ford Company (Singapore) and the fourth chairman of the EDB, who had experience being stationed in the United States over 10 years, was described by his colleagues as "Chief Salesman of Singapore"; in Chan (2002, p. 218)

[4] National Semiconductor, an American MNC, was able to start its production in Singapore in less than two months after they first made contact with the EDB by using the premises arranged by the EDB; in Chan (2002, pp. 45 and 56).

[5] Edgar Schein, who interviewed several executives of MNCs that invested in Singapore, noted the following observation in his book: "Businessmen felt comfortable in Singapore because they encountered in the EDB a group of helpers who thought like businessmen, who understood the needs of business, and who were really organized to help business"; in Schein (1996, p. 142), and "EDB members could be thought of as bureaucrats, but their mental model was clearly that of entrepreneurs, marketers, salesmen, and long-range strategy planners"; in Schein (1996, p. 164).

[6] S. Dhanabalan, former EDB staff and former PAP politician, comments, "What was there to defend if we did not have economic development? For a country like Singapore, economic development was not a choice and I was glad I chose to stick it out"; in Chan (2002, p. 31)

[7] Glaxo was not the only MNC that donated scholarships to the EDB. Sundstrand established a scholarship for the EDB in 1982, albeit the sum of donation was smaller, and Mobil, Seiko-Epson, Takashimaya and several local companies too joined in the undertaking; in Chan (2002).

[8] There are several PAP MPs and cabinet ministers who came from the EDB over the last few decades. They include S. Dhanabalan (former minister of foreign affairs), Lee Yock Suan (former minister of labour) and Yeo Cheow Tong (former minister of trade and industry), to name just a few.

References

Alten, Florian von. 1995. *The Role of Government in the Singapore Economy.* Frankfurt am Main: Peter Lang.

Castells, Manuel. 1998. *The Developmental City-State in an Open World Economy: the Singapore Experience.* Berkeley: Berkeley Roundtable on the International Economy, University of California.

Chan, Chin Bok and others. 2002. *Heart Work: Stories of how EDB steered the Singapore Economy from 1961 into 21st Century.* Singapore: Singapore EDB.

Evans, Peter and others, ed. 1985. *Bringing the State Back In.* Cambridge: Cambridge University Press.

Low, Linda and others. 1993. *Challenge and Responses: Thirty Years of the Economic Development Board.* Singapore: Times Academic Press.

OECD. 1995. *Participatory Development and Good Governance.* Paris: OECD.

Pierre, Jon and B. Guy Peters. 2000. *Governance, Politics and the State.* London: Macmillan.

Quah, S.T. Jon and others, ed. 1990. *Government and Politics in Singapore.* 2nd. ed. Singapore: Oxford University Press.

Rodan, Garry. 1989. *The Political Economy of Singapore's Industrialization: National State and International Capital.* London: Macmillan.

Schein, Edgar H. 1996. *Strategic Pragmatism: the Culture of Singapore's Economic Development Board.* Cambridge: MIT Press.

Singapore. Ministry of Information and Arts. 2001. *Singapore 2001.* Singapore.

Singapore. Public Service Commission. 1991, 2001. *Annual Report.* Singapore: PSC.

———. 2002. *PSC Scholarship Guide.* Singapore: PSC.

———. n.d. *PSC Scholarship: Management Associate Programme.* Singapore: PSC.

Soon, Teck-Wong and C. Suan Tan. 1993. *Singapore: Public Policy and Economic Development.* Washington, D.C.: World Bank.

Trezzini, Bruno. 2001. "Institutional Foundation of Malaysia's State Capacity". *Asian Journal of Public Administration*, 23(1), pp. 33–63.

Vennewald, Werner. 1994. *Technocrats in the State Enterprise System of Singapore.* Perth: Asia Research Centre. Murdoch University.

Weiss, Linda. 1998. *The Myth of the Powerless State.* Ithaca: Cornell University Press.

Woo-Cumings, Meredith, ed. 1999. *The Developmental State*. Ithaca: Cornell University Press.

World Bank. 1993. *The East Asian Miracle: Economic Growth and Public Policy.* New York: Oxford University Press.

———. 1997. *World Development Report 1997: the State in a Changing World.* New York: Oxford University Press.

Inter-Island Livestock Trade. Inter-island livestock trade is important for farmers in the dry provinces of West and East Nusa Tenggara (NTT). These relatively poor islands export livestock, mostly to Java. In 1998, NTT had a large livestock population of 803,000 (almost all cattle). Producing slaughter cattle for market was important to more than 200,000 NTT farmers (although this is merely a rough estimate). In NTB the large livestock population numbered 470,000 and was a major source of income for more than an estimated 150,000 farmers. Most of NTB's cattle were on Lombok Island (280,000).

Livestock trade was subject to both local trade taxes and inter-island shipping quotas. By mid 1997, just before the crisis, East Nusa Tenggara cattle farmers and traders had to pay a total of US$40 per cattle through 16 different kinds of taxes and levies, amounting to about 13% of the farm-gate value of a slaughter animal. On Lombok Island in West Nusa Tenggara farmers and traders paid 24 different taxes and *retribusi* on livestock trade: 3 to the central government, 9 to the province and 12 to the district. The total cost was about $31 per cattle in taxes and levies, or 5% of the $570 farm-gate value of a typical slaughter animal. In Bima (Sumbawa Island), traders and farmers had to pay the same 3 central and 9 provincial taxes and levies, plus 18 district charges. In South Sulawesi, traders bringing cattle from Bone to Ujung Pandang (five hours away) had to pay 31 different taxes and levies along the road. Of these, 6 were legal and 25 illegal. Twenty of the posts charging illegal levies were police and military checkpoints. The sum paid represented about 4% of the farm-gate value of the typical animal. A tandem-trailer truck carrying 18 cattle from Bone to Ujung Pandang had to be prepared to pay $228 in taxes and levies.

Until deregulation in 1998, the Ministry of Agriculture's Director General of Livestock set inter-island livestock trade quotas. These severely limited the number that could be marketed to at most about 5% to 6% of the local livestock populations. In fact, a well-managed herd in NTT should be able to reach between 10% and 13% off-take from a stable livestock population (ACIAR January 1998) under extensive grazing, not intensive stall-feeding management systems. Each year the DG issued a letter giving provinces annual maximum quotas for shipments. He even determined destinations (not permitting NTT to ship to East Kalimantan despite high prices and a shortage of beef for instance). Trade was restricted. The cattle quota for NTT kept decreasing each year, from 67,000 in 1994 to only 41,000 in 1997. The livestock populations were increasing, but the opportunity to market was decreasing. Livestock (and meat) prices in Jakarta rose and farm-gate prices in the outer islands fell as a result of this quota system. A large price wedge was formed, that benefited only the inter-island shipping quota rights-holders.

4.2.2 *Decentralization Era*

Efforts to reform various market distortions that proliferated in the 1980s and 1990s gained momentum between 1998 and 2000, in particular after the fall of the New Order Government. This is understandable as many of the distortions were created by or related to the then first-family or their cronies. These reforms have had some successes, resulting in improving prices received by farmers. However, the implementation of a wide-ranging decentralization and regional autonomy policy — which granted much power to district governments — starting in 2001 seems to have reversed the trend. Various forms of market distortions, which have been dismantled previously, have now revived. The only difference is that now most of the distortions are created by the district governments rather than the central government as had been the case in the past. This section discusses some examples of the new forms of bad governance but with same adverse consequences for the poor.

The costs of transporting goods from North Sumatra to Jakarta.[13]   The abundant agricultural commodities from the Karo district in North Sumatra are mostly perishable goods. Therefore, it is crucial to secure smooth and rapid distribution of these goods to maintain both the quality and the selling price at the consumer level. Consequently, farmers and traders will make every effort to expedite the delivery of these goods to the buyers, even if they have to pay various taxes and levies *en route*. These additional charges will add to the distribution cost, and will eventually lead to a higher price at the consumer level. The amount of the levies extracted is determined by measuring the tonnage of the truck at various weighing stations along the routes. Table 2.1 illustrates the number of weighing bridges and the amount of taxes and levies paid by a truck driver at each location travelling from Kabajahe, Karo district to Jakarta. A truck driver who regularly carries oranges from Kabupaten Karo to Jakarta reports that there are at least 16 truck weighing stations and several other levy checkpoints that have to be passed along the route. The table shows the number and amount of "fines" paid by truck drivers — both those who comply and those who do not comply with the weight limit at each station.

It is estimated that the total amount of levies (official and non-official) paid to transport oranges from Kabanjahe to Jakarta ranges from Rp268,500 to Rp1,008,500. Paying the lowest amount would only be possible if the truck complies with its permitted capacity. Nevertheless, even when trucks comply with the regulations, frequently drivers still have to pay levies. As a result, it is common for truck drivers to prefer to carry loads that exceed the trucks' legal capacity. The estimated value of the load of one 8-ton truck of oranges transporting approximately 120 baskets @ 65 kg at the farm-gate price of Rp1,800 for Grade A, B, C, and D oranges is Rp14,400,000. Hence, the total value of the transported goods paid out in taxes and levies is between 2% to 7%.

Table 2.1 Costs Incurred by Truck Drivers at Weighing Stations on the Way from North Sumatra to Jakarta

Province	Number of Stations	Amount of fines	Remarks
1. North Sumatra	4	Rp5,000–10,000 for each ton of excess weight	Per ton of excess weight
2. Riau	2	Rp60,000, paid by all, irrespective of weight trucks.	Fines have to be paid by both complying and non-complying vehicles, plus additional road levies: -Rp2,500 (6-ton truck) -Rp3,500 (8-ton truck)
3. Jambi	2	Rp60,000, paid by all trucks	Plus additional road levies: -Rp2,500 (6-ton truck) -Rp3,500 (8-ton truck)
4. South Sumatra	5	Fine of Rp15,000 for each ton of excess weight	In addition to the possibility of receiving a fine, there are also road levies: -Rp2,500 (6-ton truck) -Rp3,500 (8-ton truck)
5. Lampung	3	Fine of Rp15,000 for each ton of excess weight	In addition to the possibility of receiving a fine, there are also road levies: -Rp2,500 (6-ton truck) -Rp3,500 (8-ton truck)

Heavily taxed plantation sector in North Sumatra.[14] While the North Sumatra provincial government has not profited directly from the plantation sector, the commodities produced in this industry have been the target of various levies, at both the local (*kabupaten*) and the central level of government. Levies are imposed on the plantation industry starting at the production level, through to distribution and marketing of their products. According to the latest inventory released by the management of the Association of Indonesian Rubber Producers (Gapkindo) in North Sumatra, there are at least nine kinds of official levies imposed on rubber commodities (see Table 2.2).

Non-Tariff Trade Restriction in North Sulawesi.[15] The implementation of decentralization and regional autonomy has resulted in several major changes in the way that local governments exercise their autonomous rights. One of these changes has been that local governments are creating a larger number of new local laws. In the case of North Sulawesi, so far only the provincial governments have begun to create regulations that result in non-tariff barriers. However, there are also indications that district governments are also proposing to create non-tariff regulations at this level. The following is an example of non-tariff barrier found in the Province of North Sulawesi concerning regulation on pharmacies, outlined in the Governor's Decree No.4dz/03/891, 13 September 2001 (Temporary Postponement of the Establishment of Large Pharmacies in North Sulawesi). The Province of North Sulawesi has placed restrictions on the ownership of pharmacies by those who do not reside in North Sulawesi, with the aim of protecting local entrepreneurs. The following is a summary of the contents of the Governor's Decree:

1) Licences for Large Pharmacies in the Province of North Sulawesi are only to be issued to those large businesses with a central office, which own or control assets, and whose owners reside in North Sulawesi. However, these licences are not to be issued to those who reside outside of the Province of North Sulawesi, even though they may own and control assets within the province. Instead they are to be accorded the status of Large Pharmacy Branches or Representatives.

2) Large pharmacies must own a building or business location in accordance with the stipulations on ownership status.

3) Large local pharmacies are to be given priority as partners with the government in acquiring pharmacies with a value of up to Rp4 billion.

4) The establishment of Large Pharmacy Branches has to be based on the recommendation of the North Sulawesi Association of Large Indonesian Pharmacies.